THE INDUSTRIAL AGE

The Industrial Age

Economy and Society in Britain 1750–1985

Charles More

Longman
London and New York

Longman Group UK Limited,
Longman House, Burnt Mill, Harlow,
Essex CM20 2JE, England
and Associated Companies throughout the world.

Published in the United States of America
by Longman Inc., New York

First published 1989

British Library Cataloguing in Publication Data
More, Charles
    The industrial age: economy and society in Britain 1750–1985.
    1. Great Britain. Economic conditions, 1700–1985
    I. Title
    330.941'07
ISBN 0-582-03451-5 CSD
ISBN 0-582-49427-3 PPR

Library of Congress Cataloging-in-Publication Data
More, Charles.
    The industrial age.

    Bibliography: p.
    Includes index.
    1. Great Britain – Industries – History.
2. Great Britain –Economic conditions. I. Title.
HC254.5.M63 1989   338.0941   88-8990
ISBN 0-582-03451-5
ISBN 0-582-49427-3 (U.S.: pbk.)

Set in 10/12 Linotron Times Roman

Produced by Longman Singapore Publishers (Pte) Ltd.
Printed in Singapore

Contents

List of tables   vii
List of figures and maps   ix
Preface and acknowledgments   x

PART ONE   Industrialisation 1750–1830

Chapter 1   Agriculture and rural society   3
Chapter 2   Population, migration and labour supply   12
Chapter 3   Towns, transport and internal trade   21
Chapter 4   Foreign trade   30
Chapter 5   Money, banking and finance   38
Chapter 6   Manufacturing and mining   45
Chapter 7   Government, war and the economy   58
Chapter 8   The aggregate economy   65
Chapter 9   Industrial Revolution?   72

PART TWO   The Industrial Economy 1830–1914

Chapter 10   Into the railway age   87
Chapter 11   Population, migration and labour supply   99
Chapter 12   The workshop of the world: manufacturing and
              mining   111
Chapter 13   The service economy   123
Chapter 14   Agriculture and rural society   129
Chapter 15   Foreign trade and Empire   135
Chapter 16   Banking and finance   143
Chapter 17   The end of economic supremacy   150

PART THREE   Industrialisation and Society 1750–1914

Chapter 18   Incomes and consumption   163

The Industrial Age

Chapter 19   Industrialisation and the family   174
Chapter 20   Work and leisure   179
Chapter 21   Ranks and classes   191
Chapter 22   Employers and unions   198
Chapter 23   From *laissez-faire* to collectivism? Government
             economic and social policy   207

PART FOUR   Prosperity and Problems: the Economy 1914–85

Chapter 24   Britain and the world economy   221
Chapter 25   Economic performance and government
             policy 1914–39   237
Chapter 26   Economic performance and government
             policy 1939–85   255
Chapter 27   Population, migration and labour supply   279
Chapter 28   Business organisation and management   292
Chapter 29   Trade unions in the twentieth century   299
Chapter 30   Banking and finance   312
Chapter 31   Production and distribution   322
Chapter 32   Change and decay: economic performance in the
             long run   347

PART FIVE   Economy and Society 1914–1985

Chapter 33   Prosperity and poverty   363
Chapter 34   Social policy 1914–85   374
Chapter 35   Work and leisure   386
Chapter 36   A middle-class society?   400

Appendix: Changing price levels 1750–1985   406
Bibliography   408
Sources for quotations   414
Glossary of terms   415
Maps   423
Index   434

List of tables

2.1 Population growth in Britain 1701–1831 12

3.1 Urban growth *c*. 1750–1800: some examples 22

4.1 Exports of British produce 1784–1826 by commodity groups 32

6.1 Consumption of raw cotton 50

7.1 Government expenditure and income 1750–1820 61

8.1 Growth of real national income (RNI) and income per head 66

8.2 Share of sectors in national income 68

8.3 Share of value added in industry (as percentage of total industrial output) 68

8.4 Investment in the British economy 1760–1840 70

10.1 Share of sectors in national income 88

10.2 Urbanisation in Britain 1801–1901 (totals and some sample towns) 96

10.3 Population distribution by region 98

12.1 Share of staple industries in national income 112

12.2 Industrial production in Great Britain (annual average) 114

15.1 Percentage share in total exports of certain goods in 1913 136

15.2 British exports to and investment in colonial areas 141

17.1 Growth in national income productivity 1830–1913 151

18.1 Consumption per person 165

20.1 Share of labour force in sectors 181

22.1 Trade union membership 204

23.1 Government income and expenditure 1830–1913 216

24.1 UK composition and geographical pattern of exports and imports 1955–85; and share of world trade 1939–85 232

25.1 Inter-war unemployment   238
26.1 Unemployment averaged over five-year periods (UK)   256
26.2 Income and productivity growth 1937–85   256
26.3 Dates of nationalisation or denationalisation (privatisation) of major industries   261
26.4 Inflation 1939–85   268
27.1 Population 1901–81   280
27.2 Population distribution by region   285
27.3 Female participation ratio   288
29.1 Union membership   299
31.1 Productivity growth before and after the First World War   323
31.2 Income and productivity growth 1913–37   324
31.3 Productivity growth after the Second World War   327
31.4 Selected industrial output indicators   327
31.5 Agricultural statistics   333
31.6 Share of sectors in national income   343
31.7 Regional unemployment in Britain 1931–85   345
31.8 Employment in staple industries   345
32.1 International investment and productivity comparisons   351
33.1 Income and spending 1913–85   364
33.2 Income shares 1913–85   366
33.3 Income shares 1949–85   367
33.4 Women's wages 1938–78   367
33.5 Wealth distribution 1924–81   370
33.6 Housing by tenure 1914–84   371
33.7 Consumer spending 1913–85   373
34.1 Government expenditure 1913–81   375
35.1 Share of labour force in sectors 1913–74   387
35.2 Occupational class of the employed population in 1911 and 1971   387
35.3 Hours of work 1913–85   395
35.4 Participation in social and cultural activities, 1977   397

List of figures and maps

15.1 The multilateral system on the eve of the First World War   138
25.1 Inter-war unemployment   239
29.1 Days lost by strikes in the UK 1900–84   300

1 Pre-1974 counties and major towns   424–5
2 Canals and major navigable rivers in Britain by c. 1830   426
3 The railway network in 1852   427
4 Agricultural regions (by percentage of tillage) in 1871   428
5 Coalfields in Britain c. 1900   429
6 Counties and local authorities in England, Wales and Scotland in 1985   430–1
7 House price differentials in Britain in 1985   432
8 Motorways in 1985   433

Preface and acknowledgements

This book was written as a non-specialist introduction to the economic and social history of modern Britain, for students in higher education who are studying one or both of these subjects as part of a wider course in history or some other discipline. I hope it will be useful to other groups, however: students specialising in economic and social history, schoolteachers, sixth-formers and, indeed, anyone who is interested in the subjects covered.

The book contains an outline survey of the major aspects of economic activity in the past, such as manufacturing, agriculture, banking and foreign trade; and it surveys economic growth, economic change and economic problems. It covers the areas of social history which are most closely associated with economic activity – areas such as work, living standards, and the social make-up of the population. The book's main aim, though, is to make the reader think about why the economy worked as it did, why it grew, why it changed, why there have been problems, and how economic and social history relate together. So there is economic analysis, but it is kept simple. Some terms are explained in the text, while for others there is a glossary; the index indicates where to look.

The book also aims to be up to date. The statistical material, both contemporary and for the earlier periods, is drawn from the latest publications of which I am aware. Controversies which have not recently excited much attention have been left alone, but areas where historians' interpretations have recently differed are highlighted. The approach here is not to give a blow-by-blow account of the 'controversies', but rather to outline the current state of play. I have not hesitated to give my own interpretation, but have tried to make it clear when this has been done.

Naturally in writing a book like this, one uses material, most of which is not directly referenced, from many sources. So I extend thanks and apologies to all my professional colleagues who find their ideas and discoveries, unacknowledged, in the text. I hope they will not be too dismayed at the use made of their material. I am also indebted to a number of individuals. The students at the College of St Paul and St Mary, whose ideas have often been a source of stimulus; my colleagues Susan O'Brien and Charles Withers, and Peter Wardley, for their advice; Howard Gospel, for the opportunity to consult his book before it was published; my teachers at the London School of Economics, Dudley Baines, Eddie Hunt, the late Arthur John, and Walter Stern, without whom I would not have known any economic history; Homan Potterton, whose enthusiasm for the art of the farmyard showed me the significance of 'Mr and Mrs Andrews'; and Andrea Masters, who did the word-processing, for her efficiency and helpfulness. I owe a particular debt to Bernard Alford, for his many helpful comments on the text.

My greatest debt is to my wife, for her help throughout the writing of this book. I dedicate it to her.

The publishers would like to acknowledge the following for permission to use illustrative material in the text: Cambridge University Press (tables 2.1, 6.1, 7.1, 10.3, 15.1, 20.1 and 27.2), the Controller of Her Majesty's Stationary Office (tables 31.8 and 35.4), Leicester University Press (table 4.1), Methuen and Co. (map 4 and table 35.2), the Nationwide Anglia Building Society (map 7) and Oxford University Press (tables 8.1, 8.3, 18.1, 31.2 and 31.6).

To Hilary

PART ONE
Industrialisation 1750–1830

CHAPTER ONE
Agriculture and rural society

In the National Gallery, in London, hangs a portrait, 'Mr and Mrs Robert Andrews', by Thomas Gainsborough. It depicts a young squire, Mr Andrews, and his wife, in an English landscape. The landscape is not there merely as an ornament, for Gainsborough has painted his subjects on Mr Andrews' farm, Auberies in Suffolk. In 1751, the date of the picture, Auberies was a modern working farm, and in the picture Mr and Mrs Andrews are portrayed beside a field whose crop, sown in neat rows, has just been reaped. Further back is a rectangular field, gated and hurdled, which encloses a flock of sheep, while to the left cattle can be seen beside newly-built sheds. The picture is suffused by an air of quiet prosperity.

The Andrews were exemplars of the landed gentry of eighteenth-century England. The gentry and the aristocracy together constituted around 20,000 families, owning between them nearly three-quarters of the land surface of the country. Gainsborough's picture, therefore, depicts land and land ownership. Missing from it, though, are the people who worked on the land, the farmers, the labourers, the women harvesters, the carters, and many other types of worker, who comprised about one-third of the adult population. Their numbers were so large because the amount produced by each worker was low, compared with agriculture today. Unmechanised harvesting necessitated a vast labour force to cope with the harvesting period. It took endless human toil to plough the land and sow the crops, which then produced a meagre return. Although the agricultural workforce was not subject to the subsistence crises that still affected parts of Continental Europe, many of them were not far above subsistence level.

Behind their poverty lay fundamental and age-old constraints on

3

production. Technology and the understanding of plant and animal biology was limited, while isolation and lack of education hampered the transmission of better techniques from one area to another. These constraints meant that the yield ratio – that is the amount produced from each seed that was planted – was low, and hence the yield from each unit of land was low as well.

To carry pessimism too far would be wrong, however. Gainsborough's picture conveys the justifiable pride English agriculturalists felt at the relative productiveness of their farms, a productiveness in sharp contrast to other countries. Comparative yield ratios illustrate this more prosaically: in eighteenth-century Britain they were about 10 : 1, in eighteenth-century France about 7 : 1, little better than England in the late Middle Ages. Contemporary writers recorded the poverty of French agriculture compared to English. Only Holland, and a few localised farming regions in other Continental countries, could equal the productiveness of British agriculture. And although the labour force in British agriculture was large, relative to the population it was much smaller than in most Continental countries.

Farming practices in Britain were not the same all over, of course, for Britain too was divided into fairly well-defined farming regions, which still exist today in a modified form. As one progressed northwards and westwards pasture increased, with a mixed grain and sheep economy in areas like the Cotswolds and Lincolnshire wolds, and with cattle predominating further west. Cattle rearing was mainly for meat, since milk was hardly sold outside the individual farm, although cheese production and sale was important. Within the broad farming regions, there were clearly defined smaller regions, some only a few square miles in extent. Thus the coastal strip of Lincolnshire specialised in corn and the fattening of cattle; the Somerset levels in cattle rearing and horse breeding. The rapid alternation of different types of landscape and soil in Britain fostered this agricultural diversity, which was evident from the fifteenth century or earlier. It had significant effects. Farmers in different regions could grow crops suitable to the potential of their soil and landscape, and sell these to neighbouring regions. The crucial factor was that the short distances involved kept transport costs low; in much of Europe, a lack of diversity discouraged exchange, because transport costs between regions were so much greater, thus hampering agricultural specialisation and forcing peasants to remain subsistence producers. In Britain specialisation, which enhances efficiency and facilitates an active market economy, was present from an early date.

In most regions, the ownership of agricultural land and the organisation of production followed a common pattern. A large proportion of land was owned by medium to large landowners, such as Mr Andrews. Obviously there were many small landowners as well, owning less than 40 hectares each, but their numbers were declining for much of the eighteenth century. This concentration of land ownership in Britain, although increasing over time, goes back a long way – certainly to the sixteenth century. Even more important than ownership, however, were the patterns of tenure that had grown up. Elsewhere in Western Europe, most land was either owned or rented by peasant farmers using their own or their family's labour. There were still many such farms in Britain, especially in Wales and the South West, but increasingly landowners rented their land to farmers on a large scale, who themselves employed labour and sold large quantities of their produce rather than consuming it on the farm. This was particularly the pattern in Eastern, Southern and Midlands Britain.

The techniques of farming depended partly on the landscape, but also on factors such as the knowledge possessed by the farmer, the tenurial arrangements, and the methods which had become established in an area in times past. In many areas, such as the South West of England or the Weald of Kent, land had been gradually taken in over the centuries from waste or forest, the individual cultivators who did this growing hedges or putting up walls, to mark their field boundaries. This gave rise to a landscape of enclosed fields; that is, the field boundaries were delimited in some way. In other areas, including the major areas of arable farming, the earliest settlements had been marked by some type of communal farming of the village lands, and this type of farming gave rise to large open fields, divided into long strips which were rented or owned by individual cultivators. These open fields persisted over much of Britain, especially in the East and Midlands, into the eighteenth century. There was a gradual tendency for many villages to be partially enclosed by agreement among the proprietors, however, so by 1700 around 70 per cent of the land area of England was enclosed, although less in Wales and Scotland. The eighteenth and early nineteenth centuries were to see a continuation of the trend towards enclosure, so that by 1830 around 90 per cent of all land in England was enclosed. Much of the remainder consisted of the surviving commons, that is rough grazing land over which there were communal rights. (Where such land was enclosed, this denoted the apportionment of formerly communal rights rather than the construction of physical boundaries.)

In the period 1750–1830, a large amount of enclosure was by private Act of Parliament, probably because enclosures increasingly tended to encompass whole villages and thus involve more complexity, and possibly opposition, than voluntary agreements could cope with. It was at this time that the broad open fields of Eastern and Midlands Britain, as well as much heath land and other land of poor quality hitherto little used for systematic cultivation, gave way to the straight roads and rectangular fields which can still be seen in many areas today. In Lowland Scotland, where enclosure before 1750 had been limited, the change in the peak enclosure years of the late eighteenth and early nineteenth centuries was even more dramatic.

These peak years were also years of very high wheat prices. Enclosure was probably always a good investment for landowners, but for the smaller ones the cost was higher per acre, because fencing costs for small areas of land were high. It seems likely that much of the land which was enclosed late was in villages with a number of small owners, who were only shaken into activity by the high prices which resulted from demand from the growing population, and the inflation associated with the war years up to 1815.

Why was enclosure a good investment, given that with the cost of legal expenses and surveyors' fees, new roads and fencing, it was expensive? The inflation of the war years makes a definite figure meaningless – costs altered as prices rose and fell – but one estimate is that around 1800 it cost £30 per hectare, which is the amount that an agricultural labourer would earn in a year. Both contemporaries and historians suggest that enclosure freed farmers from the constraints imposed by the use of traditional and inefficient rotations on the open fields, where communal sanction was needed for change, and allowed them to follow best practice elsewhere. In fact, techniques on the open fields could be flexible, and open field farming could be as efficient as enclosed farms, but in general there was an improvement when enclosure took place, while other factors – fewer scattered fields leading to less travelling time, better roads and the better drainage that was often installed – must have helped to improve the yield of the land or to lower costs. The replacement of communal pasture rights by enclosed pasture also helped by reducing risk of disease from cross-infection. All this enhanced the attractiveness of the enclosed land to farmers and enabled landowners to raise rents.

Important though enclosure was, there were other significant changes in agriculture which had been taking place over many generations and continued in this period. These changes would no doubt have continued without enclosure, although as has been seen it did facilitate change. Probably the chief development was the spread of improved rotations. The traditional method of open field farming in England was to have two years of grain crop, which absorbed nutrients, especially nitrogen which is crucial for grain crop yields, from the soil, and then a year of fallow, which enabled the soil to regain its usual low level of fertility by the limited nitrogen-fixing activities of weeds and algae. Improved rotations, which date back to the Middle Ages but became widespread in Eastern England in the seventeenth century, might incorporate, over a period of four years or more, one year of turnips or other root crops which provided winter fodder for the animals, and also demanded thorough weeding and thus cleared the ground. Much more important was the incorporation of leguminous grasses such as clover, either in alternate rotation with grain and fodder crops or in convertible husbandry, where grass was laid down for several years, then grain crops likewise. Legumes fix nitrogen from the air and so, via the animals which ate the clover and then deposited their dung and via the plant residues left in the ground, the soil's fertility could be permanently enhanced.

There were many other agricultural improvements open to farmers in this period, many of which, like the use of leguminous grasses and root crops, were not new but simply became more widely diffused. Apart from the increased use of dung from animals, there was growing use of lime and marl, that is clay, to alter the composition of soils, especially where river navigations or canals reduced the cost of transport. Cheaper iron facilitated the greater use of iron ploughs which were lighter and more effective than those mainly constructed of wood, thus leading to savings on draught animals. Farming generally remained unmechanised, however, with the other major stages of arable farming – sowing, reaping and threshing – carried on largely by hand-wielded implements, although threshing machines were being introduced in the early nineteenth century. The beginning of the systematic cross-breeding of animals is often associated with the mid-eighteenth-century Leicestershire breeder Robert Bakewell, although interbreeding to improve characteristics was certainly not new. Bakewell and others improved both sheep and cattle, laying the emphasis on early fattening to reduce the time taken to get animals to market. Many of these earlier cross-breeds, whose bloated forms still stare out patiently from faded

7

prints on the walls of country hotels, were so fat as to be unpalatable. Nevertheless the methods of the early breeders laid a foundation for further improvements.

All these advances contributed to a slow but definite improvement in the productivity of the key inputs into farming. Estimates for yields per hectare and yield ratios are very uncertain, since they rely largely on the chance survival of farm records or the guesses of opinionated contemporaries such as the agricultural writer Arthur Young. One estimate is that yield ratios rose from 9 : 1 in the late seventeenth century to 11 : 1 in the early nineteenth. One estimate for yields per hectare – which would not necessarily change in the same proportion as yield ratios – suggests they rose as much as 75 per cent between the mid-seventeenth century and 1800; a less optimistic estimate suggests an increase of one-third from the late seventeenth to the late eighteenth century. Some historians think that the increase was slower in the later than in the earlier eighteenth century, accelerating again after the turn of the century, but no one suggests that there was an alteration in the general pattern of improvement. Another way of measuring is to look at population, which rose in Britain from around six and a half to almost eleven million between 1700 and 1800. While there was a small net export of food in 1700 and a small net import in 1800, a substantial increase in food output must still have come about, even if dietary standards fell somewhat. This also indicates that labour productivity in agriculture increased substantially, since it seems unlikely that there was much growth in the farm labour force over this period.

The advances discussed earlier supply the proximate reasons for output increase. What needs to be explained, however, is why farmers in Britain adopted these improvements. The first thing to do is to look at long-term influences on output, because the period shared many characteristics with earlier periods and cannot be sharply separated from them. One model of agricultural change, associated with Ester Boserup, suggests that it has occurred throughout history under the influence of increasing demand from a growing population. Increased demand leads to rising price, which stimulates farmers to adopt innovations in technique in order to increase production. At the same time, a denser population makes it more worthwhile to invest in expensive overhead capital, such as ships, docks and roads, which need to be intensively used to be profitable. These improved transport facilities encourage farming regions to specialise in produce suitable to their soil and climate, which further increases productivity. Furthermore, the population of towns increases, absolutely if not in relation to population in the country as a whole, and these areas of concentrated population provide a further market for intensive, specialised agriculture.

To some extent the long-term course of agricultural change in Britain fits in with this model. Population was growing, except for a lull from the mid-seventeenth to the early eighteenth centuries, and the population of towns, especially London, was usually growing even faster; agricultural prices rose sharply relative to other prices in the sixteenth century and, after dropping back, accelerated again in the later eighteenth century; the most advanced agriculture, at least in the sixteenth century, was to be found close to London. In spite of these facts, the role of population growth and demand in stimulating change should be put in perspective. Demand is more likely to stimulate change if there is a market. In economists' terms, this means not just the existence of physical market places, but any situation in which buyers and sellers are in contact and are exchanging goods for money, thus enabling prices to reflect changes in demand and supply. The more goods are actually bought and sold, and the more people who enter into trade, the more efficient markets will become. That is, the more prices everywhere for the same product will tend to be equalised, taking account of transport costs. The consequence of efficient markets is that when demand for a product rises in one part of the country, the subsequent rise in price will be transmitted elsewhere, giving producers everywhere the chance to respond to the higher price by increasing production. The more efficient markets become, the more one can talk of a national market, and this had certainly become established in Britain by the eighteenth century, if not earlier.

The growth of a national market in Britain was not just a function of increasing population, for in much of Europe the same conditions applied but did not have the same effects. Perhaps it can be traced to early agricultural specialisation, which was facilitated by geographic diversity and by naturally good transport facilities due to the long coastline and navigable rivers. The result of agricultural specialisation was a greater exchange of products over a wider area. The experience of many Continental countries in the period suggests that where well-established markets and reasonable transport links were lacking, output only responded sluggishly when population rose. Periods of desperate shortage had occurred in these countries in the late sixteenth and seventeenth centuries, and were looming again in the later eighteenth century.

While demand, which was made effective by pre-existing market mechanisms, helps to explain agricultural improvement, there may be other factors which made farmers in Britain responsive to change. Explanations which emphasise knowledge by farmers and landowners of innovations and willingness to adopt them, either to increase production at times of rising prices or simply to reduce costs, may be described as supply-side explanations, as may explanations which emphasise the availability of capital to carry out improvements. Is there evidence that could favour such explanations?

The answer is yes. The numbers of larger farms in Britain had been increasing since the sixteenth century. Farmers on a large scale, who could concentrate on organising production and selling their output and leave the manual work to others, were more likely to be knowledgeable about what the market required, were more likely to travel and thus learn about new techniques used elsewhere, were more likely to take risks, were probably more literate and thus had more opportunity to gain information, and were more likely to have access to large sums of money. The latter was important because it was not just enclosure, which the landlords paid for, which was expensive; better seeds, new ploughs, horses instead of oxen – all these cost money.

The role of landowners as opposed to farmers in improvement is undoubted, but less easy to explain. Historians of an earlier generation emphasised the importance of 'improving' landlords such as Viscount Townshend, nicknamed Turnip Townshend. While such landlords improved their own estates, their influence elsewhere could be limited, since farmers who took the risk of adopting new rotations were more likely to be impressed by other farmers' experience, rather than by the experiments of wealthy landowners. Nevertheless there is enough evidence of landowners encouraging the diffusion of new crops to show that they did have an influence. The support given by landlords to farmers, for instance by reducing rents at times of low prices or poor harvests, was also beneficial. Taking a cynical view, it seems likely that the acceptance of social obligations by landlords was underpinned by their opportunities to increase rents in the longer term through enclosure. In Highland Scotland, by contrast, landlords found that the only way to raise their income was to remove the population and convert to sheep farming. This they did in the notorious Highland Clearances of the eighteenth and nineteenth centuries. Fortunately in England and Lowland Scotland altruism largely coincided with self-interest. The example of the Highlands suggests that self-interest might have won had there been a competition.

THE LONG-TERM CONTEXT

All these factors in agricultural improvement were not specific to the period 1750–1830. In fact, given that enclosure itself was not new but only the form it took, the only really striking feature which distinguishes the agrarian history of the period is the rapid enclosure of poorer marginal land, much of it previously uncultivated in any systematic way, during the wartime years 1790–1815. This clearly was in response to demand, and much of the land went out of arable cultivation when prices fell after the war. The cultivation of this land may explain the apparent slowdown in the rate of increase of yields from the late eighteenth century onwards. Yields are likely to be lower on marginal land, and this would reduce the average. The lack of any striking innovations in this period, on the other hand, certainly reinforces the earlier suggestion that a demand-side explanation of change is inadequate by itself, as does the fact that the best period for yield increases seems to have been the earlier eighteenth century, when prices were depressed.

In a wider context, the ability of farmers to improve production and productivity should be measured against the fact that in the earlier eighteenth century Britain was a remarkably underpopulated country, with a population one third that of France. It would therefore not have been so difficult to improve total production simply by using more labour to intensify cultivation. The particular achievement of British farmers was to increase production by improved techniques which did not need large quantities of extra labour. This kept down costs and so, in the long run, moderated food price rises, thus encouraging demand for industrial goods; on the supply side, it enabled the extra workers produced by the increasing population to work more productively in industry. So in spite of its unrevolutionary nature, the steady growth of agricultural production and productivity was important to growth in the wider economy.

11

CHAPTER TWO

Population, migration and labour supply

The accelerating increase in population which began in the mid-eighteenth century is one of the most striking, and important, changes of this period, with wide economic ramifications (Table 2.1). Although it has always been difficult to estimate population figures before the first census of 1801, recent improved techniques mean that the figures given here are likely to be as accurate as is possible. To cause the increase, there must have been a fall in mortality, a rise in fertility, or both together. Here, too, data is a difficulty, for systematic civil registration of vital events, that is births and deaths, did not exist before 1837, although registration by the parishes of the Church of England had gone on for many years. But again, recent historical research has improved the quality of the available data.

Table 2.1 Population growth in Britain 1701–1831

	Population (million)	Average rate of growth per decade	(%)
1701	6.3	1701–1751	3
1751	7.4	1751–1801	8
1801	10.8	1801–1831	15
1831	16.4		

(*Source:* Floud and McCloskey, Vol. 1)

The first point to make about the population increase is that some level of growth is not particularly remarkable or surprising. More often than not from 1500 on, European population had been rising. It is true that periods of increase were punctuated by violent declines due to abnormal mortality from disease or famine, and some periods of decline lasted a long time, but the fact of a secular rise remains. So it is not the population rise from 1750 which needs explaining, but why the rise was so steady and was not punctuated by sharp declines, and why the rate of increase accelerated as time went by.

It is not difficult to offer a surface explanation of why there were no sharp declines in population, such as were caused by the Black Death of the Middle Ages. Quite simply, there were no major disease pandemics in Europe in this period. It is harder to explain why this was so. The two most plausible suggestions, which are not mutually exclusive, are that European quarantine precautions against the spread of plague, a major killer in the past, had improved, and that certain killer diseases, notably measles and smallpox, became essentially diseases of childhood, in which they assumed a milder form than previously. The change in the nature of these diseases was caused by the decreasing geographical isolation of the population as transport improved and towns grew, changes which made the diseases endemic, so that they no longer struck large groups of adults who had no resistance. In addition inoculation in the mid-eighteenth century, and vaccination in the later eighteenth, restricted the spread of smallpox still further.

The absence of severe mortality crises helps to explain why mortality fell in the later eighteenth century, something hitherto regarded as a puzzle. Recent figures, produced by the Cambridge Group for the History of Population and Social Structure, show that mortality in most years remained much the same throughout the century. The average level was higher in the earlier part of the century, but this was mainly because the late 1720s saw one final severe mortality crisis. Mortality then improved slightly in the early nineteenth century, the expectation of life at birth rising from the upper thirties to the low forties. This near stagnation is really what we would expect, since none of the evidence gives any reason to suppose that there was much improvement in either diet or medical treatment at this time, apart from the developments in the treatment of smallpox. There may have been some improvement in environmental conditions, due to the increasing proportion of brick-built housing, and by the early nineteenth century the increased use of easily washable cotton clothing and the increased availability of soap. The significance of environmental factors is given added weight by the fact that infant mortality appears to have fallen most markedly, from average levels of over 200 per 1000 live births in the seventeenth and early eighteenth centuries to around 150 per 1000 by the mid-nineteenth century. Infants are notoriously susceptible to infections harboured by dirt, and an increase in the general standard of cleanliness may have made a significant difference. Improvements in standards of child care may also have been a factor in this decline.

The most recent assessment of the reasons for the very high growth rates of the late eighteenth and early nineteenth centuries, made by the Cambridge Group, puts the emphasis on a rise in fertility, suggesting that it rose steadily from the mid-eighteenth century and sharply from the 1780s. This rise accounted for about two-thirds of the increase in the rate of population growth between the early eighteenth and early nineteenth centuries. Fertility was well below its potential maximum in early eighteenth-century Britain, not so much because of birth control techniques within marriage (although there may have been attempts to space births) as because marriage was late. The available evidence suggests the average age of marriage was around 26 years for women in the first half of the eighteenth century, falling to around 24 years by the turn of the nineteenth; the average age for men, which was slightly higher, also fell. The number of parishes investigated is small, so the evidence should be treated with some caution, but the addition of two years or more on average to women's child-bearing period must have had a major influence on fertility levels. In addition, the proportion of women never marrying fell from very high levels of over 20 per cent in the late seventeenth century, to around 5–7 per cent by the late eighteenth, the steepest fall coming in the early eighteenth century.

The reasons why people married younger, and thus had more children, are still the cause of arguments among historical demographers. It seems unlikely that it was simply a matter of greater employment opportunities in industrial areas, and almost certain that it was not due to a greater demand for child labour in these areas, as was once thought. The decline in the average age of marriage seems to have occurred all over the country, whether areas were industrialised or not, although again we should remember that the evidence is limited. The Cambridge Group's own explanation is that as real wages rose in the earlier eighteenth century, the economic constraints on early marriage were reduced. The problem with this explanation is that, by the later eighteenth century, real wages in some parts of the country were stagnant or even falling, but it was just at this time that fertility increased rapidly everywhere. According to the Cambridge Group, people took so long to appreciate their greater prosperity that they were actually getting poorer again by the time they thought they were getting richer.

It is not difficult to construct alternative hypotheses. Here is one. If we look at the motivation for marriage, we can hypothesise that there was always a desire to marry and be independent, but economic factors might strengthen or weaken this desire. In the earlier eighteenth century, a higher proportion of the rural population owned their own land, or had the expectation of renting land, than was the case later on. In these circumstances, men would wait until land became vacant before setting up an independent household, and this would decrease marriage opportunities and lead to a later age of marriage for men and women. As time went by, the decline in the proportion of small owners and tenants meant that this was less and less a feasible option. Instead, men would simply become agricultural labourers, which they could do at any age. In addition, the later eighteenth century seems to have seen contrasting trends in female employment opportunities. On the one hand, regular work for women in rural areas declined, thus reducing the attraction of remaining single. On the other hand, there were plentiful by-employments open to females, notably in textile-related occupations such as spinning as well as in diverse industries such as straw-plaiting and glove-making. Thus women had good opportunities to contribute to the family income after marriage, even if there were children in the household.

This explanation for marriage behaviour suggests that the incentive to marry is positively correlated with decreasing opportunities for achieving a position in society by postponing marriage. If you were destined to remain a labourer, why not marry now? Or as Dr Johnson put it: 'A man is poor; he thinks, "I cannot be worse, and so I'll e'en take Peggy".' One might add that Peggy may have thought the same about Hodge. Perhaps the reader, if dissatisfied with either of the two explanations so far put forward, might like to drop the idea of an economic explanation, and look towards subtle and as yet undetected shifts in interpersonal relationships as an explanation for marriage age changes. Maybe it was all due, as Lawrence Stone has suggested, to the greater availability of soap which made sex more inviting.

Explanations are easy to find. What is really needed now is more research to test these explanations. Whatever the explanation, it does seem unlikely that the fertility rise was in any simple way a response to industrialisation, as is sometimes suggested. It is also clear that although the fertility rise was important, for much of the eighteenth century it was the low level of mortality that ensured a rising population, and that this was still a factor even when fertility became the major component of population increase.

MIGRATION AND LABOUR SUPPLY

Students of internal migration in Britain in this period find it hard to decide whether to be amazed at the amount of migration that took place or puzzled that there was not even more. Massive short-distance migration of agricultural workers moving to obtain slightly better wages or conditions was nothing new and continued through-out this period. There was also a flow to London with its plentiful employment opportunities and high wages. As the eighteenth century wore on, the industrialising North, and particularly the North West, offered relatively high wages too; but all the evidence suggests that although there was in-migration, for the most part migrants came only a short distance, from the rural areas of Lancashire and Cheshire, and to some extent from the Lake District and North Wales.

There were some longer distance migrants. Small groups of highly skilled workers might travel long distances, such as the Shropshire and Staffordshire miners who were tempted by high wages to bring their expertise to South Wales in the late eighteenth century. And where there was rapid population growth and no alternative employment in the areas from which migrants came, they might also travel a long distance. Irish immigration to England and Scotland is best known, although it was on a fairly small scale until 1815, but there was also large-scale migration from the less remote Highlands to Lowland Scotland. The Irish, too, formed a high proportion of the migratory harvesting teams which proliferated at this time.

Taking all these exceptions into account, as a general rule migrants did not move far. Attempts in the 1830s by Poor Law authorities to move agricultural families from Southern England to the North had little effect, and are notable only because they highlight the fact that such people did not move voluntarily. Why was this when wages were so much better in the North? The answer seems to be that, apart from differences in wages, two other things stimulate migration: know-ledge about the intended destination, and the prior existence there of relatives or other contacts. Both these factors help to explain why most migration was short distance. In the case of migration to industrial towns in the North West, for instance, the early migrants could remain in touch with their home villages as they were still reasonably close. As time went by, these early migrants provided points of contact with later incomers, providing them with short term housing and knowledge of job opportunities.

Apart from population growth and migration, the supply of labour was affected by a number of other factors. One was the participation rate, that is the proportion of the population who worked, which is usually broken down into the male and female rate. Conceptually separate from the participation rate is the question of the hours people worked, but it is convenient to treat this and the participation rate together.

While there is no reason to suppose that the male participation rate changed significantly, since life expectancy remained short and thus there were few older workers who might be expected to work less, it seems likely that the average number of hours worked increased. There is no strong evidence that this came about through an increase in hours worked in individual occupations. Rather, it came about through the growing proportion of industrial workers, who were likely to work with more regularity than those in agriculture. The size of the agricultural labour force was dictated by the peak needs at harvest time, while for much of the rest of the year, if not actually idle, the agricultural worker was likely to be doing unproductive work. One estimate is that hours worked per year increased from 2500 to 3000 between the mid-eighteenth and the mid-nineteenth century, although there remained many whose productive working hours were considerably less.

The female participation rate is even more difficult to assess. One can start by saying that it is likely that the total amount of work done by women did not change much, if we include the massive amount of unwaged work involved in looking after the home and bringing up children. There was, however, a probable decline in non-household work, starting with the fall in female participation in agriculture as the eighteenth century wore on. Up to the early nineteenth century, domestic spinning and other rural by-employments provided alternative waged work for women, but these too were in sharp decline after 1815.

Female employment in textile factories provided some antidote to the probable decline in female participation elsewhere in the economy. But at the maximum in the mid-nineteenth century, only about 12 per cent of all adult women worked in textile-related occupations, whether in factories or elsewhere, and they were concentrated in the textile districts. In most cases the growth of industry and mining was accompanied by low female participation rates in the areas concerned. Furthermore, even in the textile areas the bulk of employment was of unmarried women; married women's participation rates were much lower. Consideration of the geographically limited nature of textile employment also highlights the fact that only a limited number of children were affected by employment in the mills. Elsewhere, child employment for the most part probably continued as it had in the past, that is intermittently up to about the age of twelve and then, for most working-class children, full time.

Just as the actual course of female participation rates in waged work is still uncertain, so the reasons for change remain shrouded in mystery. It has been argued that industrial work was physically less suited to women, but the fact is that women did not participate in many tasks which they were quite capable of doing. Clerical work, for instance, was almost exclusively a male preserve until the end of the nineteenth century. It seems more plausible to explain women's exclusion from most waged work as occurring through the interaction of economic and ideological change. Economic pressures in rural areas in the later eighteenth century, stemming from the increased supply of male labour, seem to have led to a process of social exclusion of women from waged work in order to maximise the amount available to men. The decline of small farms where the wife participated in the work may have had the same effect. The resulting sexual division of labour was carried over into nineteenth-century industry and strengthened by an ideology which increasingly glorified the home as the woman's sphere. Of course, some women may have preferred this, but speculating on whether such preferences are given, or are socially induced, takes us into the realms of psychology and is best avoided here.

In overall terms, the supply of labour for waged work probably increased faster than the population, although the increase in male hours was partly offset by a decline in female participation. But measurement of the supply of labour should extend beyond mere measurement of quantity to consideration of quality. A skilled and literate worker may be worth far more than an unskilled illiterate, although the extra value will partly depend on the type of work available. The concept of human capital is a useful one around which to organise a discussion of labour force quality. The cost of education and training can be seen as an investment which will bring in future returns, just as the cost of a road or piece of machinery is an investment. Measurement of education is difficult for this period, since there is no hard data on schooling, but literacy is usually taken as a proxy. The test of literacy is whether people could sign their names on marriage registers. It is an imperfect test, but adequate. Based on this, M. Sanderson has put forward a number of propositions about human capital formation in this period. Literacy seems to have improved little in the period *c.* 1760 to *c.* 1830, and it may even have declined in the industrialising areas of the North West. But this did not really matter, because the bulk of the workforce did not need to be literate. In fact, Sanderson suggests that it was better for the economy that investment was concentrated on physical rather than human capital. He also suggests, however, that there was a reasonable standard of education available for middle-class children in business and scientific subjects. We might add two more points. The actual standard of literacy in Britain, although not rising much, was already reasonably high by the standards of many Continental countries. In the mid-eighteenth century, male literacy in England was around 60 per cent, and it was somewhat higher in Lowland Scotland: this compares with 50 per cent in late eighteenth-century France. Second, an important part of human capital formation took place through on-the-job training, either by apprenticeship or by the informal picking up of skills. In this, Britain had the great advantage that industry and commerce were already well established. Training was therefore carried out cheaply and effectively in the course of working, and this was so whether we are talking about working-class iron puddlers, middle-class mining surveyors, or the clerk who was gaining a training in commercial skills in a merchant's office.

No doubt further investment in education would have yielded some further return by enhancing labour-force quality still more, but it is hard to quarrel with Sanderson's view that there would have been little advantage in major expenditure on education because the available type of work did not justify it. Can we come to a similar clear-cut conclusion about the effect on the economy of the rise in population in this period?

On the face of it, rising population stimulated demand and, therefore, by pushing up prices encouraged farmers and industrialists to invest more, and to innovate, in order to take advantage of these high prices. In other words, population growth stimulated economic development. The motivations for investment and innovation are not necessarily so simple, however. Earlier periods of rapid population increase, such as the later sixteenth century, were associated with declining living standards, because production had failed to keep pace. This strongly suggests that rising population does not necessarily provide enough stimulus by itself for enhanced investment and innovation. Clearly the conditions which do provide such stimuli are important in assessing the effects of population increase on economic development. Chapter 1 discussed the conditions necessary for growth in agricultural output; subsequent chapters will discuss the necessary conditions in other sectors of the economy.

CHAPTER THREE
Towns, transport and internal trade

TOWNS

'I set off for Cheltenham . . . it is to these watering places that a foreigner should be taken, in order to give him an adequate idea of the magnificent opulence and universal luxury of England.' The words of the novelist Bulwer Lytton, written in 1830, could have been used at any time in the previous eighty years, if not about Cheltenham then about equivalent towns such as Bath. Compared with most Continental countries, England was both more wealthy and more urbanised. Only the Netherlands and Northern Italy could match English levels of urbanisation, and probably only the Netherlands could match English levels of income per person.

In spite of this relative sophistication, most towns in 1750 were small both in area and population, with densely-packed housing, especially for the poor, and little of the suburban sprawl so familiar today. Apart from London, even the largest towns such as Edinburgh, Norwich and Bristol had populations of less than 50,000 each in 1750, or the size of a modern medium-sized town. There were only eight towns with more than 20,000 inhabitants in 1750, although there were twenty by 1800. London was different: already one of the monster cities of Europe in 1700, along with Paris and some Italian cities, its population had almost doubled to 950,000 by 1800, making it the largest city in Europe.

The lack of a census before 1801 makes it impossible to estimate exactly the urban population of Britain, as does the fact that a town is hard to define. A minimum population level of 2500, which would be very small by today's standards, might in the eighteenth century exclude settlements which carried out the functions of a town by providing services for the surrounding countryside. Using this 2500 minimum as the best guide we are likely to have, it is estimated that the urban population in England and Wales as a proportion of the whole rose from about 22 per cent in 1750 to about 30 per cent in 1800; Scotland was less urbanised (Table 3.1).

Table 3.1 Urban growth *c.* 1750–1800: some examples

		000s	*000s* *1801*
Birmingham	(1750)	24	71
Bolton	(1773)	5	13
Liverpool	(1773)	34	78
Manchester	(1788)	43	75
Norwich	(1752)	36	37
Worcester	(1779)	13	11

Note: Dates in brackets are of local enumerations
(*Sources*: Corfield, P 1982 *The Impact of English Towns 1700–1800*; Mitchell and Deane)

Whereas most early towns were market towns servicing agriculture, or military, ecclesiastical or administrative centres, by the eighteenth century in Britain they had developed other economic functions. Given the significance of agriculture, however, the market town function was still extremely important, and there was a market town in well-populated districts every few miles. They did not survive economically simply by holding markets, but also by acting as the centre of the local transport network, and by providing retail shops and professional services such as those of solicitors. One step up were regional centres such as Maidstone and Gloucester, which provided the same services at a more extensive level and often performed specialised non-economic functions such as holding the assizes. In addition, such towns increasingly provided a penumbra of recreational services, and a rapid increase in the number of theatres, literary institutes and assembly rooms took place in the later eighteenth century.

The growing sophistication of Britain's economy and its increasing integration as a national economy rather than a series of local economies was reflected by the development of towns with specialist economic functions. Eighteenth-century towns which had the provision of pleasure as their main function were often centred around a spring of evil-tasting water, the drinking of which was held to have therapeutic properties. With hindsight, we can see that the medical fashion which dictated this was a veil behind which the gentry and wealthier merchants and farmers could have a good time, while pretending to themselves that they were improving their health. There were many now forgotten local spas, while the existence of Bath, whose population in 1801 of 33,000 made it the twelfth largest town in the kingdom, testifies to the wide market the provision of pleasure could tap. From the late eighteenth century, seaside resorts, notably Brighton, were creeping up on the spas in popularity. Economically, the provision of recreational activities, either in specialist towns or as part of the function of other towns, was extremely important, generating building activity, and the provision of lodgings, transport and retail services.

Foreign trade was important for a more limited number of towns. London and Bristol were pre-eminent in the earlier eighteenth century, but Liverpool and Glasgow grew rapidly as the century wore on; Hull and Whitehaven also had a major involvement. It was not merely the provision of shipping and dock services which provided employment and wealth in such towns, but also the need for shipbuilding and ship repair, and the provision of warehousing and of facilities for upgrading imported goods, for instance by refining sugar. Other important ports such as Newcastle and Sunderland depended on coastal rather than foreign trade, both of these specialising in coal, while many smaller coastal towns were involved in shipping services of some kind, either in the coastal trades or in short-sea trades to Europe. Finally, Chatham, Portsmouth and Plymouth had the specialised and for them economically vital role of providing bases and servicing facilities for the Royal Navy.

Practically all the economic functions listed above except the last came together in London, the largest port and the greatest administrative centre, and a provider of services on a national and international level. An explanation of London's dominance among English towns must go back to the sixteenth century or earlier and is beyond the scope of this book, but some understanding of why it continued to be dominant can be gained. London's income depended on a multifarious range of activities. The provision of governmental services, such as they were in eighteenth-century Britain, helped to attract a social elite to London for part of the year and thus supported the provision of a vast range of recreational services. Through being the major English port, London became the centre for the provision of international insurance and banking services, still small in the eighteenth century but growing. The existence of a large and wealthy market encouraged manufacturing in the London region, and economies of scale led in some cases to London dominating the national market. This occurred, for instance, with the distilling of gin and the manufacture of pocket watches, both important consumer goods in their different ways.

The rise of manufacturing towns is the most striking feature of this period. In 1750, manufacturing in small workshops for the local market was an important function of all towns. Apart from London, however, much manufacturing for the national and international market was carried out in semi-industrial villages or in the country-side. Thus the greatest centre of cloth production was the countryside of the West Riding of Yorkshire, where towns like Leeds and Halifax acted more as trading than as manufacturing centres. (Such towns were referred to by contemporaries as manufacturing towns, since they provided services for industry as much or more than for agriculture.) Other towns such as Birmingham, which was the leading producer of small metalware, did carry on manufacturing themselves but were also centres for surrounding industrial villages. The later eighteenth and early nineteenth centuries saw the rapid growth of large-scale manufacturing in the cotton districts of North-West England and the West of Scotland, at first in the countryside but increasingly concentrated in the towns. At the same time, the general growth of industry meant that districts of industrial villages such as the Black Country and the Potteries coalesced into towns. By 1850, around 50 per cent of the population of both England and Scotland was urban.

Although the growth in towns was accompanied by intensified house-building, it seems likely that in the early nineteenth century growth was so rapid as to outstrip the ability of towns to provide an infrastructure of roads, paving, drainage and public lighting. There had been a rapid growth of such civic amenities, particularly roads and bridges, in the later eighteenth century, and to these we might add the increased provision for recreation which has already been noted. Eighteenth-century towns also benefited from the planned development of better-quality housing, as for instance at Bath and Edinburgh, while the eighteenth-century taste for uniformity stimulated much rebuilding to produce the genteel parapetted and sash-windowed houses which survive in the centre of many smaller towns today. Although it is almost impossible to quantify the provision of amenities or the standards of housing, it seems likely that rapidly-expanding towns in the early nineteenth century fell behind the standards of the eighteenth.

Some historians have pointed to the growth of towns, particularly London, as an autonomous factor in economic growth. In this model, towns acted in various ways to directly stimulate the economy, rather than merely growing passively in response to growth in other sectors. The argument should be treated with caution. In the eighteenth century, prosperous towns reflected productive agriculture. Without increases in agricultural production, the availability of food would have been less and its price more, thus cutting urban spending power and perhaps leading to severe distress among the poor. This occurred in France in the later eighteenth century. It is true that towns provided a positive function by acting as clearing houses for information and thus aided the dissemination of knowledge of improved agricultural and industrial techniques. And as social status in towns depended less on the possession of land and more on conspicuous consumption, there was a stimulus to the acquisition of consumer goods, both reflected in and accelerated by the growth of retail shops. Both the dissemination of knowledge and the stimulus to consumerism, however, were not just attributes of individual towns but functions of the sophistication and integration of society in Britain. Towns were part of that society and not something standing above it and, therefore, important though they were towns cannot be viewed simply as separate and autonomous influences for growth.

TRANSPORT AND INTERNAL TRADE

Even the smallest towns cannot survive without goods and agricultural produce from outside, and thus their existence is dependent upon some sort of transport and trade network. A sophisticated economy such as Britain's, with its numerous and specialised towns and its specialised farming regions, needed a complex network.

Water transport was far cheaper than land transport in the eighteenth century, so bulky goods went by water if possible. Britain's long, indented coastline, punctuated by a number of navigable rivers, was therefore a valuable economic asset. Important water-borne traffic included coal from the North-East to the South, particularly London, and grain and hay, which moved from small ports all round the coast to a few large distribution centres such as London and Bristol. The Severn was a major artery for mineral traffic and manufactured goods from the Midlands. And, as the eighteenth century wore on, the trade in agricultural products from Ireland grew ever greater.

The technology of sailing ships did not change much in this period, although there was a gradual improvement in efficiency. When steam vessels came into use in the early nineteenth century their high fuel costs limited them to tug-boat work, where they could work against the wind and clear ships quicker from port, and to short-distance passenger traffic, for instance between Scotland and Ulster, where speed mattered more than price. The big development in water transport in the period was the canal. These had been preceded in the seventeenth and earlier eighteenth centuries by the removal of impediments to navigation such as mudflats and rapids in many rivers. Canals were not a radical departure but the next step forward from these so-called river navigations. The first canal in England, apart from the very short Exeter canal in the sixteenth century, was the Sankey in Lancashire, opened in 1759. It was followed by the much better known Bridgewater canal of 1761, which linked the Duke of Bridgewater's coal mines with Manchester. Its engineering feats, including an aqueduct and a tunnel, struck the imagination of contemporaries. A rapid period of canal-building followed, with peaks in the 1770s and 1790s.

The development of canals has often been regarded as one of the foundations of the Industrial Revolution, but in fact they had many limitations. There was the fact, obvious to anyone who travels along one of the surviving canals or studies a map, that they usually meandered about and, when they surmounted a hill, needed numerous time-consuming locks. They were also of limited value in many parts of the country, either because of topography or because there was not enough traffic to justify them. For the latter reason and also because there was good river communication, there were few canals in much of Eastern or Southern England, while they played an insignificant part in London's economic development. The coal-mining areas of the North-East also had little use for them: Northumberland and Durham were too hilly, and the short distance from the coalfield to the river estuaries was better served by waggonways. Canals were concentrated in the Midlands and North, particularly the North-West. In the North-West they helped to widen the market for the Lancashire coalfield and cheapen carriage from Manchester to the sea. Their impact on Birmingham and the Potteries was perhaps even more marked, giving these two land-locked areas improved outlets for their manufactured goods.

While the achievements of canals should be kept in perspective, it is fair to say that they had a considerable localised economic impact in the areas they served. They sharply reduced the price of coal and other bulky commodities, both at their terminal points – it is said that the Bridgewater canal halved the price of coal in Manchester – and also in the rural areas through which they passed on the way to their destinations. The extent to which heavy traffic was suited to canals is shown by the fact that most warehousing in cities like Birmingham and Manchester continued to be located on canals even after the railways were built.

Important though water carriage was, it was inevitable that a vast proportion of traffic went by road for at least part of the distance. Although legend has it that English roads at this time were appalling, it seems likely that parish maintenance of them from the sixteenth century onwards was often quite effective, and it is a striking fact that expenditure on parish roads, mainly maintenance rather than new construction, was higher than that on any other form of inland transport infrastructure in the eighteenth century. Waggons also increased in size and sophistication from the sixteenth century onwards. Roads were further extended and improved by the growth of turnpiking throughout the eighteenth century. So-called turnpike trusts took over sections of road, levied tolls – the toll houses are still highly visible – and in return undertook maintenance and improvement. Unlike canals, which were usually financed by shareholders who sometimes reaped extraordinary profits if the canal was successful, turnpike trusts aimed only to pay a fixed percentage on the money they borrowed. Like canals, they were non-governmental institutions, even though they maintained the King's Highway, and were usually developed by groups of merchants or local residents and landowners. (The government developed a very few canals and roads for military purposes.) Geographically, turnpikes were much more evenly spread than canals, but there was a strong tendency for the most heavily travelled routes, that is the roads out of London, to be turnpiked first.

Impossible though it is to quantify, the volume of traffic that went by road was undoubtedly large and growing. Vast numbers of animals went by foot, like the cattle that were moved from Wales and Scotland to the Midlands fattening grounds, and then on to London. Stagecoach services began in the seventeenth century and developed in the eighteenth, with the Royal Mail beginning in 1784. It was only in the early nineteenth century, however, that passenger coach services reached their peak, at the same time as there was a significant improvement in road surfacing associated with the improved construction techniques of MacAdam and other engineers. As late as 1754 it took ten days from London to Edinburgh by coach, but by 1830 this was reduced to forty-two hours. In the 1820s, a medium-sized town like Cheltenham had a total of fifty-five coach departures every day, with frequent services to nearby towns like Gloucester and Tewkesbury, as well as coaches to such far-flung destinations as Liverpool, Exeter and Holyhead. Equally remarkable were the goods waggon services from this one town, daily to London and frequently to South Wales, the North and other destinations. There was a network of such services over the entire country.

While canals had the obvious effect of cutting haulage costs directly, there were other ways in which both they and improved road transport benefited the economy. A reduction of the time taken in transit, or an improvement in the reliability or frequency of the service, meant that merchants and manufacturers could keep smaller stocks of finished goods or raw materials, and yet could still be sure that they would not run short. Less money tied up in stocks meant lower interest charges and hence lower costs or, alternatively, more money available for investment. Less tangibly, the improvement in transport, and particularly in coach transport, alerted the inhabitants of the small towns and sleepy villages of England to their place in a busy consumer society, in which examples of the latest fashion in hats or copies of the latest novel sped across the land at ten miles per hour.

Dependent upon this transport network were all those engaged on internal trade. Specialised shops had been established for centuries in London and other large towns, but at the start of the period much retailing in other parts of the country, and most retailing to the poor, went on in markets or through travelling hawkers, or was carried on by independent artisans like cobblers who both made and sold their products. Wholesaling tended to be an unspecialised function, carried on by manufacturers and retailers. Henry Wood of Bridge Street, Westminster, announced on a bill of 1766 that he sold 'all sorts of China-ware, Useful and Ornamental, Laquer'd Ware, India Fans, Flower'd and Plain Glass, Best White Stoneware etc. etc. Wholesale and Retail'. As the market grew in size, shops grew in number, and wholesaling became increasingly an important activity in its own right. By the 1830s, the centre of Manchester had become less devoted to manufacturing and more to large wholesale warehouses. As with trade, the provision of transport services at the start of this period was frequently unspecialised; Yorkshire weavers, for instance, rode into market with their own cloth; shipowners often carried on other types of business. Throughout the period there was a growth of specialised transport firms, with their own specialised employees – bargees, lock-keepers, coach-drivers and guards, and so on.

Two things stand out from this survey of transport and trade. The first is that growth, particularly that of transport facilities, was primarily demand-led. If the demand had been there before, turnpikes and canals could have been built earlier than they were, since there were no major technical innovations involved in their construction. Even the raising of the large sums of money involved was not a particularly difficult task, since Britain was well used to the techniques of large-scale money-raising.

On the other hand, the very ease with which transport facilities and trade accommodated themselves to growing demand can lead to their importance being overlooked. In developing countries today the lack of a transport infrastructure is often a major disadvantage and not one which can be easily remedied, since it is so expensive to install. Britain was given the basis for a network – the sea and the rivers – by nature, and it was comparatively easy to add to this because there was a good supply of capital. The lack of an internal trading network can be an equal problem in developing countries. Trade requires skills and qualities which are not easily acquired: commercial skills, but also qualities of punctuality and reliability on the basis of which merchants can form long-term relationships without necessarily ever seeing each other. Britain had been developing these skills and qualities over centuries of internal trade, and the growing specialisation of this period was adding to an existing store of expertise. Merchants also had a dynamic role, however, since even if not innovators themselves they acted as a channel for introducing new products to the market, if there was a potential for profit.

While transport growth was demand-led, therefore, it was important that there was a good supply-side response. And in the case of trade networks, it is almost impossible to disentangle the extent to which they merely grew in response to rising demand, and the extent to which they spread knowledge of new products and therefore actively stimulated demand.

CHAPTER FOUR

Foreign trade

THE GROWTH OF TRADE

The sordid glamour of the slave trade and the sugar plantations, the
wealth of the Indian nabobs and the exploits of English seamen all
cast a haze of romance over trade, ships and the sea in the eighteenth
century. In reality, trading to far-away places was only a small part of
total foreign trade in the mid-eighteenth century. Trade was
dominated by the mundane business of selling wool textiles to
Europe and importing such staples as wine, from France and
Southern Europe, and naval stores, that is goods such as timber and
hemp, from the Baltic region. The import from the West Indies and
North America of warm-climate products such as tobacco and sugar,
and their re-export to Europe, was also important. This pattern had
not altered much since the later seventeenth century, when Britain
had risen to a major position in European trade, overtaking the
Dutch and rivalling the French. The mid-eighteenth century saw the
beginnings of further change. European trade remained important,
and by the mid-1780s accounted for around 40 per cent by value of
British exports, and a higher proportion of imports. The West Indies
and North American trades had grown rapidly, however, accounting
together for a third of exports by the mid-1780s. To pay for these
goods, mainly textiles and metalware, North America sold agricultural produce to the West Indies, which in turn sent increasing
quantities of sugar to Europe. Tobacco from Virginia was another big
North American export. These were the main extra-European
trades, since India and the Far East were not major export markets
for Britain, although there were significant imports of luxury goods
from the region, paid for partly by bullion. Woollens and worsteds

were still the main export goods, although metalwares and cotton goods were of increasing importance.

The next forty years saw further changes. The course of trade during the Revolutionary and Napoleonic wars was, not surprisingly, erratic. As Britain became increasingly predominant at sea, and as after 1790 revolution broke out in the main French sugar-producing colony of Saint Dominigue (now Haiti), Britain temporarily monopolised the re-export trade, importing West Indian and North American produce and selling it to Europe. Then in the 1800s, economic sanctions against Britain tended intermittently to depress trade with the Continent, and the need to find new markets, combined with Britain's naval supremacy which kept competitors away, meant that South America, previously insignificant in British trade, became an important destination for exports. The ending of the wars unleashed the potential of Europe as a market for British manufacturers, and by 1830 Europe again took around 40 per cent of exports. Once the initial shift towards the Americas had taken place, the destinations of exports did not, therefore, experience further significant long-term changes in this period. Australasia, Africa and even India were not of major importance as trading partners before 1830. The big change was in the products which entered into trade. Exports of cotton yarn and manufactures grew dramatically from the later eighteenth century, exceeding wool textiles in value in the early 1800s. By 1830, cotton goods were by far the largest single export product. This massive growth was accompanied by a growth in imports of raw cotton, so although the old staple imports continued to grow, and were joined by an increasing importation of foodstuffs, the cotton trade became paramount (see Table 4.1).

As the account above suggests, the aggregate growth of trade was substantial. Over the eighteenth century as a whole, the import and export trades combined grew about sixfold, considerably faster than the economy as a whole. As Table 4.1 shows, growth accelerated from the 1780s on, so that trade was doubling every twenty years.

It is a paradoxical fact that the growth of trade during the eighteenth century took place within a mental and physical framework that saw trade as static. This set of beliefs, known to later writers as mercantilism, held that the chief task of statesmen concerned with trade was to protect existing trades through laws or, if necessary, force, and to wrest as much trade as possible from other countries. Although trade was actually growing, these ideas made some sense at a time when everyone else believed them, since failure to defend existing trades might well result in their forcible appropriation by other countries. Acting, therefore, out of both genuine belief and also expediency, Britain had developed from the mid-seventeenth century an increasingly complex system of controls designed to keep trade with the colonies in British ships and also to discourage manufacturing in the colonies: these were the Navigation Acts. Their intention was to benefit Britain and British trade by bringing colonial goods cheaply to Britain and by ensuring an outlet for British manufactured goods.

Table 4.1 Exports of British produce, 1784–1826, by commodity groups; in £ million and percentages (annual average); also totals by volume

	1784–6	*1804–6*	*1824–6*
Cotton goods	0.8	15.8	16.9
(% total)	(6.0)	(42.3)	(47.8)
Woollen goods	3.7	6.2	5.7
(% total)	(29.2)	(16.4)	(16.3)
Total by value	12.7	37.5	35.3
Total by volume (index nos)	100	223	425

Note: The more rapid rise of the value over the volume totals between the 1780s and 1800s reflects the inflation of the period; the opposite in the subsequent period reflects the subsequent price fall
(*Source:* Davis, Ralph (1979) *The Industrial Revolution and British Overseas Trade*)

The Navigation Acts welded together what has since become known as the First British Empire, the important constituents of which were the North American colonies, both those which were to become part of Canada and those which were to become the United States, and some of the West Indian islands, notably Jamaica. The parts of India which were controlled by the British East India Company were of lesser importance at this time. Historians' chief interest in the Acts has been in their effects on the colonies themselves, since the Acts were such a bone of contention between the North American colonists and the British government. The general view now is that although the Acts inconvenienced some groups of colonists, their impact on the North American colonial economy as a whole was slight, because the colonists produced many things that were not affected by the Acts. Even in the case of goods that were affected, it was not necessarily disadvantageous to buy from Britain, as is shown by the fact that exports from Britain soon recovered after the War of Independence.

For Britain, the positive effects of having an Empire seem to have been even more limited than were the negative effects for the colonists. The reason for this was that the cost of protecting trade and the colonies was as great if not greater than the small economic advantages which came from selling to a protected rather than a free market. In forming a final judgement on the economic effects of British policy, however, it is worth remembering that the alternative to markets protected in favour of British goods would probably not have been a free market, but one protected against British goods. If Britain had not defended her colonial interests, then the French and Spanish, who took exactly the same beggar-my-neighbour attitude as the British, would probably have seized British colonies and hampered British trade.

This highlights the fact that without military protection, the Navigation Acts were no more than words. The British Navy was usually able to provide this protection, and Britain did quite well in the eighteenth-century trade wars, emerging victorious from the Seven Years War (1756–63), although being soundly thrashed in the American War of Independence (1776–83), in which the French and Spanish joined against Britain. The latter defeat, however, was more than compensated for by the lasting naval superiority gained during the Revolutionary and Napoleonic wars (1793-1815).

The motives behind Empire were various, and certain special interest groups did have aggressive economic intentions. But the overall economic impact of the First British Empire was defensive. It was necessary to maintain Britain's position, but it cannot be held to have positively accelerated the growth of trade, a conclusion that is supported by the fact that between 1715 and the 1780s the growth of French trade was considerably greater than the growth of British. Paradoxically, the effective end of this Empire with the loss of the American colonies was followed by a period when Britain, due both to naval and manufacturing superiority, drew decisively ahead of France as a trading nation.

If the Empire had negative rather than positive advantages, even less can be said in favour of the high tariffs which Britain inherited from the late seventeenth century. Particular industries gained advantages from these tariffs, but in the case of some products, such as wine and tea, the duties were levied to raise revenue rather than to

33

protect British goods, and were so high as to lead to the development of smuggling as a major industry. Smuggling helped to mitigate the deleterious effects which tariffs otherwise had on trade, but clearly there were still substantial extra costs involved which tended to depress trade below the level it would otherwise have reached. In the 1780s, a combination of the influence of Adam Smith, the economist who was an enemy of all sorts of economic restriction, and a commonsense judgement that lower duties might lead to less smuggling and thus higher revenue, led to a reduction on some goods. The outbreak of the wars and the consequent need for revenue made any more tariff cutting seem too risky, however, and these promising moves to freer trade were set aside for over thirty years, to be revived in a small way in the 1820s.

Since the existence of the First British Empire cannot account for the rapid growth of trade, and since the high levels of tariff would tend to have a depressing effect, there must be other explanations for trade growth. The period was one of general buoyancy in the economy of Europe and the Americas. Population and production were increasing, although not so fast as trade. Given this underlying growth, some growth in trade is hardly surprising; nor is it surprising that it should grow even more rapidly than production. There are two effects that will tend to accelerate the growth of trade beyond the growth of production. First, different countries have advantages in the production of different commodities, due to superior natural facilities or for other reasons. Thus tropical products will be produced cheaper in tropical countries than in Britain, for the obvious reason that they have to be grown in hothouses in this country. As territory in the Americas was discovered and opened up, and its suitability for growing products such as sugar and coffee came to be known, the range of products in which certain areas had such an advantage, known as an absolute advantage, steadily increased. Consequent upon this, the number of products which it was advantageous for European countries to import also increased. Thus the overall advantages of trading were enhanced, because more products were available to trade; in these circumstances, it was natural for trade growth to exceed the actual growth of production.

Second, the comparative advantage which countries have in the production of various goods will also foster trade. Suppose that there are two countries which each produce agricultural produce and industrial goods. It may be that one country has an absolute advantage in the production of both these types of good, that is it produces them with fewer inputs of labour and other factors of production. Income per head and, consequently, wages will be higher in this country (country A) because of its greater efficiency. Suppose also that country A is particularly efficient in the production of industrial goods and has a greater advantage over the other country in this sector. This being the case, the low wage costs of the other country will make its agricultural produce cheaper, while the efficiency advantage of country A will make its industrial goods cheaper. The implications of this for trade are obvious. At any one time, different countries are likely to be at different stages of efficiency in different sectors of the economy. As transport facilities improve, comparative advantages, as well as absolute advantages, will lead to increasing specialisation in products that the different countries are particularly efficient at producing. The result, again, will be that the increase in trade exceeds the increase in production.

Very broadly, we can generalise that absolute advantage does much to explain the growth of trade, particularly with the Americas, up to the end of the eighteenth century. The Americas had an absolute advantage in producing specialised agricultural produce, and Britain an absolute advantage in producing manufactured goods. After that date, while the above relationship remained unchanged, it also seems likely that Britain became more efficient than Continental Europe in producing both agricultural and manufactured goods. Her comparative advantages, however, lay in manufactured goods, and hence resources increasingly went into this sector and exports from it grew, while she imported more agricultural products. Although several sectors of manufacturing enjoyed a comparative advantage, it was largest in cotton textiles, where Britain had mechanised early. The large advantage in this industry helps to explain its rapid growth from the 1780s on.

FOREIGN TRADE AND INDUSTRIALISATION

Just as agricultural change and population growth have been seen as forces which may have stimulated the Industrial Revolution, so trade has been seen by some historians as the engine which drove industrialisation forward.

In order to substantiate this, we would need to find evidence to support at least one of two propositions. The first is that growth in export demand was such that it resulted in a significant breakthrough in methods of production in Britain. It seems clear that this was not the case. Up to the 1780s, growth in exports was in traditional sectors such as wool textiles and metalware. The cotton industry was growing up initially on the back of domestic demand, and the important innovations in spinning were all developed when exports were small. On the other hand, it is true that export growth made a substantial contribution to the general pace of economic advance, with around 60 per cent of additional industrial output going to exports in the last two decades of the eighteenth century. This proportion is strikingly high but, of course, if the export markets had not been available, the investments made in order to produce goods for export might have been used to produce goods for domestic use. Clearly exports made Britain better off, through the benefits brought by the utilisation of this and other countries' absolute and comparative advantages; and export growth fuelled by comparative advantage certainly helped to keep the cotton industry growing rapidly after its initial expansion. It is less obvious that export demand made a major contribution to technical innovation.

The second proposition is that the profits from foreign trade were an essential source of the capital needed for investment. The idea was first popularised by Marx, who was trying to explain how capital accumulated before industrial capitalism and factory industry came into being. How, in other words, were the early factories themselves financed? Marx's suggestion was that the slave trade and the sugar plantations, the riches looted from India by the early adventurers, and other ill-gotten gains, provided much higher levels of profit than were available from more mundane activities, and thus provided the capital needed for the development of industry. Although it still has supporters, this idea has been subjected to strong criticism. First of all, early industry, even early factory industry, did not need much capital, although large amounts were needed for agricultural improvement or for infrastructural developments such as canals. It is well established that such capital came from many sources, including merchants in foreign trade, but most notably from landowners themselves, as well as groups like shopkeepers and the clergy who likewise had nothing to do with foreign trade. Second, foreign trade itself amounted to a relatively small part of Britain's total national income, and much of this foreign trade was with traditional markets such as Europe where there is no suggestion that profits were unusually high. Therefore, total profits from foreign trade could not have been vast. The slave trade, notorious though it was, was a minor part of the British economy as a whole, and the same goes for other extra-European trades. P K O'Brien has shown that even if profits in these trades were abnormally high, and even if a very high proportion of these profits were reinvested, the small size of the trades meant that the reinvested profits would have accounted for a maximum of 15 per cent of total investment in the British economy. This takes no account of the fact that if merchants had not engaged in these trades, they would have engaged in some other activity and made some profit, albeit perhaps a lower one. The true figure for the proportion of investment generated by trading to or from, operating plantations in, or simply looting the non-European world was therefore much less than 15 per cent.

A distinctive contribution which exports did make was to Britain's ability to fight the Revolutionary and Napoleonic wars. Cheap cotton goods provided Britain with a unique and saleable product which was acceptable in all markets, at a time when Continental sanctions and the American war of 1812 led to rapid fluctuations in demand and the need to quickly find new outlets. Britain was able to find these outlets and continue to earn the foreign currency necessary to carry on the war. The cotton industry's contribution to victory over Napoleon should not be underestimated.

Foreign trade, and the profits accruing from it, were certainly a factor in Britain's economic growth. Trade lay behind the rapid growth of the shipping industry during this period and, likewise, behind a growth in the provision of international financial services such as banking and insurance which was to reach massive proportions by the later nineteenth century. Certain ports, notably Liverpool and Glasgow, experienced outstanding growth. And international demand for the products Britain exported helped this country pay its way during the Napoleonic wars. Foreign trade was therefore one factor in industrialisation, but not a decisive one.

CHAPTER FIVE
Money, banking and finance

A sophisticated economy requires a monetary system which achieves the following ends. First, it will supply satisfactory means of exchange so that transactions can be carried out easily and without recourse to barter or to rudimentary and clumsy forms of 'money', such as salt which has often been a favourite in simple societies. Second, it will provide mechanisms by which the savings of those whose income is greater than their spending will be transferred to those who wish to borrow money. Assuming that the credit network does achieve these ends, it may create for itself a new problem. The need to link savers to borrowers efficiently implies the existence of financial intermediaries, but savers may come to doubt the financial stability of the intermediary in which they have deposited their money, and the existence of easily transferable means of exchange will enable them to withdraw their money quickly. Such crises of confidence, however arbitrary or short term in origin, might have very damaging effects. The economy therefore needs some means of overcoming such crises.

The provision of means of exchange can be briefly dealt with. Like most countries, Britain until the end of the eighteenth century relied on precious metals (i.e. gold and silver) for coinage, with copper to provide small change; in practice, silver was little used. These were supplemented by notes issued by the Bank of England, the Scottish banks and, increasingly, by out-of-London banks known as country banks. Bankers were expected to be able to redeem their notes in gold or silver, however. Cash and notes were quite inadequate to meet the demand for credit by themselves and, since the Middle Ages, merchants had been accustomed to use various short-term credit instruments known collectively as bills. Essentially bills were orders to pay a stated sum of money at a certain date. If the drawee (i.e. the person who had accepted the order to pay) was of good reputation, then a bill could become to all intents and purposes like money, since it could be freely exchanged for cash or notes. The cheque so familiar today, drawn on an existing banking deposit, was also in use, but not to the same extent.

Before dealing with the channels by which money went from savers to borrowers, the terminology should be clarified. In everyday speech, the term investment is used to mean both the acquisition by governments or businessmen of physical assets such as buildings or machines, and also as a description of individuals' own savings or financial assets. To economists, investment is usually used in the first sense outlined above, the acquisition of physical assets. Savings are any money set aside from current consumption, whether it is put in the bank or under the mattress. An equal ambiguity attaches to the word 'capital'. It can mean financial assets, as when people refer to the lump sum of their savings as their 'capital'. Or it can mean the aggregate of a stream of investment: that is, a collection of physical rather than financial assets. Subsequent use of the terms in this book will attempt to clarify which meaning is intended, unless it is clear from the context.

Capital, whether meaning financial or physical assets, can be divided for convenience into fixed capital and circulating capital. The former denotes long-term physical assets such as buildings and machinery, or the finance necessary for them. The latter denotes the stocks of raw materials and finished goods which are necessary for carrying on a business, plus the credit advanced to customers, or alternatively the necessary finance for all this.

At the beginning of this period, the mechanics for transferring capital from savers to borrowers were primarily local networks of credit, together with a few national institutions. Local credit networks centred around solicitors or similar trustworthy intermediaries who arranged mortgages. Today, mortgages usually provide finance for private individuals to buy houses, but in the eighteenth century their function was to enable land or property owners to raise money on the security of their property. This money could then be used for investment. In addition, family and religious affiliations also provided links through which money was lent or borrowed. For instance, the Darbys of Coalbrookdale, the Shropshire ironmasters, raised capital both from fellow Quakers and from other family members. These sources were supplemented in the mid-century by the few country banks which then existed; but more often, cash-rich individuals such as brewers or maltsters lent money as a sideline.

They were largely acting on their own account rather than as financial intermediaries, and thus their resources were limited. This suggests that there was a potential gap in the lending market – a lack of sources of finance to enable businessmen without extensive family or other connections to build up their capital. They had to rely mainly on each other's bills, with the lack of flexibility and security that this implied. The gap could not be filled by the incorporation of joint-stock companies with limited liability, which would tap funds from investors looking for security and ease of investment. (Joint-stock companies had freely transferable shares; limited liability meant that shareholders who participated in profits, rather than just receiving interest on fixed interest stock or on loans, were not liable for a company's debts beyond their share.) Joint-stock companies, with or without limited liability, were restricted by the Bubble Act of 1720, which was a reaction to the collapse of the speculative boom – the so-called South Sea Bubble – surrounding the South Sea Company. Only a few large companies incorporated before 1720, such as the East India Company and the Bank of England, had the privileges of incorporation. Parliament was willing to lift the restrictions of the Bubble Act for public utility companies such as canals, but not for manufacturing companies.

Neither was the gap in the provision of finance filled by the national financial institutions, since they were limited in function. The London Stock Exchange, named as such in 1773 although in existence before, dealt mainly in the fixed-interest stock issued by the government. The Bank of England (henceforth the Bank) and the many private London banks borrowed and lent largely in the London area, the Bank's other main tasks being to issue notes, arrange sales of government stock and act as the government's banker.

The later eighteenth and early nineteenth centuries saw the rapid development of country banks, often linked to the wealthy individuals and families who had earlier lent money on their own account. By 1810 there were over 600 such banks, including such now famous names as Barclays and Lloyds. They were mostly small, because in England and Wales only the Bank of England could be a joint-stock bank. All other banks were limited to six partners, another of the Bubble Act's prohibitions. In Scotland, there was no prohibition on joint-stock banking and hence there were fewer, but larger, joint-stock banks, together in the eighteenth century with three very large joint-stock banks with limited liability. These were the Royal Bank of Scotland, the Bank of Scotland and the British Linen Bank. The Scottish banks initiated branch networks, which were virtually impossible to develop in England because of the banks' small size. Apart from issuing notes, the basic function of most country banks and Scottish joint-stock banks was, in bankers' jargon, to borrow short and lend short. That is, depositors with them could reclaim their money at short notice, while the money the banks lent could also be recalled without delay, at least in theory. In practice, one of the main ways in which banks advanced money was to purchase from businessmen the bills which the latter had received from other businessmen in payment for goods or services received. This process, known as discounting since the bills were purchased at a discount reflecting the current rate of interest, gave businessmen ready cash or a deposit in the bank, but it meant that the banks held large stocks of bills which had not yet reached their redemption date, and whose own convertibility to ready cash depended entirely on the willingness of someone else to buy them.

The development of a banking network, whether it took the form of independent country banks or the branches of larger banks, had important implications for an industrialising economy. As the century wore on, the demand for funds in industrialising areas such as Lancashire exceeded the resources of savers in those areas. These funds were needed in particular to provide circulating capital. Simultaneously agricultural areas were producing a growing surplus of savings, not all of which were utilised by investment in agricultural improvement. The banks provided a means by which these savings could be easily mobilised and then transferred from one area to another. This was done at first in England by the intermediation of private London banks, which took bills from industrialising areas and sold them on to the banks in agricultural areas. At the turn of the century, specialist intermediaries known as bill-brokers started to take over this function. The development of banking, therefore, was filling the gap in the provision of short-term circulating capital, although many banks also made loans which effectively financed fixed capital. The provision of longer-term finance for large enterprises like canals developed along the established lines of the joint-stock companies, although most canal investors and, for that matter, most turnpike investors were local. The national market for long-term capital was still concerned largely with government stock.

How adequately did the institutions and practices described above cater for the needs of a sophisticated economy, as outlined at the beginning of this chapter? There were few problems in the provision of means of exchange, although for much of the eighteenth century there was a shortage of small coin, leading some large employers to issue their own in order to pay their workmen. The coin shortage was inconvenient but not serious, since the overall need for credit within the economy was met by the growth of country banks and, in Scotland, joint-stock banks. In 1797, a different problem arose. War spending began to force up prices, thus increasing the internal demand for coinage, while at the same time stimulating imports. These factors led to a heavy drain of bullion from the Bank's resources, and the decision was made to conserve bullion by withdrawing it from its role as currency and as a backing for the Bank's note issue, a situation which lasted until 1821. Confidence in the Bank was such that its notes were acceptable without gold backing, and although the removal of a fixed monetary base exacerbated inflation during the war years, it never reached a disastrous level. Between 1790 and 1801, prices rose by about 85 per cent, and after that fluctuated with only a small further increase.

Even more important was the fact that the credit system coped adequately with the task of channelling funds from savers to borrowers. It is important to realise that the traditional system of credit continued to play a major part. As urbanisation grew, much housing was financed through solicitors who channelled mortgage funds to developers and to those who owned houses as an investment and let them out. Since housing was a major component of total investment, the continuing role of solicitors was very important. Similarly, most of the fixed assets in industry continued to be financed through local or family connections or simply through ploughing back retained profits. But the financing of industrial plant was less of a problem than the need for circulating capital. Early industrial plant was not expensive, but the uncertainties and slowness of transport systems meant that a much higher proportion of total capital than today had to be tied up in stocks. The development of London banks and bill-brokers as intermediaries between agricultural and industrial areas was therefore important because it provided circulating capital for industrialists and merchants. The growing efficiency of the financial system in channelling funds to where they were needed is indicated by the decline in long-term interest rates, from around 6 per cent at the beginning of the century to around 5 per cent at the end – and this latter figure was inflated by the very high demands for finance by the government during the wars. Increasing efficiency was only one reason for the decline, however, since the supply of savings throughout the country also increased as people grew wealthier. The interest rate reflected the growing demand for credit and the growing supply of savings, as well as increasing efficiency in financial intermediation.

The third requirement for a banking system in a sophisticated economy, the ability to withstand crises of confidence, was less well developed. Crises might occur for a variety of reasons. For instance a bad harvest, as in 1792, would cause gold to drain from the country to pay for imports of food. The reduction in their gold reserves would lead banks to reduce their other assets, in the form of loans and holdings of bills, since prudence dictated that a reasonable proportion of banking assets should be in gold in order to meet possible demands from depositors. This restriction in the supply of credit caused business failures which, in turn, reduced confidence in banks which had lent to those businesses, thus leading to the withdrawal of deposits and failures by banks which could not raise cash fast enough. In these circumstances, the proliferation of small English banks brought about by the Bubble Act's well-meant prohibition on joint-stock banking was liable to increase depositors' uncertainty about bank stability and hence increase panic. The remedy developed in the nineteenth century was a central bank, which at moments of crisis acted as a 'lender of last resort' and supplied funds to the other banks. In the eighteenth century, the Bank of England did assume this role, for instance in the panic of 1763, but it did so unofficially. Thus although calamitous collapses were averted, panics continued longer than they need have done because it was not always understood that intervention was taking place. Although the existence of the Bank was undoubtedly advantageous and enabled the growing banking system to operate without too many disasters, the Scottish banking system seems to have been more effective, since the very size of the Scottish banks made major crises of confidence less likely to occur.

Striking though the changes in banking were, the growth of credit networks tends to reflect the sophistication of an economy, rather than to exert a major influence upon it. Institutional and chance factors which impede or encourage this growth have an influence, but ultimately perhaps a fairly marginal one. Banking in Britain grew naturally from the activities of goldsmiths and other wealthy individuals who lent money, and from the activities of lawyers who refined techniques such as the mortgage in the seventeenth century. Financial intermediation was a great deal more sophisticated in 1800 than in 1700, and this was valuable in that areas of high saving became linked to areas of high investment; but of much more fundamental importance was the fact that Britain as a whole was a wealthy country generating surplus savings, and that it had a well-developed legal system and a stable government which meant that lenders could make loans in an atmosphere of security. The one important positive innovation from outside the organic growth of the system was the formation of the Bank of England in 1694 as the government's banker. This was part of a general improvement of government finance at this time which enabled eighteenth-century British governments to raise money reasonably easily. The Bank's reluctant acceptance of the role of central bank also provided a long stop in case of crises of confidence – but with a different system, crises might not have developed so frequently, suggesting that outside interference, in the form of the Bubble Act, could be negative as well as positive.

CHAPTER SIX
Manufacturing and mining

Manufacturing industry is seen by many historians as the centrepiece of economic growth in this period. It was in manufacturing that the most spectacular technological change occurred. It was in manufacturing that the most famous examples of business enterprise could be found. It was changes in manufacturing that led Arnold Toynbee in the late nineteenth century to entitle a series of lectures 'The Industrial Revolution' and begin a discussion which has never stopped since.

The growing importance of manufacturing and mining in relation to the rest of the economy can be quickly gauged by observing the growth in their share of national income, from about 20 per cent in the mid-eighteenth century to about 35 per cent by 1830. This gives an idea of the overall magnitude of growth, but to understand the nature of growth it is necessary to break industry down into sectors. This can be done in a variety of ways, but the most helpful for this period might be to think of industries as catering either for a mass market or for a very limited market. A related though not identical division would be between industries producing consumer goods (anything from beer to textiles to private carriages) and those making producer goods (items like buildings and machinery, which are used to produce other goods or services). Producer goods are usually, although not always, made in fairly small quantities; consumer goods are more likely to cater for a mass market.

As a general rule, industries catering for a mass market will exhibit a high degree of specialisation, or division of labour. In other words, producers will specialise in making only a small part of the product or performing only a small part of the service. Specialisation might occur at the level of either the firm or the individual worker, or both.

The rationale behind specialisation is best illustrated by some examples. A country blacksmith was a typical producer for the non-mass market. He would have numerous different tasks, such as shoeing horses, making agricultural implements, and mending all kinds of iron goods. Most of these tasks had to be done in a hurry, so there was little chance for the blacksmith to make a large number of items one after the other. In contrast, a Birmingham pinworks in 1810 had thirteen different stages in the process of pin making, a classic early mass market industry; each stage could be performed by a different worker.

The economic advantages of specialisation are fairly obvious. Individual workers, and also firms, gain experience in particular skills or particular lines of activity. This experience makes them quicker, or more dextrous, or more efficient in their activities, whether these are making, managing or selling. Against this must be set what economists call 'transaction costs'. The more divided up a process becomes, the more liaison will be needed between the different groups or individuals performing each part of the process. An increasing volume of production in any one industry will both enhance the advantages of specialisation and will lower the transaction cost for each unit produced. Hence the dictum of Adam Smith, the author of the *Wealth of Nations*, that the division of labour is limited by the size of the market. The larger the market, and hence the potential scale of production, the more profitable it becomes to specialise. Specialisation is one of the most important economic advantages of size, advantages which are summed up in the phrase 'economies of scale'.

Not all consumer goods industries catered for a mass market. Such non-mass-market industries are not the principal focus of attention of economic historians in this period because, by definition, they were the industries whose technology and scale of operation remained relatively unchanged. They included many trades such as baking which produced items of common consumption, but which only distributed their products locally. Apart from baking, all sorts of everyday activities, both services and manufactures, were organised in this way. As late as 1851, for instance, there were a quarter of a million shoemakers and the same number of milliners, with 133,000 laundresses to clean the clothes made by the milliners; 7 per cent of the working population were in these trades. To them can be added the producers of luxury goods, such as high-quality furniture, for which the market was small not because it was localised, but because only a few people could afford to buy the products. In few trades, however, was the market limited so much by price that there was no opportunity to specialise, because by 1750 England, and to a lesser extent Scotland and Wales, were already rich compared with most of the Continent. In London, in particular, there were enough wealthy people to almost constitute a 'mass market' themselves. Products like watches or clothes, even private carriages, had already spawned an extensive sub-division of occupations. A contemporary commentator listed nine in watchmaking, including the wheel cutter, the case maker and the assembler.

Thus there is no hard and fast division between mass-market products and other products, but a gradual shading into each other.

The mass-market product which everyone thinks about is textiles. For the obvious reasons that people both need clothes and covet them for personal adornment, the production of cloth was by far the largest single manufacturing industry. The force of demand had long ago led large parts of the industry, both in Britain and other countries, to break away from the restrictions of the urban guilds in order to utilise the cheap labour of rural areas. The system which evolved had many different forms. The basic principle was that spinning and weaving were carried on in the workers' home, and hence this has been called domestic industry. Within this framework, the detailed organisation could be very different, depending on local enterprise, the nature of the trade itself, and other factors. There was the so-called putting-out system, in which the merchant who owned the raw material also owned the machines and paid wages to those performing the manual work. Sometimes the producers were independent, buying their raw materials, completing a stage of the process, and selling the material again. In between, there was a range of intermediate arrangements.

Various elements of specialisation could exist in domestic industry. The actual stages of manufacture, in the case of woollens and worsteds, were split into washing the raw wool, carding or combing it to straighten the fibres, spinning it into yarn, weaving, dyeing, and possibly fulling to make the 'nap' of the cloth lie flat. Although households, or small groups of producers working together, might perform two or three of these stages of production, there was always a point at which the material passed to someone else for further treatment. The selling functions, too, exhibited various degrees of specialisation. A merchant might own the material throughout the processing by different groups and then handle its sale on the international market, but in other areas there were merchants who were solely concerned with marketing the finished product.

Apart from wool products, linens and silks were important textile products. The later rise of the cotton industry obscures the fact that these were fast-growing industries in the eighteenth century, responding to the demand for more varied types of cloth. The other important eighteenth-century textile industry utilised silk and linen, as well as wool. This was the hosiery industry, producing stockings (for men, who wore knee breeches, as well as for women), gloves, underwear and other products, and using the stocking frame, a sixteenth-century invention. This was the nearest thing to a mass-production clothing industry. Otherwise, clothing manufacture was a local and small-scale affair.

In the eighteenth and on into the nineteenth century, textile production went on everywhere to some extent. Wool textile production was most widespread, although lace making was a domestic industry in a number of areas. There was, however, a marked concentration of industry in some areas, so that although most production took place in the countryside, population density in the busiest areas was high and towns grew to act as centres of marketing and organisation. The main centres of the wool textile industry were the West Riding of Yorkshire, East Anglia, and the West of England, particularly Gloucestershire, Somerset and Devon. Derbyshire and Cheshire became centres of the silk industry. The linen industry was more diffused, with Northern Ireland, Eastern Scotland, North East and North West England all of some importance. The hosiery industry was centred in the East Midlands. Significantly, the linen and the hosiery industries grew in areas where there was little production of wool products and hence there was a reservoir of available labour. The same reason probably accounts for the initial development of the cotton industry in central Lancashire.

The cotton industry had developed in the earlier eighteenth century, partly because of tariffs against cheaper Indian cotton goods. In spite of this, it remained fairly small until about 1770. At that stage, cotton benefited from developments throughout the textile industry, in which the growth of production had led to increasing pressure on the supply of yarn. This always tended to be a bottleneck in textile production, as one weaver could use up the output of several spinners. The bottleneck was one factor behind a series of inventions. Carding machines invented by Lewis Paul were coming into use in the middle of the century, and in the 1760s James Hargreaves devised his spinning jenny, a hand-operated machine which enabled a number of lengths of yarn to be spun simultaneously. More important was the water-frame, using a different system of spinning. It was patented by Richard Arkwright in 1771, but was based on the ideas of a number of earlier inventors. Arkwright, a ruthless businessman, quickly set up a number of substantial factories using, as the device's name implies, water power. The spinning mule, a development of the jenny, was devised in the late 1770s by Samuel Crompton and came into extensive use in the 1780s. In improved forms it was to be the basis of the English cotton spinning industry up to the First World War. It was much more difficult to improve the loom, and it was only in the 1820s that the power loom started to make rapid progress.

Although the wool textile industry utilised the inventions, technical reasons connected with the nature of the fibre made them easier to apply to cotton spinning in the early days. Almost simultaneously, a reduction in the price of raw cotton was occurring, making the use of cotton still more attractive. As a result, until the 1820s the mills which colour our mental picture of industrialisation were chiefly limited to cotton spinning and, to a lesser extent, for worsted spinning using the water-frame. Much machinery was still used in the home or in small hand-powered mills. Water was the main power source of larger mills in the eighteenth century and continued to be important well into the nineteenth, although the use of steam power increased rapidly from the turn of the century.

Early cotton mills had been located in the Midlands as well as in Lancashire and Cheshire, but by the early nineteenth century the latter counties, Lancashire in particular, became dominant, although the West of Scotland had an important presence in the industry. Lancashire has good access to the sea and, as steam power developed, its coal supplies were an advantage. In addition, the alleged benefit of its damp climate to cotton manufacture is not just an invention by the writers of school geography textbooks. Later in the nineteenth century, when wages were based on output, it was noted that output slowed down on the fortunately rare occasions when humidity in Lancashire fell; the drier air made the threads more liable to snap.

Once the industry had begun to concentrate in Lancashire, the tendency to do so further became ever stronger. Concentration permits economies of scale through the greater division of labour it makes possible. An example would be the provision by specialists of services such as the rapid repair of machinery. Specialisation in this would be uneconomic without a large market for it. The industry in Lancashire developed an incredibly complex range of specialised activities, from the shipping firms and raw cotton brokers of

Liverpool, through the weaving and spinning and dyeing firms themselves, to the warehousemen and export merchants; not to mention the machinery suppliers, repair shops, bobbin makers, and a hundred and one other activities.

Table 6.1 Consumption of raw cotton

	Million kilos (annual average)		Million kilos (annual average)
1750–59	1.3	1790–99	13.0
1760–69	1.6	1800–09	27.0
1770–79	2.2	1810–19	42.4
1780–89	7.0	1820–29	75.5

Note: The consumption of raw cotton is the best available indicator of the growth of cotton production
(*Source:* Mitchell and Deane)

The supply changes in cotton textile production led to a continual reduction in price, and a consequent expansion in output, as shown in Table 6.1. Expansion was aided by the growth in demand from the rising population, but the main impetus to growing consumption came from purchasers at home and abroad substituting cotton goods for other textile products, and from an increase in the total market for textiles at the expense of other consumer goods whose price did not fall in the same way. Since Britain had mechanised early, her comparative advantage in the production of cotton goods was large, which accounts for her dominance.

By 1830 the cotton industry had become the largest British employer after agriculture. Even so, the wool and other textile industries remained important. Their mechanisation developed much more slowly, however, and their location and organisation did not at first change rapidly. It was only after 1815 that the post-war depression, combined with the continuing effects of technical change, put an end to large-scale textile production in areas such as East Anglia and the West Country, although some localities in the south had already experienced decline. The reasons for decline were complex and not yet fully understood, but the following suggestions have been made. The capital for the textile industries in these areas came from entrepreneurs who in the eighteenth century often turned to agriculture, where innovations and, from the mid-century, rising prices offered attractive opportunities for making money. In the

North of England, by contrast, textile industries often developed in poor agricultural areas. In other words, the distribution of activities within England can also be partly explained by comparative advantages, the south for agriculture, the north for industry. The industries in the south were characterised by a generally greater concentration of ownership, perhaps because they had been established for longer, and this gave rise to strong collective action by workers on occasion. Because of this and because workers often perceived that their industry was declining, they were much more hostile to technical change than were workers in the north, who frequently welcomed innovations like jennies which could be used at home. The growth of water-powered machinery gave the *coup-de-grace* to several southern textile regions, and steam power killed off most of the others. The south as a whole, however, had been in long-term decline as a textile-producing region long before these innovations.

Other important mass-market industries were unaffected to any great extent by mechanisation and depended for their low prices on a well-established division of labour. Among the most important industries of this kind were pottery and leather. There were potteries in many parts of the country, but north Staffordshire had already become the leading production area. Although the industry there is best known for its mid-eighteenth century entrepreneur Josiah Wedgwood, it had developed technical innovations such as coal-fired kilns before his time. And although Wedgwood's salesmanship enabled him to make his high-quality ware a popular success, pottery had effectively become a mass-market industry by the early eighteenth century. Leather, a vital raw material for shoes, gloves and saddlery and hence a major industry, was also produced all over the country but with major centres in Bermondsey, using hides from the cattle slaughtered in London markets, and in the East Midlands.

One could name a whole host of similar industries which, apart from increasing in size, did not change much in this period: watch making in London; cutlery in Sheffield; the manufacture of all sorts of small metalwares, from locks to guns to buckles and other ornaments, in Birmingham and the Black Country (manufacture of the lighter goods was known collectively as the Birmingham toy trades). In a slightly different category were mass-market industries in which production was capital rather than labour intensive. Among these were sugar-boiling, paper-making, and brewing. The latter was a major industry, and among the myriads of small local brewers there were already a number of very large-scale affairs in bigger towns, such as Barclays in London, owned by the Thrale family which befriended Dr Johnson.

While urban industries showed considerable sophistication in organisation, it is the case that early factory industry developed from the predominantly rural or small town-based textile trades. Some historians see this as more than an accidental connection and claim that the specialised and often capitalist nature of domestic industry was the true progenitor of factory industry and, indeed, of the Industrial Revolution. The phrase proto-industrialisation has been coined to describe this hypothesis, according to which the growth of rural domestic industry to escape guild restrictions and the expense of urban labour resulted in population growth in the countryside, thus providing a supply of labour for later industrial development. Domestic industry had much wider effects as well, stimulating factory production as a means of lowering costs still further once the initial economies had been exhausted, and providing a field for entre-preneurial skills to develop, and capital to accumulate.

The theory has been criticised by many economic historians, for a variety of reasons. Population growth is usually seen as multi-variate in its causation and, anyway, its links with industrialisation are uncertain. Rural domestic industry was a European phenomenon which had existed on a large scale since the sixteenth century, but had not generated large factories before the eighteenth, suggesting that there was no necessary connection between one and the other. Capital had accumulated in many ways in Britain, while the methods of mobilising it (through bills, loans, and so on) had been devised by medieval, urban Italian bankers. Sub-division of work existed, as has just been described, as much in towns as in the countryside. Finally, entrepreneurial skills and large-scale organisation were also seen in urban industries like brewing, or overseas trades like tobacco and sugar. So proto-industrialisation, as a general hypothesis to explain subsequent large-scale industrialisation, remains unproven.

Producer goods industries, which saw many of the most important technical advances, hardly fit into the proto-industrialisation schema at all. The basic industry here was iron, usually thought of as one of the core industries of the Industrial Revolution. Cheap iron was of enormous importance for the production of more efficient machin-ery, for boilers and other parts of steam engines, and for rails for the railways which were being built at the end of this period. Iron production in the early eighteenth century was based on the blast furnace, using charcoal as a fuel to melt the iron ore, a process accelerated by blasting air into the furnace. The result was known as pig iron (it was run out of the furnace into a line of oblong blocks which bore a fanciful resemblance to piglets feeding on a sow). This could be remelted and run into moulds in a foundry, the result being known as cast iron. Due to the carbon in it, it was brittle, although suitable for products such as cooking utensils or the parts of machinery which did not have to undergo stress. For iron to bear stress, the carbon had to be slowly and expensively beaten out of it by hammering in a forge. The result, known as bar iron (later wrought iron), could be reworked by a blacksmith or shaped on a lathe.

The all-important fuel supply, charcoal, was capable of almost indefinite renewal through the technique known as coppicing. In this, trees are cut back to the stump with the result that small, straight and quick-growing branches spring up, a process that can then be repeated again and again. The attentive observer can still see old coppiced woodlands today. As demand grew, however, more remote woodlands had to be used and consequently the relative price of charcoal rose from the late seventeenth century. This stimulated a search for a way to use coal in blast furnaces. Coal use had developed rapidly in Britain from the sixteenth century, and by the early eighteenth it was being used in the form of coke to smelt non-ferrous metals, to malt grain and to fire pottery kilns. (Heating coal expels the carbon, which is deleterious to industrial processes, and produces coke.)

It was not therefore surprising that Abraham Darby built a coke-fired blast furnace at Coalbrookdale in Shropshire in 1709, especially as he had started his business career by building malt mills and then become a brass founder. For a long time, the Coalbrookdale furnace and two others associated with the Darbys remained the only coke-fired ones. This was because in the early stages of coke use, the technology was still undeveloped and hence coke fired furnaces were more expensive to operate, although they did permit the production of iron suitable for thin walled castings, which Darby specialised in making. The slow diffusion of the innovation was not, as is often said, the result of lack of knowledge of the technique elsewhere. From 1750, coke smelting began to be more competitive, and its widening use was associated with a cheapening of iron and its growing adoption. Output of pig iron rose from about 28,000 tons per year in the mid-century to around 90,000 tons in 1790 and almost 700,000 tons in 1830.

An almost equally important bottleneck existed in the production of bar iron, which also needed charcoal. From the mid-eighteenth century, the potting process made it possible to use coal; in this the pig iron was placed in clay pots to prevent impurities from the coal reaching it as it was reheated. In 1783, Henry Cort patented his better-known puddling technique, which used the reverberatory furnace already developed for non-ferrous metal smelting. Here the coal is burnt in one part and the reflected heat melts the iron. The molten iron was then 'puddled', or stirred, which brought impurities to the surface where they were burned off. The potting and then the puddling processes complemented the coke-fired blast furnace by allowing the use of coal for another important stage of iron making.

Although much iron still went for the same mundane but vital purposes as before – nails, agricultural implements, and so on – an increasing amount was used by the burgeoning engineering industry. Apart from general machinery, particularly for cotton mills, there were two important sides to this. Machine builders such as Henry Maudslay greatly improved the accuracy of the heavy-duty lathe, thus enabling it to cut metal to much finer tolerances. Maudslay's innovations were disseminated by engineers trained in his workshop. Among the beneficiaries of this greater accuracy were steam engine manufacturers. Steam engines had been in existence since the early eighteenth century, and in the shape of the Newcomen engine had pumped numerous Cornish and North-Eastern mines. In 1769 the Edinburgh instrument maker, James Watt, patented the condenser, which greatly improved fuel consumption, and in the 1780s he developed mechanisms which enabled the up-and-down motion of a piston shaft to be transmitted to rotary motion. His partner, Matthew Boulton, an efficient businessman, ensured the successful exploitation of these inventions and by 1800 steam engines were already widely spread and increasing rapidly in numbers. Nevertheless, water power was still extremely important and performed numerous industrial functions such as powering machinery and providing the blast for blast furnaces.

Scientific knowledge such as Watt possessed was also of value in textile manufacture, since washing and bleaching the material was a lengthy business using traditional processes. Fundamental to the new processes was sulphuric acid. This was originally used as a bleaching agent, and the discovery of an effective production technique in the 1740s was stimulated by the particular needs of the Scottish linen industry for bleach. By 1791 a French chemist, Nicholas Le Blanc, had devised a practicable method of utilising sulphuric acid to make soda, the standard detergent in industrial processes, from common salt. This was taken up by English and Scottish manufacturers. The production of chlorine for bleaching had also been developed abroad, but it was the Scots chemical manufacturer Charles Tennant who developed bleaching powder in the early nineteenth century. Soap boiling was another important if more traditional industry which grew rapidly in this period, benefiting from cheap soda as a raw material.

A very different producer goods industry was the building industry, in which, so far as historians can tell, there was no major change in techniques in this period. Although developers might sometimes operate on a large scale, most building firms were small, often consisting simply of a skilled worker who sub-contracted different parts of the job to other workers. The industry was untouched by mechanisation.

Another industry whose basic organisations and techniques did not change radically was mining. Coal mining grew rapidly in this period, production rising from about five million tons per year in 1750 to about thirty million in 1830 but, as the first figure implies, coal was well established as a fuel at the beginning of the period. The North-East had long had large-scale operations in deep pits, hence its early use of steam engines for pumping. Mining also developed rapidly in this period in the West of Scotland, where the coal was particularly suitable for iron production, and in South Wales, Lancashire and the West Midlands. Mechanisation in mining was confined to steam pumping and from the 1790s, steam winding, which together permitted much deeper pits. 'Hard-rock' mining, mining for iron and for non-ferrous metals like tin, lead and copper, has attracted less attention but was extremely important. It was mainly located in mountainous areas of the Pennines, West Wales and South-West England, although iron mining was important in the West Midlands and West of Scotland. Some of these mining operations, such as Thomas Williams' Anglesey copper mines, were on a very large scale, while the Cornish tin mines were an important market for early steam engines, which were used for pumping.

To summarise the development of industry in this period is not easy, because developments in different sectors proceeded at different rates and involved different types of change. Certainly the most spectacular change was the application of mechanisation to the production of a mass-market good, namely cotton cloth; or, strictly speaking, since weaving was only being mechanised at the end of the period, to the production of cotton yarn. Mechanisation on such a scale was certainly a dramatic innovation, but mass-market production itself was not new, and many industries continued with little change throughout this period. The other main agent of mechanisation was steam power, but at this time steam was essentially a substitute for water power, or for horse power, which was frequently used for small mills or in pumping applications. Steam was more reliable than water and cheaper than horses, but in only a few cases, such as deep mining, did it make something possible which had not been possible before.

Concomitant with the mechanisation of cotton spinning and the growth in the use of steam power went the development of a machine building industry. Again, this was not new, since complicated machines such as wind and water mills had been erected before. The most notable feature of the industry at this time was the increased use of iron, made possible largely by its cheapening, and the development of the lathe, leading to greater accuracy in machining.

These things together led to another change, significant when taken over a long period, which was the agglomeration of industry. Much industry had been located in the countryside, to take advantage of cheap labour or give access to water power. However, by 1830, areas like Manchester, the Black Country and the Pottery towns had become conurbations. The reasons for this included the increasing concentration of mass-market industries due to economies of scale, but also the growing influence of the steam engine. By 1830, most cotton spinning was concentrated in central Lancashire where access to coal was easy. Central Scotland and the Glasgow area also saw the growth of concentrated industry based on coal, which in turn stimulated iron production, cotton spinning and machine building. In spite of this shift towards the pattern of industry which we recognise as typical of the nineteenth century, some older industrial areas, notably Cornwall with its tin mining and London with its wide variety of industries, still remained important. Others, however, did not, and one of the most important features of this period was that, for reasons discussed earlier, large scale mechanised industry grew rapidly in the North, leading directly to the decline of domestic industry in the South and East Anglia.

In spite of the increasing scale of industry, most firms were small. Specialisation could have been achieved by dividing firms into functional departments when they grew in size. In practice, specialisation usually occurred through each firm remaining small and concentrating on one part of a process: thus in textiles, the development of a factory industry was accompanied by the specialisation of firms in either spinning, or weaving, or dyeing, or merchanting, and so forth. In other words, the advantages of economies of scale were realised through external economies (i.e. economies external to the individual firm) rather than through radically increasing firm size. One reason for this pattern of development was the Bubble Act's prohibition of joint-stock and limited liability, which limited the scope for firms to raise long-term capital outside the networks of family and friends and, consequently, limited their size. However, legislation was not the only reason for the small size of firms, as is evidenced by the fact that after the restrictions were lifted in 1856, it took some time before most companies altered their traditional partnership structure.

The other big problem with size was that large firms were difficult to manage. There was little in the way of a management profession in the eighteenth century, the nearest equivalent being the land agents who managed large estates. In industry, only mining and iron production, both long established, had a cadre of managers in the late eighteenth century, such as, in iron, the Guest family of Shropshire and later South Wales. The shortage of managerial expertise reduced the scope of owners for delegation which in turn, limited the size of the firm. Furthermore, people of managerial capacity were likely to be attracted into ownership by the profits available, so making it difficult for a management profession to develop. The Guests took the step to ownership and eventually became millionaires. Another classic example was Robert Owen, the socialist dogmatist. Having started as the manager of a cotton mill in Lancashire, Owen became a partner, before moving to another partnership at a mill at New Lanark, in Scotland. The profits from this enabled him to pursue his schemes of social amelioration. Keeping firms small, so that one or more of the partners could provide general oversight, was therefore a rational response to the problems of attracting and retaining managers. Firms like Arkwright's and, later, that of the Peel family, with several mills, were exceptional. Within individual plants, control of the details of production was frequently decentralised to privileged workmen, called sub-contractors, as described in Chapter 20.

CHAPTER SEVEN

Government, war and the economy

To Adam Smith, writing in the late eighteenth century, the increase in a nation's wealth came about primarily because of the efforts of individuals. The governments of the Continent had tended to the opposite point of view: government intervention was necessary to maximise national prosperity. In Britain, typically enough, the usual eighteenth-century attitude was neither at one extreme nor the other.

The roots of the British hostility to Continental-type intervention lay far back in the past. A distinctive approach to economic policy had developed within the common law; this saw legislation which awarded special privileges to groups in society as obnoxious. Furthermore, the governmental system which had emerged from the turmoil of the seventeenth century was restricted in the initiatives it could take by its answerability to Parliament. Since the concern of many of the more independent MPs was to limit the power of central government, whether in the economic sphere or in any other, the possibility of intervention was reduced. The fact was, though, that the sort of intervention practised by the French in the seventeenth and eighteenth centuries – the setting up of substantial manufacturing industries and the construction of roads – simply did not enter into the mental make-up of government ministers, who believed in the same set of general ideas as did judges, lawyers and independent MPs, and had no conception of direct government intervention in many spheres of economic activity. Projects such as the road to Holyhead, the port for Ireland, completed in 1826, or government dockyards existed purely for strategic reasons and were quite exceptional.

In spite of these limitations, eighteenth century governments did in other ways interfere a great deal in the economy. When the interests of pressure groups who supported intervention outweighted the forces which opposed it, then it was likely to take place. The most obvious examples were the wars of the eighteenth century, which were partly commercial in inspiration. Tariffs, which had grown up and remained in existence partly for revenue purposes, were also supported by agriculturalists and manufacturers. The Navigation Acts, and the bounties given to grain exports in the first half of the eighteenth century, were other examples of intervention. Intervention in the agricultural trade reached its peak in the Corn Law of 1815, passed at a time when prices had started to fall from the peak levels induced by wartime demand and inflation. The 1815 Law prohibited imports when prices of grainstuffs fell below a certain level, which in the case of wheat was 80 shillings a quarter (weighing about 220 kilos; strictly speaking, a quarter is a measure of volume). Outside the realm of external trade, legislation such as the Bubble Act and the Usury Laws also reflect the impact of pressure groups or of some particularly striking public event.

Governments were pragmatic in their approach to the economy; if intervention would satisfy some vociferous party and did not involve the spending of money, they were quite willing to intervene. A positive drive towards the reduction of government interference came only when the latter impinged on the philosophy of judges and lawyers. The most notable example of this in the eighteenth-century was the common law's hostility to the Elizabethan Statute of Artificers, one of whose aims was to enforce apprenticeships and confine trades only to those who had been apprenticed. The law had attacked this from very early days as supporting the rights of small privileged groups over the common good, and eighteenth-century governments made little attempt to oppose the constant restrictions the courts put on the enforcement of the Statute. Although the Statute had initially been supported by masters as well as workmen, it became increasingly supported by organisations of workers alone, and it was partly their clamour for the more stringent application of its apprenticeship clauses that encouraged employers to join with lawyers in opposing it. Since they were more influential than workmen, the Act was repealed in 1814.

Hostility to the Statute of Artificers in its later years was partly class-based. In earlier years the common law and the philosophy which underlay it had contributed more positively to economic development, particularly in the seventeenth century, when sectional privileges of all kinds, such as monopolies, chartered companies with their exclusive rights to foreign trade, and guilds with their restrictions on apprenticeship and the setting up of businesses, had all come under successful attack. Entrepreneurs in Britain could therefore go about the task of making money unhindered by such sectional privileges.

The main contribution of both the law and the government to economic advance was involuntary, however. The government was stable, and the legal system well established and keenly concerned with the well-being of private property. Both these facts gave businessmen, whether in industry, trade or agriculture, a basis of security in business ventures or commercial transactions. The risks they took were the ordinary ones of trade and were not compounded by the risks of arbitrary governmental or legal action.

It is not surprising that, given the objections to government interference, government spending apart from that on war and the servicing of government debt was low. Again it was pragmatism as much as philosophy that dictated this. To the more independent MPs, government spending and tax-raising were equally obnoxious because they offered opportunities for corruption: government employees, such as customs officers, would vote for government-sponsored MPs, while the government could dispense favours through appointments to lucrative offices like the Lord Chancellorship, one of the incumbents of which, Lord Eldon, died in 1838 worth over £700,000. Striking though this example is, the actual resources of the government in this direction were very limited. Table 7.1 illustrates the very low level of government spending on everything bar interest charges and the military.

The other constraint on spending was that, in times of peace, it had to be matched by taxation. The British government could sell government debt reasonably easily in times of war because the government was seen to be stable and fiscally responsible. Hence its debt was attractive to international investors such as the Dutch, whose own economy was stagnant and who therefore looked for good investments overseas. The corollary of this was that the government had to demonstrate its fiscal responsibility in times of peace. Peacetime government spending was therefore limited by available tax revenues, and attempts to raise taxes were met by strong opposition. Thus in 1763 the government had to raise extra revenue to service the debt left by the Seven Years War, but one answer, the Cider Tax of that year, led to widespread rioting. It was the continued search for revenue in the 1760s that led the government to try to tap the North American colonies – with consequences that are familiar to everyone.

Table 7.1 Government expenditure and income 1750–1820 (£ million, nearest whole number)

	1	2	3	4	5	6	7
1750	7	78			5	2	–
1763	18	133					
1770	20	131					
1783	23	232					
1790	17	244	2	2%			
1815	113	745					
1820	57	840	9	3%	40	8	9

Key: 1 = Total central government expenditure
2 = Total government debt
3 = Central government expenditure (excluding military and debt service)
4 = Column 3 as percentage of national income
5 = Yield from customs and excise
6 = Yield from land and assessed taxes
7 = Post Office revenues and stamp duties on legal documents
(*Source:* Mitchell and Deane)

This conservatism on the part of both government and taxpayers led to the taxation system remaining in the mould in which it had been fixed since the late seventeenth century. Customs and excise duties were the chief revenue raisers, as shown in Table 7.1. Excise duties fell on goods ranging from beer and spirits, to bricks and salt; customs duties fell on semi-luxuries like tea, sugar and tobacco, but also on producer goods such as timber and necessities such as grain. The tax system was therefore highly regressive; that is, it bore most heavily on the poor. Opponents of the French government, who looked to Britain and saw land taxes and other taxes assessed on wealth, such as those on windows and playing cards, deluded themselves by thinking that the British taxation system was actually fairer than the French. The relatively low yield from such taxes is shown in Table 7.1, and although the income tax imposed in 1799 raised this yield, it was removed again in 1816.

While the incidence of tax per head fluctuated according to the wars, it is possible to make some educated guesses as to the effect of taxation on the working class. The incidence of customs and excise duties in 1800 was around £2.00 per person per annum. By comparison a skilled London craftsman earned around £60.00 per annum, and it seems a reasonable assumption that he and his family each consumed an average amount of dutiable goods. Obviously the actual amount payable depended on the size of the family, but duties must have taken a significant proportion of family income, and probably rose as a proportion as income levels fell. The usual argument in favour of this incidence of taxation was that, since the poor rarely saved, it did not discourage savings; while if taxation had been lower and the poor's real income higher, they would simply have done less work. While higher taxation on the better-off might have discouraged some saving, it seems unlikely that the poor would have worked less hard had goods been cheaper. Their growing taste throughout this period for semi-luxuries suggests rather that they enjoyed spending and would have responded to lower prices by buying more. Therefore the demand for goods would have increased, which would have increased profit margins and hence perhaps stimulated investment and saving among entrepreneurs, thus acting as an antidote to the discouragement of saving by high taxation. The whole question deserves further research and thought by economic historians.

If it had not been for war, taxation levels generally would have been much lower. Since large wars could not possibly have been financed just by taxation, but also involved issuing large quantities of government debt, the interest on this debt jacked up government expenditure, leading to permanent increases after each war (Table 7.1 illustrates this pattern). In spite of this secular increase, national income rose too, thus keeping government spending fairly stable at 12–14 per cent of national income in peacetime. During the American War of Independence and the Napoleonic Wars, however, expenditure rose to over 20 per cent of national income, and in the last years of the Napoleonic Wars to over 30 per cent. This was a massive level to sustain, and it must have had important economic effects.

Some historians have argued that wars accelerated industrialisation by stimulating the output of key industries such as iron and non-ferrous metal smelting. This stimulus was short-term, however, and it would require proof that the demand for metals for war use caused major technical breakthroughs to support the argument; there is no real evidence that war did any more to stimulate innovation than did other specialised uses. The first use for coke-smelted iron, the biggest innovation of all, was for cooking pots.

This leaves us with the short- and medium-term effects of war on the economy, which can be generalised as follows. Wars caused government spending which exceeded revenue from taxation, and both theoretical considerations and the available evidence suggest that this had what would now be called a Keynesian effect on the economy. Many people in the later eighteenth century were underemployed, notably women workers, who were becoming increasingly peripheral in the waged labour market, and agricultural labourers. High government spending stimulated employment for such workers, in the fighting services, through spending on government contracts, and through the employment of women as substitutes for men. The revenue to pay for the government spending was generated, in part, through this extra employment. It stimulated customs and excise revenue, and increased the demand for goods which in turn must have enhanced profit margins and, hence, the ability of the better-off to save and with their savings purchase government debt. In other words, to some extent war paid for itself.

Almost certainly it did not entirely do this, but also called on the current resources of the economy. The effect of taxation on living standards has already been noted. Another probable effect was on the volume of investment. This had been increasing rapidly in the eighteenth century, and increased again after the Napoleonic Wars. Its rate of increase slowed sharply, however, during the period of heavy war spending. There was not an actual fall, but investment which would otherwise have taken place was being choked off. High interest rates attracted savings to government debt and discouraged investment elsewhere; this was exacerbated by the operation of the Usury Laws, which prevented interest on house mortgages going above 5 per cent and therefore discouraged investors from mortgages as soon as the yield on government stock reached this level. House-building collapsed in the 1790s and only rose slowly thereafter, while canal-building virtually ceased after 1800. One effect of the war, therefore, was to discourage the build-up of capital stock in the infrastructure of the country. Savings had instead gone into government bonds on which interest had to be paid after the war ended, the revenue for this being raised mainly from customs and excise. At the same time, the supply of houses had been reduced, so pushing up rents. So war in general and the Napoleonic Wars in particular had a deleterious effect on living standards. Furthermore, this effect extended over a lengthy period.

In the shorter term, the living standards of poorer people were adversely affected not just by taxation and higher rents, but also by high food prices, because the Napoleonic Wars disrupted the European grain trade and hence raised grain prices – already on a rising trend because of population increase. On the other hand, high prices meant high profits for farmers and high rents for landowners – both encouragements to enclosure. In general terms, war was probably good for the better-off, not so good for the poor. However, the end of the Napoleonic Wars caused problems for everyone. The government wanted both to cut expenditure to match it to income, and to restore gold to monetary use. The beneficial effect of heavy war spending on employment therefore ceased, and it is probably no coincidence that rural by-employments and domestic industry in the South declined rapidly after this date. Prices began to fall after 1818 as government spending fell, and the downward pressure continued with the restoration of gold to monetary use and consequent reduction of the note issue in 1821. Since traders and workers were slow to respond to price reductions, economic conditions were worsened while the adjustment was made. This was a short-term effect, but the impact on farmers and traders who had incurred debt in the period of high prices, and who now faced fixed interest charges which had to be paid from a reduced income, continued up to the 1830s.

Adding to this catalogue of woes was the effect of the Wars on foreign trade. They brought an end to Britain's promising commercial treaty of 1786 with France, ensured the continuation of high tariffs, and caused violent fluctuations in foreign trade. In recompense was the opening up to British trade of the French West Indies and South America, the latter remaining an important outlet for exports after the Wars. The Wars also had a far more devastating effect on France than on Britain. However, to believe that this was necessarily a good thing for Britain would be to fall into the fallacy of mercantilism – that you can only gain at the expense of your rival. Most historians believe that Britain's economy was already stronger and more advanced than France's, and neither war nor peace was likely to make much difference to this fact.

CHAPTER EIGHT
The aggregate economy

The time has now come to draw together the different strands of economic activity dealt with in the last few chapters and look at the economy as a whole. Assembling the information which makes such an overview possible is a task in itself, since the systematic collection of the relevant data by the government only started in this century. Going back into the nineteenth and eighteenth centuries, estimates of economic activity depend more and more on intelligent reconstruction by historians from partial and limited sources. Inevitably there is continuing disagreement about many of the statistics that have been produced.

Although many figures are lacking, the sources that are available should not be underestimated. Among these are customs records, which exist right through this period. They have their own pitfalls, but the experienced historian can make allowances for these. Tax data can throw light on wealth and income levels. Patient work by the historians of individual industries has allowed many output figures to be reconstructed. Insurance valuations can give information about the cost of buildings and machinery, necessary in order to estimate capital investment in the economy as a whole. These are only some of the sources that have been used.

The measure of an economy's total output – or the income flowing to producers, which amounts to the same thing – which is produced from these and other sources has various names, but will be called here national income. If it is necessary to measure change in the national income over time, then constant prices are used for the exercise. Changes in prices upwards or downwards will make national income appear larger or smaller, when it may not have changed in reality. Figures for individual years are therefore adjusted in line with changes in the price level, to give real national income.

In this chapter, changes in national income are discussed, and also changes in three other important measures of overall economic activity, on all of which new light has been thrown in recent years. The first of these is the growth of individual sectors of the economy, and the share of each in output at different dates. The second is the changes in average income per head, that is national income divided by population. It is of interest because ultimately it is changes in income per head that affect individuals. The income of a nation may be growing fast, but if the population is growing just as fast, then individuals will not, on average, be any better off. In addition, changes in income per head give us a rough measure of how labour productivity changed.

The final area to be considered is the rate of investment. Economists separate out land, labour and capital as the three basic elements which make a contribution to the productive process, calling them 'factors of production'. Changes in the amount of physical capital are particularly important because it is difficult for production to increase over a long period without an increase in capital. Physical capital – buildings, machinery and so on – is formed through investment and, therefore, it is particularly important to know how much investment was taking place.

The outline of economic growth is shown in Table 8.1. The implications of these figures are quickly spelt out. The rate of growth accelerated at the end of the eighteenth century and into the first three decades of the nineteenth. On the other hand, the fact that population only rose slowly in the first half of the eighteenth century, and then increased at an accelerating rate, meant that income per

Table 8.1 Growth of real national income (RNI) and income per head

	Growth of R N I (% pa)	Growth of income per head (% pa)
1700–60	0.69	0.31
1760–80	0.70	0.01
1780–1801	1.32	0.35
1801–31	1.97	0.52

(*Source:* Crafts)

head rose much more smoothly. For reasons which were discussed earlier, these figures should not be regarded as absolutely precise and, therefore, not too much importance should be attached to small changes. So while it is safe to say that national income grew faster as time went by, as the changes in its rate of growth are so large, historians are cautious about attaching significance to the relatively small changes in the rate of growth of income per head. The main thing to notice here is the low rate of growth throughout, with perhaps a small improvement in the final period shown.

The growth of various sectors of the economy is the next subject. Here, recently estimated figures bear out the picture sketched out in some of the preceding chapters. Agricultural output rose fairly steadily at about 0.5 per cent per annum for most of the eighteenth century, possibly with a slowdown in the period 1760–80; the growth rate then rose to over 1 per cent per annum after 1800. Agricultural output per head of total population behaved differently because of the accelerating rise in population: it rose from 1700 to 1760, but fell after that.

Industrial output rose much more steeply. It grew at about 0.7 per cent per annum in the first sixty years of the eighteenth century – little more than the rate at which agricultural output grew – but by the first thirty years of the nineteenth century was growing at 3 per cent per annum. The increase in industrial output outstripped the increase in population throughout the period 1700–1830. The figures for service industries will not be given here. The available figures are not very helpful, because statisticians find it very hard to estimate the output of service industries in this period; many of their figures are simply based on the assumption that output grew in line with the economy as a whole.

One cautionary point should be made about these figures, and about the other statistics given here. The rates of increase in output are averages and, of course, conceal fluctuations in individual years. The apparently smooth progression over periods of a decade or longer should not blind the reader to the fact that the smoothness is a statistical artefact. Similarly, the actual dates chosen as the starting or termination points of statistical series do not usually have a special significance in themselves, but are chosen mainly for statistical convenience. This fact, and the imprecision of the figures themselves, means that it is dangerous to assume that specific dates, or even decades, are 'turning points'. We need to see substantial changes before reaching such conclusions.

Table 8.2 Share of sectors in national income

	Agriculture (%)	Manufacturing, mining, construction (%)	All others (trade, transport, services, rent, government) (%)
1760	37	20	43
1831	23	34	43

(*Sources:* Crafts; Deane and Cole)

The next step is to see how much each of these broad sectors contributed to national income. In view of the rapid growth of industrial output, the increase in industry's share is not surprising. It will not be a surprise either to find that the cotton industry played an especially large part in accounting for this increase, as shown in Table 8.3. Furthermore, in the case of both cotton and iron, high productivity growth meant falling prices and hence understate the rise in physical output. Nevertheless, traditional industries like beer, leather and wool textiles, dominant in 1770, were still important in 1830.

Table 8.3 Share of value added in industry (as percentage of total industrial output)

	1	2	3	4	5	6
1770	2.6	45.9	6.6	4.4	5.7	22.3
1831	22.4	46.0	6.7	7.0	4.6	8.7

Key: 1 = cotton
  2 = all textiles (including cotton)
  3 = iron
  4 = coal
  5 = beer
  6 = leather
Note: Shows value added to the basic raw materials during production
(*Source:* Crafts)

Growth in income per head, which was painfully slow, is shown in Table 8.1. One implication of this is that labour productivity also grew slowly. Income per head also throws light on the standard of living, which will be discussed in a later chapter. At this stage, we can note that consumption per head was growing even more slowly than income per head. This was because income per head includes two elements which do not contribute to personal consumption, namely government spending and investment. Since both of these were rising for much of the period, the share of the total going to consumption was declining.

The importance of investment to economic growth has already been sketched out. In most economies in the past, investment was at a very low level, which meant that much of it simply went on replacement, since buildings eventually fall down and implements wear out. There was little surplus over to increase the stock of physical capital.

The period 1750–1830 was marked by a steady rise in investment. The amount of investment which takes place in an economy is usually expressed as a percentage of national income, in which form it is known as the investment ratio. This is a particularly useful measure if we wish to compare investment levels with other countries or with other periods. It is also useful to know the change in actual levels of investment, because even a static investment ratio would result in an increase in total investment, given that national income was itself increasing. Table 8.4 gives the relevant figures. As with all other statistics for this period, there is a considerable margin of error, in this case by perhaps as much as 25 per cent.

The most important changes can be quickly highlighted. The figures for total investment grew rapidly from 1760 on, but this partly reflected the growth in national income, especially from 1780 on. After this date, the investment ratio continued to rise, but at a slower rate. It was only in the second decade of the nineteenth century that it spurted again, to reach the 11 per cent level by 1820. The slowdown in the rate of increase more or less coincides with a long period of war, and the connection between the two was discussed in the previous chapter.

As time went by, the composition of investment changed in predictable ways. In the later eighteenth century, as much as a third of investment may have gone on agriculture, both on obvious things like enclosures and also on increasing and improving the animal population. About a quarter went on industry and trade, and another quarter on house-building, with the rest going on transport. Stocks of goods, or circulating capital, were a high proportion of total capital in industry. Around a sixth of investment in the later eighteenth century went to stock building, so the amount going into industrial buildings and machinery was minuscule. By 1830, the proportion of investment going to the different sectors had changed significantly. Agriculture now took less than 15 per cent, while industry and trade accounted for a third. Housing at this stage also took a third. Transport was only to increase its proportion substantially when the great age of railway building got under way in the 1840s.

Table 8.4 Investment in the British economy, 1760 –1840.

	Investment ratio %	Total investment (£ m, pa)
1760	5.7	
1780	7.0	
1761–90		8.0
1801	7.9	
1791–1820		17.0
1831	11.7	
1821–40		33.5

(*Source:* N F R Crafts 1983 British economic growth 1700–1831: a review of the evidence. *Economic History Review* 2nd series, Vol XXXVI (No. 2): 177–99)

We can summarise the changes in investment as follows. Total investment increased rapidly. In relation to population and national income, however, the increase was much slower, since these were also rising quite fast from the later eighteenth century. Within the rise in total investment, there were significant changes. By the nineteenth century there were big economies on stocks, as would be expected after the improvements in transport. Stocks did not actually fall, but became a much less significant part of total capital. Conversely, a higher proportion of total capital was devoted to industrial buildings and machinery. So while total capital per person rose only slowly, the amount of machinery per industrial worker, while still very small, did rise quicker.

This picture of a fairly steady rise in investment fits in well with the earlier discussion of the aggregate economy. Change was rarely dramatic. National income rose more rapidly as time went by, but income per head rose slowly throughout, implying only a low rise in output per worker. This also fits in well with what is already known from earlier chapters about individual sectors of the economy. In agriculture, for instance, it is well established that output per head of the total population fell from the later eighteenth century onwards. Output per worker in agriculture probably rose, but most historians think the rate of increase was slow. Industrial output did rise rapidly but, apart from the iron and textile industries, there was only limited technical change in this period and no reason to believe that output per worker in most industries changed much.

While the statistical material presented in this chapter coincides with much of what is known about the economy from other sources, it is important for the reader to realise that the material is based on recent revisions which mark an important change from previous interpretations of the aggregate economy in this period. The most important change results from the assumption that the early eighteenth-century economy was much larger than historians had thought previously. The result of this reinterpretation needs only a brief spelling out. A much larger starting point for the economy, with a similar destination point, means that the growth rates in between are smaller. The revisions therefore indicate a much lower growth rate for the late eighteenth century than had previously been accepted by historians, and less dramatic change over the whole period, particularly in the rate of growth of income per head.

CHAPTER NINE
Industrial Revolution?

The underlying theme of the chapters so far has been the slow but steady growth of the British economy between 1750 and 1830. This growth manifested itself in a number of ways. In agriculture, both output per hectare and output per person rose, while the amount of land that was regularly cultivated also increased. In manufacturing industry, there was spectacular growth in output and labour productivity in two industries, cotton textiles and iron smelting. Output growth in other industries was slow, however, and most industry remained unmechanised until the mid-nineteenth century or later. In trade and transport, there was a response to growth in the form of greater specialisation, as well as capital investment in canals and roads. In the national economy as a whole, output rose at an accelerating rate, reflecting the acceleration in population growth – population more than doubled in this period. However, output per person only grew slowly, because in so many sectors productivity growth was slow. As a result, living standards only rose fitfully, and for many people not at all.

Yet it is in this period of slow and painful economic growth that historians usually place the Industrial Revolution. The phrase 'Industrial Revolution' is now so familiar that it is enshrined in the English language. Most people know roughly what it means, but exact definition is more difficult. Historians tend to use it in up to three different ways, although these are not mutually exclusive. Sometimes it is taken to be the very rapid growth of certain sectors of manufacturing industry, in particular cotton and iron, from the later eighteenth to the earlier nineteenth century. This usage connects it with the growth of factories and the use of steam power, both of which developments were only really marked in these industries, and is perhaps the nearest to the popular idea of the Industrial Revolution. Alternatively, it is taken to be the structural shift in the economy occurring over a longer period between the mid-eighteenth and mid-nineteenth centuries, which saw Britain change from a nation in which agriculture occupied the largest proportion of the population, to one in which manufacturing and mining fulfilled this role. A final meaning attached to the phrase is more complex. The 'Revolution' in this case is seen as one in which the entire economy broke out from a state in which total national income grew only intermittently, if at all, into a state in which there was continuous advance in national income. This idea has been enshrined in W W Rostow's phrase 'Take-off [to] a self sustaining growth process'.

Rostow's detailed explanation of why this take-off occurred is associated with the idea of a leading sector, that is a sector of industry which grew so rapidly and was so important that it led to change in many other sectors of the economy. Rostow's argument is that the cotton industry was a leading sector. The productivity increases which took place in cotton textile production led to reductions in the relative price of cottons and, hence, a rise in consumption. This made investment in the cotton industry so attractive that total investment in the economy rose sharply, providing a stimulus to growth. Furthermore, the cotton industry itself needed producer goods from other sectors, such as coal and machinery. This leading sector argument is thought-provoking, but it has serious limitations. As the previous chapter indicated, the cotton industry did not need heavy capital investment and hence the 1780s and 1790s, the period on which Rostow focuses, did not see an exceptional rise in investment; nor was there a significant rise in real wages and hence the overall ability to consume, because productivity advances in cotton were not matched elsewhere in the economy. It was rather that consumption shifted away from other goods towards cottons. Dethroning the cotton industry from a position of centrality in the explanation of industrialisation leaves an explanatory gap, however. To fill it, an alternative model (a simplified explanation) will be put forward to clarify the main factors involved, which will then be explored in more depth.

The causal factors in industrialisation were, first, certain demand-side stimuli. What is meant by this is not simply that demand grew, but that by doing so it exerted an upwards pressure on prices and therefore gave producers an incentive to produce more by whatever means they thought fit, such as installing machinery. The main demand-side stimuli were increasing population and foreign trade, although a shift in consumer tastes towards industrial goods might also be a factor. Technical change in agriculture might also lead to increasing demand for industrial goods. There were also forces on the supply side which cheapened the cost of production and hence widened the market. These included the availability of capital, since the more capital that is available the cheaper it will be; the availability of labour; the improvement of technology, either from an increase in know-how or from the application of science; and finally 'entrepreneurship', the willingness to take risks in developing business activities. Vital to the effectiveness of all these stimuli to growth was the existence of a market. Without the ability to buy and sell goods freely, the price signals from increasing demand or the cheapening of supply will not get through to producers or consumers.

Now to examine the process of industrial growth in more detail, beginning with demand. The starting point here will not be industry, but agriculture. There were two aspects of agricultural performance which were of crucial importance to the growth in demand for industrial goods. One was the growth in agricultural output, the other the growth in efficiency which cut the costs of production. The two are analytically separate, since output could grow independent of efficiency, for instance by the use of more labour. In practice, they usually went together. The growth in total agricultural output enabled Britain to minimise imports of European grain as the population increased. Such growth therefore limited, though it did not prevent, the upward pressure on prices which came from rising demand in a European grain market which was frequently undersupplied. Price rises of this kind transferred income from the urban population, and from all wage-earners whether urban or rural, to farmers, landowners and, in the case of imports, to foreigners. This was likely to reduce demand for industrial goods. Farmers and landowners were already a relatively high income group who would not have been tempted to spend all their extra gains; while there was no guarantee that foreigners would spend their gains on British goods.

The growth in agricultural efficiency benefited all parties. Because farmers' costs fell, they received an additional stimulus to increase output at the ruling price. In the long term, and without any intervening factors, the rise in output would exert a downward effect on agricultural prices. In reality, there was an intervening factor in the form of the upward pressure on prices from rising population. But the net effect of efficiency growth was to moderate price rises, by stimulating faster output growth than would occur just from increasing inputs of labour and capital. The combination of output growth and efficiency gains, the first partially the result of the second, meant that agricultural outputs rose more or less in step with population, and consequently that while food prices rose, they did not rise too fast. This was of importance because food formed a major segment of consumers' expenditure. To increase food prices relative to incomes means that effective purchasing power would be cut. Agriculture's achievement was to ensure that this did not happen to a serious degree and, therefore, to ensure that rising population was translated into rising demand for consumer goods.

Agriculture had two other linkages with industrial growth. Investment in agriculture itself resulted in demand for industrial goods, for instance iron, used in agricultural implements, nails for fencing, and so forth. Although this was an important component of demand, it was not one which by itself was large enough to stimulate large-scale industrial growth. Agriculture's other, more pervasive, link with industrialisation was through the supply side. Because it achieved much of its increasing output through efficiency gains, agriculture economised on capital and labour. Although much capital was needed for enclosures and other agricultural investment, there was still a surplus which flowed, for instance, into transport investment or into financing industrial stocks through the banking system. Similarly, agriculture did not need to absorb labour from the rising population; labour could move instead into industry. In effect, the growth of agricultural efficiency not only helped to maintain a growing demand for industrial goods, but also supplied part of the capital and labour needed to make those goods.

Agriculture's effects on the supply side should not be over-exaggerated, however, since in a wealthy country such as Britain there were other sources of capital, while the rise in population guaranteed a rise in the industrial labour force irrespective of growing agricultural productivity. Furthermore, much labour remained underemployed in agriculture and did not move into industry. The most important role of agriculture was a passive one. By supplying the growing population with food at not too excessive prices, it enabled that growing population to buy more of the products of industry. Added to this rising domestic demand was rising foreign demand, although the latter was much smaller. The effects of the growth of demand on industry can be generalised as follows. It stimulated the growth of total output, which could be met by increasing inputs of capital and labour, particularly labour. To a large extent, these were the only responses in traditional industrial sectors.

Demand growth also made it possible to reap economies of scale, for instance in the provision of transport systems which raised the efficiency of the economy as a whole. There may also have been economies of scale in manufacturing itself but, in practice, there is not much evidence that these increased substantially over and above those already available in eighteenth-century Britain. This leads on to an important question: How far did demand growth lead to innovation, either in manufacturing processes or in the introduction of new products? An acceptance of demand as a factor in innovation implies that innovation results partly or wholly from changes in relative prices. The further implication of this argument is that there was not necessarily any special quality of inventiveness, or special kind of knowledge, needed for innovation.

It is easy to find examples of how demand changes did spur inventiveness. Anxiety to reduce the cost of labour, which was rising in response to increasing demand, was clearly one factor behind the innovations in textile machinery. The search for an effective coke-fired blast furnace was encouraged by the rising price of wood fuel, caused in turn by rising demand for wood. As the discussion of agricultural innovation in Chapter 1 suggested, however, factors on the supply side which stimulated change independent of demand might be very important. In the case of coke-firing, for instance, J R Harris has suggested that one reason for its success in Britain was that British workmen had long experience of using coal as a fuel. Coal had been mined and used extensively in Britain since the sixteenth century, while coke had been used as a fuel since the seventeenth. In France, when coal or coke was introduced into various processes where formerly wood had been used, enormous trouble was experienced in getting the process right. Since knowledge of the process was held in the minds of often illiterate workmen and, unlike details of machinery, could not be written down in books, it was very difficult for the French to adopt it on a wide scale.

Other innovations, such as those in the chemical industry, needed a knowledge of pure science, and scientific knowledge helped in many other fields, such as the development of the steam engine. Many of the best-known eighteenth-century industrialists, such as Wedgwood, Boulton, and John Smeaton the civil engineer, were interested in science and had close contacts with scientists. Education fostered this, for there was a considerable amount of scientific education available, both in Anglican schools and in the 'Dissenting Academies' which flourished because Dissenters were excluded from the old universities. Matthew Boulton and John Roebuck, one of the pioneers of sulphuric acid manufacture, were two of a number of industrialists who had been educated at Dissenting Academies. This interest in science permeated down to the ranks of skilled artisans, among whom it was a reflection of a more general interest in self-education, which was fuelled by a tremendous growth during the eighteenth century in itinerant lecturers, public reading rooms, and the number of books and booksellers.

The interest in science clearly aided innovation and invention, but where did this interest come from? Scientific knowledge, like craft knowledge, was not something which had sprung up in a few years, but was rather the accumulation of research and thought which had been going on since the Ancient World and had accelerated sharply from the sixteenth century. This process was, of course, European and not just British. French scientists played as important a role as British in the eighteenth century, if not more so, while interest in the pursuit of knowledge in general was also international, part of the process known as the Enlightenment. The famous Lunar Society in Birmingham, a venue for industrialists and scientists, was only one of many discussion societies in France and England. Yet the contacts between science and industry seem to have been stronger in Britain. There are a number of possible reasons for this. In Britain, contact between industrialists and other groups was easier because it was a smaller country, in which concentrations of industry had developed earlier. There was a higher level of literacy in Britain which facilitated the transmission of ideas to those lower down the social scale. Finally, the higher levels of real incomes in British society must have helped the diffusion of books, both scientific and practical. All these things meant that, although the inherited skills of practical workmen fostered innovation in particular industries, there were an increasing number of professional inventors. They were produced by the cultural *milieu*, but they were also responding to demand. The patent system, although not perfect, worked well enough to ensure that most successful inventors gained a reasonable reward from their discoveries – so giving them an incentive – but their inventions were eventually made available for others to exploit freely.

While the preceding discussion has emphasised the economic and cultural factors which fostered invention and innovation, some historians, those who like to explain most events in history as stemming from the actions of individuals, see entrepreneurs as the heroes of the Industrial Revolution. Rather than the inventors, it is those who put the inventions into effect – the entrepreneurs – who deserve the credit. The whole argument about entrepreneurship is a complicated one which often suffers from a lack of specification. As usually put, it suggests that there were various special qualities in British society which produced people who were more likely to invest and take risks than not, or who simply liked to make a lot of money; other societies at the time lacked such qualities and, hence, such people. There are various ways of testing these arguments.

One way would be to examine whether Britain was a more open society than most, where business enterprise was socially esteemed or was the path to social success. Alternatively, some historians have looked for the origins of psychological characteristics which might influence attitudes towards money-making and found them in religious doctrine. Another test would be to look at the actual attitudes of businessmen: did they show a strong desire or willingness to take risks in eighteenth-century Britain, as compared with other countries or other periods?

Social emulation with a view to reaching the pinnacles of society has often been suggested as a motive which might spur businessmen to success. Recent thinking by historians, however, tends towards the view that the peerage in Britain, far from being open, remained remarkably closed to outsiders in this period. Furthermore some of the most successful entrepreneurs, such as those whose interest in science was noted above, actually espoused fairly radical views about the unrepresentative nature of political power in Britain, views which hardly suggest that their holders' motive in life was simply to join the landed aristocracy. Looking at social mobility in the other direction, that is the participation of the landed classes in industry and enterprise, suggests more openness, but not enough to be really significant. Just as the landed classes would listen to ideas for agricultural improvement which would increase their rent roll, so they were quite willing to lease off their lands for mining or other industrial activities, from which they could collect royalties or rent without necessarily actively participating. Upper-class families did make some direct contribution to the ranks of industrialists, but a comprehensive survey, discussed later, suggests that it was relatively small. Younger sons would go into the Church or the armed services, but not often into industry.

The argument that psychological characteristics enhanced entrepreneurs' desire to make money goes back to Max Weber's thesis on the effect of the Protestant ethic. To Weber, Protestantism encouraged the pursuit of rational capitalism which he identified with the orderly conduct of business and the systematic pursuit of profit. Weber's thesis was originally put forward to explain the growth of capitalism in Europe from the sixteenth century, and this broad thesis does not concern us here. It has often been suggested, however, that certain dissenting groups, such as the Quakers and the Baptists, particularly stressed these characteristics in the eighteenth century, giving them a special role in economic growth. The most objective survey available, however, a study by W D Rubinstein of the very wealthy with non-landed fortunes who were born between 1720 and 1860, shows that 15 per cent were dissenters. Since the proportion of dissenters in the population increased from about 5 per cent in the mid-eighteenth to about 15 per cent in the mid-nineteenth century, this suggests that there was some over-representation of them among the very wealthy, but that it was not very great.

Did businessmen in Britain, whether dissenters or not, show an exceptional desire to take risks and expand by investment of profits? What is rather remarkable is the evidence to the contrary. Overall growth rates in output per person were low outside the cotton industry, much lower than for most of the nineteenth or twentieth centuries. Few industrialists in the eighteenth century are more famous than the Darbys of Coalbrookdale, who were businessmen, innovators, and Quakers to boot. Yet these heroes of industrialisation took forty years or so to develop the coke-fired blast furnace to a state where it could be widely used; hardly rapid progress. In another field of enterprise, the West Riding woollen industry, businessmen's investment policies often seem to have been defensive responses to competition, rather than innovatory.

It seems that British businessmen were often not particularly dynamic or risk-taking. They may have liked money, but that is hardly an uncommon trait. In that case, what is left of the entrepreneurial thesis? The answer lies in the social origins of entrepreneurs, about which there have been several recent studies.

The clear conclusion from these is that successful businessmen tended to come from families which already had a trading or manufacturing background, often in the same trade or industry. F Crouzet's summary of this research gives the occupations of the fathers of 226 industrialists who founded large industrial undertakings in Britain between 1750 and 1850: 23 per cent were in trade, 19 per cent were manufacturers or industrialists, another 19 per cent were farmers, some of whom were also manufacturers. Rags to riches stories are sadly rare, with only 7 per cent of the industrialists coming from working-class backgrounds, although another 8 per cent had craftsmen as fathers. The scarcity of those lower down the social scale was matched by the scarcity of those from the top: only 9 per cent had fathers from the aristocracy or gentry.

There are fairly obvious reasons why entrepreneurship in industry should have been, as Katrina Honeyman says, almost an hereditary occupation. Those whose families were already engaged in trade or industry were brought up with a knowledge of it. In many cases, this knowledge was transferable across to related industries: just as Abraham Darby moved from brass to ironfounding, or many merchants dealing in some sort of textiles moved across to become merchants or manufacturers in the cotton industry. Secondly, families with some wealth would provide starting capital for their children, either from their own resources or from the resources of friends or colleagues in business or with a shared religious background. Provision of capital was important because many business-men who started with too little capital failed.

The implications of these findings are extremely important. On the one hand, it is fair to say that businessmen in eighteenth-century Britain were not individually remarkable, in the sense that they were no more dynamic than other businessmen in other places or periods. On the other hand, and this is the crucial point, there were large numbers of businessmen, because of the prior existence in Britain of both industry and, more generally, of enterprise and wealth. These had been fostered by active trade, both domestic and foreign, and the commercial orientation of the agricultural sector.

This is not to suggest that there were no factors which affected the quality of entrepreneurship. The exclusion of religious minorities in England (and to a lesser extent Scotland) from the universities and from public office may have encouraged them to devote their energies to business, and also fostered the dissenters' development of a network of schools orientated towards practical education. And precisely because the dissenters were excluded from much social activity, they tended to form close-knit groups in which a high level of trust existed, facilitating the development of credit networks.

Even if dissent did play a part in fostering entrepreneurship, however, there is no need to postulate that businessmen in Britain were exceptionally dynamic. Given developed markets, economic advance will take place anyway. Improvements, whether in agricul-ture or industry, occur through the slow accretion of practical know-how, or the more dramatic work of a few inventors. The significance of the market is that it rewards the adoption of these improvements through the price mechanism. Those who can produce more cheaply will increase their profits. However, the market also punishes those who will not adopt innovations. As an innovation becomes more and more widespread, the supply of the product in question will increase and its price will fall. Those who stick with the old ways will fail. In an active market economy, therefore, improvement will take place without any conscious search for efficiency on the part of most businessmen; the market in itself ensures economic advance.

The existence of active markets and numerous businessmen in Britain goes back a long way. Market-orientated agriculture can be traced back to the sixteenth century or earlier, while trade and industry grew rapidly from the late seventeenth century, thus increasing the supply of businessmen for the future. The emphasis in this chapter has been on how these forces for economic advance were complemented by others, the sources of which can also be traced back to the seventeenth century or earlier. Tenurial arrangements which encouraged farming on a large scale, so that individual farmers were better educated and less averse to risk-taking than their contemporaries on the Continent, facilitated growth in output and efficiency in agriculture. This ensured two things. First, that the growing population did not suffer a declining standard of living, which in turn meant that the growth of population led to growth in overall demand. Second, that agriculture released labour and capital which could be used in other sectors of the economy. If we look outside agriculture, then a long-term view seems just as appropriate. The foreign demand for industrial goods, especially the colonial demand which was the most dynamic element in the eighteenth century, has its roots in the European overseas expansion of the sixteenth and seventeenth centuries. Probably more important, the development of a large-scale market for consumer goods in Britain goes back a long way. A relatively highly urbanised society, as Britain already was by the early eighteenth century, fostered the exchange of information and hence the desire for consumer goods by both the middling and lower groups in society. Good internal transport links, which existed even without the help of turnpikes and canals because of Britain's extensive coastline and river system and lack of mountain ranges, also helped to spread consumerism.

Finally, the supply side of industry was responsive to demand, and was also an independent force for growth. Industrial growth was facilitated by Britain's favourable resource endowment of coal, which increasingly provided the raw material and motive power for the iron and cotton industries. Coal availability was not a major cause of industrial growth before 1800 or so, but it helped to ensure the continuation of rapid growth as the demand for power grew. There were also less tangible influences which improved the supply side's ability both to initiate and sustain growth. As with demand factors, the roots of these go back a long way. There was adequate capital available, because of the country's existing wealth and because people were accustomed to supplying capital to family and friends, or to using local attorneys as intermediaries. The existence of a strong framework of law which laid down the relationship between debtor and creditor was helpful here; by comparison, the development of the English banking system in the later eighteenth century was at first only of moderate importance. The growth of trade, manufacturing and mining over the previous century ensured a supply of business-men, while the growth of scientific knowledge and the slow build-up of craft know-how can be traced back to the sixteenth century.

The former was a European rather than a purely British phenomenon, and this highlights the fact that most of the changes outlined were not confined to Britain. The Netherlands was also wealthy in terms of per capita income, was as highly urbanised, had a similarly commercial farming sector, and a similarly large middle class. But the Netherlands was a much smaller country, which may explain its relative stagnation in the eighteenth century. Foreign trade was a very important part of the Dutch economy, rather than a fairly small part as it was in Britain, and the Dutch from the late seventeenth century lost ground against Britain and France in trade because of a lack of naval strength by comparison with the larger countries. France was poorer than Britain in terms of per capita income, less urbanised in relation to population, and with much more peasant farming; but it did have large areas of commercial farming, great cities such as Paris and Lyons, a thriving foreign trade sector, and a strength in science. France's main problem compared with Britain was the relative lack of integration of its economy, and the relative weakness of its farming sector, which could not increase production in line with population growth.

Britain did not, therefore, enjoy a set of completely unique economic privileges. Rather, her economy shared with the whole of Europe a number of common features which had been present since the Dark Ages. These included rising population, apart from the major setback of the plague period in the fourteenth century, increasing urbanisation, technical advance and agricultural specialisa-tion. Until the eighteenth century, population growth had over long periods tended to outrun the growth in agricultural production, so that periods of falling living standards had followed advances in population. By the eighteenth century, there were signs that this was coming to an end all over Europe. It was the British economy, however, which responded most positively. This was largely due to agricultural advantage, although in other aspects too the British economy was relatively dynamic. Then at a crucial time during the period of accelerating industrialisation, Britain's main industrial rival, France, already suffering from a more backward agricultural sector, was racked by Revolution and then fought a series of wars from which Britain gained more commercial benefit. While there is no reason to suppose that the absence of war would have been deleterious to Britain, it is probably true that without it the French economy would have expanded faster and Britain's economic lead in the early nineteenth century would not have been so striking.

How far do the processes of change which have been outlined above fit in to the varying concepts of Industrial Revolution discussed at the beginning of the chapter? Certainly the period between 1750 and 1830 saw rapid growth in the cotton and iron industries, although the development of steam power and factories was limited otherwise. Certainly this same period saw a decline in agriculture's share of the labour force and a corresponding growth in manufacturing and mining; although the large size that this and the services sector had reached by the middle of the eighteenth century, in comparison with the Continent, is just as remarkable. Whether or not either the rapid growth of a few industries or the broader sectoral shift deserve to be called an Industrial Revolution seems a matter of taste; probably the phrase is too deeply ingrained to be jettisoned now. In one respect, its survival is a pity, because it obscures one of the most important features of the economic history of the period: the rise of the North and the relative decline of the South. In terms of population and wage levels, a major shift had begun which continued until the end of the nineteenth century, and whose impact is discussed in Chapters 11 and 18. So the Industrial Revolution was a localised one: its centres were the Midlands and North of England, and parts of Wales and Scotland.

One final question. Did the period from the mid-eighteenth to the early nineteenth century see a 'take-off' to self-sustaining growth, from a previous state when growth had not been self sustaining. This would be really revolutionary, but is much more problematical. Agricultural and industrial output, trade and income per head had all been growing from the late seventeenth century. It is true that population only grew markedly from the mid-eighteenth century, and so the period 1750–1830 saw a more rapid growth in total national income than before. However, the ability to sustain this growth, and to accelerate growth by innovation, was not something which had developed only in this period. As this chapter has shown, it had its roots in a long history of agricultural, commercial and industrial developments. It is an attractively simple idea that in one short period a revolutionary advance occurred in man's control of economic change. Unfortunately, history is not that simple.

PART TWO

The Industrial Economy 1830–1914

CHAPTER TEN

Into the railway age

THE GROWTH OF A MATURE ECONOMY

The mills of Lancashire and the blast furnaces of South Wales were visible manifestations of the classic period of the Industrial Revolution, from the 1780s to the 1820s. In other areas of the country, however, the impact of industrial change was less visible, and in many it was barely perceptible. The next thirty years, though, were to see the scope of industrialisation widen. A national network of railways developed, bringing those smoking harbingers of the industrial world almost to the doorsteps of the population. The coal, iron and engineering industries became relatively more important, and textiles, although still the pre-eminent manufacturing industry, no longer dominated the industrial scene. The subsequent fifty years, from the 1860s to the eve of the First World War, were to modify the type of economy which had come into existence in the mid-nineteenth century, but not essentially to alter it.

It was an economy in which, as in the earlier period of industrialisation, agriculture became less and less important. But whereas at the end of the earlier period, in 1830, agriculture had still played a major part, by the 1900s its contribution to national income was almost insignificant. Another difference between the two periods is that, in the earlier one, it was manufacturing's share of output that had grown at the expense of agriculture; but in the later period, it was the services sector whose share grew the fastest. There are two fundamental reasons for these developments. First, the apparent growth in the provision of services is to some extent a statistical artefact. This is because services were increasingly provided as a separate activity, when in the past they had been undertaken by those also engaged in agriculture or manufacturing. The farmer's wife would make the butter (agriculture) and take it to market (service); likewise, the Yorkshire weaver might manufacture his cloth, and transport and sell it. However, the advantages of specialisation increasingly led to the separate provision of services. This means that the figures shown in Table 10.1, and those for the earlier period shown in Table 8.2, cannot be precise.

Table 10.1 Share of sectors in national income (per cent)

	Agriculture	Manufacturing mining, construction	Other
1831	23	34	43
1913	6	38	56

(*Sources:* Deane and Cole; Matthews *et al.*)

Nevertheless, there were major shifts in demand and supply which meant that important changes did occur, and the figures in Table 10.1 do represent real trends. When incomes rise, the demand for agricultural products rises more slowly. In economic terms, demand for such produce is relatively inelastic in response to income changes. Combined with rising efficiency which kept agricultural prices down, and the continued shift of comparative advantage in favour of manufactures, the decline in agriculture's share of national income was inevitable given rising real incomes. Demand for manufactures and services, on the other hand, was income-elastic. In other words, growing incomes led to a rapid growth of demand, the exact relationship differing for different products and types of service. Manufacturing also experienced rising efficiency and, as with agriculture, this ensured falling or static prices relative to the general price level. Falling relative prices combined with growing physical output to ensure for manufacturing an almost static share of national income. Services, on the other hand, probably experienced much lower levels of efficiency increase: hence relative prices rose and, combined with the growth in output, led to a rise in services' share of national income.

The decline in the importance of agriculture also caused changes in the rhythm of economic activity. Throughout history, economic activity had suffered from violent shocks caused by harvest fluctuations, exacerbated by factors like war. The British economy had long escaped from the position of subsistence economies, where successive bad harvests could cause widespread malnutrition or even starvation. Increased economic complexity, though, brought other problems. Bad harvests cut consumers' purchasing power by raising grain prices, so depressing activity in other parts of the economy. A bad harvest would also lead to gold draining from the country in order to pay for imports of food. The adverse effects of this on credit provision were described in Chapter 5. In the early part of the nineteenth century, these fluctuations had been exacerbated by the Napoleonic Wars, and up to the 1830s had been superimposed on structural changes associated with the decline of domestic industry. The result had been frequent periods of misery and unemployment for large groups of workers.

As the nineteenth century wore on, the impact on the economy of random shocks from poor harvests diminished. An increasing proportion of food was imported as a matter of course, and this provided a cushion against food price fluctuations. Fluctuations in economic activity – booms and depressions – still occurred, against the backdrop of secular growth; but they manifested themselves in a different way. They were particularly evident in the heavy industries, metal production and engineering, which depended on investment – this tended to be more volatile than consumer spending. Even so, unemployment among trade unionists, many of whom worked in the heavy industries, never exceeded 10 per cent in the later nineteenth century, and then only for a short time. There has been considerable debate among economists and economic historians as to how far fluctuations formed a pattern of regular cycles, caused for instance by changes in investment intentions, and how far short-term economic changes were still caused largely by random shocks. What is clear is that the latter were still important, even though they were not now associated with bad harvests. The restriction on cotton imports during the American Civil War of 1861–65, the 'Cotton Famine', had a serious effect on the cotton industry. The failure of the City of Glasgow Bank in 1878, caused by fraud, sent shock-waves through the British economy; in Scotland, the impact of the failure lasted for years.

In spite of these shocks, the pervasive impression is of greater stability as economic activity became more diversified. This diversification coincided with the growth of the railway network. Not surprisingly, historians have in the past attached great importance to railways as a factor in economic growth. Rather than take this view for granted, the approach recently has been to identify and if possible quantify the specific economic effects of railway building and operation. The next section will outline the early development of railways, then consider the extent to which they actually improved economic efficiency, when operating, and will then look at railway building and its effect on the economy.

THE IMPACT OF RAILWAYS

Waggonways, built first of wood and then of iron, had been in use since the seventeenth century. An early one formed a line of defence in the Battle of Prestonpans in 1745 between the Jacobites and the forces of the Crown, foreshadowing the later importance of railways in military activity. These waggonways were found particularly in mining areas, such as South Wales, North-East England and the Lowlands of Scotland, where it was too expensive to link any single pit to the canal network. As steam engines developed, attempts were made to harness them to locomotion, either on or off rails. Primitive efforts to this end dated back to the eighteenth century. By the 1820s, various steam locomotives were running, and it was a matter of chance as well as engineering skill that led to George Stephenson being remembered as the 'Father of Railways'. If Stephenson had not built locomotives successfully, no doubt someone else would have done. He built the Locomotion for the Stockton and Darlington Railway, a short line in the North East, which was the first railway both to use locomotives and to carry passengers and freight; it was opened in 1825. Then he built the Rocket for the Liverpool and Manchester, a much longer line, opened in 1830.

By the end of the 1830s, several important main lines, such as the London and Birmingham, and the Great Western to Bristol, had been built or were almost completed. There was then an ebb in construction until the Railway Mania of 1844–6. This was the period when lines were being frantically promoted, and just as frantically supported by investors who were carried away by greed brought about by the prospect of apparently unlimited profits from this new industry. While the mania itself subsided quite quickly, lines were still being constructed rapidly up to 1850, as there was an inevitable time-lag between promotion and construction. Much of Britain was affected by the vast mobile building sites which marked the progress of railway building. By the end of the 1840s, the railway network had emerged in a recognisably modern form, although there were big gaps. There was not yet a continuous line west of Plymouth, while hilly, less populated areas, such as Central and North Wales and northern Scotland, had few railways. There were relatively few smaller branch lines as yet. Most major towns, however, were now connected to the main network, and the total route length in 1850 was 9800 km, compared with 2900 km in France, and 5900 km in Germany. Although signalling systems and rolling stock were still primitive, these aspects were developing along with the growth of the network.

The railways had a dramatic effect on the landscape of Britain: did they have a similar effect on its economy? The method of argument which has been used to assess the effects of railway development on economic efficiency is the 'counter-factual'. This involves posing an alternative scenario to that which actually happened – so in this case the scenario is that the railways were not built – as a means of estimating their impact on economic activity. It is worth reflecting that many questions in history involve the making of counter-factual judgements, even if these are not spelled out. Their use in economic history involves the formulation of a specific hypothesis to focus the investigation on measurable phenomena. Here the hypothesis is that the spending of capital on the railways made the whole economy more efficient, even if the capital would have been spent on something else had railways not existed. The gain from this spending would become apparent when a substantial mileage of railways had been built and, therefore, the date taken to measure their effect is some time after their initial development.

In order to test the hypothesis that the economy gained from railways, the following measurement needs to be made. The total amount charged by railways in a particular year for moving goods and passengers is estimated. The amount which would have been spent to move the same number of passengers and tonnage of goods the same distance by water or road is also estimated. This is the alternative scenario. The difference between the two is then a measure of the benefit conferred on the economy or, in other words, the economy's increased efficiency as a result of railways. The benefit is sometimes referred to as the 'social saving'. The assumption made in calculating this is that railways made a normal rate of return on the capital invested in them, which it seems that, on average, they did. (If the rate of return had been very low, then the railways would have conferred the benefit on the customers, but their own shareholders would have lost, so the net benefit would have been reduced.)

However simple in theory, the measurement of benefits in this way is fraught with the many pitfalls that lie in wait for historians

dealing with statistics. It is not always easy to find comparable costs
for the different means of transport. This is particularly the case with
passengers, where no means of transport before railways offered
anything like their speed or comfort. Even with freight traffic, the
speed and regularity of railways were important because they enabled
traders to keep down stock levels. It was therefore worth a cash sum
which is not reflected in the railway charges, and is difficult to
estimate. The methodological, as opposed to purely evidential,
difficulties are even greater. One problem is that there is no means of
estimating how much technical advance would have taken place in
other means of transport if railways had not been built. Another is
the inbuilt bias in favour of railways which arises from measuring
their effect some time after they were built. Naturally, after a period
of time, industries located themselves where they could most
effectively use railway transport; if railways had not been built,
industries might have located themselves elsewhere to save on
transport costs. Measuring the simple difference between railway
charges for freight transport and the costs of transporting the same
amount of goods by other means might therefore be misleading.

Overcoming or ignoring these pitfalls, G R Hawke has estimated
that in 1865, when railways were well established, the economy
would have been somewhere between 7 per cent and 11 per cent
worse off if they had never been built. The rate of growth of real
income per person in the mid-nineteenth century was slightly over 1
per cent per annum, a proportion of which was contributed by the
enhanced economic efficiency which railways brought about. So had
railways not been built, Hawke's figures imply that with a growth rate
of about 1 per cent per annum, it would have taken another seven
years, if not more, before people's incomes reached their actual 1865
level. The uncertainty of the estimate arises because of the difficulty
of making any comparison with pre-railway passenger transport.
Comparing railways with stagecoaches gives the lower figure;
comparing them with private carriages, which is possibly a better
comparison, the greater, because private carriages were more
expensive per passenger/mile than stagecoaches. A benefit which is
not brought into the computation (but could be) is that accruing to
Britain from railways built abroad. Much of the social saving from the
railways which helped to open up the hinterland of the New World
eventually came to Britain through lower food prices. However,
given the difficulty of calculating the social saving because of the
problems mentioned earlier, readers may feel that even the one made
for Britain alone is completely meaningless. Or they may feel that

some measurement, however inadequate, is better than none.

If it is difficult to measure railways' impact on overall economic efficiency, it is relatively easy to measure their impact on individual industries. Studies of the iron industry have shown that although the demand for iron from railway construction was very large at certain periods, this increase in demand did not lead to any major changes or innovations in the industry. In other words, it did not have a significant qualitative impact. It seems likely that the picture is similar for engineering, since major sectors, such as textile machine and steam engine construction, were already well established and growing rapidly. Railway demands, including growing export demands, made these industries larger than they would otherwise have been, but not fundamentally different.

Measuring the extent of the short-term boost which railway building gave to the national economy is a more difficult problem. Its possible impact can be demonstrated using Keynesian assumptions. Very briefly, since his ideas are dealt with more fully later, Keynes suggested that a lack of investment opportunities could arise in a capitalist economy, the result being a long-term unemployment of resources. A Keynesian view of Britain in about 1830 might argue that this state of affairs would have been a possibility if railways had not become technically viable. Because railways lowered charges for many services and gave new standards of service, they offered a massive new profit opportunity and tempted investors once more. The result of this investment was not just the long-term benefits which have already been discussed, but also a short-term boost to the economy through the spending power unleashed by railway construction. The figures for employment, showing that around 250,000 navvies were employed in the peak construction year of 1847, are certainly impressive. To these might be added those who gained employment as the navvies spent their wages and all those in ancillary industries, such as iron and brick manufacture, who were given employment by railway construction. Whether or not the argument could be sustained would depend on a more sophisticated calculation than is possible here. The implications of the argument are interesting, since the 1840s was a time of serious political discontent, which might have been exacerbated by a deterioration in economic conditions. If there is any truth in this argument, it also suggests that the opportunity cost of building railways was lower than a straightforward measure of capital expenditure would imply. In other words, if railways had not been built, the economy did not necessarily forgo opportunities to invest the capital elsewhere, because without railway building many of the resources would simply have lain idle. If this was the case, then the long-term social savings generated by railways would be enhanced, because it would not be legitimate to make the assumption that the capital invested in railways would be earning a return elsewhere in the economy. This, in turn, throws a more optimistic light on the impact of railways. Maybe economic historians should return to their computers.

What can be concluded is that the building of railways and their subsequent operation did make an important contribution to the transition to a more regular cycle of economic activity which was discussed earlier. Railways may not have changed the iron and engineering industries qualitatively, but they enlarged these industries' importance in the national economy and thus reduced its reliance on cotton and agriculture. Railways also improved opportunities for migration from the rural south of England. Although the rural south was to remain poor, the deterioration in its inhabitants' standard of living relative to other areas now ceased.

The other manifold effects of railways are well known. Their economic effects are in theory 'captured' by the social saving measurement, but the uncertainties of this mean that it does not adequately describe the full impact of railways. They had many intangible effects on, for instance, the spread of commercial contacts among businessmen (although the electric telegraph, developed at much the same time, was probably equally important here); on holidaymaking, and on urbanisation, discussed in the next section. One effect which is often attributed to railways, the spread of Greenwich Mean Time throughout Great Britain to replace many local times, in fact occurred because of the uniformity brought about by stagecoach schedules. This emphasises that, important though railways were, their impact should not be over-dramatised, for Britain was already a commercially integrated society when they were no more than primitive tram roads.

URBANISATION AND REGIONAL CHANGE

The impact of economic change in the nineteenth century took its most dramatic form in urbanisation. The reasons for urbanisation are complex and are not simply accounted for by the growth of manufacturing, but also by the form which that growth took and by other factors, including the growth of services. Economies of scale in manufacturing industry encouraged concentration, while the growth of steam power stimulated industrial development in areas with access to cheap coal. Both these factors contributed to the fact that large-scale industrialisation was confined to a limited number of areas. Since for most of this period the ability of working people to travel more than a short distance to their place of work was constrained by the relatively high level of fares on public transport, industrialisation was almost inevitably accompanied by increasing urbanisation in these areas. At the same time, the rapid growth of specialised retail shops at the expense of markets, and the general growth in demand for services, meant that the number of urban service employees grew even faster than the number in manufacturing.

As in the eighteenth century, however, many towns also had specialised service functions of various kinds. The growth of railways not only created manufacturing towns almost entirely devoted to their needs, notably Swindon and Crewe, but also generated substantial activity through the development of goods yards, terminal stations and so forth. An even more significant generator of urbanisation was the provision of facilities for pleasure and leisure. In the eighteenth and early nineteenth centuries, spa towns were the focus of these activities, but in the nineteenth century the range became wider. Railways clearly facilitated this trend, but their influence should not be overstated, since towns like Bath, Cheltenham and Brighton had grown to a substantial size before railways were built. The provision of holiday facilities in rapidly growing late Victorian resorts like Blackpool or Eastbourne was part of the continuing expansion of the leisure industry; but equally important, if less noticeable, was the provision of facilities for those who had the means to forgo paid work. In a country like Britain, there was a numerous middle class of manufacturers and merchants, many of whom would expect to save enough to retire. Added to these were public servants on pensions, including military officers and those who returned from service abroad; others who had made money abroad privately and retired to Britain; and not least the middle-class widows and spinster daughters who lived on annuities or inherited capital. All these groups had been growing since the eighteenth century, when they populate the novels of Jane Austen. In 1901, the census showed a quarter of a million men and unmarried women living on their own means, and without occupaton. (There was also a separate category of retired, but it includes paupers and lunatics so isn't much help.) This army of the non-employed, with their domestic servants, gravitated towards seaside towns, spas, and London – with its clubs, theatres and fashionable shopping facilities.

Table 10.2 Urbanisation in Britain 1801–1901 (totals and some sample towns)

	1801 (000s)	1851 (000s)	1901 (000s)
Birmingham	71	265	760
West Midlands conurbation	n.a.	n.a.	1483
Blackpool		3	47
Bradford	13	104	284
Bristol	61	137	329
Cardiff	2	18	164
Glasgow	77	375	762
Clydeside conurbation	n.a.	n.a.	1343
Greater London	1117	2685	6586
Manchester	75	338	645
S.E. Lancashire conurbation	n.a.	n.a.	2117
% population urban in England and Wales	30	50	77

Note: 1801 Towns of 2500 +
      1851 Towns of 2000 +
      1901 All areas classed as urban sanitary districts. Birmingham, Glasgow and Manchester totals include districts incorporated in the cities subsequent to the date shown
(*Sources*: Corfield, P F 1982 *The Impact of English Towns 1700–1800*; Halsey, A H (ed) 1972 *Trends in British Society since 1900*; Mitchell and Deane; Weber, A F 1899 *The Growth of Cities*)

Financial services constituted another group of service industries which were closely associated with urbanisation. Here, London was even more prominent, although most large provincial cities developed a stock exchange and other financial markets associated with their dominant industry, such as Cardiff's Coal Exchange and Liverpool's Cotton Exchange. London, and to a lesser extent Edinburgh, were major international financial centres, generating much wealth at the top end of the income scale but also a growing volume of employment. The other major international service industries were shipping and the provision of port facilities, both of which generated high levels of employment.

The pattern of urban growth shown in Table 10.2 highlights the pattern of regional specialisation and regional prosperity which had developed as a result of industrialisation and its associated changes between 1750 and 1830. Manufacturing areas were high-wage areas. This applied by 1830 to London, Lancashire and parts of Yorkshire, the North East and the West Midlands. With the growth of metal manufacture and coalmining, Central Scotland and South Wales joined the group over the next fifty years. The relatively high wages in these areas applied to agricultural as well as to industrial work, as industry's demand for labour pushed up wages in all sectors in the regional economies concerned. Conversely, in other areas, particularly the rural south, mid-Wales, the Scottish Highlands and East Anglia, wage levels remained relatively low, dragged down by the supply of surplus rural labour. Although migration away from rural areas increased from the 1840s, it was able to do no more than prevent further relative deterioration in wage levels. The regional impact of industrialisation is demonstrated in Table 10.3. The relative share in population of the North West and to a lesser extent Yorkshire grew steadily from the inception of large-scale industrialisation and throughout the nineteenth century. Even after the initial stage of growth centred around the textile industry, these areas continued to attract capital because of their cheap coal and the economies of scale they offered. Other regions which contained important industrial areas, such as Wales, Scotland and the North, failed to increase their population share because they also included large rural areas. The sharpest decline, however, was reserved for the regions of agriculture and declining industry, that is the South West and East Anglia. London's predominance ensured that the South East's share continued to grow, markedly in the later nineteenth century as the service sector became relatively more important.

The late nineteenth and early twentieth centuries saw the beginnings, but only the beginnings, of change in this pattern. Relative wage levels shifted slightly in favour of the poorest areas, and the urbanisation which was associated with the provision of leisure and retirement facilities began to have a significant impact in some seaside areas, in low-wage counties such as Sussex and Hampshire. On the other hand, the employment provided by such services was often just as seasonal as in agriculture. There was also some growth in manufacturing industries outside the established areas. The mechanisation of agriculture from the mid-century promoted the growth of agricultural engineering firms, which were often located in agricultural marketing centres such as Lincoln and Banbury. With their expertise in portable machinery, these firms later diversified into products such as road rollers and internal combustion engines. The growth of light engineering, which needed few inputs of heavy materials in relation to the value of its output, also had some effect on industrial dispersion. London, which had seen the decline of its own shipbuilding and engineering industry from the 1860s, experienced a new growth in light engineering from the 1890s, and a number of smaller southern towns, such as Chelmsford, where Marconi Radio started in 1898, also benefited. One other effect that these developments had was the rescue of one of the oldest industrial areas, the West Midlands, where coal production had stagnated and iron ouput declined, as the area became less competitive from the 1870s. By the 1900s, this area was benefiting from the growth of the cycle, motor and allied component industries.

Table 10.3 Population distribution by region (per cent)

	1751	*1801*	*1851*	*1901*
South East	22.8	23.8	24.5	28.4
East Anglia	6.6	5.9	4.9	2.9
South West	15.0	13.0	10.7	7.0
West Midlands	7.5	8.1	8.2	8.1
East Midlands	7.5	7.6	6.8	6.5
North West	5.8	8.3	12.0	14.1
Yorkshire/Humberside	5.1	6.7	7.7	8.7
North	6.7	6.1	5.6	6.8
Wales	6.1	5.6	5.7	5.4
Scotland	16.9	14.9	13.9	12.1

(*Source:* Lee, C H 1986 *The British Economy since 1700*)

CHAPTER ELEVEN

Population, migration and labour supply

INTRODUCTION

The population explosion of the later eighteenth century meant that by the turn of the century, the population of Britain was growing at over 15 per cent per decade. After 1850, the growth rate settled down at about 12 per cent per decade, and over the whole nineteenth century, the population grew from eleven million to thirty-seven million. This level of growth is low by comparison with some underdeveloped countries today, but extremely rapid by any previous standard. The rapid population growth had important economic implications. There was a high level of demand throughout the century for food. Until the mid-century, imports were limited for various reasons, and most food was still provided from indigenous resources, keeping food prices relatively high and therefore preventing major improvements in living standards. From the mid-century on, and particularly from the 1870s, new sources of food supply were found in the temperate lands of the Americas and Australia. Just as the British population provided much of the demand for these foodstuffs, British capital went in large quantities to open up the lands which supplied them. The demand for overseas investment was thus another result of population increase. Throughout the century, another large proportion of investment went into housing for the growing population, and the provision of urban infrastructure, such as roads and sewers. Up to the mid-century, such investment could do little more than keep pace with the population increase, but from then on improvement did take place.

The fact that the natural rate of increase was as high in rural areas as in the towns meant that rural labour continued to be in surplus, with a deleterious effect on rural wage levels. As the inhabitants of rural areas became increasingly aware of opportunities elsewhere, migration increased. The population as a whole also became more aware of opportunities abroad, and emigration increased to provide the third pillar for the economic development of newly-settled countries, together with land (which they already had in abundance) and capital. The quantity of emigration suggests that throughout the century there was no shortage of labour, and so labour supply is not a problematical subject, although changes in participation rates and the quality of the labour force present features of interest.

POPULATION

Since mortality in nineteenth-century Britain was still high, the continued population growth depended on high fertility. So far as is known, fertility did not exhibit striking class differences in the early part of the century: parents from all walks of life had large families. By contrast, mortality was a function of class and geography, of who you were and where you lived. In Manchester in 1842, the average age of death was eighteen; in Bath it was thirty-one. Manchester was more working class, and a larger proportion of the population was grossly overcrowded: both these contributed to the high death rate. Farm labourers, in spite of their miserable standard of living, had a relatively low death rate.

Measurement of both fertility and mortality becomes easier during this period as civil registration of births and deaths began in 1837 for England and Wales, and 1855 for Scotland. In the 1820s, fertility had declined slightly from its peak levels, but then remained more or less stable until the 1870s, when it began a rapid and continuous fall. This decline was most marked and most rapid in the middle class, from the higher professions down to the more lowly clerical workers, but it extended to the working class as well. As the decline got under way, it led to the emergence of striking class differences in fertility. By the Edwardian period, a middle-class wife would more likely than not have no more than two children. By contrast, groups like miners and farm labourers frequently had families of five, six or more. In spite of these differences, it was the general fact of decline that was most marked. The crude birth rate fell from around thirty-five births per thousand population, at which it had stuck since the 1830s, to under twenty-five by the eve of the First World War. Just as the Third World today, with its high fertility, is full of children, so was Victorian Britain. By the First World War this state of affairs was coming to an end.

Although by the early nineteenth century, mortality was at a slightly lower rate than in the late eighteenth century, there was very little further improvement before the 1870s. It is likely that the mortality experience of individual groups in the population became rather better, but that this was cancelled out by the increasing proportion of people living in the unhealthy towns and cities. Evidence to support the suggestion that mortality lessened for individual groups comes from a comparison between mid-eighteenth- and early nineteenth-century London, which shows it falling from around forty-eight per thousand to around twenty-five. Appalling though the conditions and mortality rates of early nineteenth-century towns were, they were almost certainly better than those of eighteenth-century towns. From the 1870s, the favourable influences outweighed the unfavourable, and crude death rates in Britain fell sharply, from around twenty-two per thousand to around fourteen per thousand just before the First World War. By far the greatest fall occurred in the mortality of children and young people and, from the 1890s, of infants.

In the course of fifty years or so, a great demographic transition had occurred. Up to the mid-century, population growth had been close to the pre-industrial pattern, with very high fertility outweighing high mortality. From then or a bit later, both fertility and mortality fell rapidly, to arrive by 1914 at what we think of as the modern pattern of low levels for both.

The fall in mortality is easiest to explain, although there are many uncertainties. Most of the improvement can be related to the reduction of specific diseases, such as cholera, smallpox and tuberculosis. The increasingly effective separation of water supplies from sewage undoubtedly helped to stem water-borne diseases like cholera, a dreaded killer in early nineteenth-century cities. But impressive though the achievements of the Victorian sewer builders like Joseph Bazalgette were, their importance in cutting the death rate was at first fairly limited although, of course, if improvement had not been undertaken the problem would have become worse as cities grew larger. Advances in medicine had even less impact, being mainly confined to the further spread of vaccination for smallpox. Any reader of Conan Doyle's medical stories will know how bizarre many medical theories were in the late nineteenth century. On the other hand, the growth of hospital provision may have had beneficial side-effects through providing better nutrition for the sick, while also helping their families by reducing the burden and expense of care. The hygiene of hospitals, which had been a major health hazard in its own right, greatly improved from the 1870s. However, the major impact on mortality probably came from improvement of the domestic environment and the rising standard of living, which helped to reduce diseases like tuberculosis (TB). TB, or consumption, was by no means confined to the poets with whom it is romantically associated, but affected the poor to a much greater extent. Its decline has been particularly associated with increased resistance to disease, due to improvements in diet and housing. The quality of food remained poor for the working class throughout the nineteenth century, however, and it seems likely that the main effect of rising incomes was to lessen the impact of crises, such as the unemployment or illness of the breadwinner, on the entire family. It was not so much the normal diet that improved, as the diet at times of crises, thus increasing resistance to TB and other diseases.

The later fall in infant mortality seems puzzling, but can be explained. The sewers of the Victorian engineers mainly serviced middle-class water closets. Earth closets and midden heaps were still a feature of the working-class quarters of Victorian towns, while horse dung was ubiquitous. The persistence of such conditions goes much of the way to explaining the continuing death toll among infants, who are particularly susceptible to intestinal infections which spread easily in these circumstances. At the very end of the nineteenth century, water closets became cheaper and many working-class homes acquired them, while local authorities, conscious of the link between filth and disease, began a drive to clean up the worst areas. Another factor was the substantial increase in the availability of milk, and the development of pasteurisation.

The decline in fertility is harder to explain. It occurred mainly through limitation within marriage, and was not merely a reversal of the previous change and a return to later marriage. The mechanisms for change seem to have been either abstinence or the age-old standby of *coitus interruptus*. There was an increase in the availability of artificial methods of preventing conception, but they were not of major importance. What are hard to establish are the motives for change.

Economic change must provide part of the explanation. Children became increasingly costly to keep as schooling spread and became compulsory in the 1870s. The educational standards required before children could leave were progressively tightened up over the next forty years, thus forcing up the leaving age. Evidence for this as a motive is provided by the fact that parents were not postponing the first birth of a child but, rather, limiting births after families reached a certain size. In the days before compulsory education, working-class parents could be sure that after they had had three or four children, the eldest would be going out to work so they could afford to have more. This was decreasingly the case. Complementary to this were the falling prices of consumer goods relative to the price of having a child. When such goods were effectively out of reach of most families, there was no point in forgoing the pleasures of having another child. As consumer goods became more affordable, the incentive to forgo childbearing became stronger. In the 1930s there was a saying, 'A baby or a baby Austin' which, translated back to the 1880s, when pianos rather than cars were the height of desirability, would have gone, 'A baby or a baby grand'. (Or, for the working class, an upright in the front parlour.)

J O Banks has put forward a different argument. To him, it was the growing expense of certain necessary items of middle-class expenditure, such as education and domestic servants, that led to the fall in fertility for that group in society. In order to maintain their life style, they reduced the number of their children, which brings the non-economic element of status into the argument. To this particular non-economic element could be added others, such as the growing secularisation of many groups in society. How far groups were integrated into society and influenced by its dominant values is also important. Two of the most socially isolated groups in society, miners and farm labourers, experienced the smallest fall in fertility.

Equally if not more important is the question of whether women or men, or both together, were the influence behind the transition. For instance, the growth of education in the period, of particular benefit to women because they started from lower levels of literacy, may have made them more aware of the arguments for family limitation which were being increasingly propagated in the late nineteenth century. These then became a matter for family discussion. Much work still remains to be done on this fascinating subject; the arguments put forward are highly tentative because of the difficulty of establishing exactly what values were at work and how they were transmitted.

MIGRATION AND EMIGRATION

Migration increased still further from its already high levels before industrialisation. The greatest volume of such migration arose within counties, and was not usually recorded in any official published statistics. Only local studies give us some clue as to how much there was. A large part consisted of rural adolescents and young adults, both male and female, moving to towns in search of work. Ernie Bevin, the illegitimate child of a poor mother, moved from the depths of rural Somerset to become a carter in Bristol docks. No other working-class migrant went on to become leader of the Transport and General Workers Union and Foreign Secretary, but his first move was typical, as many Bristol dockworkers came from the adjacent counties of Somerset and Gloucestershire. Similarly, the majority of female domestic servants who looked after the houses of the middle classes in Cheltenham came from within the county of Gloucestershire. In industrial areas, men would usually move within a limited area in search of work, due to the importance of personal contacts in the process of finding a job. The main exception to this was migration to London, which more ambitious skilled workers saw as a good place to acquire extra training.

In spite of the continued prevalence of short-distance moves, there was an increase in longer-distance migration and important shifts in migration patterns. Previously, most rural migration had been between villages; many young migrants became servants on farms before marrying and setting up for themselves. The increasing job opportunities provided by urban growth, even in areas like the South of England, meant that rural migrants were increasingly moving to towns. Most moves, even if within counties, would therefore be over longer distances than before. An even more marked break with eighteenth-century patterns was the growth of migration to industrial areas, supplementing the existing focus of long-distance migration – London. In this, the railways seem to have played an important part. It was not so much the easier travel they provided as the increased awareness of outside opportunities which they brought that was the spur to move. Mining areas were a particular focus, for coalmining in boom phases offered plentiful and well-paid job opportunities to unskilled workers. The coal mines of South Wales, for instance, were magnets for Central Wales and even the West of England in the later nineteenth century.

Emigration, the most striking of all types of nineteenth-century migration, was no different in kind from other types of migration.

Rather, it showed many similar patterns. It was strongly influenced by knowledge of the intended destination, coming either from family members or former neighbours who were already there, or increasingly as the century wore on from newspapers or information disseminated by emigration agents and shipping companies. Improved technology contributed to the growth of emigration by reducing the cost of travel, but the effect of this should not be overestimated. Passage by sailing ship was cheap before steamers were introduced, and the main effect these had in the later nineteenth century was to improve conditions and cut the time spent in travel. As well as encouraging more emigration, therefore, steamships encouraged a higher rate of return to the home country.

Before the mid-nineteenth century, the number of emigrants was relatively small. They tended to have above-average incomes, and were unlikely to return: emigration was final. From the 1850s, emigration patterns became much more diversified. Emigrants came from all areas of the country and walks of life, rural and urban, skilled and unskilled, working class and middle class. If skilled, they tended to take up their old occupation in their new home; if unskilled, they mostly went to the towns where work was easy to get, even if they were rural in origin. The most notable and tragic group of skilled workers to move were the Cornish tin-miners, whose industry declined from the 1860s, and who moved in droves to the mines of Australia and the Rocky Mountains. Most emigrants did not move because of excessive poverty, however, but simply because the opportunities seemed better elsewhere. Up to the 1890s, this was the USA, but in the last great wave of emigration from 1905 to 1914, it was the Empire countries, Australia, Canada and New Zealand, which were the most attractive. In all these cases, wage levels were significantly higher than in Britain, but in spite of this emigration was not so final as it seemed. Perhaps as many as 40 per cent of all emigrants returned, some of them permanently, some of them short-term returners in industries where there was a frequent temporary migration across the Atlantic, such as coalmining. Middle-class emigrants included the professionals and businessmen who staffed the Indian and colonial Civil Services, who ran the plantations and mines in British ownership overseas, and who served in the army, a large proportion of which was always in India. Many of them came back to Britain at the end of their service to retire. Farmers, and younger sons of farmers, were another important group of emigrants, particularly after agriculture became depressed in the 1870s.

The idea has been put forward that high levels of emigration and internal migration alternated, in line with the observable swings in investment between home and abroad. On this argument, increased investment overseas heightened employment opportunities overseas, thus stimulating emigration; increased investment at home stimulated internal migration. The evidence for a close link between changes in the direction of British investment and changes in the direction of migration is not good, however. Total population movements in the boom emigration decades of the 1880s and 1900s were higher than in the 1890s, when emigration fell sharply but internal migration did not rise enough to compensate. Decisions on migration were affected by a variety of factors. People in certain areas, such as the West Country, always had a high propensity to emigrate, perhaps because information about it was particularly good in that area. People in East Anglia or North Wales were less likely than the average to either emigrate or move within Britain. So in spite of the similarities between emigration and internal migration, the decision as between the two courses of action was not a simple trade-off, dependent on whether economic conditions were better abroad or at home.

Migration and emigration had major effects on population. The two combined caused rural population to increase only slowly after the mid-century, while in areas such as Central Wales and the Highlands of Scotland the population fell, in spite of high birth rates. Emigration affected the entire country, since many emigrants were from urban areas. In the peak decades of the 1880s and 1900s, respectively, gross emigration (i.e. not counting returners) came to 1.75 and 2.25 million people. Since emigrants were mainly young, the effect of their departure was to reduce the population still more below what it would have been had they remained, as their future children became Americans or Antipodeans rather than British.

While there were fewer immigrants to Britain than emigrants from it, their story is equally interesting. Ireland was politically part of the United Kingdom at this time, but it is usual to regard movement from Ireland to Great Britain as immigration to the latter. Irish immigration increased rapidly as the food supply in that country worsened from the 1820s and reached a peak in the years after the potato famine of 1845–6, when half a million Irish settled in Britain. Immigration then continued at a slower rate and as time went by the relative number of Irish-born decreased. As cultural and religious links between those of Irish ancestry remained strong, however, the Irish presence became if anything more marked, with Irish communities in most large towns. In Liverpool and Glasgow, the Irish were omnipresent, with around 20 per cent of each city's population in 1851 being Irish-born. Similar forces to those which led to Irish immigration also caused an equally dramatic if smaller scale migration in the mid-century, from the Highlands of Scotland to the Lowland cities. Jewish immigration from Eastern Europe increased rapidly after 1880, mainly to London's East End, Manchester and Leeds. Apart from that, foreign immigration was restricted to small pockets. There were, for instance, Polish steelworkers in Scotland and German miners in the North East. Small though these pockets were, they do illustrate that Britain had relatively attractive wage levels compared with most of Continental Europe. Apart from these working-class immigrants, Britain as a tolerant society with many commercial opportunities played host to foreign businessmen and intellectuals of all descriptions. Hermann Sipf, the author's grandfather, came from Frankfurt in the later nineteenth century and set up an insurance brokerage specialising in German business. A rather better-known German immigrant, this time an intellectual rather than businessman, was Karl Marx.

LABOUR SUPPLY

While population growth was by far the biggest influence on labour supply, changes in participation rates and hours worked might also have been significant. Changes in the quality of the workforce also need to be considered. The discussion below looks first at participation rates and hours worked, then at labour-force quality.

Participation rates for adult male workers, who constituted by far the largest part of the waged workforce, were probably stable, with a high level of participation throughout. The evidence on hours worked is much more uncertain. First of all, there was much underemployment, among both rural and urban workers. The mid-century journalist Henry Mayhew recorded the great variety of workers in London with intermittent occupations, from coster-mongers to street-sweepers. The street scenes of Victorian novelists are full of men waiting – cab-drivers, men who held horses for sixpence, men who groomed horses, or simply 'loafers'.

Little empirical work has been done on the extent of underemployment in the nineteenth century, or on changes in its extent. There was undoubtedly a great deal of casual work in the late nineteenth- and early twentieth-century cities, particularly in the docks. It does seem likely on *a priori* grounds, however, that work was far more irregular earlier in the century. As industrial capital increased, employers needed to utilise it to the maximum, and this encouraged them to have a stable, fully-employed workforce. Compared with most big industrial towns, London was notorious for a high level of casual work; but even here there is ample testimony, in Charles Booth's monumental survey of London industry, to the spread in the late nineteenth century of factories employing a stable, semi-skilled workforce. These developments would have tended to increase hours of work over the century. Another influence in the same direction was the decline among more skilled industrial workers of frequent unofficial holidays and Mondays off. Offsetting these trends was a reduction in the standard working week from the mid-century, which was particularly associated with the growth of the Saturday half-holiday. For many workers, a regular work week of around 56 hours became established by the late nineteenth century, as compared with an irregular one at the beginning, nominally of 60–70 hours but possibly of less. From the 1890s there were further reductions, particularly for shift workers like railwaymen who had not benefited much earlier. Whether the net effect of all these conflicting influences on hours of work was positive or negative is, it seems to the author, quite uncertain in the present state of knowledge.

Measured by published statistics, the participation rate of women workers did not change much. Around a third of women did waged work, increasingly concentrated in domestic service, textiles and clothing. Their exclusion from other paid work reflected their own lack of power, and was exacerbated by the strengthening of the ideology of domesticity, in which women's sphere was the home. Although this exclusion was sometimes maintained by unions, as in the case of printing, it was usually accepted unquestioningly by employers as well as male workers. Hence the decline in fertility levels in the later nineteenth century was not marked by any increase in the proportion of women in the paid workforce. Even in the growing non-manual sector, women were only employed in large numbers as nurses and teachers – clerical work and typing were largely male preserves until the 1900s.

In less easily measurable ways, the amount of paid work for women may have increased as the nineteenth century wore on, thus reversing its probable decline earlier on. Urban living led to a vast demand for lodgings for single people. Meeting this demand, and doing associated work such as taking in laundry, was a very important activity for many working-class wives but hardly shows up on published census statistics. It can only be studied through examining the details of individual households and is, therefore, an excellent subject for local study. Much part-time children's work, such as newspaper selling, likewise escaped the employment statistics. Although many children had part-time sources of income, their disappearance from the full-time workforce through the pressure of legislation and the growth of schooling was one of the bigger changes of the nineteenth century. Paradoxically, the century which is most associated with full-time child labour is the one in which this virtually ceased to exist for the first time in history.

Schooling was the most striking way in which the quality of the workforce could be improved. Significant increases in the proportion of those being educated seem to have occurred as the population growth rate began to slow in the 1840s, with many working-class parents paying for some education or obtaining it for their children through Sunday schools. Religious and state support for schools increased rapidly, and by 1900 most school leavers possessed basic literacy. By most accounts, schools did not teach much of value otherwise, but even basic literacy was important to a growing range of jobs. These included railway work, which depended heavily on written rules and instructions, the Post Office, jobs connected with warehousing and carting, and the growing amount of clerical work. Among skilled manual jobs, engineering was becoming increasingly dependent on blueprints and instructions rather than rule of thumb, while occupations like gas-fitting and electrical installation needed sophisticated technical knowledge which depended on basic literacy for its acquisition.

In spite of this trend, learning skilled work in industries like engineering, shipbuilding and printing depended largely on apprenticeship, in which skill was gained over a lengthy period by watching and imitating, or 'sitting by Nellie'. By the 1900s, around 20 per cent of all manual workers had served an apprenticeship or a learnership, which was similar though rather less formal and often shorter. Apprenticeship was a relatively cheap method of acquiring skill, since the young worker also performed useful work rather than merely sitting in a classroom. It was attractive to employers and the state because its cost was borne by the young worker, who earned less than he would have done in unskilled occupations. In terms of Britain's industrial development, apprenticeship was reasonably efficient because there were already large numbers of skilled workers who could pass on the necessary techniques. It could be criticised, however, for encouraging old-established rule of thumb methods. To counter this, technical education was growing rapidly, often in association with apprenticeship, from the 1890s. Much of it took place through evening classes, which not surprisingly suffered from poor attendance, while there were complaints that the students' basic level of education was too low to enable them to fully benefit from technical education. Nevertheless, the criticisms that are often directed by historians against Britain's technical education for manual workers at this time are quite misplaced. In relation to Continental countries, provision was quite good. Problems came rather in technical education at the managerial level, which will be discussed in a later chapter.

In spite of the potential importance of education to economic growth, physical capital is also needed to make human capital fully effective. Thus nineteenth-century Sweden had a highly educated workforce but, for much of the century, could not use its skills for lack of physical capital. Conversely, in early nineteenth-century Britain it may have been economically rational to build up physical capital and not bother too much about education. Even subsequently, it seems likely that, although educational provision in this country was never outstanding, it increased fast enough for most of the century to service the economy adequately. Towards the end of the nineteenth century, however, it might have been beneficial economically to have had better basic education, which would have improved the adaptability of the workforce and its receptiveness to technical training.

CHAPTER TWELVE

The workshop of the world: manufacturing and mining

THE GROWTH OF INDUSTRY

By 1830, Britain had already become an industrial nation, in the sense that manufacturing exceeded agriculture in its contribution to the national income. Manufacturing's importance was partly due to the rapid rise of the cotton industry, and by 1830 this was by far the largest manufacturing industry. However, by 1850, cotton's pre-eminent position in manufacturing was being eroded, while iron and engineering were becoming more important. The rest of the period up to 1914 saw these trends continue. Cotton and other textiles remained extremely important, but their importance relative to other manufacturing industries was reduced. In this same period, cotton ceased to be the only large mechanised industry and was joined by many others. These included not only iron and steel and engineering, but also important consumer-goods industries such as clothing and footwear, as well as the major sector of transport, encompassing railways and shipping.

This process of mechanisation was a direct cause of the rise of the producer goods industries, which helped to ensure the continued growth and prosperity of the regions associated with coal and metals production. Between 1855 and 1913, the growth rate of producer-goods industries averaged 2.5 per cent per year, as compared with 1.6 per cent per year for consumer-goods industries. There was a vast increase in the use of steam engines to drive machinery and power transport, of coal to fuel the machines, and of iron and later steel to build them. The scale of mechanisation was far broader than in the eighteenth and early nineteenth centuries, and this is reflected in the figures for horsepower of steam engines in industry, which rose from

Table 12.1 Share of staple industries in national income (%)

Approximate dates	All textiles	Cotton	Coal	Iron and Steel*	Iron and steel Products†
1820	14	5	1		3.5
1860	10	4.5	3		7.5
1907	5	3	6.5	2.0	6.0

* Includes iron ore mining

† Includes engineering and shipbuilding. Up to the 1860s, the great bulk of iron industry products were very simple, e.g. rails, constructional girders; by the 1900s, the more complex products were far more important.

Note: All figures given are net output, i.e. after deducting inputs from other industries (raw materials, coal etc.). Adding these would make cotton relatively larger in 1820, since it was highly mechanised compared with other textile industries

(*Sources:* Deane and Cole; Lewis, W A 1978 *Growth and Fluctuations;* Feinstein)

about one million in 1870 to over seven million by 1907.

Mechanisation outside the cotton industry was only starting in 1830, however, and it is essential to an understanding of the mid-nineteenth-century economy to realise that at this time the majority of workers were still in non-mechanised handicraft trades such as shoe-making and tailoring. It is estimated that in 1851 only 25 per cent of industrial workers were in mechanised industries, and a number of these were in mining, which was only mechanised in the sense that steam engines were used for pumping. The relative proportion of workers in handicraft industries did, of course, fall steadily throughout the period, as trades like shoe-making and tailoring became mechanised from the mid-century on; but certain major occupations remained almost untouched by mechanisation up to the end of the century. One of these was building, which employed 9 per cent of the adult male workforce in 1911. Bricks, and to an extent joinery, were by that time machine-produced, but the actual process of building remained little changed since it is difficult to subject it to mass-production techniques.

Mining, in which coalmining was predominant after the collapse of the Cornish tin industry from the 1860s, employed the same proportion of the workforce as building in 1911. Coal output had increased in all areas over this period, with particularly rapid expansion in South Wales, Scotland, Yorkshire and the East

Midlands. Steam pumping had been introduced in the eighteenth century, but otherwise mechanisation was virtually non-existent. The nineteenth century saw the introduction of much improved shaft-sinking techniques. These, along with improved ventilation and drainage, enabled mines to go much deeper. The shafts had steam-wound cages in sliding runners to facilitate the transport of miners and coal. Underground, efficiency was improved largely by the introduction of existing ideas from the outside world, such as the use of ponies and, later, steam winding for haulage, or by reorganisation of the methods of working. The main change here was the gradual spread from the West Midlands to all areas except the North East of the long-wall method of working. This extracted all the coal from a face, whereas the old pillar and stall method left 'pillars' of coal behind. What is notable is that mechanisation in the form of coal-cutting machinery made little progress. The actual extraction of coal was largely manual, the only innovation being the use of explosives to undercut the face. The lack of major innovations meant that output per worker only increased slowly until the 1880s. It used to be thought that there was subsequently a fall in labour productivity up to 1914, but recent research has shown that this was not the case. Output per man hour stagnated but did not fall, although as hours were reduced, output per worker did decline. Revenue per worker rose, however, because of investment in facilities which enhanced the saleability of 'small coal', for instance by washing it. Previously, much coal had been unsaleable because it was mixed with dirt and stones. This example shows the drawbacks of relying on simple output per person calculations as a universal measure of productivity. The economic performance of the coal industry, previously much criticised, appears more favourable if measured on a revenue basis.

In spite of slowly rising productivity, wages rose faster, so the price of coal at the pithead increased over the period, while other wholesale prices fell. Transport improvement meant that coal prices away from the coalfields did fall gradually; but the rise in coal output owed itself more to increased demand than to supply-side cost reductions. Exports, shown in Table 12.2, gained more from reduced transport costs and therefore grew particularly fast. Mechanisation of industry and transport in other countries which had poorer indigenous supplies of coal also contributed to export demand.

The mechanisation of most industries in the nineteenth century depended upon the use of steam. The thrust of all steam engine development, from James Watt onwards, was to reduce fuel consumption, and to achieve lighter and therefore cheaper engines.

113

This was done by slow, incremental improvements in design, aided by the development of metal-working techniques which enabled boilers to sustain higher pressures and moving parts to fit together more accurately. Steam engines remained essential for pumping in mines, and were later essential for the great urban water-supply schemes of the later nineteenth century. The main use of steam, though, was to provide rotative motion, to locomotive coupling rods, ships' paddle wheels or screws, and factory shafting. Since it was impractical to have small steam engines for each machine, the flexibility of factory layouts was limited by the necessity to link individual machines, via leather belting, to steam-driven shafts running through the factory.

Table 12.2 Industrial production in Great Britain (annual average)

	Raw cotton* (million kilos)	Coal (million metric tons)	Coal exports (million metric tons)	Pig Iron (000 metric tons)	Steel (000 metric tons)
1830–39	146	36	1	892	
1865–74	476	117	11	5731	485†
1900–09	792	246	52	9318	5564

* Including Ireland
† 1871–4
(*Sources:* Church, Roy 1986 *The History of the British Coal Industry,* Vol 3; Mitchell and Deane; Riden, P 1977 The output of the British iron industry before 1870. 'Economic History Review' 2nd series, Vol XXX (No 3); 442–59)

One late but major innovation was the steam turbine, one version of which was produced by Charles Parsons in 1884. The turbine was developed for electricity generation, its main use today, and to some extent for marine engines; but apart from these, the reciprocating steam engine still remained supreme, although gas engines and internal combustion engines were beginning to challenge it for low horsepower applications by the end of the period.

The development of iron and steel technology also largely involved improvement rather than radical innovation, although cheap steel was a major exception to this. In the first half of the nineteenth century there was an increase in blast furnace size, which cut capital costs per unit of output, and gradual improvements in technique which cut fuel consumption and raw material wastage. A dramatic change began in 1856, when Henry Bessemer, a professional inventor, announced his process for converting pig iron directly into what is now called mild steel. This was cheaper than wrought iron, more consistent in quality, and capable of being produced in much larger sections, although it was less resistant to corrosion. Further advances in steel making included the Siemens-Martin open-hearth furnace developed in the 1860s; it had different advantages to the Bessemer process, so both methods continued in operation. They needed non-phosphoric iron, much of which had to be imported. Two chemists, Sidney Thomas and Percy Gilchrist, discovered a method of using phosphoric ores in 1879, but at first this process was more used abroad. Steel took some time to be accepted for rails and shipbuilding, two of the main uses for wrought iron, and wrought iron production continued to grow up to 1882. By the 1870s, however, steel production was increasing rapidly, and this increase continued until the 1890s, when the rate slowed. Over the whole period, Scotland, Cumberland and the North East all grew to importance as iron- and steel-producing areas; South Wales' relative importance diminished, while the old West Midlands area, including Coalbrookdale, became a quite insignificant producer.

The British iron and steel industry had been the world's largest until the 1880s, and the technological leader. By 1914, the total size of the industry, and the average size of its plants, was small compared with the USA and Germany, while the plants were less modern. Two important reasons for this were external to the industry. The population of both these countries was growing faster and, naturally, this generated a higher growth of demand for steel. Furthermore, both America and Germany had tariff protection, while Britain was a free-trade nation; this meant that while the British industry did make substantial exports, there were also big imports, particularly from Germany. Both the factors noted above meant that the natural growth rate of British production was likely to be slower than her competitors' and, hence, there was less incentive for large, modern plants to be built.

Complementary to iron and steel manufacture was the heavy engineering sector, which turned metal into machines. It encompassed the construction of machine tools to shape the metal, of railway engines and rolling stock, of steam engines, of textile and agricultural machinery, and of a host of other machines catering for all the industries which mechanised in the nineteenth century, such as paper, printing and grain milling. Similar in its techniques, although important enough to count as a separate sector, was shipbuilding. For all these industries, it was again incremental advances in the

115

technology of metal working and the adaptation of machines for particular purposes, rather than spectacular breakthroughs, which constituted the major part of technical change.

Before 1850, Britain was the dominant world supplier of this type of machinery, although outside Britain herself demand was limited. As world demand grew, production and exports also continued to grow rapidly, although by the end of the century Britain remained predominant in only some of these lines, such as textile machinery and ships. In shipbuilding, Britain suffered from severe American competition in the mid-century, when wood, cheaper in the USA, was the main raw material. The use of, first, wrought iron and, then, steel increased from the 1850s, until by the late 1880s the latter was the standard material for British-built ships. The industry became increasingly concentrated where its raw material was cheapest, on the Clyde and, in the North East, on the Tyne and Wear. Its competitive position improved, so that by 1900 Britain's share of world shipbuilding output had stabilised at about 60 per cent. There were a variety of reasons for this dominance, including the strength of the British shipping industry, whose owners found it easier to liaise with British builders, the stimulus of building for the Navy, and the availability of cheap steel from Germany. It is also clear, though, that British shipyards were more efficient than foreign competitors. The differential can be put down to concentration and the consequent internal economies of scale, which enabled designs for certain types of vessel to be standardised and production runs lengthened, together with external economies from the availability of skilled labour and the proximity of ancillary suppliers.

Light engineering as an industry is almost impossible to define. Originally light metal objects, such as cutlery, pots, pans, stirrups, nails and so on, had largely been produced by hand, although the use of treadle-powered machines for pressing and stamping had developed in the Birmingham area in the eighteenth century. Much of the industry remained little changed until the mid-nineteenth century, when workshops in Birmingham began to operate on a larger scale and use steam power. The growth of consumer incomes had provided a growing demand for household utensils and metal ornaments ever since the seventeenth century, but the process accelerated in the mid-nineteenth century as real wages began their sustained rise. As the century wore on, new products, such as gas and later electrical appliances, bicycles and, in the 1900s, motor vehicles, became important. Light engineering therefore grew rapidly in the late nineteenth and early twentieth centuries and became essentially a mechanised factory industry. Its growth was particularly rapid in the traditional areas of light metal goods production, notably London and the West Midlands.

In spite of the growing demand for consumer durables, textiles remained the most important consumer-goods industry, although its relative importance declined and its markets changed. Up to the mid-century, the drastic reduction in the price of cotton goods had enhanced cotton's attractiveness for clothing, but slower technical change after that date meant that there was no subsequent comparable price fall. At the same time, consumer incomes were rising, and part of the increase went on better-quality clothing – made out of wool. Thus the temporary fall in cotton's share of the home market, caused by the high price and shortage of cotton in the American Civil War, became permanent. So the wool textile industry, having been overtaken by cotton in the early nineteenth century, regained some of the lost ground later on, although it always remained smaller. Exports became increasingly important to the cotton industry, due to the stagnation in its home market, and it still provided around 25 per cent of Britain's exports of goods in 1913; but whereas it had dominated world markets up to the mid-century, in the later nineteenth century exports to Europe and the USA became increasingly hampered by tariffs; as a result, exports were more and more directed towards countries with less tariff protection, and by 1913 over 50 per cent went to India and China.

Technically, this period saw the gradual mechanisation of the whole of the wool textile industry, which was increasingly centred in Yorkshire. In cotton, rapid technical change continued with the adoption of the power loom, beginning on a large scale in the 1820s and more or less complete by 1860; and the adoption of the 'self-actor' or fully automatic spinning mule, perfected by Richard Roberts in 1830. Productivity continued to grow rapidly until the 1850s, but from then on improvements were, as in other industries, incremental rather than sudden. Lancashire, which remained the centre of the cotton industry, did not adopt the alternative technology of ring spinning, popular in other countries. Almost certainly this was due less to inertia or conservatism and more to the fact that Lancashire increasingly specialised in finer cotton goods, which were more economically spun on mules.

Whereas major technical changes in textiles had almost run their course by the mid-century, technical change in other consumer-goods industries was just beginning. However, there were some exceptions. Gas production and gas lighting had developed since the eighteenth century, although the incandescent mantle for more efficient lighting and the slot meter, which together made large-scale domestic consumption of gas possible, were only developed after 1880. The birth of rotary printing, which made high-speed production of newspapers possible, can be dated to Koenig's press, used by *The Times* in 1814. At the other end of the century, newspaper production was further revolutionised by the Linotype machine, an American invention, which mechanically cast and set type. Newspaper production became a major industry. Printing was also aided by the reduction in paper prices consequent upon the development of the paper machine from the 1800s, a development largely carried out in Britain although the inventors were French. These advances in paper making and printing depended, of course, on the improvement in engineering technique.

The increased circulation of newspapers facilitated advertising and, hence, the ability to build up brand loyalty for consumer goods, the demand for which was underpinned by growing consumer incomes in the later nineteenth century. The production of items like cigarettes, packaged biscuits, chocolates and soap rose on the back of this demand, while brands like Wills Woodbine cigarettes, Huntley and Palmers' biscuits, Cadbury's chocolates and Pears' soap became household names. Mechanisation facilitated the growth of all these consumer-goods industries and many others, such as linoleum manufacture and the production of canned foods. Other old established industries were changed by mechanisation: these included milling, in which the introduction of roller milling from the 1870s, combined with the shift to foreign wheat, led to the decline of the rural mill; clothing, where the sewing machine, an American invention of the 1850s, facilitated the development of a factory industry making ready-made clothes alongside the existing workshop industry; and shoe-making, where a host of machines introduced from the 1850s led to a mechanised industry by the early 1900s. While mechanisation was a major force for change, many of these industries had other significant characteristics: they often used high proportions of cheap, unskilled and/or female labour, as in the case of cigarette, biscuit and chocolate making, and in the clothing industry where this feature was as notable as mechanisation; they depended on rapid distribution; and they depended upon, as well as helping to create, mass consumer demand.

PATTERNS OF CHANGE

The growth of light engineering in response to rising consumer demand highlights a development which has aroused great interest among historians. From as early as the 1850s, it was evident that the USA, although at that time backward in many branches of industry, had developed novel methods of production in those where consumer demand was high, such as locks and guns (a consumer durable in the USA). Basically, these methods involved the use of numerous specialised machine tools to produce different components; these were made to close tolerances and hence could be assembled without further filing to shape. The 'American system', recognisably the same system used today in any mass-production engineering industry, allowed the use of semi-skilled labour to be maximised, whereas in Britain the shaping of components on lathes and the subsequent fitting were skilled tasks. As time went by the American system became more and more characteristic of American industry, extending to products like sewing machines, typewriters and, later, cars. British engineering firms, however, largely retained their existing methods. While there has been much debate about the relative merit of each country's methods, it seems likely that British techniques, when applied to heavy products, were quite appropriate. Such products were made in small quantities with frequent changes in specification and therefore, highly specialised machines were inappropriate. Furthermore, the cost of skilled labour in Britain, if measured by wage differentials between skilled and unskilled, was relatively low compared with the USA. The problem was that British engineering techniques were less appropriate to mass production. Although the bicycle industry adopted American techniques and machines quite successfully in the 1890s, the fledgling car industry was notoriously poor at standardised production in the 1900s. It seems likely that many British firms were lacking in the organisational skills and knowledge of techniques appropriate to mass production; this did not matter for most of the nineteenth century, when demand for consumer durables was low, but was to matter in the twentieth.

An even more serious problem was Britain's deficiency, apparent by the late nineteenth century, in technically advanced industries, the most notable being chemicals and electrical products. Britain was still an important producer of many basic chemicals, but by 1913 the German chemical industry was twice the size of the British, even though total German industrial output was only slightly greater. In particular, the British industry was weak in the production of advanced chemicals; on the eve of the First World War, 90 per cent of the artificial dyes used in this country were imported, and the British army used German dyes for its uniforms. The electrical industry exhibited similar weaknesses. The large-scale development of electrification in this country, for tramways and factories only began at the very end of the 1890s, some ten years after America. Britain also lacked major home-based producers of electrical equipment; a number of the larger firms before 1914 were subsidiaries of German or American companies, and the most technically advanced products often came from abroad.

As mechanisation came to affect more sectors of the economy, this period saw a more radical change in industrial organisation than had the previous eighty years. The 'domestic system' of production in homes gradually disappeared, except in clothing and a few other 'sweated' trades in large cities where there was a reservoir of very cheap labour and no pressing technical reasons for large-scale production. The factory became the dominant place of employment for industrial workers, workshops surviving mainly as repair shops or in a few luxury trades. Most workers were in factories with under a 1000 employees, however, and the average size was smaller than in Germany or America. There were a few large plants employing 5000 workers or more, among shipyards, steelworks, and the occasional big engineering firm, like Platts of Oldham, who made textile machinery.

Most firms remained single-product concerns, owning only the one plant. The fact that in the late nineteenth century most manufacturing concerns of any size became limited companies, rather than partnerships, made very little difference, since most companies remained private rather than issuing shares to the public. There were some large integrated manufacturing firms in the armaments and shipbuilding sector such as Vickers and John Brown; and a few American-style 'trusts', amalgamations which controlled a high proportion of output in one industry, developed from the 1890s. Examples were the United Alkali Company of 1890 and the Imperial Tobacco Company of 1901. At the time, much was made of the 'trustification' of British industry, but the actual proportion of large firms, in comparison to USA and Germany, was small. This was partly because there were many informal price-fixing and market-sharing agreements among groups of firms. These developed in the late nineteenth century, in response to the falling prices and depressed conditions which marked the 1880s, and also as self-protection when old local monopolies were eroded. With such agreements, there was less incentive for formal amalgamations. Although the intention behind informal agreements and formal amalgamations was to limit competition, their effects were probably not great. Free trade made it easy for foreign firms to enter the British market, so that there only seem to have been a few examples, sewing thread being one, when monopolies or near monopolies pushed up prices significantly. Furthermore, some of the firms in this position, such as Levers the soap manufacturers, used their high profits in a dynamic way, to invest and expand.

The small size of most British manufacturing firms was reflected in their simple organisational structures. The idea of functional departments covering the main areas – production, sales, personnel and so on – had hardly evolved. 'Personnel management' was still largely the remit of the foreman on the shop floor, who had the power to hire and fire. Production in many industries throughout the nineteenth century was also the responsibility of the foreman and of the skilled workers themselves; or, in many mines and iron and steel works, of sub-contractors who were paid for a tonnage of output and given *carte blanche* to run the operation. By the later nineteenth century, however, larger plants would have works managers and costing departments. Nevertheless, the lack of management theory meant that even large amalgamated firms often failed to develop a sensible management structure. The Calico Printers Association, one such firm, continued to operate after amalgamation with a central board of eighty-four directors. Most such firms confined themselves to central control over pricing and possibly purchasing, and otherwise allowed their component plants a high degree of autonomy. There was a marked difference between the progress of large American firms in centralisation, and the concentration of production on the most efficient plants, and the much looser organisation and local autonomy of most British amalgamations. In Alfred Chandler's view, American firms gained significant advantages from substituting the 'visible hand' of central management co-ordination in functions such as accounting and research, instead of the 'invisible hand' of the market.

In fairness to many smaller British firms, one reason for the rarity of separate sales departments was the fact that the owner or managing director was often personally responsible for sales. Historians have criticised the sales efforts of British firms, particularly abroad, but recent research suggests that much of the criticism is misplaced. Where sales volume was substantial, firms sent in their own travellers and produced catalogues in the appropriate language. Agricultural and textile machinery makers, and machine tool companies, seem to have been particularly active, while warship building firms hawked their wares with, in Eric Ambler's words, 'tireless internationalism'. In smaller foreign markets, where the expense of individual sales drives would be unjustified, British firms gained from the well-established network of British merchant houses which handled a range of goods. Here the invisible hand was still a beneficial force.

In domestic markets, the growth of the consumer-goods industries and the technique of branding suggest that British firms were willing to adopt innovative sales techniques, in spite of their backwardness in other managerial functions. Wills, the tobacco firm, recruited high-quality travellers, paid considerable attention to packaging, which was an important element in establishing awareness of branded goods, and produced new brands of cigarettes to appeal to specific markets. Their attention to sales reinforced their adoption of new technology, in the form of the Bonsaek cigarette-making machine of the 1880s, and helped them to withstand strong American competition in the cigarette market. While more comparative research on sales techniques in different countries would be helpful, it seems likely that in this area many British firms were fully competitive.

CHAPTER THIRTEEN

The service economy

To the Victorian middle classes, the growth and proliferation of specialised service activities was far more visible than the developments in manufacturing, which were well-hidden in workshop or factory. The convenience of numerous bank branches, the provision of more and more luxurious rail travel, the ability by the end of the century to telephone a department store and order at short notice clothes for the family's summer holiday at a seaside resort – such is a small sample of the services which were available to those with sufficient income. The great majority of the population could not aspire to bank accounts, frequent rail travel or summer holidays, but most people did enjoy a substantial range of services undreamt of at the beginning of the nineteenth century.

Even those with sufficient income to afford frequent rail travel would usually start their journeys by horse-drawn transport, for up to the 1890s this comprised the great bulk of short-distance transport. The number of horses in Britain reached its peak in the 1900s, and the majority of these were urban horses, pulling cabs, buses, carts and the carriages of the better-off. Grooms and carters were as much urban workers as were bank clerks or factory operatives. Carting was an enormous and diverse activity, as road haulage is today, the firms engaged in it ranging from large specialist carriers like Pickfords or the railway companies, down to local builders or shopkeepers with a single cart. Horse-bus services had developed out of short distance stagecoach services, and were complemented from the 1870s by horse tramways over routes where the volume of traffic justified the investment. Trams cut costs compared to buses, because one horse could pull a much heavier load. Both means of transport were slow and relatively expensive at a penny a mile or more, so they catered largely for the middle-class man going to work or his wife going shopping. It was not until the early 1900s that the electric tram, the 'gondola of the people', became widely adopted, some ten years later than in the USA. The delay has been attributed to the Tramways Act of 1870, which gave municipalities the power to purchase horse-tram lines after twenty-one years. Tramways built in the 1870s may have been reluctant to electrify in the 1890s because of this possibility. When electrification was adopted, frequently as a result of municipalisation, its results were remarkable. Fares fell to a halfpenny per mile, services speeded up and, important to workmen, started earlier. The traffic increase was striking: in Leeds, for instance, ten million passengers were carried in 1891 compared with ninety-three million in 1914.

Over the century, improvements in urban transport had enabled a section of the population, from the level of clerical workers upwards, to live some distance from their place of work. The impact was therefore mainly on the middle classes of large commercial cities, and it was only the electric tram which began to open up wider possibilities of decentralisation. Ironically, its development coincided with the beginnings of motor transport, which was to kill both the tram and horse-drawn transport. By 1914, buses in London were motor powered, while taxis had replaced horse-cabs.

The volume of horse-drawn traffic meant that central streets in large cities were often heavily congested. This was partly due to the traffic generated by railway stations, as they moved in from their original location on the outskirts. This move highlights the continued growth of the railways since their dramatic inception. Measured by the number of passengers and volume of goods moved per employee, their efficiency appeared to decline from the 1870s. This, however, is a misleading measurement. Hours of work for railway employees, and particularly their liability to remain on duty for long stretches at a time, were substantially reduced, while standards of service rose. Traders obtained more rapid and frequent goods services, which enabled them to cut stocks. The rise in standards of passenger service was symbolised by the abolition of second class by the Midland Railway in 1874, since third class standards were now equal to second; other lines followed later. Most regular railway travellers were still businessmen, commercial travellers, and an increasing number of better-off commuters, then called season-ticket holders. Cheap excursions were increasingly available for the working-class holidaymaker, however, while on a few lines there was a substantial provision of workmen's trains, running early and offering very low fares. However, apart from the eastern suburbs of London and a few other areas such as the Clydeside conurbation, regular working-class patronage of trains was limited.

The railways constituted the largest commercial organisations in the British Isles, having by amalgamation formed themselves into about a dozen large companies. Railway managements succeeded in organising large numbers of employees and providing high standards of service, but after 1870 the rate of return on capital fell. Railways' commercial freedom of action was increasingly constrained by legislation over fares and rates, and a strong public lobby which kept a watchful eye on service levels. Nevertheless, there were clearly management defects. The statistics collected were inadequate, and this contributed to a failure to control costs: British freight trains, for instance, carried just a quarter the tonnage of American trains in 1900, and not all the difference could be put down to higher levels of service or geographical differences.

Only comparable in size to the railways was the Post Office, which had burgeoned since the penny letter post was introduced in 1840. Run on hierarchical, semi-military lines rather similar to the railways, it too provided steadily improving standards of service, such as the parcel post introduced in 1883. The Post Office also increased its hold on telephone services, which it and private companies had started in the 1880s, and which were beginning to supersede the telegraph for urgent internal messages. By 1912 the Post Office had a virtual monopoly of the service, which by 1913 had three-quarters of a million lines. It was becoming an essential tool for commerce, although its domestic use was still limited to the better-off.

The telephone added to the conveniences of life, as even more strikingly did the growth of shopping facilities. For the middle class, there was the department store, such as Whiteleys, the Universal Providers, opened in 1863. Retailing, like the postal service, experienced no major technical revolution throughout this period but, rather, organisational change and growing specialisation. Department stores grew at the high-class end of the market, but their overall market share, at around 2.5 per cent in 1915, was not great. Unless they were exceptionally well run, economies of scale were limited, so their main advantage was their convenience to the shopper. The department store therefore appealed to the middle-class woman who was not so concerned with price.

Lower down the market, the first thing to notice is simply that shops proliferated as consumer incomes rose and the population became more urbanised. With this came many other changes: the open-air market with its naphtha flares gave way more and more to the gas-lit shop; small producer–retailers, such as cobblers and tailors, to the specialised retail outlet; the practice of higgling to the fixed price, backed up by heavy advertising. The most striking organisational change was the development of the cooperative store and the multiple retailer, which each in 1915 held around 8 per cent of the market. The beginnings of retail cooperation are usually dated to the founding of the Rochdale Pioneers in Toad Lane, Rochdale, in 1844. Cooperatives, which were strongest in the North of England, were usually small local organisations, although the English and Scottish Cooperative Wholesale Societies operated on a large scale. The societies appealed to the thriftier and better-off among the working class, since cash payment and the distribution to customers of a dividend on profits were two features. They also emphasised pure food, important in the mid-century because of the problem of adulteration. While the smaller societies offered a channel for working-class people to exercise responsibility, the larger ones developed as commercial organisations similar to any others, if based on different financial principles.

Multiples, that is firms with several branches, specialising in one type of product, proliferated from the 1870s on in food retailing, with firms like Sainsburys and Liptons. They specialised in mass-market foods such as butter or packaged tea, and tended to handle the cheaper imported produce which appealed to the working-class consumer. The growth of other mass-market industries was reflected in the subsequent growth of multiples in retail trades such as footwear, men's suits and bicycles. Multiples were *par excellence* an organisational innovation. Individual stores were small, but there were economies of scale in purchasing and the provision of finance. It is perhaps the problems of management control which provide a clue to their relatively slow development and the continued dominance of the small business. Multiples sprang up in trades where the manufacturer provided a predetermined product, branded and possibly packaged. The skills of the shop manager were therefore limited, and so people with ideas might still prefer to set up a shop of their own. Owner-run shops also had attractions for the customer: they could and did provide high levels of service. Ernst Dückershoff, a German miner working in the North East, noted in the 1880s how the wives of miners had their groceries delivered, while for the middle classes delivery was a *sine qua non*. Owner-run shops, especially the ubiquitous corner shop, also had the advantage of local knowledge in the allocation of credit, which was essential to many working-class purchasers and seems to have been expected by middle-class ones.

The decline of producer retailers and, in the food trades, the move away from local to national markets through the development of the railway system led to an increase in specialist wholesaling. Wholesalers also seem to have taken on more responsibility for packaging and preparing goods, leaving retailers freer to concentrate on advertising and selling. The degree of pre-packaging was still small, however; the colourman still had to mix paint, the grocer to cut sugar from a sugar-loaf.

Shopping was both a necessity and a leisure activity. The provision of unadulterated leisure was also a growing industry. The seaside holiday had become commonplace among the middle and upper classes, while other leisure interests were pursued on an increasing scale, as described in Chapter 21. What were the economic implications of the leisure industry?

Essentially, the provision of leisure responded to demand, rather than creating it through the introduction of major innovations. This can be seen by considering the continuing central role of the public house. From the 1830s, small taverns or ale houses were giving way to crystal palaces of ornamental glass and gas-lighting – but the centrality of drinking to leisure had not changed. Similarly, music hall grew out of pre-existing establishments which catered for both drinking and singing, and the holiday was already a middle- and upper-class pastime, albeit at first in spas rather than at the seaside. This is not to deny the existence of entrepreneurs or the importance of their role. It was rather that they served to channel investment in one direction or another, without altering the basic current of demand which was always for the age-old leisure activities of drinking, sport, or going away in pursuit of health or recreation.

The entrepreneur, or possibly a go-ahead municipality, would provide attractions such as piers and winter gardens at seaside resorts. Companies which bought the land and developed the infrastructure for whole resorts, as at Lytham St Annes, were another example of entrepreneurial activity. However, much of the capital for the development of lodgings for holidaymakers, and an infrastructure of dwellings and facilities for the resident population, came from small local investors. Lodgings, as in the eighteenth century, were usually furnished rooms which were taken by a family, so the unit of investment was small; but there was a growing provision of large hotels, such as the Grand at Brighton, costing £160,000 in 1864.

Luxury hotels, together with a range of humbler 'commercial' and 'temperance' establishments, were also developed in cities for the businessmen and commercial travellers. Again, these were not a fundamentally new departure, but were rather the successors of the old coaching inns. The growth of specialised restaurants may have been more significant, as the increased volume of travel and the separation of work from home led to a growing demand for meals eaten out. The neglect of the economic and social history of both hotels and restaurants prevents many generalisations. One which can be made is that large numbers of employees in the industry were foreign, German waiters being particularly prominent. A more tentative generalisation is that this was a period when the British, whose inns were once renowned by travellers in comparison to the mean and dirty hostelries of the Continent, began to confuse opulence with excellence and began also to lose the skills of providing food and accommodation, as foreigners more and more did it for them.

Finally, there was investment in a miscellaneous but collectively extensive range of leisure activities, such as football grounds, racecourses and ice rinks. Whether or not the late nineteenth-century British businessman was competent at managing steel mills or chemical works, he showed himself fully responsive to the demand created by the national mania for sport which was so deplored by the more moralistic of contemporary observers.

CHAPTER FOURTEEN

Agriculture and rural society

'While the reaper yonder slashes at the straw, huge ships are on the ocean rushing through the foam to bring grain to the great cities . . .' Richard Jefferies' overheated late-Victorian prose explains vividly why the significance of agriculture, on which the first chapter of this book laid so much stress, gradually declined. In prosaic economic language, Britain's comparative advantage in industrial goods and services increased, and it became more worthwhile to exchange these for agricultural goods from abroad. The price of foreign agricultural produce was reduced by productivity gains in transport and by the availability of cheap land in the Americas and Antipodes. The long-term reduction in food prices was still important to the national economy, but the reduction was partly achieved outside Britain.

The erosion of agriculture's importance in the economy had social and political implications. Agriculturalists had succeeded in maintaining protection, via the Corn Laws, until 1846, and lost it only amidst severe political turmoil. For thirty years after that the loss of protection seemed to have few deleterious effects upon agriculture. Its share of national income shrank still further, but in absolute terms agricultural output increased. By the time the sharp price fall induced in the 1870s by trans-Atlantic wheat occurred, the slow attrition in economic position had lost landowners and farmers a further proportion of their political influence. They were ill-equipped to mount a successful political battle for the renewal of protection, as happened throughout most of the Continent, and so there was no protection for agriculture in Britain before the First World War. The failure to gain protection ensured that the proportionate share of agriculture in the economy shrank even faster, while the absolute number of those working in it fell. Hence by the eve of the First

World War, agriculture formed a minor part of the British economy.

At the beginning of this period, agriculture was still in the throes of a period of relatively low prices which lasted for twenty years or so after the high-price period of the Napoleonic Wars. Prices after 1815 were still much higher than anything that had been seen before the 1790s, and the problems of many farmers in this period were also due to the burden of high borrowings taken on during the inflated price level of the wars. Nevertheless, given that the population was still increasing rapidly, and given the existence of protection, any fall in prices seems surprising. The main reason seems to have been the continued growth in yields, which may have speeded up after 1815. There were no special reasons behind this, but rather a continuation of the trends described in the first chapter: rotations improved with benefits to soil fertility; more fertilisers were used, aided by the growth of towns, which produced more horse dung and night-soil, and the continued improvements in transport; and iron implements increasingly replaced wooden ones, although this mainly benefited animal and labour productivity, rather than yields. As a result, the output of British farms more or less kept pace with population increase until the 1840s. A corollary of this was that higher levels of efficiency kept up farmers' incomes and kept down costs, thus mitigating the effect of the price fall.

By the late 1830s, grain prices had improved, ushering in what is sometimes called the 'Golden Age' of British farming. The repeal of the Corn Laws did little to upset this, but not for the reason which is sometimes given, which is that repeal made no real difference to internal British price levels for grain. It is clear that protection had pushed British prices up, something which can be easily demonstrated by looking at Continental prices. These were considerably below prices in Britain for much of the 1820s and 1830s, and then entered a long-term rising trend – almost the complete opposite of British wheat prices which, for the twenty-five years after 1846, were on average lower than in the 'depressed' period after the Napoleonic Wars. The prosperity of agriculture in the third quarter of the century owed itself rather to its response to price signals and a continued improvement in efficiency. Wheat acreage fell, so that by the 1860s, 40 per cent of wheat was imported, but there was a steady swing towards livestock. Meat prices were firmer, because the rise in working-class incomes was largely directed towards diversification of diet, which meant that more meat, as well as milk, butter and cheese, was being consumed; wool prices were firmer, because another slice of the increased incomes went on wool clothing in preference to cotton. As yet, foreign competition in these commodities was limited, so the demand changes helped to buoy up prices.

At the same time, fertiliser application, new techniques and mechanisation continued to improve the productivity of land and labour. Guano, the accumulated droppings of seabirds, imported from Peru, fertilised the soil of Victorian Britain; from the 1860s, chemically produced potash was applied. Labour productivity increased through the much wider use of the scythe rather than the sickle for the grain harvest. The scythe economised significantly on labour, but involved higher waste. Grain prices fell and wages rose between the second and third quarters of the century, so its adoption was a clear-cut case of reaction to changes in input prices. The reign of the scythe was short, however, for from the mid-century the mechanical reaper, an American invention which further economised on labour costs, was increasingly used. This and the threshing machine, an older invention also coming into widespread use at this time, were the first examples of large-scale mechanisation in farming. Fertiliser use and mechanisation were two pillars of 'high farming', essentially meaning farming with high inputs of capital to achieve high output. The other pillar was heavy investment by landowners in buildings and drainage – investment which rarely provided a decent return, for the 'Golden Age' only lasted a short time.

By the 1870s, railways had opened up the American prairies, while other wheat-producing areas, notably India and Argentina, were also expanding production. Ocean freight rates fell steeply, so the cost of freight formed less and less of a barrier to imports. The expansion of overseas production extended to animal products, notably wool but also meat. The first consignment of frozen meat arrived from Australia in the 'Strathleven' in 1880, while importation of chilled beef from USA had begun in 1875. The price of wheat fell to a low point of 23 shillings per quarter in 1894, and its average level for the twenty-five years from 1878 was 60 per cent of the prices ruling between 1847 and 1872. Wool prices also fell sharply: many farmers in the Midlands and the southern corn and sheep areas went bankrupt. In response to the signals of the market, wheat growing declined until by 1913 about 80 per cent of Britain's wheat was imported.

In spite of the apparent contrast between the late nineteenth-century agricultural depression and the previous twenty-five years, many of the late nineteenth-century changes were a continuation of previous trends. The old staple of wheat had long been declining in relative importance. Meat output continued to grow during the depression, because home-produced meat commanded a premium price over chilled and frozen imports. Milk production was an important diversification. The railways made it possible for rural dairy farmers to compete with cows kept in towns, hitherto the main source of urban milk, while the demand for milk rose sharply. Milk production became of major importance, symbolised by the milk churn, a familiar sight at country railway stations. The dairying and meat-producing regions of the North and West therefore suffered much less from the depression than other areas. The prices and acreage of barley and oats, in demand for beer and horses respectively, also suffered less than those of wheat, the acreage of oats actually rising. Technically, mechanisation continued, with the reaper/binder replacing the reaper. Total capital inputs stagnated, however, as landlords became reluctant to invest. The period saw hedgerows flourish uncut and farms decay picturesquely, to create that apparently timeless rural England which delighted sentimental water colourists but was the despair of farmers.

The later nineteenth century has been seen as a time when the dynamism of British farmers, so evident during the eighteenth century, decreased. In truth, there had always been many backward farmers, and there is no evidence that farmers in general were less responsive to change in this period than at earlier times. The halving of wheat acreage in the twenty years from the late 1870s and the shift to milk production, both suggest a rational response to changing prices. Even the failure of wheat yields to improve from the 1880s is explicable in the same terms: fertiliser was expensive and low prices reduced the cash advantage from increasing yields.

What can be said about the agricultural depression is that it saw the beginning of the end of the old set of social relations in the countryside, a set which had had a powerful impact in society as a whole. The way of life of the great landowners, the aristocracy and gentry, had often aroused the antagonism of groups of the urban middle class; but for other members of the middle class, it had been a model for emulation. In the mid-nineteenth century, the continuation of agricultural prosperity had ensured that landowners continued to hold their position as the group with both the greatest collective wealth and also the highest status. The two were closely connected. Their wealth gave them the wherewithal to maintain their status, which they did in a variety of ways: by taking a political and social lead in the county or, for the wealthiest, at national level; by employing numerous servants; and by dispensing patronage to the labourers in the form of cheap coal and blankets or, rather more expensively and rarely, improved housing.

The agricultural depression was one major factor behind the gradual erosion of this position. The financial position of landowners worsened as a result of falling rents. An added factor, although it was much less significant, was the graduated death duty introduced in 1894. It is true that many landowners were insulated from these pressures by their interests in industrial wealth, such as mines sunk on their land, or by their holdings of urban land which rose in value as towns grew in size. By the mid-century, the Duke of Northumberland's mineral royalties were running at around £25,000 per year, while the Duke of Portland got £50,000 per year from his London rents; other great urban fortunes included the Grosvenor family, also with London estates, and the Duke of Devonshire, who owned much of Eastbourne. Furthermore, other landowners, such as the third Earl of St Albans, consciously diversified part of the family fortunes into stock market investments in the late nineteenth century. Another form of income, for the titled at least, was to become the director of a public company. All these trends marked a growing coherence between industrial and urban wealthholders on the one hand, and rural landowners on the other. This coherence combined with the growing unattractiveness of land as an investment to reduce both the distinctiveness and the desirability of the rural landowner's position. Social status still accrued to it, and in an attenuated form does today; but increasingly the newly ennobled, such as the financiers of Edwardian England, were content to do without a large country estate. Even the existing owners' faith in land as a permanent store of value had been gradually sapped, both by the depression and, for those with long memories, by the fact that the heavy investment of the mid-century had never paid a decent return. The slight recovery in agricultural prices in the 1900s led to a gentle rise in land values, providing a stimulus for sales to tenants. The Liberals' land valuation proposals of 1909 sparked off fears of future land taxes and led to more sales. It was the further increase in prices and values resulting from the First World War, however, together with the increased incidence of death duties, which unleashed a flood of selling. It was only then that the old tripartite landlord/ farmers/labourers division was broken for ever; but the causes of its breakdown stretched back forty years or more.

Farmers' incomes too were hit by the depression, although those in dairying and stock raising were much less adversely affected. Those in areas favourable to market gardening, such as the Vale of Evesham or parts of Kent, also benefited from the buoyant domestic demand for vegetables and bottled jam. Farm labourers also suffered less than other agricultural groups. Their standard of living continued to be much lower than that of the average industrial workers, with those in the South earning the lowest wages, but their real wage had increased by around 20 per cent between the mid-century and 1870. It remained around this level until the mid-1880s, after a brief upward flurry during the trade boom of the early 1870s. By the 1890s, however, the reduction of the agricultural workforce through migration and emigration had reduced the glut of agricultural labour and enabled real wages to rise another 10 per cent or so by the 1900s. Although labourers fared rather better than farmers or landowners during the depression, their real wages increased much less than the manual worker average. Back-to-the-soil romantics notwithstanding, there was little to envy in the lot of most agriculturalists in the late nineteenth and early twentieth centuries.

CHAPTER FIFTEEN

Foreign trade and Empire

To many contemporaries and historians, it was the vast overseas commerce of the Victorian era which ensured Britain's prosperity. The great industries of cotton and iron depended upon exports for their prosperity, and these exports paid for growing imports of cheap food, as well as a thousand and one luxuries. How far this view is justified it is one of the tasks of this chapter to consider.

Between 1830 and 1870, the rate of growth of exports accelerated even from its high levels of the previous fifty years. While Britain's share of world trade, already high, may have increased still further, the main proximate reason for rapid export growth was the increase in total world trade. Behind this lay reasons which were both internal and external to Britain. The internal reason was the continuing rapid growth, up to about 1860, in the productivity of the cotton industry and the consequent fall in the cost of cotton textiles, which meant that foreign sales of British textiles also grew rapidly. The external reasons, which held good throughout the nineteenth century, included the exploitation of new land, the fall in shipping costs, and the fact that different countries gained comparative advantages in different products. Up to the 1870s, there was in addition a reduction in tariffs in many countries, although subsequently tariff levels rose again.

The composition of British exports naturally changed over the nineteenth century. Up to the 1850s, exports of iron and machinery were increasing rapidly, but were still small in relation to exports of cotton textiles, which provided most of the motive power for growth. From then on, iron, machinery and coal became more and more important. Export growth slowed down sharply from the 1870s, but these staples, along with wool textiles which had always remained important, continued to dominate the export trade to a quite remarkable extent, as shown in Table 15.1.

Table 15.1 Percentage share in total exports of certain goods in 1913

	Coal	Cotton textiles	Iron and steel	Machinery	Wool textiles
	10	24	11	7	6

Note: Figures are for United Kingdom, i.e. they include Ireland, but omission would not make a significant difference
(*Source:* Mitchell and Deane)

Imports also became more diversified as the century wore on. Up to the mid-century, they had largely consisted of raw materials to be used in manufacture, such as cotton, and warm-climate products, such as sugar and tobacco. In the second half of the century, food imports increased vastly as the combined effects of cheap land overseas and improved transport reduced the prices of overseas products. Imports of other raw materials continued to grow, while in the later part of the century there was also a growing import of manufactures, ranging from steel to electrical machinery to cheap German toys.

One of the most striking facts about British foreign trade throughout this period is that imports exceeded exports. In economic language, there was a deficit on visible trade, hardly a fact which fits in with presuppositions of Victorian thrift. On the contrary, the Victorians loved to consume foreign goods of all kinds, luxuries and necessities. How were they able to finance these imports and yet send vast quantities of capital overseas? The answer lies in the invisibles-earnings from shipping, financial services such as banking and insurance, and miscellaneous overseas activities such as contracting for railway building and other civil engineering projects. Earnings from these were able to provide Britain with a small but persistent surplus on the current balance of payments. This provided the wherewithal with which foreign assets were acquired; the interest on these further swelled the surplus and helped to finance further acquisitions. Later in the century, even exports and invisibles combined could not always match imports; but by that time, investment income was large enough to ensure a continuing surplus.

Shipping, the largest single contributor to invisible earnings, was one of the major British success stories of the period. Up to the

1860s, most long-distance cargo was still carried in wooden sailing ships, since steam engines consumed too much coal to make them economic except for short sea trades. American competition was strong because wood was cheap in the USA and their ships were better designed. Technical developments in engine and boiler design from the 1860s, concomitant with the improvement of techniques for iron shipbuilding, made iron- and later steel-hulled steamships increasingly competitive. Britain had a natural advantage in building these, but American owners could have bought them freely, so it seems that they were inefficient in not adopting them as rapidly as did British owners. By 1900, Britain had around a third of the world's merchant fleet, a proportion that was effectively higher because her fleet was more modern than her competitors'. Shipping earnings were one-fifth the value of merchandise exports.

Financial services were also important. Banking is discussed in Chapter 16. Insurance, like banking, benefited from Britain's long-established position in world trade. This meant that British insurers, both companies and the Lloyds unlimited liability market, had built up a store of expertise on shipping and cargo insurance. This gave them a strong position in the world market which in turn led to economies of scale and thus a further strengthening of their position. Of course, Britain's position in providing international services arose partly from the simple fact that much world trade went to or from Britain, and British shipowners, bankers or insurers had the advantage of close contact with cargo consigners. By itself, this factor was not sufficient, however, as is shown by the American shipping success in the mid-century; so the British service industries deserve credit for their international competitiveness.

Notwithstanding her continuing strong position in the provision of international services, Britain's share of world manufactured exports declined from 1870 from around 40 per cent to around 25 per cent in 1913. But in spite of the decrease in market share, exports still played as important a part as before in the British economy, because total world trade continued to grow rapidly. This growth was associated with a growing interdependence in the world economy. From at least as early as the eighteenth century up to around 1870, world trade could be characterised as taking place within a number of separate multilateral payments networks. In other words, there were different sets of countries, within each group of which imports and exports balanced. A classic early example of this, dating from the eighteenth century, were payments between Britain, North America and the West Indies. Britain had a payments deficit with the West Indies, counterbalanced by a surplus with North America, which in turn had a surplus with the West Indies. Not surprisingly, Britain was at the centre of several of such networks. As interdependence grew, the settlements pattern became more complex until virtually every area was within a world multilateral system. Britain played a major role in this, while the USA became increasingly important. Figure 15.1 demonstrates the pattern.

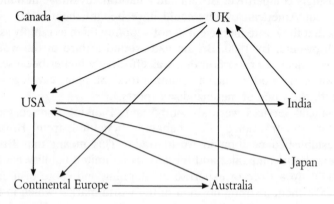

Note: The diagram has been simplified to omit certain trading areas. The arrows point towards the country with a payments surplus, e.g. India imported more from the UK than she exported to the UK and, consequently, the UK had a payments surplus with India

(Source: after Saul, S B *Studies in British Overseas Trade 1870–1914,* 1960)

Figure 15.1 The multilateral system on the eve of the First World War

Figure 15.1 shows that the UK had deficits with North America and Continental Europe, which were partly financed by India and other tropical countries not shown on the diagram. These ran a deficit with Britain, but a surplus with the USA. It is ironic to note that Japan, as an industrialising country, also ran a deficit with Britain, but this and other countries' deficits were small compared with India's. The ability of India to export raw materials to industrialised countries and to act as a customer for British goods became extremely important to Britain after 1870. In total merchandise trade Britain, as stated earlier, ran a substantial deficit, countered by a surplus on invisibles.

The multilateral payments system was also connected with the pattern of overseas lending, which is discussed in Chapter 16.

Developing countries such as Australia were liable to run current-account deficits which they financed by importing capital from countries with current-account surpluses, notably Britain. To some extent, Britain's surplus actually depended on the export of capital, since the money which was lent was often used to purchase British capital goods (and therefore in reality never left the country, but merely existed as book entries in the ledgers of British banks and industrial companies). The linkage between the export of capital and the export of goods should not be overstressed, though. There were not necessarily any ties between the banks or stockbrokers which organised foreign loans and British industry. British dominance of railway building and management in India did lead to heavy purchases of capital equipment from Britain, while in Argentina and other Latin American countries, railways were often built by British engineers who specified British equipment. In Australia and Canada, however, American engineering equipment was becoming increasingly popular. And while British investors subscribed over 40 per cent of railway loans to China between 1898 and 1912, only 13 per cent of this came back as orders for British equipment.

The proportion of national income accounted for by exports of goods and services rose from around 15 per cent in the early nineteenth century to almost 30 per cent by the 1870s, and then remained fairly stable. This apparently supports the view that exports fuelled Britain's prosperity. A moment's reflection will modify this opinion. As in the eighteenth century, trade was beneficial to national income because of the exploitation of comparative advantage. For example, putting resources into building locomotives which were exported, rather than growing food, enabled this country to acquire a larger volume of food from elsewhere than it would have been able to grow itself. Exports, however, were not essential to growth in industrial output, although they contributed to it. They would only have been essential if all innovations and new investment had sprung from demand growth caused by exports. It is clear, however, that innovations were forthcoming even in industries where exports were small, such as the consumer-goods industries or agriculture, while population increase in Britain provided a continuing source of demand growth.

This puts into perspective the effects of free trade, the pros and cons of which dominated public debate about economics at several periods between 1830 and 1914. The sun of free trade glimmered in the 1820s, rose above the horizon with the repeal of the Corn Laws in 1846 and the Navigation Acts in 1849 and, after the steady dismantling of tariffs in the 1850s, reached its zenith with the Cobden–Chevalier treaty between Britain and France in 1860. Tariffs remained on goods like sugar and tobacco, but they were revenue raising and not protective, since there were no indigenous industries to protect. Free trade was the source of bitter political conflict in the 1840s when the Conservative Party split over the repeal of the Corn Laws; and free trade in the 1900s was still a strong enough slogan to win the Liberals many votes when it seemed under threat. Given that Britain's imports and exports had increased rapidly when protection was at its height before 1840, however, and given that foreign countries' progress towards free trade in the 1850s and 1860s was relatively limited compared with Britain's, the impact of free trade on trade growth was less than its protagonists believed. Free traders argued that enhanced British purchases of agricultural produce from abroad enabled foreigners to purchase more British industrial goods. This no doubt occurred but, as the discussion of the multilateral payments system shows, it was not inevitable that the industrial goods would come from Britain. Free trade did, of course, have other economic effects. It affected the distribution of income within Britain by keeping down agricultural product prices and, therefore, shifting incomes away from landlords and farmers to everyone else, just as protection had done the opposite.

Later in the century, the revival of higher levels of protection in many foreign countries had deleterious effects on various industries, particularly iron and steel. However, as with agriculture, the loss of markets experienced by this and other manufacturing industries had a number of causes, including the growing competitiveness of foreign manufacturers and, possibly, the slowness of technical change in British industry. The loss of foreign markets by industry caused free trade to become once more the subject of political strife in the 1900s, although a brief and rather feeble revival of protectionist sentiment had occurred in the 1880s. The belief of contemporaries that free trade and protection were important should not blind us, however, to the fact that the growth of British foreign trade in the nineteenth century depended on many other factors apart from the level of tariffs at home and abroad, while foreign trade itself was only one of several factors which contributed to economic growth.

Attempts to revive protection were one response to the competitive pressures on British industry. Imperial expansion has often been seen as a similar, but European-wide, response to economic pressures, which made the opening up of Africa and other colonial areas essential to give further opportunities for investment and trade.

This was the view of V I Lenin, but in different forms it was put forward by other contemporaries with less extreme political viewpoints. This book is not the place to discuss the real motives behind imperialism, but it should say something about its effects. As Table 15.2 shows, the actual quantities of trade and the investment opportunities generated by countries which were politically controlled by Britain were relatively small, with the exception of India. India was obviously different in magnitude, while its significance in the multilateral payments system has already been noted. The point that was made earlier still applies, however. Just as exports were only one contributor to Britain's growing prosperity, so trade with India was only one contributor to the growth of exports. So far as investment is concerned, it is worth noting that Britain's domestic investment ratio was well below those of America and Germany, suggesting that even if India and other colonies had not been available as destinations for the export of capital, there were potential opportunities at home. Furthermore, a recent study by L Davis and R Huttenback suggests that there were only small differences between rates of return on Empire securities and on other securities, so there were no excessive profits to be made; while defence of the Empire was a net cost to the British taxpayer. In economic language, one can say that there was no exploitation in a neo-classical sense. There is a lot of truth in the remark that Britain was not rich because she had an Empire, but had an Empire because she was rich.

Table 15.2 British exports to and investment in colonial areas

| | % share in 1913 of total | |
	Exports	Foreign investment
Africa	7	12
(excluding N Africa)		
India	13	9
West Indies	1	negligible

(*Source:* Exports – Mitchell and Deane; investment – Crouzet)

While exports were not by any means the only source of Britain's growing wealth, they were important enough to mean that the slowdown in their growth in the later nineteenth century was a proximate factor behind the decelerating growth rate of the economy as a whole. This has implications for an assessment of the causes of the deceleration. The export slowdown might have been caused by a loss of competitiveness *vis-à-vis* other countries due to domestic reasons, or it might have been caused by factors external to Britain. Possible domestic causes are dealt with in Chapter 17, while external causes are discussed below.

There were certain external factors which made it likely that the very high export growth rate in the second and third quarters of the nineteenth century would not be sustained. The increase in tariffs in most industrialising countries, evident from the 1870s, was one such factor. More fundamental was the fact that, up to around 1880, Britain had retained a commanding advantage in both the older textile industries and the newer iron and machinery industries, at a time when the demand for these products in industrialising countries was growing rapidly. From then on, several countries began to catch up in both those sectors and could, therefore, meet more of their needs from domestic production. Britain was therefore forced to direct exports to less developed countries such as India, whose income levels and capacity for absorption were lower than those of the USA and Continental Europe. A subsidiary factor, not external to Britain but effectively beyond her control, was the fact that productivity growth in cotton textiles became much slower since the major innovations had now been adopted. Hence prices ceased to fall, and sales to rise, so rapidly. Britain's ability to switch to new products was initially limited because until the 1880s important new products, notably electrical equipment, were simply not ready for large-scale production.

While these factors all must have had an effect on global trade growth rates, which did indeed slow down, they would not necessarily have cut Britain's market share of manufactured exports, as was the case from 1870 on. Furthermore, the hiatus in the development of new products for export was not necessarily beyond the control of British businessmen. It was one of their tasks to adapt to changing conditions, and failure to do so is an adverse reflection on their business ability. While lower export demand certainly contributed to the slowdown in British export growth and, hence, in the growth rate of the British economy, the foregoing discussion suggests that there were also domestic factors reducing the competitiveness of British industry.

CHAPTER SIXTEEN
Banking and finance

To Marx, writing in the 1840s, the manufacturer was the apostle of capitalism. To Lenin, writing in the 1900s, 'finance capitalism' had taken over this role, and the top-hatted banker became an established element in the demonology of socialism. Banking did not, in reality, have the primacy which Lenin attributed to it. However, it is true that there was a growth in banking activity throughout the century: bankers became involved in the sale of securities to finance investment outside Europe; the structure of banking changed; and the money market – that is, the provision of short-term trade finance and inter-bank dealings – grew rapidly from its small beginnings with the bill-brokers in the early nineteenth century.

The changes in the structure of banking were associated with various pieces of legislation which were designed to meet real or fancied problems. The inflation during the Napoleonic Wars had been caused, it was thought, by the excess issue of banknotes. Hence one concern of legislation, when gold backing for the currency was restored in 1821, was to limit the issue of notes. Another worry was over the instability of the banking system, an instability exacerbated by the small size of many English banks. Legislation was therefore designed to remove impediments to larger-scale banking, on the model of the successful Scottish system. Thus in 1826 an Act allowed the setting up of joint-stock banks outside a 65-mile radius of London; the restriction was designed to protect something of the Bank of England's monopoly of joint-stock banking, but it was rescinded by a second Act in 1833. This Act also forbade banks set up under its provisions to issue notes. Finally, in 1844, came the Bank Charter Act, so-called because it amended the Charter of the Bank of England. The Bank's note issue was strictly limited, while no other banks were allowed to issue notes over and above their existing totals. Any bank which ceased to issue notes or amalgamated then lost the privilege permanently. It is a striking fact that outside Scotland, where the existing system continued, the currency needs of Victorian Britain were met by a limited quantity of Bank of England notes of not less than £5 denomination, by a dwindling quantity of private bank notes, and by coinage.

In practice, the legislation both did and did not meet its objectives. Joint-stock banks, after a shaky start, grew in size and helped to bring stability to the banking system. By 1914, amalgamation between banks and the absorption of many small country and private banks resulted in a much more concentrated banking system: the Midland, Lloyds and Barclays all had over 500 branches; there were, however, twenty other banks in England with more than 100 branches, so the banking system was still some distance from today's oligopoly. On the other hand, the attempt to limit the note issue and hence, it was thought, prevent destabilising expansion of the money supply was nugatory because there was no limit on bank deposits. These grew rapidly from the mid-century, a growth associated with the increase in the use of cheques, and the consequent decline of bills.

The main function of the clearing banks, as those within the system came to be called, remained the raising of short-term deposits and the provision of short-term finance for trade, industry and agriculture, rather than long-term investments in industry. In practice, it is difficult to separate out short- and long-term finance, since firms might have loans outstanding from banks for many years. Nevertheless, it can be said that it was not the prime aim of banks to provide finance for industrial investment. It has been suggested that the growth of larger joint-stock banks at the end of the century reduced the willingness of banks to adjust lending to their customers' requirements, since local links were broken. In fact, banks like the rapidly-growing Midland seem to have been better able to tailor lending to demand, since they could call on a much wider supply of funds. They were also better equipped to service the large corporate customers that were now emerging. The clearing banks still did not take long-term stakes in industrial firms, but they had reasonably close relationships with industrialists. Apart from this, the main effect of changes in banking was probably to improve services, through the multiplication of branches and the development of cheque facilities, and through the growing habit of paying interest on deposits. All these had developed much earlier in Scotland, whose banking system may well have influenced developments in England.

The other major development in domestic banking was the changing role of the Bank of England. Although it was still a private company, the directors came to accept that its duty was to maintain the stability of the financial system, rather than to maximise profits for its own shareholders. The Bank came to act consistently as a central bank for the system, a function it had performed intermittently from the eighteenth century. At times of crisis, it would act as a 'lender of last resort'. Banks which faced heavy calls on their resources could rediscount bills at the Bank of England in return for credit, and thus meet their liabilities. The Bank's new position was aided by the Bank Charter Act, which paradoxically had aimed to reduce the Bank's ability to create credit: the Act was taken as final, and so the Bank was left to evolve its techniques free from further legislative interference. In 1866, the Bank acted for the first time openly as a lender of last resort in the Overend, Gurney crisis, involving the failure of a large discount house. Although the crisis was serious, public knowledge of the Bank's activities helped to prevent a major financial panic. The severity of such crises was also reduced by the use of Bank Rate, which developed as a means of maintaining the Bank's gold reserve. Raising Bank Rate, the rate at which the Bank rediscounted bills, raised the general level of interest rates in the country and attracted an import of gold. Usually, however, Bank Rate was above the market rate of interest, so the Bank first had to push up the market rate in order to force other banks to borrow from it at Bank Rate. This it did by selling government securities on the open market, a technique known as 'open-market operations', which was in regular use from the 1870s. The Bank's primary motive was to protect its own reserves and therefore maintain sterling's international financial credibility, as the ability to meet liabilities with payment in gold was of course necessary for the maintenance of the Gold Standard. In practice, the policy also reduced the incidence of severe financial crises within Britain by attacking their causes, which had been the over-extension of credit by banks combined with a drain of gold from London – the result could be a sudden shortage of liquidity and a crisis. Active use of Bank Rate usually prevented such situations from becoming serious. The failure of the City of Glasgow Bank in 1878, discussed in Chapter 10, was an exception because fraud was involved within the bank, so external measures could not save it, and because the bank itself was so large. The Companies Act of 1879, a direct result of the Glasgow crash, tightened up requirements for the proper auditing of banks.

London's pre-eminence in world financial markets, of which the Bank was so aware, revolved around merchant banks, known in the nineteenth century as accepting houses. Many of these were foreign in origin, such as Rothschilds and Barings, but they were drawn to London as the pre-eminent centre of world trade and hence of trade finance. Accepting houses 'accepted' bills from overseas – that is, took on the liability to pay – for a commission. Other specialist banks then discounted the bills. The process indicates the benefits of specialisation. The banks built up a fund of knowledge of creditworthiness and could therefore judge how much to charge for accepting bills, while traders could sell their goods knowing that they would receive prompt payment. Lombard Street, the collective name for the institutions of the money market, became the centre for the provision of financial services, not just for trade to and from Britain, but also in trades involving two overseas countries where there was no other financial institution available. Foreign confidence in sterling's soundness was of course one reason for this. As they had intimate connections with and knowledge of foreign affairs, the banks involved became drawn into the business of issuing foreign securities on the London market, whether for governments or for railways and other commercial enterprises. Like the clearing banks, however, they did not concern themselves with the provision of long-term finance for British industry. Here there was something of a gap in the London financial market, in contrast to certain Continental countries where investment banks were important suppliers of long term capital to industry.

The sale of securities to provide finance for transport and other capital-hungry projects was one of the main growth areas of the nineteenth century. Joint-stock companies with limited liability had been the standard form of organisation for canals, and railways followed this pattern, which was suitable for projects where large sums of money had to be raised from investors with no personal interest in the business. Railways were typically financed by a mixture of fixed-interest stock for those requiring security, and equity stock for those willing to bear more risk. Other organisations, such as docks and gas undertakings, were financed in the same way. When railways came to be built abroad, the capital often came from Britain, as a country with a developed capital market which could absorb large issues. As the century wore on, the capital market widened still further. Joint-stock banks drew on it, then in 1856 the restrictions on limited liability which had hitherto applied unless companies were incorporated by Parliament (as were railway and canal companies) were lifted. While this led to further expansion of the joint-stock banks, it was some time before manufacturing companies took advantage of it. By the end of the century, however, many companies in industries like brewing, shipbuilding and engineering had issued stock, although even by 1913 only 8 per cent of the value of the securities quoted on the London Stock Exchange was in industry. Meanwhile, overseas investment had widened to include mines, tramway companies, rubber plantations and much besides, while there was also a substantial issue of foreign government loans in Britain. All the securities referred to were tradable on the London, or one of the provincial, stock exchanges.

Putting money into the stock exchange was the prerogative of the wealthier investor, but during the century other financial institutions developed to provide savings opportunities for the working and lower middle classes. Among these were the Post Office and Trustee Savings Banks, and building societies. Savings in all these were low, however, in relation to the total volume. Far more members of the working class subscribed to friendly societies and industrial insurance companies, whose premiums constituted a form of saving. The former were voluntary associations in origin, although some of them, such as the quaintly named Manchester Unity of Odd Fellows, grew quite large. The latter, of which the Prudential was the best known, were commercial companies. Both provided various types of benefit, such as sick and funeral benefit, in return for a regular subscription. They were inefficient as a form of saving, because the expense of collection and the risk of subscriptions lapsing were both so high, but nevertheless subscribing to them may have been a rational response, given the financial position of many working-class families. These were likely to find high levels of saving unrewarding or difficult. Investment in human capital, by financing apprenticeship training, offered a much better rate of return, albeit one which benefited the children rather than the parents. More important was the fact that for many of the working classes, even at the end of the century, incomes were so low that the chances of worthwhile saving were small. In these circumstances, providing against the most likely crises, which were sickness or the death of a member of the family, may have made more sense than providing against old age, which many of the working classes would not live to see. Conversely, a middle-class man would expect to reach old age, and it was individuals from this social group, saving for retirement, who provided much of the savings of Victorian Britain.

Whether these savings were directed in a way which was most

beneficial, either for the country or for individual savers, is an important question. The attention of both contemporaries and historians has been caught by the large sums of money which flowed abroad, possibly totalling as much as £4000 million by 1914. (The figure has been questioned, but no agreement has been reached on an alternative and at the moment it is the best estimate we have.) This was equal to twice the annual national income. Between the mid-nineteenth century and the First World War, around a third of the investment financed by British citizens was overseas.

The largest part of overseas investment was 'portfolio' investment – the purchase of stock in foreign companies; a very small part was direct investment by British firms in subsidiaries overseas; and a significant part, which is classed as direct, was the purchase of stock in firms which were owned and controlled in Britain but operated entirely overseas. This was common in mining, a famous example being the Rio Tinto iron ore mines in Spain. Both this and portfolio investment were what the nineteenth century called blind investment, as the investor had no direct interest in the company concerned, but merely wished to maximise his income. By far the largest part of overseas investment, some 70 per cent between 1865 and 1914, went into infrastructure – that is, railways, docks, tramways and the like – and another 12 per cent went into agriculture and mining. Much early investment went to European governments and railways, but from 1865 two-thirds or more went to the regions of recent settlement – temperate climate countries such as the USA, Canada, Australia and Argentina. The volume of overseas investment fluctuated, of course, both in total and between countries, depending upon the demand for investment in Britain and abroad.

This volume of overseas investment was one reason why Lenin paid so much attention to finance capitalism. Lenin's view was that a lack of investment opportunities in the industrialised nations led capitalists to exploit the rest of the world. More recently, historians have been struck rather by the differences between Britain and other industrial countries. The ratio of domestic investment to national income was far lower in Britain than in Germany and the USA, while the ratio of foreign investment was far greater. This suggests that there was no shortage of investment opportunities in most industrial-ised countries, but that there was something odd about Britain.

One line of argument is that financial institutions in Britain biased British investors away from domestic investment. The banks which handled many of the issues of overseas stock, such as Rothschilds or Barings, were banks of very high reputation, so that issues to which they put their name were sought after. If bias existed, then it would make a low rate of return on foreign securities acceptable. In other words, if the return on foreign securities had been lower than the return on British securities, we would infer that there was a stronger demand for foreign than for British securities; and that this demand was not generated by the underlying merit of the securities in question, but by the favourable publicity attached to them. It seems, however, that British securities over the period from 1870 to 1913 offered a lower rate of return than foreign securities, while the risk level of was similar. These facts suggest that British investors actually had a preference for British securities, since they needed an extra yield incentive to make them purchase foreign securities. The question of why British domestic investment was so low will be taken up again in the next chapter.

The changes in banking in the nineteenth century made it a more central part of economic activity. However, it did not, at least in Britain, have a predominant role. Banks and industry largely kept each other at arm's length, and where there were amalgamations in industry, banks in Britain did not, as they did in some countries, play any special part. Banking's growing importance can be attributed to certain long-term factors. These included the benefits of specialisation, which led to people entrusting their finances to banks rather than looking after them personally. Thus banks took over activities, such as the making of loans, from the non-specialised intermediaries such as solicitors who had provided such services in the past. Another reason for banking growth was Britain's pre-eminence in world trade, which led to the centrality of 'Lombard Street' in trade finance. Finally, there was the increase in world-wide capital formation, which necessitated much more complex arrangements than in the past for the control and distribution of capital.

CHAPTER SEVENTEEN
The end of economic supremacy

Between the mid-eighteenth and the early nineteenth centuries, the British economy became the world's largest. Its pre-eminence remained unchallenged until the 1870s. From then on, Britain's economic standing declined relative to other industrial countries, particularly the USA and Germany. This decline has puzzled economists and historians ever since.

The decline is demonstrated in various ways in Table 17.1. National income grew more slowly, as did real income per person – which also provides a rough measure of labour productivity. The proportion of national income which was invested remained much the same as before, but since the 1850s more had gone abroad and less to home investment. Furthermore, labour productivity growth and domestic investment became increasingly out of line with Britain's main rivals.

When, in the 1880s, contemporaries first became aware of economic problems, they attributed them to what was known at the time as the 'Great Depresssion'. This was not just a British, but a world-wide, phenomenon. It was marked by price falls, particularly of food and other raw materials, and, it was thought, by a declining rate of profit. The probable reason for the price fall was the increased supply of, and increased efficiency in, the production and distribution of food and raw materials. The decreased rate of gold production may also have been a factor. In spite of the use of the term depression, world output continued to grow at the same rate as before over the whole period, which is usually taken to be 1873–1896. This indicates that the British growth slowdown cannot be attributed to the Great Depression as a world phenomenon. ('Depression' is a potentially misleading term. There was no long-term depression in output.) Furthermore, when in the 1890s prices began to rise again, Britain's growth rate remained sluggish and her economic performance relative to other countries' remained poor. The problems which contemporaries focused on in the 1880s were not the fundamental ones, but rather those of structural change in sections of the economy. There were pressures on branches of the iron industry in particular. Pig-iron producers in some older areas such as the Black Country were being squeezed by competition in areas with cheaper raw materials, such as Teesside, while the wrought iron industry was coming under increasing competition from steel. Falling prices added to the difficulties of producers with high fixed costs, but the essential difficulty in certain branches of industry was that falling prices were accompanied by falling or static sales.

Table 17.1 Growth in national income and productivity 1830–1913 (Great Britain and Northern Ireland)

	National income (1)	Real income per person employed (2)	TFP (3)	Domestic investment ratio (%)(4)
1831–1850				12
1831–1860	2.5	1.1	1.0	
1856–1873	2.4	1.2	0.9	9
1873–1913	2.0	0.9	0.5	9.1

Columns 1–3: Annual average percentage growth.
Column 3: Measured in man-years, and includes in TFP possible changes in labour quality; includes Southern Ireland (omission would not make significant difference).
Column 4: Fixed capital investment only (not stock building) from 1856–1913. Inclusion of stocks would make little difference.
Total investment ratio (including foreign investment) from 1830 onwards was 13%.
(*Sources:* Feinstein in Floud and McCloskey, Vol I [1831–50]; Crafts [1831–60]; Matthews *et al.* [1856–1913])

While the effect of the price fall, and of changing technology and factor endowments, drew loud complaints from sectors of British industry and agriculture in the 1880s, the real problems were much more fundamental. By the 1890s, there was some grasp of this, and attention shifted to the threat posed by German and American competition. The 1900s, however, which historians now see as one of the worst periods for underlying competitive decline, saw a more complacent attitude emerge. Exports were buoyed up by a rise in overseas investment and strong demand from India, and the consequent prosperity of the staple industries allayed the earlier fears. This was no doubt one reason why Chamberlain's campaign for protection was unsuccessful. Here, however, our concern is with underlying trends, rather than short-term fluctuations.

There were three underlying forces which may have adversely affected Britain's rate of economic growth, relative both to its own previous growth rate and to that of other countries. One was a fall in the rate of growth of total factor productivity (TFP). To understand what is meant by TFP, it is helpful to first consider labour productivity, a familiar concept: it is an indicator of the output per unit of labour input. TFP, in theory, is an indicator of the output produced by a composite unit of input, consisting of labour, capital and land, aggregated in the proportions each contributes to output value. And just as labour productivity rises when the output produced rises faster than does the labour input, so TFP rises when output rises faster than the increase in the composite total of all inputs. The output in question can range from that of a single factory to that of the entire economy. Our concern here is with the latter. In effect, TFP captures changes in output which do not originate from changing factor inputs, but from technical progress, managerial improvements, and other more or less intangible factors. It is sometimes called 'the residual', because changes in it are measured by taking the input of land, capital and labour at different points of time, and subtracting it from output; TFP is what is left over.

Economic historians discovered TFP measurement, hitherto a rather esoteric branch of the economist's art, about twenty years ago and became very excited about it. The findings seemed particularly relevant to the debate about British economic performance because, according to some estimates of TFP, the British economy performed quite well between the 1870s and 1914. In other words, TFP rose at the same sort of rate as in other countries. More recently, TFP has rather lost favour as an indicator of economic performance. There are considerable practical difficulties in measuring it accurately: for example, the human capital represented by the educational level of the labour force, which strictly speaking is an 'input' just like physical capital, is very hard to measure and is often counted as part of the residual. An even more cogent criticism, however, is that measuring the increase in the residual only gives a very partial picture of a country's overall economic performance. It is the growth in labour productivity that is in the long run the main determinant of per capita income; this growth depends on inputs of capital and land, as well as increases in the residual. In only a few economies in the nineteenth century was there much enlargement of the land area, and Britain was not one of them. Capital was increasing everywhere, however, and so to understand the growth of labour productivity in individual economies, we must look at capital inputs as well as at TFP growth. The investment ratio, and its determinants, therefore constitute the second set of factors which may have adversely affected Britain's growth rate.

In any period, investment and productivity are partly under the control of businessmen. However, to some extent businesses are influenced by factors external to individual producers, and these factors constitute the third possible force behind Britain's relative decline. External factors will be discussed now before returning to TFP growth and investment.

First, there was a slight decrease in the rate of population growth (Ch. 12). This could lead to a decline in overall growth, as total demand growth would slow up, and also to a slight decline in the investment ratio as less capital was needed for housing and infrastructure. On the other hand, it is unlikely to have had any significant effect on labour productivity growth or on TFP growth. Second, there were exogenous factors which reduced the rate of growth of exports (Ch. 15), which would in turn have reduced the overall growth rate. It might also have adversely affected the rate of growth of TFP, since most industries will experience economies of scale, and lower growth rates would prevent them realising the full benefit of these economies. The same comment would apply to industries which were affected by import competition, notably steel. Here, however, the fact that steel-using industries benefited from cheap imported steel was a counter to the adverse effects. These external factors may well account for much if not all of the relatively small difference (none at all on some measurements) between TFP growth in Britain and that in other countries in the late nineteenth century. Similarly, external factors help to account for the decline in the TFP growth rate between the 1856–73 and 1873–1913 periods. It seems likely, therefore, that internal influences on the rate of TFP growth were not a serious problem in Britain's relative economic decline. But what still needs to be explained is a large gap between Britain and other countries in the investment ratio. From the mid-century on, the domestic investment ratio in Germany and the USA was around 20 per cent, compared with 9 per cent in Britain. In the long run, this had a serious effect on labour productivity. What can explain this reluctance to invest in Britain?

While there was no strong bias in the flow of funds as between home and foreign investment, the evidence from rates of return indicates that there was a strong reluctance to invest in manufacturing industry. The net profit rate (i.e. profits after depreciation) on all business averaged around 15 per cent in the 1900s, a figure somewhat lower than in previous years. At the same time, the rate of return on government stock was about 3 per cent. First-class railway bonds usually paid 1 or 2 per cent more. There is a huge gap between these bond yields and the net profit rate. Surely anyone with an ounce of enterprise would want to build a factory?

The problem of deciding why people were reluctant to invest is not so simple, however. The nearest the average investor was likely to come to a factory was the purchase of equity shares. Only a few people were in a position to build factories with their own money. And the rate of return on equities was different from, and usually lower than, the rate of return on the underlying assets, which is the figure quoted above. This is because equity dividends did not always reflect underlying profits and also because the capital value of equities could fluctuate in ways unrelated to the underlying profitability of the business. There now seems more reason for the low investment in manufacturing. Why invest in risky equities, when you could buy a safe government or railway bond? Or, in other words, investor behaviour was rational, given the available information. The equity market was unattractive to investors because it was a small market, which was notoriously vulnerable to the activities of speculators. Taking advantage of a wave of fashion for a particular industry, such as electricals in the early 1880s, promoters would launch companies at inflated prices, taking large profits for themselves. It was not surprising, therefore, that dividends were low in relation to the issued capital, since this was above the value of the underlying assets; or that the subsequent capital value of the equities concerned was adversely affected.

In some countries, notably Germany, banks provided a large slice of the investment capital for industry. Although this was not so marked in Britain, banks still played an important role in financing circulating capital – items like stocks and debtors. Much more important than the lower level of bank financing for manufacturing was the relatively small size of firms in Britain, and the dividend policies which firms followed. Large firms had important advantages in making new investments. As their total internal cash flow was far greater, they could better afford to move into new markets which initially needed heavier capital requirements. Small firms, even if they reinvested a high proportion of their cash flow, would not be able to mobilise such large absolute quantities of capital. Large firms could also afford specialist research facilities, increasingly important in fields such as chemicals and electrical engineering. The small size of British firms has been seen as an institutional constraint which was beyond the control of British businessmen. Even when firms did amalgamate, however, they often failed to pursue aggressive policies of rationalising production on the most cost-effective plants (Ch. 12). The railways, which were giant organisations, failed to control costs adequately (Ch. 13). In addition, smaller firms could have done more to help themselves. By the late nineteenth century, they were no longer atomistic entities at the mercy of competition. Even if they did not enter formal amalgamations, they were, increasingly, forming collusive agreements with other producers over prices and production levels. It was but a small step from these arrangements to amalgamation, had firms wished to go that way.

Furthermore, most British firms, large or small, seem to have followed a policy of distributing the bulk of their profits to their partners or shareholders, rather than retaining them for reinvestment in the business. This can be inferred from the fact that, comparing the late nineteenth with the mid-twentieth century, corporate investment as a proportion of national income rose, even though the profit rate declined. The failure of existing firms to invest puts the drawbacks of the equity market into perspective. A better organised equity market would have been helpful, but it was not essential. The low propensity to invest in Britain was critically affected by the attitudes of the owners and top managers of existing businesses, which did not depend on the equity market for capital. It was they who resisted effective amalgamations and who followed a low investment policy.

Both investment and the rate of TFP growth may also have been affected by another factor, the lack of highly-trained managerial and technical staff. British technical education has been heavily criticised, both at the time and by historians, but these criticisms need to be put into perspective. Low-level technical education, complementing the existing system of apprenticeship, was probably as good as anywhere abroad. Higher-level education mainly took the form of premium apprenticeships, high-grade apprenticeships in which the pupil experienced all sides of the business; university departments of engineering, metallurgy and chemistry were developing, but slowly. In Germany and the USA, far more formal technical and managerial education took place, but there were criticisms of their own methods in these countries, where the British method of on-the-job training was thought to have some advantages. And undoubtedly practice, or 'learning by doing', is vital to efficient production. Many of the more exaggerated prejudices against British technical education, which have been uncritically repeated by some historians, should therefore be discounted. Nevertheless, the lack of formally trained technical and scientific staff in industry does seem one likely reason for the failure to successfully seize new opportunities for investment in high-technology areas such as electrical equipment and organic chemicals. And while some older industries such as cotton seem to have remained competitive, a lack of managerial as well as technical competence may have held back efficiency in others such as inorganic chemicals and railways.

The problem about on-the-job training is that, whatever its merits, it is not conducive to knowledge of new technology or products, since the nature of the training is to expose the pupil to existing practices. Of course, professional associations and journals did help to provide new knowledge, but a largely practical education would not equip businessmen to grasp what were increasingly complex scientific problems. The lack of formal management training, and adequate training in allied fields such as cost accounting, was also a weakness, evidenced in the poor management structure of large amalgamated firms. A further point, although it is not one where formal education would necessarily have helped, is that British managers were not used to mass-production techniques. Here the drawback was a lack of practical experience in a particular technique, which was becoming increasingly important with the growth of light engineering.

Many other explanations have been put forward to account for poor economic performance from the 1870s on. It has been said that there was entrepreneurial failure, presumably meaning a declining willingness to take risks. On the face of it, the unwillingness to invest in new products indicates that there was failure, but in actual fact there were probably as many who were willing to have a go at business as there had been in the past. There was no shortage of firms in a new industry like car manufacturing – the problem was efficient production; while food processing and retail trade were two areas where entrepreneurship was both prevalent and successful. It may be that there were fewer risk takers than in the USA or Germany. American and German investment, though, was increasingly carried out by large firms which could spread risk. So the problem, again, may have been the structure of industry and management, rather than attitudes to risk taking. Studies of consumer-product producers and various export-orientated firms indicate that many were willing to adopt aggressive sales techniques, and so suggestions of marketing failure are unproven (Ch. 12). A contemporary criticism, echoed by some historians, was that trade-union restrictive practices held back progress. Again, there seems little evidence for this. Only a minority of workers were in unions, although the proportion was growing. Even strong unions were unable to enforce practices which employers found seriously inconvenient. The Amalgamated Society of Engineers was forced in the 1900s to accept piece-rate methods of payment, something which it had long opposed. This union had also been the focus of complaints against its excessive manning requirements on new machinery, but individual piece rates were antithetical to excessive manning, since with piece rates, each worker's concern was to maximise individual output. Many other unions, for instance in cotton and shipbuilding, had always accepted piece rates.

An excessive interest in the problems of British industry can divert attention from the more positive aspects of the late Victorian and Edwardian economy. The positive effects of investment abroad are worth examining first. This was almost certainly implicated in the stabilisation in the terms of trade which occurred in the 1850s. The terms of trade are simply an index of the average price of exports divided by an index of the average price of imports. The result is usually multiplied by 100 for convenience of expression. A rise in the terms of trade implies that a given volume of exports will purchase more imports, and vice versa. For most of the nineteenth century, therefore, the terms of trade effectively portrayed the relationship between the price of Britain's manufactures, which formed the bulk of her exports, and the price of her raw materials and foodstuffs, which were increasingly imported. Up to the mid-century, there had been an almost continuous fall in the terms of trade, because productivity in the cotton industry increased rapidly, with a consequent fall in the price of cotton textiles. This helps to explain why rapid productivity growth in the manufacturing sector at this time did not give rise to as rapid an increase in the standard of living. Foodstuffs failed to fall in price at the same rate as manufactures. The subsequent stabilisation in the terms of trade, whose long-term trend then became gently upwards, can most plausibly be explained as the result of an acceleration in productivity growth in raw material and food production. This occurred because land, capital, technology and labour came together – land in the Americas and Australasia, capital from Britain and other industrial countries, technology in the form of railways and steel ships, and labour in the form of European emigrants. The result was that all the fruits of productivity growth in manufacturing fed through to those engaged in it, rather than being partially siphoned off to agriculturalists at home and abroad.

Changes in the terms of trade were not solely attributable to British capital and labour, since the producer countries themselves had their own resources, and could also draw on other industrial countries. Nevertheless, the British contribution was substantial, and so the private return on capital invested abroad does not fully capture its value to Britain. Part of the benefit from lower food prices should be added in. If we cast the net still wider and count as 'British' anyone who emigrated from Britain, then the benefits from overseas investment become greater still, since emigrants enjoyed higher wages than they would have received in Britain. From the narrow view of national income accounting, these high wages counted as part of the national income of the host countries. From another point of view, they accrued to erstwhile British citizens.

Whether or not British citizens ultimately gained or lost from the pattern of British investment is not, therefore, a simple question to answer. It seems likely that, on balance, they lost, since much of the benefit of the overseas investment went not to Britain or even British emigrants, but to other European emigrants. Concluding that British citizens lost, however, assumes that productive use could have been made of the investment in Britain. Since this would have depended on better technical and managerial education, it is too simplistic to think that domestic investment could have been usefully increased without other changes having been made.

Another question which might alter the view taken of Britain's economic performance is related to the measurement of service-industry output. The estimates of output and efficiency growth on which most of the discussion has been based are most uncertain when it comes to service industries, because their output is very hard to measure. The quality improvement which undoubtedly took place in services such as transport and banking has not been incorporated in the available figures, and to that extent they understate output growth, particularly in the late Victorian and Edwardian period.

Taking a very long-term view, the lag in growth from the 1870s is only surprising when it is set in an international context. The changes compared with the previous forty years, especially when exogenous factors are taken account of, were actually very slight. The domestic investment ratio fell after 1850, the proximate cause being the decline in railway construction. The ratio rose again slightly after 1873, however, which suggests that, since profit rates between 1856 and

1873 were higher, there was just as much a 'failure to invest' then as later. Compared with the Industrial Revolution period from 1750 to 1830, growth in significant indicators such as output per person was higher after 1870, which should make us wary of easy comparisons between the dynamism of the early period and the lethargy of the later. Perhaps it was the entrepreneurs of the Industrial Revolution who were slothful. Only in the Edwardian period does TFP growth appear to slow down markedly. This is a relatively short period, though, and it may be that the published figures are misleading, for reasons noted above.

Even in an international context, there were some strong elements in British economic performance during the period. Dominance in the field of international financial services continued, although the USA provided a growing challenge. The shipping industry was very successful. The manufacturing sector, however, failed to move quickly enough into the production of more sophisticated goods, while some existing industries' performance may have been less than optimum. The failure to invest enough, and to exploit new technologies, can be linked in particular to the existing organisation of industry and the unwillingness to change it, and to the lack of adequate technical and managerial training.

PART THREE

Industrialisation and Society 1750–1914

CHAPTER EIGHTEEN
Incomes and consumption

INCOMES

Between 1750 and 1914, Britain was transformed from an agricultural to an industrial country. The landscape was changed, large sums of capital were poured into mines, mills and railways, the bulk of the population became urban instead of rural. Whether or not most people became better-off during this great transformation is another question.

As with most subjects in the period demanding quantitative measurement, the available figures are infuriatingly uncertain. Wage figures were not collected systematically by the government at any time, although there were wage censuses in the 1880s and 1900s. Trade-union wage rates provide reasonable coverage for much of the later nineteenth century, but as one goes back in time the available wage figures become sparser and sparser. Wage rates do not always reflect earnings, which may well have been affected by underemployment or unemployment. Furthermore, family earnings, comprising women's and children's wages as well as men's, are even harder to assess.

Money wages by themselves are of no use unless the prices of goods are known too. Dividing money wages by prices gives real wages, that is the real purchasing power of wages. Carrying out this procedure involves the reconstruction of a price index for much of the period, since official indices only started in 1892, and even these were not complete. Reconstructing prices is even more difficult than reconstructing wages because the index must reflect accurately the amount of each product purchased by the average consumer as well as its price. Of course, there is no such person as an average consumer, although one can get closer by sticking to sub-groups, such as agricultural labourers. Even so, gaining reliable price information from the eighteenth and earlier nineteenth centuries is extremely difficult. Prices of goods purchased by large institutions, such as hospitals, are sometimes available but are not necessarily representative of what the average consumer paid.

Another way is to take national income and estimate the proportion going to investment and government expenditure: the residue is available for consumption. This can then be divided among groups in society, wage-earners, upper income-earners, and so on, to arrive at per capita figures for each group. Given the problems posed by wage figures, it may be best to start this way, one which highlights the extreme inequalities of income in this period.

In Jane Austen's novel *Pride and Prejudice*, written in the 1790s, Mr Darcy, a wealthy landowner, had an income of £10,000 per annum. This was 400 times as much as a farm labourer in the South of England, whose average earnings would be around £25 per annum. A London carpenter, a member of a skilled trade in the city with the highest wage levels, earned around £60 per annum at the same time, if he worked full-time, while middle-class incomes started at about that level and had no defined upper limit. These examples highlight an inequality which may have increased in the early nineteenth century. It has been estimated that the top 10 per cent of the population received 44 per cent of national income in 1800 and 53 per cent by the mid-century, although these figures are fairly hypothetical. The top income receivers gained at the expense of the in-between groups rather than the very poor. The bottom 40 per cent of the population continued to receive around 15 per cent of national income.

In the long term, income gain for all groups was to depend more on the growth of average income per person than on redistribution. Up to the 1820s, however, average income per person grew very slowly, as Table 8.1 showed. Investment grew more rapidly, which reduced the growth rate of consumption still further. Since wage-earners seem to have taken a fairly constant share of consumption, the inescapable conclusion is that real wages also grew slowly up to that date. From the 1820s there was a speed-up in the rate of increase, although there were sharp fluctuations due to the severe unemployment that characterised some years in the 1820s, 1830s and 1840s. Table 18.1 shows per capita consumption, which is a fair proxy for real wages. It indicates virtually no change, or even a decline, for most of the eighteenth century, and then an increase of about 20 per cent between 1780 and 1821, and an increase of about 25 per cent between 1821 and 1841.

Table 18.1 Consumption per person (1700 = 100)

1700	100
1760	96
1780	96
1801	107
1821	117
1841	149
1851	169

(*Source:* Crafts)

These figures are borne out by the wage evidence or, rather, the arguments over it. Enormous amounts of time have been spent by historians on the question of real wages in the Industrial Revolution, a debate known as 'Standard of Living Controversy'. Since a number of eminent historians have come to quite contrary conclusions about living standards, conclusions usually categorised as 'optimistic' or 'pessimistic', their inability to agree is itself quite a good reason for supposing that there was not much overall change, at least in the earlier part of the period. Where there certainly was change was in the experience of occupational or regional groups in the population, figures for whose wages are not subject to so much disagreement as are national averages. In particular, there was a major long-term gain for wage-earners in the Midlands, Lancashire, northern England and Scotland. Industry's demand for labour in these areas transformed them from relatively low to relatively high wage regions. Although wages in all occupations benefited, the highest rates were earned in industrial occupations such as mining and engineering. But even the wages of northern agricultural workers went up by 50 per cent between 1780 and 1824, while throughout the South of England the wages of such workers stagnated or declined. Southern agricultural labourers were also affected by the erosion of common land which resulted from enclosure, although allotments were sometimes allocated in lieu of customary rights to graze animals on the commons. (It is also true that the more intensive farming of the commons which enclosure made possible may have enhanced employment opportunities and hence prevented wages from sinking even lower.) Evidence from Bath and London shows that even in southern towns there was no increase in real wages. One group of workers who had prospered in the late eighteenth century and who were particularly hard hit from the 1820s were the handloom weavers, whose earnings were seriously affected by machine competition. Their sufferings were worst in the southern textile towns like Bradford-on-Avon, where there was little alternative employment.

There has been intense debate over the standard of living in this period, not so much because it is an interesting question, but because it is linked with political standpoints. These can be boiled down to the different views taken of industrialisation and the capitalist system which brought it forth. An adverse view tends to lead to negative feelings about the likely course of the standard of living, and vice versa. If we look at what actually happened, it is clear not only that there was not much change for a long period, but also that what happened was not just linked to industrialisation. As in the past, the standard of living was linked to population pressure, and it was the rapid rise in the population which put such strain on living standards up to the 1820s. If industrialisation was actually a factor behind rising population, this could change the picture yet again, but there is little evidence that it was. On the contrary, industrialisation provided employment for the burgeoning population; if industry had not continued to develop, then more capital would presumably have been invested in land, but the work created would have been much more seasonal.

A further factor for much of the period was the impact of the Napoleonic Wars, discussed in Chapter 7. On the one hand, the wars increased total employment opportunities and provided a last burst of prosperity for domestic industries, many of which were located in the South. On the other hand, the wars probably depressed overall living standards for working people, an effect which lasted until well after 1815 because high taxation continued in order to pay the interest on government debt. There was a transfer of resources from the less well-off, who paid a high proportion of taxation, to bondholders.

The ending of the wars saw reduced employment opportunities and a rapid decline of domestic industries in the South. This decline, which had started in some cloth regions in the eighteenth century, highlights the fact that while industrialisation may have been beneficial to employment nationally, its regional effects were very different. The relative improvement in the North's wage levels was not just due to industrialisation in that part of the country, but also to the decline of domestic textile industries in the South. This reduced total employment in the South, and hence alternative opportunities for the agricultural population, as well as reducing the number of better-paid jobs in the more skilled textile occupations. Maxine Berg has suggested that the increase in capital and hence employment in the textile industries of the North took place at the expense not just of the physical capital, but also of the human capital, of the South; in other words, the cheapening of production was achieved partly by dispensing with old skills, and thus represented a direct transfer of resources from relatively highly-paid labour in certain textile occupations like weaving to the consumer who benefited from lower prices. Any assessment of the overall impact of industrialisation on living standards in this period needs to take into account its deleterious impact on the South as well as its more favourable impact on the North.

While industrialisation may have improved overall employment and wage levels, it has often been suggested that any final verdict must go against industrialisation because cities were such unpleasant places in which to live. It was the quality of life, not just wages and prices, which according to this argument was what mattered. Of course, industrialisation by itself did not necessarily create cities: the surroundings of many mines and mills were often rural. By comparison, the incredible squalor of eighteenth-century London, not a city created by the Industrial Revolution although it had much industry, has been graphically recorded by Hogarth. In spite of this, urbanisation was to a large extent the result of industrialisation. Urbanisation created pollution and was associated with high mortality; aesthetically, the early industrial towns were grim places, unrelieved by many amenities or buildings of merit, although in the early nineteenth century they were still small and there was reasonable access to the countryside. P Lindert and J Williamson have suggested that if people moved to cities, they were making a reasoned choice in favour of high wages over these other disadvantages. It is unlikely, however, that most migrants from rural areas had much idea of the very high urban mortality rate. The high wages were more obvious. One final point is that made by E P Thompson. People felt they were worse off by comparison with others – a point which has some validity since while wage-earners' share of national income stagnated or possibly fell, the very wealthy increased their share.

The trend towards a more definite improvement in real wages, evident from the 1820s, became more marked from the 1840s. Between 1850 and 1900, the usual measures give an average rise in real wages of between 70 per cent and 80 per cent. About a third of this is accounted for by the shift of the population from less to more highly paid occupations, in particular from agriculture towards mining, metals and engineering. Individual occupations, in other words, experienced a lower rise of about 50 per cent. The acceleration in the rise in earnings, compared with the early nineteenth century, is quite easy to explain: productivity was increasing that much faster than before. For this to feed through directly to increased real wages, it was important that productivity should be improving in agriculture as well as in industry, otherwise the growing population would still have had to pay higher prices for food. British agriculture had succeeded in improving productivity in the early period of industrialisation and, indeed, beyond; but inevitably as the population grew, more food had to be imported. The cheap land of the New World, which the products of industrialisation, particularly ships and railways, had helped to open up, now played a major part in raising agricultural productivity on a world-wide basis and thereby keeping food prices down.

From about 1900, real wages appear to have stagnated. Historians are still not certain about the reasons for this. The slowdown in productivity growth, some reduction in hours worked, and the growing share of national income going to central and local government expenditure are all probable factors.

In spite of the rapid increase in real wages, poverty was still endemic at the end of the nineteenth century. The social investigator S Rowntree found that about 15 per cent of the working-class population, or about 10 per cent of the total population, were in poverty in York in 1899. Rowntree's investigation is a classic of middle-class meddling, which has been given a degree of credence it does not fully deserve. His apparently objective level of poverty, based on estimates of the food consumption possible at a given level of income, would probably be adjusted downwards in the light of modern nutritional knowledge; the later nineteenth-century Irish diet, which consisted largely of potatoes and milk yet provided higher nutritional levels than the English diet, proves that reasonable nutrition is consistent with very low incomes. Having said that, the fact remains that many people in Britain were very poor. The causes of poverty were not so much old age, as is so often the case today. When the poor survived into old age, they either continued to work, or lived with and were maintained by relatives, or went into the workhouse which was felt to be degrading but ensured a reasonable standard of nutrition and shelter. Poverty in nineteenth-century Britain was most often a function of low wages, often combined with larger than average families. Another frequent cause was the death of a young parent. One result of this was that a high proportion of children were in poverty. Rowntree should be given credit for drawing attention to the poverty cycle – the transition in many people's lives from poverty in childhood, to relative prosperity as young adults, to poverty again as their family grew, to relative prosperity as the children grew up, and perhaps to poverty again in old age. This dreary existence was the lot of many throughout our period, but was much more marked in the South, whose low wages relative to the North persisted throughout the nineteenth century. A survey of 1914, using similar criteria to Rowntree's, found that in Reading 29 per cent of the working-class population were in poverty. By contrast, the coalmining town of Stanley in Durham and the shoe manufacturing town of Northampton had levels of poverty of 6 per cent and 9 per cent respectively. The picture of poverty at the end of this period is not all black, therefore, while the improvement since the mid-century, when wages were so much lower, was massive. An estimate for York suggests that, on Rowntree's criteria, all married labourers were in poverty in the 1850s, as well as many skilled workers, who mainly escaped poverty by the 1890s.

The improved living standards of manual workers were paralleled by improved living standards both for the middle class and for the very rich, although agricultural depression from the 1870s had an adverse effect on the incomes of farmers and landowners. Up to that time, landowners had dominated the wealth stakes, a dominance which highlights the emphasis this book has put on the persistence of the old amidst the new. After landowners, it was not iron or cotton masters who formed the most numerous group of millionaires, but bankers, followed by brewers. The highest proportion of the very wealthy in relation to the population in the later nineteenth century was not in Manchester, not in Glasgow, but in Burton-upon-Trent.

CONSUMPTION

The increased consumption of goods and services is ultimately what economic growth is about. Economic growth cannot affect our spiritual welfare. It can be diverted to purposes which are damaging to others, such as the construction and use of weapons, or which are positive in the long run but have no immediate effect on welfare, such as investment. This leaves increased consumption as the only end for which economic growth is much use, at least to the people who are there while it is taking place. Consumption of some important things, like leisure, is dealt with elsewhere. This section looks at the consumption of goods.

After 1815, relatively little was spent on weapons and war. Other forms of government expenditure also remained low. Investment, which rose as a proportion of income until the mid-nineteenth century, was stable thereafter. By a combination of their own volition and the actions of the outside world, the British people spent most of their extra income from economic growth on consumption.

At the basis of consumption for most people in this period was food and drink. In poor societies, people inevitably spend much of their income on food. For poorer members of the working class in the early part of the period, this proportion was around three-quarters. Much of this expenditure went on bread, and it was a measure of English wealth as compared with the Continent that the English mainly ate wheaten bread, made as white as possible by milling out the husk. This was more expensive but offered a higher protein content than rye bread. More important to the consumer, it was digestible. When bread was the main item of diet, an excess of fibre, the Holy Grail of modern diet, was as unpleasant as its absence can be deleterious. By contrast, in Scotland, originally a much poorer country, oats had been and remained an important part of the diet, their persistence in the menu showing the importance of custom as well as income in dietary habits. Although bread was the mainstay of the working-class diet in the eighteenth century, tropical luxuries were penetrating working-class homes as they were middle-class. Consumption of sugar and tea in particular was burgeoning. The relative wealth of Britain at this time, and her access to cheap supplies of these commodities, fixed an enduring taste for them in this country.

As income rose, diet diversified, although food and drink still dominated working-class budgets, food alone accounting for over 50 per cent of working-class spending in 1914. Tea and sugar consumption went on rising throughout the nineteenth century. Contrary to the fears of contemporaries worried about its effect on the health of the nation, tea is quite good for you. However, most foodstuffs were not bought for health but to provide variety, although they might bring nutritional benefits. Meat, milk and butter consumption all rose steeply in the later nineteenth century. Not shown on the statistics, but often referred to in accounts of working-class life, were tinned salmon and pineapple. There is substantial oral evidence that much of the benefit of this diversification went to working males in the family, who were thought to need meat in particular. The continued heavy spending on food has been represented as an adherence to traditional patterns of consumption, but a moment's thought shows that diversifying a diet consisting largely of bread and potatoes would be anyone's priority in the same position. This diversification could only be achieved by buying more expensive foodstuffs such as meat. It was human nature rather than tradition which accounted for the continued predominance of spending on food in family budgets.

Alcohol consumption rose until the 1870s, to a level of 270 pints of beer and 1.5 gallons of spirits per person, per year; most was consumed by adult males. In the 1870s, a shift of tastes seems to have set in. The rising real wages of the next twenty years were not marked by any further rise in alcohol consumption, and in the 1900s it declined. At its peak in 1876, it took 15 per cent of consumers' expenditure. No wonder brewers were so rich.

Middle-class eating habits are best summarised by this extract from a middle-class budget in Rowntree's survey of York. A typical menu consisted of: breakfast – fried bacon, bread, butter, marmalade, toast, cream, tea; lunch – pea soup, mutton, potatoes, greens, fruit tart, rice pudding, cheese, butter, biscuits, coffee, cream; tea – bread, butter, hot toast, cake, tea; dinner – soup, blackcock, bread sauce, greens, toast, anchovy cream, dessert, tea, cream. To be fair, this was probably a wealthier family – other middle-class families had their main meal in the middle of the day, with only a light supper.

Although the middle classes didn't stint themselves on food, they still had much more disposable income than other purchasers. In the eighteenth century, their consumption of semi-durables like china has already been noted as an important component of demand. The proliferation of cheap Staffordshire ware in the early nineteenth century shows that these tastes extended down to the working class when they could afford to indulge them. Clothing was the most important semi-durable, although with the reduction in the cost of material, the actual proportion spent on it may not have changed much. Of equal or greater importance than semi-durables as an item of consumption was housing, spending on which was growing rapidly throughout the period. The substantial detached villa of the middle-class Victorian family must have been much more expensive than the neat Georgian terrace. Inseparably connected with villadom, as an item of consumption, was travelling to work. This was increasingly part of the middle-class life style as they moved their homes from the towns and city centres. Much of middle-class spending must have gone on furnishing these houses, as Victorian taste called for large quantities of furniture and ornaments. In the later nineteenth century, the ability to buy these products was further enhanced by mechanisation in carpet and wallpaper manufacture, and the development of new products such as linoleum.

Working-class housing improved too. This was not very difficult, for both rural housing and the houses in early industrial towns were in different ways appalling. Most farm labourers' families in the early nineteenth century did not live in the cosy nooks which estate agents today call country cottages; such houses were occupied by artisans or farmers. Labourers' cottages typically consisted of one or two ground-floor rooms and, possibly, an attic bedroom. By contrast, early industrial town housing had two stories with three or four small rooms, built in terraces with a consequent lack of air, light and waste-disposal facilities. A small minority of workers lived in better houses, usually built by employers in remote spots to attract a workforce. A much larger minority lived in poorer dwellings: cellars, mainly inhabited by Irish in the highly overcrowded cities of Liverpool and Manchester; and older houses in multiple occupation, a feature in some towns like Plymouth throughout the century. The back-to-backs which often stand as a symbol of bad housing were actually not so bad. They were, quite simply, two rows of houses built with common back walls and with no intervening yard or garden. People liked them because they were easy to keep warm. Their main disadvantages were lack of light and the virtual impossibility, as there was no yard, of having an earth closet for each house. Common in the Midlands and North, their building was banned in most cities in the later nineteenth century. In Scotland, the standard form of housing was based on the one-room rural Scottish cottage, with sleeping compartments partitioned off from the main room. One- or two-room apartments of this kind, raised into the sky in tenements four or more storeys high, made Scottish cities distinctive throughout the century. Scotland reflects the fact that there were regional differences in housing which did not necessarily correspond with regional prosperity. Much southern housing was quite good by the later nineteenth century, since low wages meant low building costs and hence low rents, while the worst overcrowding in this period was in Scotland and the North East.

Warming homes throughout Britain, and frequently providing cooking facilities as well, was the open hearth. It was wasteful of heat, but coal was cheap and it provided a focal point for Victorian domesticity. Towards the end of the century, the domestic gas cooker came into widespread use, encouraged by the development of the slot meter. In Leicester, for instance, a third of consumers cooked by gas in 1898, and four-fifths by 1914. The slot meter revolution must have affected the lives of many women for the better.

The later nineteenth century saw a significant improvement in housing standards, although there was only a slow fall in the average number of occupants per house. Houses became better built, rooms became larger, and four or five rooms became standard in new-built urban housing in most areas. Building regulations meant wider streets and larger back yards, which made one closet per house feasible. There was undoubtedly improvement in furnishings as well, although spending on this continued to be low: only 5 per cent of total spending, by all classes, went on durables in 1900. Enhancement of the structure of the home, however, should not be seen just as a continuation of 'traditional' patterns of consumption. In effect, the water closets and gas fittings which became increasingly common in middle-class homes from the mid-century, and in working-class homes towards the end, were the Victorian equivalent of today's durable goods.

Writing in the early 1900s, the industrial correspondent of *The Times*, Arthur Shadwell, painted a picture of extensive if modest prosperity in Britain's industrial heartlands. Of Bolton, a Lancashire textile town with a population of 170,000 in 1901, he wrote this: 'Of course in a town the size of Bolton, poverty, misfortune, illness, vice and dirt occur; but the proportion of them is surprisingly small; they need a good deal of looking for. On the other hand the evidences of a decent standard of living meet the eye at every turn. The houses are tidy and tidily kept. The people respect themselves and like to have things nice about them in a plain way.' By the 1900s the economic system, whatever its drawbacks, provided this modest prosperity for a large proportion of the population.

CHAPTER NINETEEN

Industrialisation and the family

Ever since the early years of industrialisation, commentators have lamented its deleterious effects upon family life. In recent years, however, research has begun to modify many of the myths about industrialisation and the family. Historians of the family are concerned with the structure of the family, a term which refers to questions such as whether families lived in nuclear groups (spouses and children) or with a wider range of kin (relatives) in one household; they are concerned with affection within the family; the history of the family impinges upon historical demography, which has been dealt with elsewhere, and can include the study of how work is organised within the family, an aspect which will be dealt with in the next chapter.

In peasant societies, the family is the unit of production as well as of consumption. Patterns of marriage are likely to be strongly influenced by the need to work the land and pass it on to the next generation. Marriage may be arranged rather than based on affection, although this does not mean that affection is necessarily absent. An increase in wage labour would loosen both these constraints, and hence the suggestion in Chapter 2 that the growing difficulty of establishing or inheriting farms may have contributed to the fertility rise of the later eighteenth-century. It is far too simple, though, to assume that eighteenth-century Britain saw a transition from a peasant economy to a proletarianised labour force. At the beginning of the eighteenth century, there were already large numbers of urban middle class and of wealthy farmers; significant numbers of non-agricultural manual workers, both rural and urban; and many landless farm workers. The divorce of work from land ownership was already taking place. It continued throughout the eighteenth century and into the nineteenth, although its form changed as industrialisation accelerated and more workers became urbanised, some of these moving into factory work.

Reflecting this slow change, many features of family life in pre-industrial Britain had very deep roots. The basically nuclear family structure, involving relatively late marriage, seems to go a long way back into both British and Western European history. Within this basic pattern, some families would deviate at any one time by having kin, such as grandparents, a sibling (brother or sister) of one of the parents, or an orphaned nephew or niece of one of the parents, living with them. Furthermore many families, if slightly higher up the social scale, would have young servants of either sex living with them. These were not so often the specialised domestic servants of Victorian times, but apprentices to urban tradesmen, or farm servants. The importance of service, in learning a trade or just getting a job, meant that many families had few of their own adolescent children in their household, although they might have children from other families.

With the growth of factories, the condition of working-class families ceased to be something which was taken for granted and became an issue among contemporary moralists. Many contemporaries expressed the view that factories had adverse effects on family life, by forcing the wife as well as the husband to go out to work. Census evidence, however, suggests that the proportion of married women who worked in factories was not that high. In Preston, a large Lancashire factory town, 26 per cent of married women did such work in 1851. Even where wives did work, they might well be younger women without families, or older women whose families had grown up. Wives with young children might go out to work, but co-resident kin such as grandmothers might then look after the children. A final and most important point is that throughout the nineteenth century, cotton factory employment was the only major occupation in which a substantial number of married women did go out regularly to work. In other words the problem, if there was one, was occupationally and geographically limited.

Moving away from the myths put about by the moralists of the day, we come to the much more interesting subject of family structure as it had evolved during industrialisation. Our knowledge of this rests heavily on M Anderson's study of working-class family structure in mid-nineteenth-century Preston; there is no way of knowing, without numerous other studies, how typical Preston was, but there is no reason to suppose the families in it were markedly different from anywhere else in industrial Lancashire. Anderson's families, like eighteenth-century ones, were basically nuclear, but co-residence of kin was not uncommon. In 1851, 23 per cent of households included kin outside the immediate parent/child relationship, which was higher than the proportion in most pre-nineteenth-century English households. Taking the entire life cycle of a family, co-residence of kin at some stage would be quite probable. Furthermore, there is evidence that kin frequently lived close to each other, so that a fair degree of contact among the extended family – that is, the kin outside the nuclear family – seems likely. While a majority of Preston adolescents and young adults lived at home, a substantial minority moved away. For instance, 20 per cent of males and 33 per cent of females aged 15–19 lived away from home. While a number of girls were domestic servants, many of the boys had moved into lodgings, either in Preston or elsewhere.

Anderson suggests that the relationships which bound kin together were based on the construction and maintenance of reciprocal obligations, rather than on pure affection. There were strong pressures in society towards a high degree of independence for individuals or nuclear family groups. Adolescents and young adults had good work and earnings opportunities and could move away from the parental home, while migration to urban areas might physically separate kin from kin. There were also strong pressures in the opposite direction. Crises in family life, through the illness of a parent or unemployment of the breadwinner, were frequent. There was no social security for these, only the Poor Law which existed as a safety net, but one which carried a social stigma and enforced the separation of family members. Neighbours could give help, but at a time of great fluidity people might not be neighbours for long. Kin were always kin, and the existence of mutual obligations strengthened the ties of blood. Benefiting from kin in times of trouble also meant accepting the obligations of kinship even if there was no immediate reward. Hence grandparents or orphan nephews and nieces might be supported. However, in an individualistic society, these ties were not limitless and such dependents might be able to render some immediate reciprocal service to strengthen their claim. Grandparents might look after children if the mother went out to work, for instance.

Anderson does not deny the existence of affection, particularly between parents and children; Elizabeth Roberts, using oral evidence to study Lancashire family life in the early twentieth century, suggests that affection and a sense of duty could be the main factors in kin relationships, which consisted of more than just the maintenance of a set of obligations. For instance, one family in Barrow-in-Furness struggled to keep a grandmother from the workhouse, even though the old lady was addicted to drink and pawned the family furniture to buy it.

Moving on another fifty years, studies in the 1950s of family life in another working-class area, Bethnal Green in East London, reveal a community where contact within the extended family was frequent. It was based not so much upon obligation, because the growth of state welfare had reduced the need for help in times of crisis, but upon affection and a sense of relationship.

These findings bear out the idea, familiar to historians of the family, that over time there has been a trend towards the greater independence of family members. Proletarianisation, which was exacerbated but not initiated by industrialisation, freed family members from the need to centre their attention around the family land, but in its early stages meant that they still had to concentrate on maximising the family income, which was now earned through labour. Industrialisation also led to an increase in migration and a set of new circumstances for family members – the trauma of settling in a new town and finding a new job, possibly greater exposure to life crises caused by economic depression or high urban mortality. These countervailing forces often separated people from their kin, but gave strong motives for continuing relationship with kin in some form. Migration slackened in the late nineteenth century and this, combined with the existence of outside sources of welfare, heightened the opportunity for more affectionate and less contractual relationships with kin.

Although industrialisation and urbanisation shaped family strategies, they should not be seen as all-powerful forces. To some extent, industrialisation was itself shaped by families: many employers recruited through the families of their employees, while in the early factories, whose isolated position and large size meant particular problems in the recruitment and control of labour, it made good sense to carry out these functions by employing entire families. Family responses to industrialisation were shaped by the transmission of existing values and practices and by non-economic forces. Changes in fertility, for instance, were influenced by cultural factors as well as economic changes. In middle- and upper-class families, it is even harder to link change directly with industrialisation; rather, it seems connected to more general changes in mores, changes with deep social and intellectual roots. One example of this is the Victorian cult of domesticity, a convenient label for the heightened interest, by both wife and husband, in their home and immediate family. The appeal of the sampler over the mantelpiece saying 'Home Sweet Home', and the slippers by the fireplace, was strong throughout the social spectrum. The idea of domesticity implies close relationships within the family, although not necessarily equality. Lawrence Stone has suggested that for the middle and upper classes, an increasing degree of partnership in the eighteenth century was followed by a regression towards patriarchy in the nineteenth. Certainly the image of Victorian male dominance is hard to shake off; thus the doctrine of separate spheres, which allowed the male the dominant role outside the home, made the home the women's sphere, and so women's autonomy was not entirely denied, although it was limited. Furthermore, an idea is not necessarily a guide to everyone's practice. Oral evidence for the Edwardian period indicates that for the working and lower middle class, marriage was frequently a genuine partnership. George Bourne noted that in Surrey, 'it is quite the common thing in the villages for a man and wife to lock up their cottage on a Saturday evening, and go off with the children to do the week's shopping together'. Many husbands handed their wage packet to their wives, to receive back a small allowance for beer and tobacco. The view that patriarchy and male domination was universal in Victorian and Edwardian society is far too simplistic. This has implications for the degree of change which occurred in nineteenth-century marriages, but at the moment we know too little about eighteenth-century working-class marriages to make judgements about change.

This cursory glimpse of family relationships is a reflection of the paucity of serious writing on the subject, although there is plenty of oral and literary material available as raw material. Enormously important subjects such as childhood, sex and the treatment of death in Victorian families have been omitted on the grounds that a very brief treatment would be of little use. The reader should look at the excellent material which has appeared elsewhere. If there is a subject which is crying out for more to be written on it, it is that centre of human relationships and emotions, the family.

CHAPTER TWENTY

Work and leisure

OCCUPATIONAL PATTERNS

In spite of the many changes that the nineteenth century brought about, the broad division between middle class and manual groups in the population seems not to have altered much. In 1867, Dudley Baxter, using income as the criterion, could estimate that around 20 per cent of the occupied population was upper or middle class. Only a minuscule proportion were upper class, and less than half of the whole group had an income of much over £100 a year, which was scarcely wealth. Most of those who fell into the middle-class category were wealthier farmers, professional men, clerks, people living on pensions or savings, and employers in industry and commerce. Most of the last group would employ quite small numbers: the small workshop was still prevalent in industry, while retailing was dominated by small firms. So it would be incorrect to equate 'the middle class' with non-manual workers. Many smaller shopkeepers and employers must have done some manual work as a matter of course.

Baxter's proportion of a fifth as middle class is probably roughly correct for the earlier nineteenth century, too. In the eighteenth century and earlier, however, the distinction between groups was increasingly blurred, since a higher proportion of the population owned some property, as small farmers or tradesmen, but also did manual work. Going forward to 1911, and using Guy Routh's computation which is made on an occupational rather than an income basis, the proportion of upper and middle classes was still 20 per cent. On the other hand, the unoccupied are not counted in Routh's figures. Their inclusion might raise the proportion of the middle class in the whole population by several per cent – although the inclusion of children would lower it again for the Edwardian period, since working-class families were larger. Although the share of the middle class in the total population had not altered much, its composition was changing. By 1911, the proportion of clerks and lower-paid professionals such as teachers and nurses was around 8 per cent of the occupied population of eighteen million: it had increased throughout the nineteenth century. There were still almost twice as many employers as there were managers, however (6.7 per cent against 3.4 per cent of the working population), reflecting the continued importance of small firms in the economy, especially in retailing.

The work experience of a large proportion of the poorer four-fifths of the population changed much more sharply. Table 20.1 shows how the agricultural workforce, including farmers but predominantly labourers, declined as a proportion of the total. The change probably occurred more between generations than in each generation as the children of agricultural workers moved to other jobs.

Another way of measuring the manual workforce is by broad skill composition. Baxter, in 1867, estimated that 10 per cent of the population were skilled manual labourers, 40 per cent were lower skilled and factory workers, and 30 per cent unskilled and agricultural workers. The figure for skilled workers seems low: it may understate the true total because using income as a criterion, as Baxter did, could mean that skilled workers in low-wage areas did not get counted as such. Equally, agricultural workers, although badly paid, might exercise more skill than factory workers. By 1911, on Guy Routh's compilation, 30 per cent of the occupied population were skilled workers, around 35 per cent semi-skilled, and 15 per cent unskilled, again counting agricultural workers in the last group. Routh's figures are more likely to be accurate than Baxter's, and tally quite well with the author's estimate that only about 20 per cent of adolescent males in the appropriate age group were apprentices in the 1900s, since a fair proportion of skilled work was not learned by apprenticeship. Within these broad categories, certain groups became more and more important. Mining employed over a million male workers by the 1900s, and the whole category of metal manufacture and engineering employed 1.75 million. In the service sector, railways employed almost half a million, and there were increasing numbers of shop assistants of both sexes. Many of these might consider themselves as middle class on status grounds, although not counted as such in the figures given earlier. Another group with an ambivalent status were domestic servants who, along with groups like laundresses and chambermaids, comprised roughly 15 per cent of the occupied population from the mid-century. Around four-fifths of these were female: two million testimonials to the inequality, both social and sexual, of Victorian and Edwardian society.

Table 20.1 Share of labour force in sectors (per cent)

	Agriculture	Manufacturing, mining, construction	Other
1831	25	41	34
1913	8	46	46

(*Source:* Deane and Cole)

THE EXPERIENCE OF WORK

In the eighteenth century, as today, types of work were so different that it is impossible to summarise all their varieties. A skilled London craftsman in a 'high-class' trade such as coachmaking or high-quality tailoring would work in a small workshop with a few other journeymen and one or two apprentices. In theory, a day's work was twelve to fourteen hours, but payment was by the piece (i.e. the amount produced) and so hours were not strictly controlled. Such a craftsman and his fellow workers would have full control over the life of the workshop: the employer provided the building, ordered raw materials and sold the finished product, and as long as workmen produced good work they would be left alone. By contrast, a Black Country nailer worked in much cruder conditions, in his own home, doing much less skilled work. He worked under a variation of the domestic system, with an ironmonger providing his raw material and selling the finished product. With relatively little skill, nailers were open to exploitation and had low earnings. In spite of this, their control over the pace of their work was as absolute as the skilled craftsman's. Weavers in the later eighteenth century were often prosperous but, like nailers, they worked under the domestic system with the autonomy that implied. Furthermore, in Yorkshire and Lancashire the weaver was often independent of the merchants, buying his own yarn and selling the cloth. In contrast to all these, a farm labourer had little autonomy. Big farms, particularly in arable areas, had a large labour force which worked under the close supervision of the farmer.

If many male industrial workers had control over the pace of their work, most women who worked for money did not. Apart from housework, women's work included helping in the processes of domestic industry. Thus weavers' and nailers' wives and children would help the man of the household, and although women might become weavers themselves at times of labour shortage such as the Napoleonic Wars, usually their position was subservient. Hand-spinning, an exclusively female occupation, had low productivity and low earnings compared to weaving. Rural women in the arable-dominated eastern counties were also becoming increasingly confined to low-grade occupations in agricultural work, such as gleaning after the harvest. Some of the possible reasons for this are discussed in Chapter 2.

The nineteenth century saw a steady increase in the degree of control by employers over their employees' work habits, control which took the form both of written rules and regulations regarding conduct, and an insistence upon strict timekeeping. Enhanced control was associated with mechanisation, which involved investment in expensive machinery and the use of steam power. Employers did not want their machinery to lie idle or their steam engine to use up coal, while production was under the maximum because workers were taking time off. Coal mines, in which only the winding gear was powered, and shipyards, where mechanisation was limited, remained remarkably slack about timekeeping up to the end of the century; but when discipline was important, as in the observation of safety regulations in mines, enforcement was rigorous. This strongly suggests that, although employers in these industries complained about poor timekeeping and attributed it to the laziness of the workforce, they could have improved it had it been worth their while to do so. Thus after the West Midlands' metal trades started to mechanise in the mid-nineteenth century, employers successfully enforced regular hours on their workers, hitherto notorious for their addiction to heavy drinking on Sunday followed by the observation of St Monday (Monday off work), and sometimes St Tuesday and St Wednesday as well. Textile workers, one of the earliest groups to be so controlled, remained the largest. In the 1880s, Beatrice Webb stayed with textile workers in Bacup, a small Lancashire town, and found an unquestioning acceptance of the regular habits of work which were required. Work discipline had become internalised.

Another form of control over the workforce was sub-contracting, in which one worker, the contractor, would employ one, two or a number of others. The contractor was fully responsible for the others' work; typically he was paid by the piece, and paid his underworkers by the hour, a system which could lead to exploitation as he worked them as hard as possible to maximise his own earnings. Sub-contracting allowed the ultimate employer to lay off responsibility for employee relations and thus simplify the task of management. It was not a common form of employment in skilled occupations, but was prevalent in industries which needed large quantities of semi-skilled labour, such as iron and steel making and coalmining. It seems likely, therefore, that it grew in the nineteenth century with the growth of these industries. In iron and steel, the development of union organisation among semi-skilled workers at the end of the century gave them the strength to successfully oppose sub-contracting. In mining, it continued to be endemic in some areas like the Midlands until much later.

Although industrial workers' control over their timekeeping and pace of work declined during the nineteenth century, there is little evidence that the skill needed in work was reduced. The figures cited in the preceding section, while they should be used with caution, suggest the opposite. Naturally there were conflicting trends: the proportion of agricultural workers, whose skills had been diverse if limited, was reduced; crafts such as coachmaking continued to flourish, although rural crafts such as wheelwrighting and black-smithery began to decline from the mid-nineteenth century; new skills, particularly in engineering, flourished. Even in industries requiring new skills, there was change, with an increase in the degree of knowledge required and a decrease in the degree of manual skill. The proportion of white-collar and technical staff increased in the late nineteenth century, due to the growth of routine clerical work as more formal accounting systems came into use, but also because of the continued development of scientific and engineering techniques. Industries like steel and paper-making were appointing chemists by the end of the nineteenth century, while accurate draughtsmanship became more important as machinery became more complex. At the lower end of the scale, the growth of factories saw a rise in the proportion of semi-skilled workers, although the nineteenth century would not have recognised the term, calling them instead 'intelligent labourers', or operatives if in a factory. Semi-skilled work typically involves mastery of a limited number of techniques, with training lasting from a few weeks to six months. Factories, apart from those in predominantly skilled trades such as engineering, were likely to employ semi-skilled workers because they were mass-production enterprises, which meant that work could be sub-divided. Hence textile factory workers were the first large group of semi-skilled workers. As mechanisation developed from the mid-century, they were followed by workers in the shoe industry, then in diverse industries involving light engineering or consumer-goods manufacture in the later nineteenth century. Transport workers, too, could often be classed as semi-skilled.

Some commentators have seen the changing conditions of work for men as one aspect of a qualitative deterioration in manual workers' lives brought about by large-scale industrialisation. The enhanced control by employers over workers in matters such as conduct in the workplace and timekeeping, and the need to work at the pace of the machine rather than at the workers' own pace, are often put forward as facets of this deterioration. While there were obnoxious innovations in the nineteenth century such as sub-contracting, the fact is that eighteenth-century working conditions can be easily romanticised. Many workers, notably farm labourers, were already closely supervised by their employers. Wives and children working in the family economy of the domestic system were subservient to the husband. Often work may have been arranged to all parties' mutual satisfaction, but the impression given by the evidence is that male groups like the metal workers of the West Midlands arranged work for their own satisfaction, without much regard for anyone else.

Furthermore, to see closely supervised factory work as typical of the nineteenth century is to gain an incorrect impression of work in the period, and of the contrast between the eighteenth and nineteenth centuries. Outside factories, handwork was still predominant: occupations like building and mining, each by the 1900s employing around 10 per cent of the male labour force, continued to rely almost exclusively on the skill and strength of the individual worker. For men who preferred freedom from immediate supervision, there was railway work or carting, both of which could involve some autonomy. Even in factories, many of the tasks involved transport and maintenance work and so were not machine-tending jobs. Furthermore, machine-tending jobs themselves were not all the same: engineering was largely skilled work involving a variety of operations; some less skilled workers like cotton spinners established a degree of autonomy, albeit of a limited kind, through setting their machines in an individualistic way so that only they could operate them; other factory workers, as in the boot and shoe industry, learned by working a variety of machines and thus were not confined to one process. Whether machine-tending, repetitive or not, is more soul-destroying than sewing countless buttonholes or making nails on a forge day in and day out, both typical occupations for poorer handworkers of both sexes, seems to the author a moot point.

The approach which associates industrialisation with a deterioration in working conditions is influenced by the views of Marx, who was keenly interested in the labour process, as he called the organisation of work and the technology associated with it. In Marx's view, a long-term process of sub-division of work was taking place under capitalism, with the intention of reducing the skills of labour in order to reduce the costs of production. Historians and sociologists who have been influenced by Marx have elaborated his ideas. Thus H Braverman has suggested that the aim of 'deskilling' the workforce by sub-dividing work was not just to reduce costs, but also to reduce the workers' control over the labour process; by doing this, employers would enhance their own opportunity to extract the maximum profit from the labour process, since workers would no longer be able to contest with them on the basis of equal or superior knowledge.

There are two problems with this approach. The first is that, although increased sub-division of work has undoubtedly taken place over time, and this has often resulted from a desire to simplify tasks and so cut costs, sub-division is also bound up with the increasing complexity of work as knowledge increases. Thus industries like engineering adopted more complex techniques as time went by: overall skill levels did not decline, but workers became more specialised because of the growing complexity of the tasks involved. The second problem is rooted in Marx's simplistic view that a businessman's prime aim was to reduce labour costs. In reality, businessmen were and are concerned with reducing costs and improving efficiency in many different areas, encompassing control of capital investment, raw materials, sales and so on. Therefore they might have many different attitudes towards their workforce, depending on whether labour was a large part of the cost of production, on whether high-quality work was important, or on other variables. They might want to reward labour for its skill; to control it strictly, with fines for the slightest misdemeanour, as in some early factories; or to minimise their direct control rather than strengthen it, as with sub-contracting. Finally, individual employers might have moral views which directed them to act towards their workers in certain ways. Paternalism, considered in Chapter 20, was one result of this.

Where the labour process approach has been of value is in drawing attention to the fact that gradations of work, and the occupational classifications which correspond to them, are not an inevitable outcome of technology, changing only as technology changes. The division of labour in a particular place of employment might arise from the employer's strategy, or it might be influenced by unions' attempts to maintain certain work for skilled workers. The cost of training might be a factor: for instance, the high proportion of skilled workers in nineteenth-century Britain as compared with the USA may have been influenced by the low cost of apprenticeship as a means of training, leading in turn to low differentials between skilled and unskilled workers' wages and, hence, an incentive to employ the former. Old-established practices could also be important. Miners in different areas of the country had many different ways of organising their work, some of which had no basis in the differing technology or geology of the coalfields and can only be explained by custom.

At the end of the day, it seems likely that technology, taken together with the type of market and whether it called for mass production with sub-division of work or small-scale production using skilled workers, were probably the paramount influences on how work was divided among male manual workers. However, the subject remains open to further study.

The social influences on divisions of work are highlighted by the sexual division of labour, as the tendency for women to be confined to certain types of work was heightened in the nineteenth century. Homes became ever more central as places of paid work for women, whether this was taking in lodgers, laundry work, or domestic service which dominated the work experience of unmarried girls, except in a few areas such as Lancashire and the West of Scotland where alternative textile employment was available. The preference of girls in these areas for factory work, despite the fact that by the end of the century wages were little different in the two occupations, clearly indicates that when there was a choice, girls preferred independence. Having said that, domestic service offered many advantages. By 1900, wages were around £18.00–20.00 per annum clear of bed and board. Much of this could be saved, although some might be sent back to the parents in poorer families. A girl starting service at fourteen could save a substantial sum by marriage, and acquire a training in housework, something which working-class mothers themselves thought was desirable for their daughters. In turn, middle-class women devoted a great deal of time to supervising their servants. This constituted a large part of the 'work' of most upper-middle-class women, together with voluntary activities, such as philanthropy with its time-consuming demands for fund raising, committee work and visiting the poor; canvassing at elections, too, was as much a female as a male activity although women did not have the vote. There were, of course, many gradations within the middle-class, and the wife of a clerk with one servant, such as Carrie Pooter in the *Diary of Nobody*, spent much of her time doing lighter housework.

Unwaged work in the home – that is, housework, bringing up children, sewing and cooking – was the central activity of most Victorian working-class women. There is little evidence of major change in the duties these activities entailed, although the spread of urban water supplies eased the tasks of fetching water and of cleaning while, earlier in the century, cotton clothing and cheaper soap must have made life a bit more bearable. On the other hand, the amount of cleaning presumably increased as houses grew larger and more cluttered with furniture and ornaments. Much of this activity, the constant washing of net curtains and scrubbing of front doorsteps, was part of a complex ritual involving status and self-respect. Like the work of middle class women, it was not strictly functional – but then how much work is?

Working-class cooking was sharply constrained by the ubiquity of open hearths. Gas appliances were rare until the 1890s. Nevertheless, oral evidence indicates that many working-class women possessed good cooking skills, despite the patronising tone adopted towards them by middle-class commentators like Seebohm Rowntree. For the very poor, however, cooking strategies were sharply limited by their very inadequate equipment and reliance on hand-to-mouth purchasing of food.

LEISURE

If we go by the artefacts and the buildings that remain, only the middle and upper classes had much leisure in the eighteenth century. The theatre, balls in the assembly rooms which proliferated during the period, reading novels, and perhaps a month or more in a spa like Bath or Cheltenham, were some of the leisure activities available to those with money to spare. Most of this leisure was not sex-differentiated, although it seems to have played a more central part in women's lives than in men's, who also had their work. Poorer women, by contrast, had limited leisure time. Such as existed was centred around community activities, involving the exchange of information, which could be done while working; child-centred activities; and to the extent that it was economically possible, the purchase of consumer goods such as clothing which might confer status or personal satisfaction.

Male manual workers in the eighteenth century did have more leisure although, as with women, it was not so often available in regular blocks but taken irregularly, in the interstices of work. Drinking, either at work or afterwards with workmates, was probably the biggest single leisure pursuit, especially for skilled workers. Industrial workers were often followers of activities like bull-baiting and cock-fighting, legislated against in 1833 as cruel sports. An image of drinking and violence does a disservice to many manual workers, however, especially those in more sedentary occupations like weaving, who were often readers. Subjects like science and politics were popular, although the most widely read book was of course the Bible. The largest single occupational group, farm labourers, had little time for leisure or money to spend on it; what time they had might be spent on tending a few pigs or geese on the common land, or working the allotments they were sometimes given when commons were enclosed.

On the face of it, the nineteenth century saw vast changes in leisure habits, particularly for working-class men and to a lesser extent for women of all classes. For middle-class women there was a new leisure activity, associated with the increased production of consumer goods: shopping for non-essentials. 'Comparison' shopping was already important in the eighteenth century in any fair-sized town, although country dwellers could only patronise itinerant salesmen. By the late nineteenth century, urbanisation and transport improvements had made shopping a major social and leisure activity, as shown by the rise of department stores. Although economics constrained the ability of working-class women to shop for non-essentials, growing female literacy enabled them to read more. In Middlesbrough in the early 1900s, Lady Bell found that women in at least sixty out of 200 working-class families questioned did some regular reading. Music-making must have increased with the spread of pianos to all but very poor homes, even if many of these were for show. And when working-class families did take seaside holidays, women had a genuine break. Outside Lancashire, however, where high family incomes made them commonplace, such holidays were largely confined to skilled workers and their families, since practically no manual workers had paid holidays. For most, a day-trip organised by employer or church was all they could expect.

For working-class men, leisure became more commercialised and more segregated from work, but the activities most associated with leisure remained remarkably similar. The shorter but more rigorously enforced hours of work, and the Saturday half-holiday which spread rapidly from the 1850s, cut down workplace drinking, but the public house was still central, with the amount of drink consumed per person increasing for much of the century. Pubs were largely though not exclusively male preserves. From the pub, and from pleasure gardens like Vauxhall which had been fashionable in the eighteenth century, emerged the idea of a mixture of variety entertainment, drinking and audience participation which became music hall. The first specialised music hall, the Canterbury Music Hall, was opened in London in 1851, and by the 1860s there was seating for 50,000 in the largest music halls in the capital. If London was the centre of the music hall, so the North and Scotland were centres for commercialised sport although, of course, both forms of entertainment spread nationwide. As the century wore on, professional cricket and football, and gate-money horse-racing, replaced cruel sports and the horse-races held on downs and commons. Entrance fees for football matches were introduced in the 1870s and, symbolically, the amateur and upper-class Old Etonians were defeated by the proletarian Lancashire lads of Blackburn Olympic in the 1883 Cup Final.

Another innovation was off-course cash betting. This was illegal until betting shops were sanctioned in 1960; but a combination of low-level bribery of the police, a network of lookouts, and the technical innovations of the electric telegraph and cheap press (*The Sporting Life* was founded in 1863), meant that such betting flourished from the later nineteenth century. The study of form is extremely time-consuming, so this and the following of other sports through newspapers could be private activities, as could hobbies such as gardening, pigeon-fancying or fishing. Ross McKibbin has suggested that hobbies are deeply rooted in the English way of life; certainly ones like gardening depend on space which Continental and Scottish apartment dwellers simply did not possess. More certainly, both hobbies and sport were male-centred. Nevertheless, some occupations did bring husband and wife together, including holidays, day-trips and the music hall, but also music-making or simply reading. Since many men lacked either the cash or the inclination to be regular drinkers and did not necessarily have other male-centred hobbies, the extent to which men and women participated together in informal leisure activities may be greater than at first seems apparent.

To the more serious of the middle class, there was a disappointing lack of intellectual interests among working people in the later nineteenth century, in spite of the provision for 'rational recreation', such as museums and public libraries, which was increasingly developed from the mid-century. Although this patronising attitude may well have missed much intellectual activity which did take place, there is no doubt that many people preferred reading about sport, or a day-trip to the seaside, to reading about philosophy or a day-trip to the British Museum. Whether this preference was a response to poor education, the result of boredom at work or merely human nature is a pertinent question. The answer may be human nature, since the middle and upper classes possessed the advantages which the working class lacked, but had basically the same interests. The middle and upper classes also went to seaside resorts, while patronising different sections within those resorts; they also went to race meetings, even if they had separate enclosures; they also watched cricket, while playing as amateurs rather than professionals; they did not watch soccer much, but played golf instead.

Apart from human nature, leisure pursuits were shaped by custom as much as by technical innovations or by entrepreneurship. Certainly entrepreneurs were active in the provision of leisure activities, and 'supply-side' innovations such as the music hall or the cinema, which was becoming popular before the First World War, should not be ignored. Essentially, however, leisure provision responded to demand, with sport and entertainment, albeit in changing forms, remaining overwhelmingly popular. A classic example of this response to demand is contained in the reply of Samuel Smiles, the standard-bearer of Victorian ideas of thrift and sobriety, to a question on why the railway company for which he worked ran special trains to a prize fight. Smiles pointed out that demand was irresistible. However much elements of the middle class may have wanted to shape working-class leisure, the lure of profit triumphed over morality.

The increasing separation, or delimitation, between work and leisure also shaped leisure by placing the focal points of male leisure in the home or community rather than in the culture of the workplace. In theory, this gave men much greater leisure opportunities, as they were freed from the tyranny of custom. In practice, as has been shown, the taste for leisure remained essentially conservative.

CHAPTER TWENTY-ONE
Ranks and classes

The growth of class and class feeling is often seen as the most important social change generated by industrialisation. Sociologists use class terminology as a means of describing social groups who have a similar economic position. The significance of this similarity is enhanced if class becomes a source of solidarity in society, something which in turn might lead to conflict between one class and another over the distribution of wealth. There are, of course, other sources of solidarity, for instance religion, local community, or association with one's family or clan or tribe. The focus of this chapter, however, will be on class. This is not necessarily because class is more important, but because of the connection in the minds of historians and sociologists between industrialisation and class.

Placing someone in a class can be merely a neutral description of their occupation. This applies to the census authorities' 'social classes', used in presenting government statistics, which are arrived at by using an individual's occupation as a basis for allocation to a particular social class. If we are interested in class as a source of solidarity and conflict, and in the meaning that individuals attached to belonging to a class, then we need to make judgements about the classes into which society should be categorised. Most people in nineteenth-century Britain saw landowners as upper class, the middle class as the section of society ranging from big businessmen and professional people down to clerks and shopkeepers, and the working class as comprised of manual workers. An alternative view was that of Max Weber, a German sociologist writing in the early part of this century, who suggested that at the top of society in Western industrialised nations were those privileged through the possession of property or education. In other words, Weber classed wealthier businessmen and professionals as part of the elite. This identification of a fairly large privileged class makes quite good sense for late nineteenth-century Britain, as by that time there was little conflict between landed interests and business interests. The really important thing about Weber's categorisation, however, is that it suggests that the possession of educational qualifications was a form of privilege which could be equated with the possession of tangible property, such as houses or stocks and shares. Educational qualifications, leading for instance to a career as a lawyer or doctor, are like property in that they produce for their possessors a stream of income over and above what they would get otherwise. The concept of human capital, discussed in Chapter 2, is an expression in economic terms of the same idea. Obviously there are some differences between property (or physical capital) and human capital: for instance, the latter is more difficult to inherit; but even here much can be done to transmit human capital, by an educated person using part of their income to pay for their child's education.

More recently, it has been suggested that the existence of meaningful class boundaries can be measured by the degree of social mobility in society. This idea also makes good intuitive sense. If membership of economic groups was ephemeral, something that could be changed by marriage or accident, or was not transmitted to one's children, then the significance of class must be reduced.

While Weber saw class as a possible focus for solidarity between individuals and hence conflict with other classes, he recognised that there were other foci for solidarity. One of these was status, meaning the degree of social esteem accorded to an individual, either by himself or herself or by others. People's status may vary according to the observer.

In contrast to Weber, who did not think that class conflict was inevitable, Karl Marx thought that the economic foundations on which class rested gave rise to irreconcilable conflicts. During the early modern period the conflict had been, according to Marx, between the landowners and capitalist merchants. By the eighteenth century capitalism, meaning the system in which property was freely transferable and was owned by individuals, was triumphant in Britain, and large-scale industrialisation was under way. In Marx's view, there was now an irreconcilable conflict between the capitalists who owned property and the proletariat who did not, because capitalism's lust for profit ensured a steady increase in the soul-destroying division of labour at work and prevented technology enhancing the lives of workers as it should. Class was therefore an economic category with a vengeance: one where conflict with other classes was ultimately inevitable, because of the fetters that capitalism placed on man's freedom to develop his faculties to the utmost extent. Nevertheless, merely to categorise people into a particular class did not necessarily mean that they were aware of their exploitation by capitalists. Arrival at this feeling of solidarity with other workers is termed 'class-consciousness'.

By the nineteenth century the language of class was ubiquitous, although people tended to identify an upper or landed, a middle and a lower or working class, rather than Marx's two classes of capitalists and proletariat. Before the middle of the eighteenth century, however, the word class was hardly used. Position in society was denoted by reference to a person's rank, which expressed much finer gradations and was as much an indicator of status as of economic position. Thus Gregory King, who drew up an estimate of England's population in 1688, divided it into twenty-six ranks, from 'Temporal Lords' through the 'Better Sort of Freeholders' down to 'Vagrants'. This lack of emphasis on links between people in a similar economic position was partly because economic and social solidarity was often between people of different rank – that is, it was vertical rather than horizontal. Patronage – that is the distribution by the powerful of favours such as government contracts or jobs – led to such a vertical bond, between patrons and potential beneficiaries. It can be seen as a modification of the family or clan linking mentioned earlier, family connection often being one of the claims to patronage. Lower down the social scale, the rural poor, if in a village owned by a reasonably generous landlord, might identify their interests with his and his family's. Other manual workers possessed horizontal solidarity, but in the form of solidarity between members of a community rather than a class solidarity. Community solidarity found expression in riots, over issues as diverse as Catholics, bread prices, or wages, mingling in the latter case with strikes. There was little awareness of a wider 'class' of working people and, so far as manual workers did feel moral affiliations beyond the bounds of community, it was with other free-born Englishmen against politically-oppressed, poverty-stricken, wooden shoe-wearing unfortunates such as the French, or superstitious subverters of the Constitution, as Catholics were regarded.

The language of class came into increasing use from the mid-eighteenth century. Its origins seem to have lain in growing urbanisation, which was producing larger and more visible groups of business and professional people who could not be easily fitted into the old categories and whom it was convenient to call 'middle class'.

At first, the language of class was used descriptively, without any hint that its use implied economic solidarity. By the early nineteenth century, however, class was an important issue. Business and professional people felt that they had common interests, for instance in political reform to enhance their voice in Parliament, or in reform of the Corn Laws to lower food prices and stimulate trade. Among manual workers, some stirrings of a working-class consciousness had been awakened by eighteenth-century radicals, and was stimulated further by the French Revolution. The growth of large urban areas and cheaper and more easily distributed newspapers converted community solidarity into class solidarity, at least among some groups of workers in areas like London and Lancashire.

Class solidarity or class consciousness was defined earlier as a consciousness of solidarity with those in a similar economic position. In fact, among both middle and working classes, class consciousness also had other implications, in that demand for a political voice, independent of any economic claims, was strong. Where there were economic claims by the working class, they were not so much claims against capitalists as against the owners of landed property, for exploiting the fruits of labour in rent, and the holders of government debt and government offices, whose demands were thought to lie behind the high levels of taxation. These working-class claims were not so different from those of the middle class, and this is not really surprising because many of the 'working-class' leaders, particularly in London, were artisans or small tradesmen who possessed skill, and sometimes property, and were themselves on the boundaries of the middle class. A classic example of this was Francis Place, a retired master tailor and one of the leaders of moderate radicalism in the 1820s and 1830s.

This pattern was reflected in Chartism, the apotheosis of the working-class movement in the first half of the century. Although some Chartists were hostile to capitalism, in most cases their demands stemmed from the preoccupations of traditional radicalism. It seems, therefore, that urbanisation and the factory system, in spite of the strains that they imposed on people's lives, were not a source of class conflict along Marxist lines, except perhaps in a few areas. Indeed, as prosperity increased from the 1840s, the opposite occurred and some wealthier factory owners successfully recreated the paternalistic atmosphere of the eighteenth-century village, by rewarding their workers with reading rooms and days off to celebrate the birth of an heir to the family.

The failure of the British working class to develop class-consciousness along Marxist lines after the mid-century puzzled Marx and his collaborator Friedrich Engels, since they had wrongly interpreted Chartism as a great anti-capitalist movement. Later in the century, Engels observed that British workers had become divided into a privileged 'aristocracy among the working class' of trade unionists and an unprivileged remainder. The idea was taken up by Lenin who suggested that this segmentation had sapped the strength of the working-class movement. Subsequently, historians have spent a great deal of time trying to identify the exact membership of this 'labour aristocracy', although there is general agreement that it was drawn from skilled workers. Since recent interpretations of the earlier part of the century suggest that capitalism was never the enemy identified by most workers, the decline from the mid-century of working-class activity directed at fundamental political and social reform can be explained quite easily, without suggesting that there developed a clearly identifiable group of labour aristocrats with interests different to those of other workers. It is hard to support this idea, because while skilled workers did enjoy much more favourable conditions than unskilled, there were many intermediate groups, such as miners, railwaymen and textile workers, who cut across any neat division between skilled and unskilled.

It is easier to explain the decline of working-class activity by pointing to the amelioration of the grievances which had been expressed by the Chartists and earlier radicals. On the one hand, those bastions of landed wealth, the Corn Laws, were abandoned, while government spending and hence taxation declined steadily as a proportion of national income. On the other hand, working-class leaders were incorporated into political liberalism which continued to criticise landed wealth and privilege, and also stood for low taxation. Other factors, such as growing prosperity and factory paternalism, also contributed to social stabilisation.

The lack of class-consciousness in a Marxist sense raises the question of how far there were classes in the later nineteenth century. In economic terms, there clearly was still a fundamental split between those possessing large amounts of physical capital and those possessing hardly any, namely most manual workers. If, however, we extend the idea of human capital to include skill as well as education, then there was a large grey area between classes. The fruitfulness of regarding human and physical capital as synonymous is illustrated by considering skilled workers who often saved money to purchase a small shop or house property for their retirement. At any one time, only a fairly small proportion of skilled workers, the older ones, would have much physical capital; but a much larger number would have the potential to save, as their earnings were usually 50–80 per cent higher than those of unskilled workers. This potential to acquire property raises the question of how easy it was to pass from one group in society to another.

There is a lack of historical research on social mobility, but one thing which clearly emerges is that there were barriers between groups in the working class as well as between classes. This arose because of segmentation, both occcupational and geographic, of the labour market. Recruitment to skilled work, if by apprenticeship, took place at fourteen or fifteen, and apprentices had lower wages than other young workers. This meant that those in the right place, that is industrial towns, and those with reasonable family incomes, that is skilled workers, were more likely to get their sons apprenticed. It was therefore difficult for poorer or rural workers to take a step up the ladder of skill. By contrast, skilled workers could afford to keep their children at school longer, giving them the additional chance of getting jobs in the growing middle-class occupations of clerical work and, for girls, teaching. This factor, together with the ability of skilled workers to purchase property and the existence of labour-market segmentation, reduces the degree to which the economic position of different groups of manual workers could be described as similar.

On the other hand, there were influences which mitigated the effect of labour-market segmentation. Less skilled workers could gain promotion in many jobs, for instance railway work, while evidence from Rochdale on marriage patterns suggests that there was little segregation between skilled and unskilled families. This may partly reflect the influence of status. Working people achieved status, in the eyes of themselves and others, by 'respectable' behaviour, which ranged from the regular washing of curtains to the avoidance by women of quarrelling in the street and by men of swearing in the home, and was something which cut across divisions of skill. Oral evidence from two other towns in the North West, Preston and Lancaster, also suggests that by the early 1900s neither skill nor the achievement of respectability lessened the conviction among manual workers' families that they were 'working class'; although this conviction was not held in a Marxist class-conscious sense but as part of a fatalistic acceptance of their position in society.

There is, therefore, contradictory evidence as to how far working people actually formed a rigidly segregated class and how far they could experience upward social mobility or, alternatively, remain in segmented sub-classes. Although the fatalistic view of class position as fixed was undoubtedly a realistic estimation of many people's chances in life, one must remember that much can happen in a lifetime and many children born into working-class families in the 1900s would eventually become middle class by one route or another. The same was probably less true of earlier periods, in spite of the potential some workers had to acquire property, because the overall proportion of manual workers was not shrinking as it has done in this century. The predominant form of social mobility in the nineteenth century was rather the shift from rural to urban work.

Looking at British society in the late nineteenth century, one has the clear impresssion that there were groups, albeit not totally homogeneous ones, in a similar economic position and, hence, there were classes in a sociological sense. The existence of class-consciousness in this sense, however, is more questionable. Middle-class groups who early in the century had been conscious of their economic position *vis-à-vis* the landed interest now became less so as the latter's importance diminished. Working-class feelings of economic solidarity often lay with their employers, either as part of a naked calculation that this was in their interests or because of deference, that is respect for what was believed to be the superior judgement of employers. Deference was often found among workers who experienced the sort of paternalistic behaviour described earlier. Where there was horizontal solidarity among workers on economic issues, it was most likely to apply to small groups of workers in the same occupation who were affiliated in unions. These form the subject of the next chapter.

The language of class, of course, was universal as a self-description by all groups in society. Its use, however, was in sociological terms much more a status description, with even the term 'working class' carrying to those who applied it to themselves complex connotations of respectability, independence and not aping those in other classes. In the later nineteenth century, most people's moral affiliations outside their family were shaped by status, politics and religion, with a diffuse patriotism in the background, and not by class as sociologists use the word.

CHAPTER TWENTY-TWO
Employers and unions

Much historical writing about trade unions has been bedevilled by a tendency to see their history as a long march of progress towards the sort of trade unionism we have today. The title of a book of the 1950s about unions, *Magnificent Journey*, sums up this attitude. To look at unions from this point of view is to distort their history. Like every other institution, they responded to contemporary ideas and economic and social pressures, and made their own contribution to these things. Their history was no more a predetermined journey than was the history of any other institution.

Outside a few large towns, trade unions were not important in the eighteenth century. Paternalism was a strong influence in the countryside and brought some real benefits. Farmers and landowners kept labourers on over winter when work was scarce; allotments were granted and charities supported. The motive for paternalism was often altruism, and this may have strengthened as the influence of Evangelicalism strengthened in the early nineteenth century. Frequently, however, the *quid pro quo* for the generosity of the paternalist was that the beneficiaries should show deference towards him and his family. This was easy enough to extract in 'closed' villages, where the landowner owned most of the houses and in which the villagers were bound to him by a combination of genuine loyalty, gratitude, and fear of being evicted. Deference was less easily obtained in 'open' villages, in which land ownership was scattered among numerous owners and there was no-one to keep a watching eye on behaviour. Villagers in such settlements were less likely to be the recipients of charity and more likely to be the source of rural anti-landlord activities such as poaching.

Large industrial employers in the eighteenth century were even less likely to be paternalistic, since most did not own their workers' housing. A few such as the Darbys of Coalbrookdale might, for ethical reasons or the need to keep a labour force in an isolated area, build housing and other amenities for their workers. Most employers were anxious to reduce rather than increase their responsibilities, and this facilitated the growth of family employment in the early cotton mills, since the entire workforce could be recruited and disciplined through the direct employment of the heads of the households. The similarities between this and sub-contracting, discussed in Chapter 20, are obvious. The anxiety to be free of responsibilities for workers' welfare was not the reflection of some new, more cash-orientated, ideology, however. On the contrary, the domestic system which preceded the factories was based on an impersonal cash relationship between merchants and workers.

Within the domestic system, this relationship had found expression in frequent antagonism between the two groups, resulting in rioting, machine-smashing and, occasionally, striking. West Country textile workers engaged in endemic machine-smashing, for instance of spinning jennies, in the eighteenth century. Best known are the Luddite riots in Yorkshire, Lancashire and the East Midlands from 1811–13, directed against new machinery and new techniques in the textile industries. Ned Ludd, the leader, was a mythical figure, as was Captain Swing of the agricultural labourers' Swing riots in the southern counties in 1830–1, directed against threshing machines. It is significant that Swing rioters seem to have been drawn more from open villages or those where less paternalistic relations obtained, implying that the rioters' only relationship with farmers and landowners was the wage they were paid.

In contrast to the community solidarity found among workers in domestic industry, the craft workshops which formed the other lynchpin of eighteenth-century British industry were cradles of vertical solidarity between employers and workers. The dominant economic idea of both parties was defence of the trade. This idea had originally found expression in guilds, organisations encompassing masters and workmen. From the seventeenth century, restrictive practices of guilds such as the prevention of unapprenticed individuals from setting up in a trade had come under attack from English common law, which saw these practices as restrictions on freedom; while from the outside, guilds in more commonplace trades were undermined by competition from industry in the countryside or unincorporated towns. Furthermore, the advantages of the division of labour meant that even in workshop trades, employers often withdrew from manual labour to take on an organising and selling role. In spite of this and the decline of guilds as formal organisations, the old relations between employers and workmen did not change too dramatically in luxury trades or those catering for an established local market. Eighteenth-century London trade unions such as hatters and cabinet-makers regulated hours of work and wage rates, and insisted on apprenticeship; so long as employers could be sure that their rivals were not undercutting these rates, they did not seriously object to unions.

In a modified form, it was the idea of defence of the trade, rather than the drama of machine-smashing, which formed the basis of trade unionism as it evolved in the nineteenth century. Defending the trade implied the existence of a firmly held concept of what the trade was, and a clear idea of the market and the competition. This was possible in old-fashioned luxury trades, but increasingly difficult in amorphous industries like engineering. Nevertheless, skilled workers still saw themselves as 'tradesmen', having mutual interests with those in the same occupation. In these circumstances, a common occupation remained the criterion for union formation (hence the phrase trade unions), but the aim of the unions became the protection and enhancement of the wages and conditions of particular occupational groupings, rather than of an entire industry. Exclusion of other workers from skilled work, thereby limiting the supply of labour, became the key to fulfilling this aim. Union policy therefore reinforced the existing segmentation of the labour market, the implications of which were spelled out in the previous chapter. Exclusion was most often enforced by limiting the numbers of apprentices, combined with controls over the tasks which unapprenticed workers were allowed to carry out. In the eighteenth century, unions in larger and more competitive trades such as London tailoring had already developed along these lines. By the early nineteenth century, they were joined by localised trade unions in the building trades, among turners, millwrights and patternmakers in engineering, and among other skilled groups. Although employers were frequently hostile to unions, this hostility was sporadic and lukewarm, because in most industries skilled workers were necessary and apprenticeship was a reasonably efficient method of training them.

As time went by, employers' and society's view of unions was tempered by the unions' increasing acceptance, within limits, of the ideas of *laissez-faire* economics. By the later nineteenth century, union leaders portrayed themselves as engaged in the commercial activity of selling their labour at the best possible price, just like any businessman selling a commodity. This portrayal glossed over their attempts to restrict the supply of this commodity; but it meant that leaders and members were quite genuinely non-antagonistic to capitalism. They might, of course, be antagonistic to individual employers, since stealing a commercial advantage over an employer was to do no more than one businessman would do to another.

Although protection of groups of workers bound together in trade unions, and protection of the trade as a whole, seem to be different ideas, they are both concerned with the furtherance of the economic conditions of one small group in society against other groups. Robert Currie has suggested that this pattern of behaviour reflected the way people in Britain thought about their relationship with other people and with society. Relationships were essentially contractual, and there was no concept of the over-riding importance of some superior collectivity, such as the state. Unions likewise were not regarded as collective organisations superior to the individual, but merely as an effective means of promoting the individual's economic interests. Hence unions were not an expression of collectivism, but of individualism.

The policies of most employers also reflected this individualism. Although the idea of paternalism, which could be seen as opposed to individualism, was taken up by some large employers who valued it as a means of creating a contented labour force, it was never of overwhelming significance. The attitude of many employers was summed up instead by a factory owner's reply to the Factory Enquiry Commission of 1833: 'There is no control or superintendence exercised over [the workers] when out of the mills: they are respectable, and left to arrange their families and habits of life in the same manner as all other classes who do not work in factories.' Employers who were not concerned with their employees' welfare could hardly express moral indignation at the idea of unions, and although some employers resented the 'interference' implied by union rules on apprenticeship, others put up with unions much of the time, with occasional expressions of frustration. In the 1850s, both engineering and building employers tried to get their workers to sign the 'document', a promise not to join unions. In spite of bitter strikes, unionism in these industries was not significantly affected in the long term. As time went by, employers began to value union officials as sensible men who prevented the workforce acting rashly: a management textbook of 1896 advised that if the men should strike 'under some sudden impulse', the manager should immediately contact the union, as the author (the manager of an engineering works) had 'universally found the heads of societies or unions to be men of good sense, and amenable to reason and businesslike arguments'. By the end of the century, unions had become accepted as part of the scheme of things in major British industries such as engineering, cotton, mining, shipbuilding and footwear.

Underpinning the growing acceptance of unions was the attitude of the state and the law. Governments in the early nineteenth century were torn between their dislike of combinations of workers as flouting *laissez-faire* principles and also because they might pose a political threat, and their need to demonstrate acceptance of the equality of all before the law. The belief by most people in England, rich and poor, that they were fortunate to be English depended partly on the maintenance of this equality, or at least on not violating it too blatantly. Destroy that belief, and social order might be even worse disrupted than by combinations of workmen. Thus the Combination Act of 1799, which allowed prosecutions against unions and was sparked off by the French Revolution and the fears it brought of sinister conspiracies, was modified in 1800 by another Act allowing prosecutions against combinations of masters. In practice, neither was much used. The Combination Acts were repealed in 1824, and another Act in 1825, strongly supported by government ministers, kept unions within the law, although restricting their activities somewhat. Governmental attitudes were most clearly revealed in the case of the 'Tolpuddle Martyrs' of 1834. Six farm labourers from Tolpuddle in Dorset were prosecuted, not for joining a union, which was of course legal, but for swearing an illegal oath. They received seven years' transportation to Australia; but the government, having supported the case initially, took fright at the strong opposition to the sentences among all groups in society and granted the men a free pardon in 1836. Governments, along with most of the upper and middle classes, did not like unions much; but the rules of fair play meant that they had to put up with them. By the 1870s, calls for further reform, orchestrated by the Trades Union Congress, founded in 1868 as a pressure group, had increased. A series of Acts were passed, notably in 1875 the Conspiracy and Protection of Property Act, which sharply reduced the opportunities of prosecuting trade unionists for offences like obstruction and, hence, made peaceful picketing legal; and the Employers and Workmen Act, which ended the unfairness by which breach of employment contract was a criminal offence for workers but a civil offence for employers. One feature of these Acts was the lack of serious opposition to them:

equality of employers and workers before the law was now accepted.

Although formal membership of unions remained small throughout the nineteenth century, union activity touched many workers at some time or another. This might be through temporary membership, for instance of the Grand National Consolidated Trade Union (GNCTU) of 1834, to which the Tolpuddle Martyrs belonged. The GNCTU predictably failed, since its attempt to protect all workers was far too big an idea for those concerned with protection of their trade to understand; but many other unions waxed and waned, drawing in members at times of boom. Many workers experienced elements of unionism, such as joining in strikes and subscribing to strike funds, without formally belonging to unions. Nevertheless, vast numbers of workers, including many in agriculture, most in the service industries, and the great majority of women, were untouched by unionism throughout the nineteenth century.

In the mid-nineteenth century, unions were locally-based organisations; even in those with a central office, such as the Amalgamated Society of Engineers founded in 1851, the local branches set wage rates which differed widely from one part of the country to another. Wages were not negotiated with employers but instead relied on unilateral regulation, in which the stronger side laid down wages which the other could take or leave. As unions grew more widely accepted, however, they began to engage in collective bargaining with employers. This was supplemented in some industries by Conciliation and Arbitration Boards, which included neutral parties to help settle disputes, and thus represented the growing acceptance of unions within society. One of the most famous of these was the Nottingham Hosiery Board of 1860, in the area where only fifty years earlier Luddism had prevailed. The industrialisation of whole regions stimulated the employers to form federations for bargaining purposes, such as the Employers Federation of Shipbuilding and Engineering Trades. This further widened the scope of collective bargaining, enhanced the status of union officials, and encouraged some centralisation of union policy-making.

The beginnings in 1889 of so-called New Unionism, organising less skilled workers in industries like the docks and gas-making, seemed to represent a shift away from the cautious market-based bargaining of the older unions. At first the new unions emphasised aggressive strike action, together with state intervention in favour of measures like the eight-hour day. The shift was more apparent than real. The older unions were aggressive if necessary, as in the refusal of engineering workers in London and Lancashire to work overtime, which led to a three-month lockout in 1852, and the five-month strike in the cotton industry in 1892–3. Where possible, however, they sensibly preferred to obtain their ends peacefully. And while most unions had pressed for the 1870s reforms in order to keep the law out of industrial relations, some workers in the past had called for state intervention when they were not strong enough to take on employers. Most notable was the pressure for the Factory Acts, discussed in Chapter 23. The new unions did not represent a radical breach, therefore. Their own policy was essentially as sectional as that of the old unions, beneath their veneer of socialism. Illustrative of this was the call made by the dockers' leaders for a pre-entry closed shop, that is the limitation of employment to those holding union cards. The similarities with the skilled unions' attempts at apprentice limitation are clear enough.

Table 22.1 Trade union membership

	Metals engineering, shipbuilding	Mining and quarrying	Textiles	Total	Total as % of male work-force paid	Total as % of total work-force
1850	n.a.	n.a.	n.a.	c.250,000	4	3
1888	190,000	150,000	120,000	c.750,000	8	5
1913	550,000	920,000	520,000	c.4.1m	32	22

(*Sources:* Numbers in trade unions – Hunt, *British Labour History*; numbers in workforce – Mitchell and Deane)

The 1890s saw moves towards an alignment of old and new unions. The old unions saw threats to their freedom to picket from court decisions, while union activists were turning towards socialism. The year 1900 saw the formation, with support from some unions, of the Labour Representation Committee (LRC), intended to secure greater representation for labour in Parliament. Union suppport for this was increased by the Taff Vale decision of 1901, which secured damages for the Taff Vale Railway Company against the Amalgamated Society of Railway Servants for picketing. Previously it had been thought that unions could not be sued; now the tacit withdrawal of the law from industrial relations seemed to be under further threat. This threat was removed when the Liberal government of 1906 gave the unions complete immunity from damages. The LRC continued under its new name of the Labour Party but, with their main aim achieved, the unions remained wary of political involvement. The strike wave of 1910–14 and the rapid increase in union membership, particularly in mining and among unskilled workers, had practically nothing to do with politics. They were related rather to the stagnation of money wages before 1910, in the face of rising prices; and the spread of collective bargaining over larger areas, so that larger numbers of workers became drawn into any one dispute. The Miners Federation of Great Britain, for instance, had by 1908 united all the old district unions of the miners. Almost a million men were involved in the coal strike of 1912.

Historians, who have written numerous tomes about trade unions, have very rarely attempted to estimate their actual effects on workers' pockets. At first sight, it seems clear that unions had only a peripheral effect on the great rise in real wages which gathered pace after 1850, because most workers were not union members but still shared in the rise. Simple economic theory predicts this outcome. As productivity increased in an industry, employers' profit per worker, at the old wage rates, increased; the possibility of increased profit tempted capitalists to invest more and hence increased the demand for labour; this enhanced demand led to increased wages. This process can be generalised to explain the rise in wages throughout most of the economy.

Nevertheless, unions may have had some important effects. One was deleterious, at least to unskilled workers: this was the skilled unions' support for the segmentation of the labour market, which may have increased differentials between skilled and unskilled, and certainly made it that much more difficult for unskilled workers to get better jobs, either for themselves or for their children. On the positive side, unions may have accelerated wage rises which would have eventually come about through the pressure of demand for labour. The skilled unions watched the industrial scene carefully, and were quick to press demands when they saw an upturn in trade. In 1910–14, the growth of unskilled workers' unions may have had the same effect on these workers' wages, which had tended to change very infrequently in the past.

Potentially more significant than these effects, but very hard to quantify, is the possibility that, by pushing for rises above the rate of productivity growth and resisting wage reductions in spite of falling prices, unions forced employers to become more efficient in order to maintain profit margins. In an age when long-term price levels did not change much, employers could not simply pass on wage rises by increasing prices, a fact which strengthens the likelihood that there may have been an effect of this nature. If this was the case, then unions contributed to the rise in productivity throughout the economy and thus did help to stimulate the long-term gains in real wages, as well as achieving small temporary advantages.

CHAPTER TWENTY-THREE

From laissez-faire *to collectivism? Government economic and social policy*

'It was the age of *laissez-faire*', said the Liberal *Yellow Book* of 1928 when describing the nineteenth century. Meaning 'let be', or leave alone, the phrase *laissez-faire* implies that government policy towards social and economic affairs was dictated by an ideology, albeit a negative one, that intervention was likely to be harmful.

It is certainly easy to find influences which led contemporaries towards a belief that *laissez-faire* was the right attitude to adopt towards the economy. The ruling intellectual tradition in economics, given a powerful impetus in the late eighteenth century by Adam Smith and continued by economists such as David Ricardo and Nassau Senior, held that, in most activities, interference with the free market would be harmful, although important exceptions like education were admitted. An older strand of thought which led in the same direction was embodied in the common law, which disliked monopolies and other devices which restricted the freedom to carry on lawful activities. Legislators were open to influence from pressure groups, however, and so restrictions did exist on some types of activity through the medium of tariffs, the Navigation Acts, and other pieces of legislation. This was the situation in the early part of the century. Does the course of events bear out the description in the Liberal *Yellow Book*?

During the nineteenth century, government policy towards specific economic interests falls into two categories. In commercial policy, free-trade ideas became increasingly dominant. Tariff liberalisation was cautious in the 1820s, vigorous from the 1840s. The breakdown of protection was not just due to new ideas, however. There was the increasing influence of cotton manufacturers, who relied heavily on exports. They argued that duties on raw materials and food imports prevented foreign countries selling these to Britain and thus acquiring sterling to buy British goods. This argument turned Adam Smith's ideas upside down, since he had stressed that free trade would benefit the consumer. The 'Manchester School', as the free-trade manufacturers were called, believed that the producer would also gain. These arguments, vociferously expressed by the Anti-Corn Law League, must have had some influence, although the precise reasons behind Sir Robert Peel's support of Corn Law repeal in 1846 remain the subject of controversy. In general terms, one can say that Peel had come to believe that repeal was inevitable and, in that sense, was influenced by the ruling set of ideas; but he also believed that repeal's deleterious effect on agrarian incomes would be mitigated by high farming. The Irish potato famine of 1845–6 was more an excuse for repeal than an underlying reason.

Subsequent policy towards India illustrates the self-interest lurking behind much free-trade propaganda. Lancashire pressure helped to ensure that Indian import tariffs were low and that they discriminated in Britain's favour; while a small increase in the tariff in 1859 was bitterly resented and rescinded in 1862. More generally, although somewhat hypothetically, it has been argued that British interests at this time implicitly supported an 'imperialism of free trade': Britain's hegemony over world markets for industrial goods was such that her interests were best served by global free trade, which would ensure that foreign competitors could never build up manufacturing industries since British costs would always be lower. If this was believed, it was singularly unsuccessful, at least after 1870. Nevertheless, the self-interest among many advocates of free trade should be clearly recognised.

Once free trade was established, its theoretical hold became if anything even stronger, even though other aspects of *laissez-faire* came to be questioned; while the theoretical arguments for free trade were buttressed by cheap food, which benefited everybody except the dwindling band of landowners and farmers.

The government's attitude to other specific economic interests was shaped much more by pragmatic considerations, although *laissez-faire* ideas can be detected behind the repeal of various pieces of grandmotherly legislation such as the Usury Laws (in 1854) and the restrictions on joint-stock banking and limited liability. The two latter restrictions had embodied the idea that lack of direct responsibility for a business's activities and debts would encourage lax commercial morality. Abolishing them substituted the principle of 'caveat emptor'. The Bank Charter Act, on the other hand, did not embody any particular views for or against *laissez-faire*, but was concerned with the technicalities of banking regulation. In dealing with a major new commercial activity, the railways, the government took a different attitude again. Parliamentary sanction was not given to every proposed line, to prevent excessive and wasteful overbuilding. At the same time, the monopoly powers of those schemes which were sanctioned were subject to restrictions. The 1844 Railway Act laid down certain minimum conditions of service, established a safety inspectorate and, most strikingly, provided for government purchase after twenty-one years, although this was never carried out in the nineteenth century. Later Acts required railways in urban areas to provide cheap fares for workmen. Goods tariffs were left without regulation until 1893, when legislation set maximum rates.

Finally, the government did run some industries. These included government dockyards and arsenals, and the Post Office. The gradual extension of the latter's commercial activities, to include the telegraph and telephone service, was paralleled by the growing provision of services by municipalities. The provision of even basic amenities such as paving and lighting is of course an economic activity, which in the eighteenth century had usually been the responsibility of Improvement Commissioners and was paid for out of the local rates. The reform from the 1830s of the political and administrative structure of local government facilitated the centralisation of these activities within the new municipal corporations, which frequently added provision of gas and water and, towards the end of the century, electricity supply and tramways. The lack of a local-authority capital market, as well as *laissez-faire* ideology, hampered municipal trading up to the 1840s. Water-supply provision increased rapidly after that, with Manchester, Leeds and Glasgow all assuming control of their water supply in the 1850s. Efficient water-supply provision provided important beneficial externalities, that is benefits which accrued beyond the immediate consumer. Health benefits were one such, but improved fire-fighting capabilities may have been equally in people's minds, while the whole local economy gained from the provision of greatly improved industrial water supplies for processes like chemicals and paper making. Municipalities therefore engaged in water supply partly at the instigation of large manufacturers, and it seems likely that municipal enterprise in other directions was spurred by the realisation that other services also provided external benefits. In Birmingham, for instance, the industrialist Joseph Chamberlain promoted programmes of slum clearance and street improvement as well as municipal trading. 'Gas and water socialism', as it came to be called, was sponsored by unlikely socialists.

Municipal provision of services can be categorised as both 'economic' and 'social'. The growth of intervention in broadly social areas by central government has been the subject of an explanatory model put forward by Oliver MacDonagh. According to this model, such intervention was limited in the early nineteenth century, not so much for ideological reasons but because it did not occur to governments that they should intervene in broad issues of social policy – that is, health, housing, conditions of work and so on. In a largely rural society, such things, however unsatisfactory, were hardly in the limelight. As urbanisation and factory industry developed, they generated more visible evils. Legislation followed, usually put forward by pressure groups rather than by the government itself, and this legislation might involve the creation of an inspectorate. The inspectors themselves began to develop a professional ethos and quickly discovered faults in the legislation which had been watered down to mollify those who opposed it. The inspectors would then press for loopholes to be closed, and the legislation would become more effective and wider ranging.

The actual process of change frequently bears out this model. A good example is provided by the Alkali Acts. In the process of manufacturing soda, fumes were given off which came down as dilute hydrochloric acid. Landowners and farmers in the affected areas, St Helens in Lancashire and the North East, objected to this, not very surprisingly, and formed a pressure group to obtain legislation. The manufacturers gained some remission over the original proposals, however, and the inspectors appointed to monitor the original Act of 1863 used the expert knowledge they gained to press for improvements, granted in 1874. The Alkali Acts were unusual in that property owners supported legislation, whereas frequently legislation was concerned with protecting the weak against the power of property. In most instances, however, there was some pressure-group support, although once a case was argued it was not difficult to obtain more general backing. Many contemporaries supported the sanctity of *laissez-faire* when contracts between free and equal agents were concerned, but also accepted that the weak should be protected. As Macaulay said when discussing the Ten Hours Bill, which proposed to limit children's working hours, in 1846, 'it is not desirable that the State should interfere with the contracts of persons of ripe age and sound mind, touching matters purely commercial . . . but you would fall into error if you apply [that principle] to transactions which are not purely commercial . . . '. Macaulay's words highlight the fact that interventionist legislation was not just the result of interest-group pressure or organic change: there were ideological reasons for favouring intervention. The belief that the weak should be protected was itself partly a product of new ideas – of the more humane attitudes which had been developing since the eighteenth century, and of the rise of evangelicalism, which in the person of Lord Ashley (later the Earl of Shaftesbury) was an important prop to legislation over working conditions.

Rather different in kind was the set of ideas known as Utilitarianism or Benthamism, after its founder Jeremy Bentham. This cannot really be fitted into a neat framework in which *laissez-faire* is opposed to intervention. It is more constructive to see it as a set of ideas which, in aiming for 'the greatest happiness of the greatest number', might advocate more or less intervention. In practice, it urged less, in the case of the Poor Law, and more, in the case of public health. Benthamism also highlights another problem in deciding whether *laissez-faire* is a helpful term. Much of the debate at the time was about centralisation versus local autonomy. Benthamites, of whom the most active was Edwin Chadwick, disliked local autonomy because they considered it inefficient. Practically everyone else supported it: traditionalists because such welfare as existed in the past had always been locally controlled; rate-payers, who disliked spending local money at the dictate of central government; and the central government itself, who wanted to pay for as little as possible out of central government revenue.

One of the first major reforms owed as much, in its outcome, to this debate as it did to the principle of *laissez-faire*. This was the reform of the Poor Law, which dated from the sixteenth century and aimed to give a basic level of support to the destitute. It had come under increasing strain from population growth and from the economic problems of the rural south. One response to this in the later eighteenth century had been the supplementation of wages by the Poor Law authorities, according to the size of the family and price of bread. This was seized upon by *laissez-faire* economists as an example of the detrimental effects of intervention. According to Thomas Malthus, whose 'Essay on the Principle of Population' was published in 1798, population naturally tended to rise faster than the food supply. Poor relief of any kind only exacerbated this tendency, since it allowed those without work to have families. The practical effects of wage supplementation on population growth were, probably, zero. It was an effect rather than a cause. But that was not apparent to Malthus and his fellow economists, whose views became influential.

The eventual legislation, however, was much more of a compromise than economists like Malthus or Ricardo would have wished. The Poor Law Amendment Act of 1834 set up a central Poor Law Commisssion, and enforced the union of parishes to form large groupings, in order to aid efficiency. The intention behind the Act was for the unions to build workhouses where these did not exist, for all relief eventually to be restricted to the workhouse, and for conditions for able-bodied males to be made so unpleasant that they would be effectively deterred from the workhouse and forced to work. The practical effects of all this were different again. The intentions of the Act were never fully put into effect, since outdoor relief continued. On the other hand, the number of able-bodied males receiving relief did fall to very low levels and, to the extent that residence in the workhouse was seen by the working class as conferring a moral stigma, the Act was effective. Yet the new Poor Law also acted, paradoxically, as an agent for increasing intervention. The Poor Law medical service expanded greatly over the century. From the 1870s, Poor Law Guardians increasingly built specialised hospitals, such as fever hospitals and lunatic asylums, while from 1885 receipt of medical attention from the Poor Law did not lead to electoral disqualification, as receipt of other assistance did.

The growth of this service clearly fits in to the type of organic, step-by-step change outlined by MacDonagh, as does something which was much more beneficial to health – the growth of public health provision. This is a catch-all phrase which encompasses the provision of clean water, sewerage, the removal of 'nuisances', meaning anything from slaughterhouses to piles of manure in back yards, and, later on, housing improvement. Here it was not so much the influence of a professional inspectorate which provided expert support, but growing medical professionalisation, The effect of professionalisation in any occupation is to develop a set of imperatives which are specific to that profession and, not necessarily, market-orientated. In the mid-century, the improvement of public health was the imperative for influential medical men, such as Dr John Snow and Dr Thomas Southwood-Smith. The weakness of unsupported ideology in promoting change is illustrated by the fate of the Benthamite Central Board of Health, set up in 1848 with Chadwick as one of its Commissioners, and intended to promote public-health measures. Local opposition and Chadwick's abrasiveness helped to negate its activities, and it was abolished in 1858. Change came more because of the combined influence of doctors and businessmen, who were motivated by local pride and, more hard-headedly, wanted to maximise external benefits. Local initiative, strengthened by the Public Health Act of 1872 which divided the country into sanitary districts, each of which had to have a Medical Officer of Health and an Inspector of Nuisances, gradually led to the building of effective sewers and a general clean-up of urban areas. Progress was slow, however. Joseph Bazalgette's system in London, an underground wonder of the world finished in the early 1860s, was exceptional in its completeness and because it discharged at the mouth of the Thames, well away from populated areas. Urban sewerage systems which fulfilled these conditions were not universal until the turn of the century.

In spite of a spate of national legislation in the 1870s, the provision of housing illustrates the limits of intervention before 1914. There was little slum clearance outside a few large cities. The actual provision of houses by local authorities, although legally sanctioned from 1890, was negligible in quantity before 1914. Most significant were by-laws, frequent from the 1870s, which enforced wider streets and higher building standards – although to what extent improvement might have taken place without legislation is an unanswered question.

Another field of legislative activity was working conditions. The genesis of the early legislation again illustrates the disparate forces behind reform. The limitation of working hours in factories, the initial target of reformers, was opposed by many factory owners and by most economists, but supported by a mixture of evangelicals such as Ashley, Tory paternalists such as Richard Oastler, and some large factory owners such as John Hornby of Blackburn, as well as by factory workers. Many people such as Macaulay, cited above, did not see such reform of working hours for women and children as antithetical to the general principles of *laissez-faire*, and also supported it. Once the first significant Act was passed, in 1833, the growing weight of the professional factory inspectorate was put behind further reform, and the decisive Act of 1847, the Ten Hours Act, limited the hours of women and children to ten. From then on, there was further legislation in the same vein. In 1867, for instance, hours limitation was extended to factories in many industries outside cotton and to workshops.

Late nineteenth-century Britain, with government or local government intervention operating in so many areas, could be described as a collectivist or at least quasi-collectivist state. Whether or not this is an accurate description depends partly on definitions of collectivism. If it is taken in the Continental sense, to mean that the state is morally superior to the individual, few contemporaries would have accepted it as applicable to Britain. If it is taken in a more limited sense, as meaning that intervention would be beneficial in certain circumstances, then most educated late Victorians would have agreed. Nevertheless, most of them would have excluded a wide range of possible activities.

Among the exclusions were, as has been seen, large-scale intervention in the economic sphere. In the social sphere, provision by the Poor Law of health care and unemployment relief were still regarded as safety net services. It was much better that private citizens should provide for themselves. The extent of private provision was considerable: it is estimated that by the end of the nineteenth century, 80 per cent of adult males had some sick benefit coverage through friendly societies and trade unions. This was supplemented by the voluntary hospitals, which relied largely on charitable support. The continued reliance on non-collectivist solutions is illustrated by the more general importance of charity in the social framework. This ranged from long-established almshouses, to *ad-hoc* relief measures such as the Mansion House Fund set up for the London unemployed in the hard winter of 1886, to the Charity Organisation Society, which distributed relief on a case-by-case basis. Charity provision was frequently moralistic and judgemental, the relief provided was usually scanty, and large sums were no doubt diverted into the pockets of the paid employees of institutions like hospitals and almshouses. Nevertheless, it must have had some redistributive impact – which, as far as the author knows, has never been measured.

The limits of collectivism in the late nineteenth century are outlined above. Nevertheless, the scope of acceptable state intervention had greatly increased by the 1870s, and continued to increase. Education became compulsory for all in 1880, although public provision for full-time education beyond the age of fourteen remained very limited before the First World War. Old-age pensions were seriously discussed in the 1890s, although financial stringency prevented their introduction until 1909. These two changes cannot be easily fitted into a particular set of ideas, but other changes towards the end of the century clearly received an impetus from developments in thought. Unemployment and poverty among the able-bodied came to be seen by some thinkers not as the result of individual moral defects, the idea which underlay the Charity Organisation Society approach, but as the result of systemic collective influences which could only be dealt with by collective means.

In the 1880s the problem was identified as the pernicious nature of city life, which led to physical, and in the more extreme views moral, deterioration. At first the influence of this idea was limited, but by the 1900s it provided one impetus behind measures such as provision for local authorities to subsidise school meals (1906) and medical inspection of schoolchildren (1907), both designed to improve the physique of the future labour force. Most important, it fuelled support for compulsory health insurance. This was realised in 1911, using the existing friendly society mechanism and giving an element of state subsidy. By the 1900s, the problems thought susceptible to a collective solution included the defective workings of the labour market and unemployment due to business cycles. So, along with health insurance, compulsory unemployment insurance was established in 1911 for a limited range of occupations which were liable to cyclical unemployment. It was preceded in 1910 by labour exchanges, to improve information and mobility in the labour market, and by the Trade Boards Act of 1909, which introduced compulsory wage boards into certain low-wage occupations, the so-called sweated trades. This was an interference in wage setting which went beyond any previous 'conditions of work' legislation, and seems to have been passed because of concern over physical and moral deterioration due to overwork.

While changing perceptions of social problems influenced the Liberal welfare reforms, as the legislation of the 1900s is called because of its sponsorship by Liberal governments, there were other influences. The MacDonagh model would suggest that intervention carried its own impetus. As we have seen, there is plenty to support this in the mid-century, and a change which was evident by the 1870s made it likely to continue. This was the growth of government-initiated legislation, evident not just in public health and welfare, but also in fields such as safety legislation on the railways and in the mines. Behind this, two broad trends can be discerned. First, the growth of a professional civil service, with its own ethos and priorities. Second, the extension of the franchise which increased the pay-off, in terms of votes, of redistributive legislation. The second explanation should not be carried too far, however. All the evidence suggests that, with the exception of pensions, the Liberal welfare reforms were not especially popular among the working class.

The relative ease with which much interventionist legislation was accepted can also be explained partly by the fact that it was paid for by rising national income, as shown in Table 23.1, and did not until the 1900s lead to any increase in tax rates. In fact the opposite occurred at first, for in 1830 much of the government's revenues had gone on servicing the national debt but, as national income grew, the relative burden of debt service became much less onerous. The Boer War initiated a break in trend. Expenditure grew sharply, and then fell back, but to a much higher level than before. Local-authority spending also increased more rapidly. One result of this was that fiscal policy changed significantly for only the second time since the Napoleonic Wars. The first had been the reintroduction of income tax on the better-off, at the level of 7*d* in the pound, in 1842. This made up for the drop on customs revenues following tariff reform. At one time in the 1870s, income tax dropped to 2*d* in the pound, but in 1901 it rose to 1*s* and never fell below that level. Furthermore, surtax on larger incomes was introduced in 1911.

Table 23.1 Government income and expenditure 1830–1913

	Central govt revenue from taxation (1) (U.K.)	*Local govt income from rates (2) (Great Britain)*	*Central govt expenditure on debt service*	*Columns 1 & 2 as % of UK gross national income*
1830	55.3	*	29.1	16†
1871	68.2	19.6‡	26.8	9
1899	117.9	42.6	23.6	9
1913	188.2	75.6	19.9	11

All figures in million pounds
* No reliable figures
† Column 1 used in calculation for 1830
‡ Scottish rates estimated for 1871
(*Sources:* Mitchell and Deane; Deane and Cole; Feinstein)

In spite of these increases, the redistributive effect of government spending was small, even in the 1900s. The poor had done badly from taxation in the early nineteenth century, when income had been redistributed from them to bondholders. Their gain later on was very moderate, and insignificant compared with the benefits from rising real wage levels. To be fair, government intervention probably had substantial benefits, but they were either directed towards specific groups or spread among most levels in society. The more extreme forms of exploitation, of labour and natural resources, were reduced by hours legislation and measures such as the Alkali Acts. Public health and education, the main targets of extra spending before the 1900s, benefited most groups in society, not just the poor.

The relatively low levels of government spending might seem to justify the phrase, 'the age of *laissez-faire*'. However, intervention could be carried out without heavy spending, as in the case of factory reform. There is other evidence to support the idea that the 1840s, the decade of factory reform, was the decade when intervention became respectable. Parliament began to oppose unbridled *laissez-faire* in industrial policy, by accepting that wasteful competition should be curbed and the resulting monopolies subject to restriction. This occurred with railways, while with gas and water undertakings, Parliament began to favour municipal ownership or, alternatively, controls on private company profits. So the triumph of *laissez-faire* in commercial policy coincided with the beginnings of more active intervention in domestic affairs. Perhaps G R Kitson-Clark was right to say that 'the conception of a 'period of *laissez-faire*' . . . is an encouragement to error'.

Prosperity and Problems: the Economy 1914–85

CHAPTER TWENTY-FOUR

Britain and the world economy

INTRODUCTION

In 1914, London was the financial capital of the world and Britain was still, by far, the world's largest trading nation. The so-called staple industries, coalmining, textiles and the metal industries, depended on exports for a large part of their prosperity. They were the industries whose workers enjoyed, on average, the highest level of wages. The advantages of Britain's central position in the world economy extended from the City of London and the workers in the staple industries to the upper and middle classes. As J M Keynes wrote, the inhabitant of London, by lifting his telephone and while sipping his morning tea in bed, could:

> order . . . the various products of the whole earth, in such quantity as he might see fit, and reasonably expect their early delivery on his doorstep . . . could adventure his wealth in the natural resources and new enterprises of any quarter of the world, and share without exertion or even trouble in their prospective fruits and advantages . . . could secure forthwith, if he wished it, cheap and comfortable means of transit to any country or climate without passport or other formality, could despatch his servant to the neighbouring office of a bank for such supply of the precious metal as might seem convenient, and could then proceed abroad to foreign quarters . . . .

The First World War ushered in, and helped to cause, a fundamental change in Britain's position in the world economy, that position which had helped to make possible the things which Keynes itemised. It was a change which was to affect coalminers and cotton-spinners, shipyard workers and steel-smelters, as well as the middle class sipping morning tea in their beds. After the First World War, Britain was never again to exert the same degree of influence on

221

the world economy. She was now far more vulnerable to economic pressures from the outside world. The chief theme of this chapter is the way these pressures impinged on the British economy.

1914–45

So wealthy was Britain in 1914 that the enormous expense of the First World War was borne with only relatively small sales of overseas assets. Inevitably exports fell off as production was directed to war material, but nevertheless in 1918 Britain still had substantial foreign investments. The country's apparent financial strength, however, was based on much less secure foundations than it had been previously.

One major problem was home-grown. The war had seen rapid increases in wages, and manufacturing costs were increased further by a sharp cut in working hours instituted in 1919. The effect of this on export prices was mitigated for a time by the decision in 1919 to allow the pound to float against the dollar, as the strain of war and post-war spending on Britain's balance of payments temporarily became acute. The pound's value declined, reducing the dollar price of exports. However, the intention was always to return the pound to the Gold Standard at roughly the old pre-war parity of £1 to $4.86, and while British manufacturing costs fell in the slump of 1921–2, they still remained relatively higher than USA costs, as compared with each country's position in 1914. When the return to the Gold Standard was achieved in 1925, British goods were priced at a relatively high level, in dollar terms, compared with before the war, while this overpricing was exacerbated by the undervaluation of the franc, which made French exports cheap. The exact effect on the competitiveness of British exports is uncertain, as in the case of certain goods, which sold on the basis of quality as much as price, some rise in the relative price level may not have mattered much. The overvaluation of the pound did have a severe effect on the coal industry, still a major exporter.

Exports suffered in other ways. Markets in Central and Eastern Europe were badly affected by the disorganised state of many countries' economies after the war, the widespread raising of tariffs, and the multiplication of tariff barriers which resulted from the break-up of the Austro-Hungarian Empire into a number of smaller countries. In the important Indian and Far Eastern markets for cotton goods, Indian and Japanese producers had made big inroads during the war, because of restrictions on British exports as manpower and shipping space was switched to the war effort. The continuing decline in the British share of the market after the war strongly suggests that loss of competitiveness in the face of low-wage competition would have occurred anyway at some stage and, perhaps, 1913 would have been the zenith of the Lancashire cotton trade even without the war. But almost certainly the decline would have been much slower without the artificial boost the war gave to producers in the East, especially the Japanese. Finally, these adverse influences on British exports, and on world trade generally, led to a slowdown in the demand for new ships once war losses had been made up. The combination of all these factors led to unemployment levels averaging over 8 per cent from 1921–29, with coal, cotton and the metal industries faring particularly badly (Table 25.1).

Serious though these problems were, an even graver one in the long term was the shift the First World War caused in the multilateral payments system. Britain's current account surplus, which before 1914 had financed a large slice of the deficits of less developed countries, was smaller in the 1920s because of the difficulties of exporting. The USA became the dominant creditor nation. Britain's foreign lending revived somewhat in the 1920s, but not at the levels of the past. Furthermore, this lending was not covered by Britain's current account surplus. Britain herself was borrowing, largely from lenders in the USA and France, the other main creditor nation.

A changing pattern of payments flows was not inevitably a problem for the world economy. It could simply reflect a situation in which one country's loss was another's gain. There were, however, two important side-effects of the changes which had taken place. The first was that a larger proportion of post-war borrowing consisted of so-called hot money – that is, money lent for short periods of time – which could in consequence be withdrawn rapidly. The second was that both the USA and France tended to accumulate gold, a trait exacerbated in France's case by internal policy which encouraged the holding of large amounts. Gold flowed from debtor nations, reducing their internal purchasing power; but the French and US monetary authorities did not allow an equivalent increase. There was, therefore, a tendency for world-wide purchasing power to decline.

Many historians consider one other factor to have contributed to instability. Raw material prices had continued their pre-war tendency to increase during the war, but fell rapidly from 1921 on. Primary producing countries such as Australia therefore constituted one important group running current account deficits, while farmers in all countries suffered from the low prices. The war was not a direct cause of this, since primary-product prices were likely to have fallen at some stage due to heavy pre-war investment in raw material production. Nor was this transition from price rise to price fall a new occurrence, since the Great Depression of the later nineteenth century had largely been a depression of primary-product prices. The decrease of prices in the 1920s would not necessarily have been a problem by itself, therefore, but it did weaken the financial position of many countries and make them more vulnerable to the world-wide depression which started in 1929.

The probable explanation for this depression was the simultaneous occurrence of internal problems in Germany and the USA, which the international economic system, weakened in the ways described above, could not accommodate. US lending overseas, a vital source of capital for many countries now that Britain's lending was diminished, had virtually dried up from 1928 as a result of high US interest rates and the attractions of financial speculation on Wall Street. As a result of this, debtor countries had to run down their gold holdings, with adverse effects on domestic money supply, or raise interest rates to retain foreign hot money. When a severe internal recession began in the USA in 1929, primary product prices and consequently primary producers' export earnings were further depressed, leading them to cut back on imports. In Germany, the capital market had been weakened by the war and its aftermath, and in 1929 its problems caused investment to be severely cut back. The US recession then hit German exports, reinforcing the contractionary effect in that country. The result was a rapid slide into world-wide depression.

As this excursion into world economic history suggests, Britain had little part in causing the world depression but, naturally, was seriously affected by it. Exports fell and so, consequently, did the current account surplus. In order to retain hot money, interest rates had to remain at the high levels established in the 1920s to support the value of the pound. By 1931, there was a current account deficit and unemployment had reached 15 per cent. Furthermore, nervousness in the world money markets was intense, partly as a result of financial crises on the Continent in the summer of 1931. The first major political impact of Britain's changed place in the world economy was now felt. The instability in the money markets and the current account deficit led to the removal of hot money from London; Britain was running out of reserves of gold and foreign currency, and had to turn to foreign bankers for a loan. Bankers were reluctant to lend unless the government's own financial deficit, which was held to be a force for inflation, was reduced. The Labour government split over the size of cuts to be made in government spending and was replaced by a National government in August 1931. Even this did not halt the selling of sterling, however, and in September 1931 Britain left the Gold Standard.

The crisis masked a significant change in many of the principles which had governed Britain's economic relationship with the outside world for the previous century. The pound, which was allowed to float (i.e. fluctuate in value against other currencies), at first fell rapidly and was then stabilised by the Bank of England. Tariffs, up to now limited in scope, were extended over a wide range of goods. Since other countries increasingly pursued similar policies, or even more restrictionist ones involving quotas or restrictions on convertibility, world trade could not revive, in spite of improvements in most countries' domestic economies from 1933 onwards. By 1937, exports contributed only 16 per cent to Britain's national income, compared with 32 per cent in 1914.

The direction of exports also changed, as restrictions increased in previously important export destinations such as Germany and Central Europe. Exporters turned increasingly to the Empire and, between 1935 and 1939, almost half Britain's exports went to Empire countries, compared with about a third in the five years before the First World War. This trend was aided by the institution of imperial preference in 1932, by which Britain gave tariff concessions to Empire countries, and received concessions in return. In practice, most concessions by the autonomous Empire countries, such as Canada and Australia, consisted of raising duties to non-Empire countries still further, and so the system had little positive impact on total trade levels. Feeble as it was, imperial preference illustrates a paradoxical fact about the inter-war period. The age of aggressive European imperialism had passed and, in retrospect, the British Empire in the inter-war years was, politically, a fragile entity. However, that was not how it seemed to many contemporaries, including manufacturers. To them the Empire was one of the few areas where British goods enjoyed a reasonable competitive position *vis-à-vis* the exports of other industrialised countries.

The decline in world trade was accompanied by a particularly rapid fall in Britain's earnings from invisibles such as shipping and banking, as trade volumes and prices fell. Earnings from overseas investments were also hit as dividends declined. Since it was these invisibles which had always covered the deficit on visible trade, the current account of the balance of payments remained fragile in spite of tariffs. The position worsened from 1936 as Britain's improving domestic economy attracted increased imports, and a substantial payments deficit again appeared. The difficult balance of payments situation was therefore one constraint on rearmament, which led to increased economic activity, thus increasing imports still further. By 1938, rearmament had to take precedence over all other considerations, and during the war there was a rapid run-down of Britain's foreign investments, which were compulsorily acquired by the government and sold to release foreign currency. Unlike the First World War, there was no initial current account surplus to cushion the cost of acquiring arms overseas, while the payments position was worsened by the inevitable decline in exports as resources were diverted to the war.

From 1941 the war was increasingly financed by lend-lease, which was technically the 'loan' of munitions, raw materials and so forth to maintain the war effort; the obligation to repay lend-lease debts (or return the munitions, which would have been even more difficult) was rescinded in 1945. Taking account of British contributions, such as the maintenance of American bases in Britain, the net American contribution by 1945 was around five billion pounds, with Canada contributing another one-and-a-half billion pounds. Another important source of finance for expenditure overseas were the sterling accounts of Egypt and India. From 1939 the pound had been made inconvertible, that is it could not be exchanged for other currencies without permission. For a country likely to be running a large current account deficit, this was an essential move as it made it possible to control the purchase of imports. Certain countries, however, including most Empire countries, remained within the so-called sterling area, within which sterling was convertible. These countries kept much of their reserves, denominated in sterling, in London. Thus Britain could accumulate paper debts and not use scarce foreign currency.

The international repercussions of the First World War and the world depression had had one other, more positive, effect on Britain. The fall in raw material prices swung the terms of trade in Britain's favour. By 1933 the price of grainstuffs relative to the general price level was just above half its 1914 level; other raw materials suffered similar falls. The price fall caused misery and unemployment in the primary producing countries, but benefited the British consumer.

1945–73

In spite of lend-lease, the financial strains of the Second World War left Britain with, in effect, zero net overseas financial assets (the exact figures are highly uncertain due to the lack of satisfactory wartime figures). Yet although she ended the war with none of her once massive overseas wealth, Britain's post-war economic growth was far more rapid and sustained than in the inter-war period. Much of this improvement can be put down to the changed conditions in the world economy. The impact of external economic affairs on Britain can be conveniently divided into two parts, the post-war recovery phase which is usually held to have ended by 1951, and the longer-term impact.

The critical problem in the short term was the lack of foreign currency for imports. Britain now lacked any cushion of earnings from investment overseas and, furthermore, was keeping up substantial overseas armed forces even after the war had ended. The shortage was primarily of dollars, reflecting the central position the USA was now to play in world economic affairs.

This centrality was reflected in the influence of American economic ideas, as well as by the post-war strength of the dollar. For a variety of reasons, policy-makers in the USA had come during the war to reject the traditional isolation of American foreign policy, which in economic affairs had expressed itself in high tariffs. The USA now became an apostle of the resurrection of free trade. To this was linked the American dislike of British imperialism, a dislike which had roots deep in American history, and in the context of trade expressed itself in hostility to imperial preference. The USA's position was, by and large, adopted at the international financial conference held at Bretton Woods in New Hampshire in 1944. Much of what was agreed there harked back to the old Gold Standard system, although gold itself was not now a necessary part of it. Discriminatory trade barriers, such as imperial preference, were frowned upon. Currencies were to be kept stable against each other, and to be made freely convertible. Finally, Bretton Woods set up two institutions, the International Monetary Fund (henceforth IMF) and the International Bank for Reconstruction and Development. The latter was to play little part in British affairs; the role of the IMF, as envisaged, was to help countries in temporary balance of payments difficulties by loaning them foreign currency, and also to supervise exchange-rate adjustments, which were sanctioned for countries with chronic payments problems. The IMF played little part in the early post-war years, but will enter the story later.

While Bretton Woods was of great long-term significance, the changing USA attitude which it symbolised was of greater importance in the short run. The post-war shortage of dollars, or the 'dollar gap', affected not just Britain but most of the world. Wartime destruction in many countries had left the Americans the suppliers of much of the world's raw materials and manufactured goods. The aim of the US was to induce European countries to increase their productive capacity, ease the dollar gap, and thus make it possible to introduce convertibility. To that end the USA lent Britain $3750 million in 1945, while Canada lent $1250 million, on condition that convertibility would be restored in 1947. Marshall Aid from the USA to Europe was instituted in 1947, when the Americans perceived slow economic recovery in Europe as laying the way open for an increase in Communist influence; Britain received about $3 billion by 1952. In 1949, as the dollar shortage showed no sign of easing, the IMF encouraged a series of European devaluations. The pound was devalued from £1 = $4.03, the level established in 1939, to £1 = $2.80.

The remarkable thing about these American efforts was their limited effect on British policy. The desperate post-war shortage of dollars of course constrained policy, as resources had to be diverted to exports and investment in export industries. Nevertheless, the British managed to construct the welfare state and nationalise numerous industries, hardly policies which could have appealed to the Americans, who still doled out Marshall Aid. In 1947, Britain did restore convertibility as the USA wished, but as there was a rush to convert sterling into dollars, it was suspended three weeks later. The 1949 devaluation, although not desired by the British, found a certain *post-hoc* justification in its durability, lasting as it did until 1967. Finally, the British maintained imperial (subsequently called Commonwealth) preferences, which the Americans disliked as a discriminatory trade practice.

World trade in the post-war period grew at unprecedented rates. Between 1950 and 1973, the combined exports of all the major industrialised countries grew at 8.5 per cent per year; that is, they doubled every nine years or so. The developments we have already traced played an important part in this. An important constraint had been eroded when the diversion of US productive capacity back to war materials at the time of the Korean War effectively ended the dollar shortage. This allowed the liberalisation of trade which had been signposted at Bretton Woods to make real progress. The 1950s saw the restoration of convertibility by many European countries, with Britain freeing current account transactions in 1958. Tariffs were slowly reduced under the aegis of an international body, the General Agreement on Tariffs and Trade, or GATT. While economists disagree over the proportion of world trade growth which can be attributed to tariff reductions, what is indisputable is the contrast with the inter-war period. There the trend throughout, and especially from 1930 on, was for increasing restriction. In the post-war years, the opposite was the case and, as we have seen, the changed attitude of the USA was a crucial factor in this. Even if the structure of the post-war international economic system was not the only or even the most important reason for trade growth, it deserves considerable credit for the avoidance of the kind of breakdown which occurred between the wars.

For the major underlying causes of trade growth, most economists look to the unprecedented growth of output in most major economies in this period. There are two basic explanations for this, which are not mutually exclusive. One points to the increasing growth of the supply of goods made possible by more rapid technical change, which in turn encouraged businessmen to invest heavily in order to take advantage of the new opportunities. The other explanation points to the existence of high and stable demand in most major economies, associated in particular with high levels of government spending. World trade grew even faster than world output as a result of the continuing growth of specialisation, aided of course by the progress of trade and payment liberalisation described above.

This rapid growth in world trade and output goes a long way to explaining the post-war prosperity of Britain, itself a major trading nation. There were, however, also problems which the increasingly liberalised world economy posed to this country.

In the post-war period, sterling had retained importance as a large-scale trading currency, or 'key currency', because of the existence of the sterling area. As currencies became convertible, the sterling area declined in importance, but the City of London's financial expertise reasserted itself so that sterling continued to be a 'key currency', with other countries finding it convenient to carry out transactions in sterling. What this meant in practice was that banks and companies world-wide held stocks of sterling to finance trade. If they lost confidence for some reason – for instance, if they thought that high inflation in Britain would jeopardise British exports by increasing prices to an excessive extent, thus raising the prospect of a sterling devaluation to maintain competitiveness – these institutions would run down their sterling holdings, a process which might in turn lead to a greater crisis of confidence and even heavier sales. A further, although lesser, threat was posed by the sterling area countries with large balances in London, who might be tempted to follow the same course. To maintain confidence in sterling in these circumstances, the British government could raise interest rates or institute fiscal policies, with the intention of reducing demand in the economy and hence reducing inflationary pressures. Crises in which sterling came under severe selling pressure occurred in 1947, 1949, 1951, 1955, 1957, 1961 and from 1966–7. Although the root of most sterling crises was the fear that exports would become uncompetitive and lead to current account deficits and ultimately devaluation, the fact was that there was no long-term deficit on the current account in this period. Over the sixteen years from 1952 to 1967, Britain had a total net current surplus of £400 million. The problem was that this translated into only a relatively small annual surplus, and in some years a deficit. This thin black line was to foreign holders of sterling the ultimate guarantee of Britain's ability to pay. Britain's defences against a loss of confidence by these holders were too weak. The only remedy apart from deflationary measures at home was to build up government or central bank holdings of foreign currencies. This was expensive because the interest payable was small, which probably accounts for Britain's persistent reluctance to follow this course of action. It is worth noting, however, that Britain's reserves have consistently been much lower than the average for Western industrial nations.

The IMF's intervention averted a crisis in 1966, but in the long term even the IMF could not hold back market forces, as the trend in the current account position was deteriorating. In 1967 a final sterling crisis resulted in devaluation to £1 = \$2.40, a level which, it was hoped, would guarantee a large enough current account surplus to restore confidence. The gradual breakdown of the sterling area as some countries converted their reserves of sterling to gold or dollars also reduced the potential threat to sterling posed by the existence of these reserves. Unfortunately, these changes coincided with growing instability in the world economy. The dollar was itself devalued in 1971, and the British current balance again worsened. In 1972 the pound was allowed to float. By 1973 most major world currencies were floating, a development which marked a partial breakdown of the Bretton Woods system. The commitment to freer trade did, however, remain.

While world trade grew rapidly, Britain's more modest trade growth rate meant that its share of world trade fell from the high level of the late 1940s, when Germany and Japan were still recovering from the war. The fall occurred even though Britain was well represented in growth industries. Immediately after the Second World War, Britain was a major supplier of most manufactured products, including cars and a wide variety of engineering goods, while coal and cotton were much less important than previously. There was, however, a heavy concentration on the old Empire markets, a legacy of the inter-war years. These markets were to prove less satisfactory for British exporters in the 1950s and 1960s, for a variety of reasons. As the general level of tariffs declined, the value of imperial (now Commonwealth) preferences to British exporters was eroded. At the same time, the process of decolonisation during the 1950s and 1960s reduced the advantages accruing to Britain as a colonial power, such as preferential government purchasing of British goods. In spite of these problems, many British firms remained heavily committed to Commonwealth markets, presumably because they were still relatively easier to penetrate than European ones. However, the share of trade with Europe did steadily increase, as shown in Table 24.1.

This trend was encouraged by Europe's own rapid growth rate, and by the two institutions which lowered intra-European tariffs. Britain was a founder member in 1959 of one of these, the European Free Trade Association (EFTA), which eliminated tariffs between the members, mainly the smaller European countries. In 1973, Britain left EFTA to join the European Economic Community (EEC). The EEC also has free trade between members, and with members of EFTA, and a common external tariff. The immense political excitement caused by joining the EEC has in many ways not yet manifested itself economically. Free trade within the EEC was available to Britain as a member of EFTA; measures such as harmonisation of product quality standards, which were meant to aid the creation of a large internal market to rival the USA, have proceeded slowly; the Regional Development and Social Funds, which should have benefited the poorer and more depressed countries such as Britain, have never had substantial funds allotted to them because of the burdens of the agricultural budget; and the Common Agricultural Policy itself has been a disaster from Britain's point of view, as is shown in Chapter 31.

In terms of commodity structure, the period was marked by a rising share of manufactures in the import total, reflecting a growth in

Table 24.1 UK composition and geographical pattern of exports and imports 1955–85; and share of world trade 1939–85 (percentages – rounded to nearest %)

	1937–8	1950	1955	1970	1985
Composition of imports:					
Food, drink, tobacco			36	23	11
Fuel			10	10	12
Raw materials and semi-manufactures*			48	43	31
Finished manufactures			5	23	44
Composition of exports:					
Fuel			5	3	21
Semi-manufactures*			30	26	20
Engineering products			36	44	34
Origin of imports:					
Western Europe			26	41	63
USA			11	13	12
Canada, Australia, N Zealand, S Africa			22	15	5
Japan			1	1	5
Destination of exports:					
Western Europe			29	46	58
USA			7	12	15
Canada, Australia, N Zealand, S Africa			25	14	5
Japan			1	2	1
Share of world exports of manufactures	21	25	20	11	9

* Products such as textiles, chemicals, metals
(*Sources:* Prest, A R 1970 *The UK Economy*; Artis)

import penetration of the home market for manufactured goods. Given the process of international specialisation, which was increasingly applied within manufacturing sectors, a rising import share is not in itself surprising and was paralleled in other industrial countries. The rate at which import penetration rose in Britain, however, was much faster than elsewhere. Between 1959–60 and 1972–3, for instance, the share of manufactured imports in national income grew at 6 per cent per year, compared with 3.5 per cent in Germany, both countries starting at similar levels of import penetration. Invisible earnings from insurance and banking were reasonably buoyant, but shipping no longer registered a substantial surplus. Furthermore, a large part of the trade surplus on invisibles was swallowed up by government expenditure abroad; almost two-thirds of this was military expenditure, and most of the rest economic aid.

The terms of trade between raw materials and manufactures may have been another factor promoting the beneficial economic climate of this period. The Second World War and subsequently the Korean War raised raw material prices sharply above the depressed inter-war levels. They then declined somewhat relative to the prices of manufactured goods, but not enough to seriously damage the purchasing power of the producers. The danger of sharp price falls had been demonstrated in the inter-war period; the danger of sharp price rises was to be demonstrated from 1973 onwards.

1973–85

The economic history of this period is dominated by the effects which flowed from the success of the major oil-exporting nations in raising the price of a barrel of oil from $2.46 in 1972 to $9.76 in 1974. They were able to do this by organising themselves as a cartel, the Organisation of Oil Exporting Countries (OPEC), whose effectiveness was aided by inflationary pressures which had been building up in the world economy for several years. The result was a sudden large transfer of income, away from the countries which bought the oil, and to the exporters, who at first had few means of spending the money and could only save it. This in turn temporarily reduced puchasing power and precipitated a recession: 1975 saw the first actual drop in output and trade in the Western world since 1945. The recession was short-lived, partly due to the successful recycling of surpluses from OPEC countries to finance the deficits of less developed countries.

The result of this recycling, however, was that when oil prices jumped a second time, from $12.70 a barrel in 1978 to $28.67 a barrel in 1980, the world economy was in a more precarious position than in 1973. Industrialised countries, faced with inflation and balance of payments difficulties, carried out deflationary policies, which hit exports from the less developed countries. In turn, the latter's balance of payments difficulties became so acute that bankers became reluctant to lend. The result was a severe and prolonged world recession. Fortunately, coordination between world financial institutions, aided by the IMF, was far better than in the inter-war period, and less developed countries, although severely affected, were not forced into the repudiation of debt or massive cuts in their ability to import, characteristic of the early 1930s.

Britain was not immune from these effects, as a major participant in world trade, and as a major oil importer in the 1970s and exporter in the 1980s. The much slower growth rate of world trade affected Britain adversely, while the oil price rise increased existing tendencies to internal inflation, and in 1973–6 also caused severe balance of payments problems which impinged on Britain's internal economic policies.

The initial effect of the price rise on the current account was to cause a massive deficit, since Britain was a large oil importer. At first, foreigners had been willing to finance the deficit in the expectation of eventual oil self-sufficiency from the North Sea, but by 1976 rising government expenditure and high inflation were sapping confidence and leading to sales of sterling. Since the pound was floating, the government did not have to worry about devaluation; but an excessive fall in sterling, by forcing up import prices, had inflationary implications, and the government had to turn to the IMF for a loan. Since the IMF believed that the government's financial deficit was a force for inflation and that it sucked in imports, it insisted that the government reverse its reflationary policy. The effect of the oil price rise in 1979–80 was very different. By this time, Britain was a substantial producer of oil and soon to become a net exporter. The current account was expected to benefit from an oil price rise, sterling was therefore popular with investors, and the value of the pound rose sharply. Even leaving aside the short-term influences, the effect of an additional stream of foreign earnings from oil exports would be to push up the long-term value of the pound. Oil was not the only reason for this, though: agricultural subsidy was another important long-term influence. By pushing up agricultural production in Britain, this reduced food imports, as shown in Table 24.1. Reducing the amount of foreign currency spent on food exerted an upward pressure on the exchange rate. The increased value of the pound, together with internal reaction to the threat of further inflation from the oil price rise, posed problems for the British economy which are discussed in Chapter 26.

Britain's pattern of trade in this period saw an acceleration of the trend towards Europe, an increase in exports to the major oil-producing countries, and the emergence of Japan as a major exporter to Britain. Changes in the pattern of commodities reinforced the trends of the previous twenty years, with the continued rise in the share of manufactured imports the most striking feature (see Table 24.1). By 1985, the composition of Britain's trade in goods was completely different from thirty years earlier or, indeed, from what it had been since the early nineteenth century. Instead of exporting manufactures in exchange for food and raw materials, much of it from the Commonwealth, Britain was now largely exchanging manufactures for manufactures, although with a substantial export also of oil; and, instead of earning a large surplus on its manufactured goods trade to pay for food and raw materials, it now experienced a deficit. Net earnings from invisibles, on the other hand, continued to rise, with tourism becoming in most years a substantial net earner of foreign currency.

In the early 1980s, Britain achieved what had eluded all governments since the Second World War – a massive current account surplus. The reasons were simple, and largely beyond government control. Oil imports fell and exports rose, at a time of very high oil prices. The increased value of the pound also raised the value of other British exports and reduced the price of imports; although the long-term effect of this was to reduce export volumes and increase imports, its immediate effect was to increase foreign earnings. The payments surplus was invested in overseas assets, which then appreciated in value, so that by 1985 Britain was once more a major creditor nation, with foreign assets of £80 billion, compared with under £3 billion in 1975.

The discussion above enables us to summarise the effect of North Sea oil on the economy. By raising the exchange rate, it deleteriously affected manufacturing and, probably, service output and, therefore, employment. On the other hand, it did create a substantial number of jobs itself, mainly in the more depressed areas of the country. Most significant was its effect on national income and wealth. The windfall profits from high oil prices passed partly to the British government and hence partly to the British taxpayer, rather than to OPEC governments. Living standards were therefore kept up in spite of difficult world conditions. At the same time, the accumulation of foreign assets which oil made possible will provide a stream of foreign currency earnings in the future which will provide some support to the international value of the pound.

As mentioned above, the changing balance of trade in oil and food has had an adverse effect on exports of manufactures. Much of the poor performance in this, however, can undoubtedly be attributed to the deficiencies of British industry, discussed in Chapter 32. One other significant external factor was Japanese competition, a characteristic of which was extreme pressure applied on a relatively limited number of industries. In the 1960s, relatively small industries such as motorcycles were virtually destroyed by the Japanese. In the 1970s, major industries such as car manufacture were menaced, while the Japanese dominated new industries such as video recorders. The intensity of competition led to successful pressure for unofficial quotas on Japanese products. Cars, for instance, were limited by agreement between the manufacturers, policed by the Japanese Ministry of Trade and Industry, to 11 per cent of the British market. While the general reasons for the efficiency of Japanese industry are well-known, the intense competitive pressure applied in certain industries did not just stem from efficiency. Taken overall, the Japanese economy is not notably efficient: the distributive sector, for instance, is notoriously inefficient. The result of this was that Japanese wage levels were not until recently high by world standards. Certain industries could therefore manufacture at a very low cost as they enjoyed high efficiency but paid modest wages.

In comparison, the threat posed by competition from low-wage underdeveloped countries can be overstressed. It is inevitable as time goes by that labour-intensive processes will tend to move to low-wage economies, as cotton textile production had started to do before the First World War. If the low-wage economies are successful in developing industry, they become high-wage economies. Only if they follow a Japanese pattern of selective modernisation, concentrating on specific industries, are they likely to prove a sudden and severe threat to industry elsewhere.

CHAPTER TWENTY-FIVE

Economic performance and government policy 1914–39

INTRODUCTION

The period between the wars has a special place in British economic history, for reasons which the previous chapter will already have made clear. With the exception of a few years during the First World War and just afterwards, it was a period of high and persistent unemployment (see Fig. 25.1 and Table 25.1). Furthermore, this unemployment was worst in the industries and the areas which had been most prosperous before the war. Steel, shipbuilding, cotton and coal (the staple industries) were the industries worst hit by adverse world conditions; Lancashire, South Wales, the North East, the West of Scotland and West Cumberland the regions worst affected. From 1929 to 1932 the world depression further reduced economic activity, but subsequently there was a sustained recovery, although its impact on the worst affected industries was limited. The First World War and its aftermath of depression also led to changes in the way that politicians, civil servants and economists thought about central government's relationships with the economy, although these changes were slow. This chapter will examine governmental attitudes and their impact, look at alternative views of what the government might have done and examine the reasons for economic recovery in the 1930s. The problems of the staples, which were primarily caused by world conditions, were examined in the previous chapter.

THE AFTERMATH OF WAR

Before 1914, it was generally believed that the only significant way in

Table 25.1 Inter-war unemployment

	1	2	3	4	5	6
1919	n.a.	n.a.	n.a.	n.a.	n.a.	3.4
1921	n.a.	n.a.	n.a.	n.a.	n.a.	11.3
1929	19.0	20.1	25.3	12.9	11.0	7.3
1930	20.6	28.2	27.6	32.4	14.6	11.2
1931	28.4	45.5	51.9	43.2	21.5	15.1
1932	34.5	47.9	62.0	30.6	22.5	15.6
1933	33.5	41.5	61.7	25.1	21.3	14.1
1937	16.1	11.4	24.4	10.9	11.3	7.8
1938	16.7	19.5	21.4	23.9	13.3	9.3
1939	12.5	15.1	20.9	16.9	11.7	5.8

1 = Coalmining (% of insured workers)
2 = Iron and steel (% of insured workers)
3 = Shipbuilding and repairing (% of insured workers)
4 = Cotton textiles (% of insured workers)
5 = Total (% of insured workers)
6 = Total (% of all workers)
Column 6 is lower as unemployment among non-insured workers (largely in clerical work, domestic service etc.) was lower than unemployment among insured workers
(*Sources:* Mitchell and Deane (columns 1–5); Feinstein (column 6)

which the government could affect economic activity was through the imposition or non-imposition of tariffs. The First World War itself did not immediately bring about a major shift in this belief. What it did bring about was a mass of practical problems which needed some sort of action – action which frequently involved the government. And when some of the immediate legacies of the war had been dealt with, its longer-term economic legacy, the dislocation of the world economy, remained. In spite of this, the thrust of government policy for most of the period was to try to reduce or minimise government intervention in the economy. One of the key reasons for this was the desire to reduce government spending and keep it at as low a level as possible commensurate with defence and social-welfare commitments. As economic intervention was likely to involve spending, it was an obvious target. Governments wanted to reduce spending for a variety of fairly obvious reasons: because it was potentially inflationary, because levying the taxes to finance it was unpopular, and perhaps most of all because the majority of people still retained the pre-war belief that individuals were entitled to retain the bulk of their

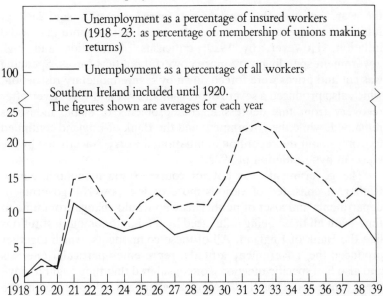

− − − Unemployment as a percentage of insured workers
(1918 − 23: as percentage of membership of unions making
returns)

——— Unemployment as a percentage of all workers

Southern Ireland included until 1920.
The figures shown are averages for each year

Figure 25.1 Inter-war unemployment rates in the UK (percentages) (based on Feinstein; Mitchell and Deane)

income themselves, and not have it taken away from them.

During the war, taxation had been raised substantially, but a very high proportion of spending had been financed by borrowing, which rose from a total of around £700 million in 1914 to £7.5 billion by 1919. The interest on this debt had to be paid after the war. The war had also been accompanied by high inflation, as a large amount of government spending had been financed by borrowing direct from the Bank of England. The effect of borrowing, and then immediately spending the money, was that cash soon found its way to all the other banks, via the accounts of those who received the money, and thus increased the banks' deposit base and enabled them to lend more. (The old restriction on bank lending which had been imposed by the need to keep gold in a certain proportion to liabilities was circumvented by issuing currency notes unbacked by gold.) Very high government spending, monetary expansion and virtually non-existent unemployment were classic ingredients for so-called demand inflation, in which a growing supply of money chased a fixed quantity of goods and labour. Retail prices doubled during the war, reaching a peak of two and a half times the pre-war level in 1920. High spending and monetary expansion had continued unchecked for a time after

239

the war, because the government feared recession and lack of fulfilmnet of its wartime promises for social reform more than it did inflation. However, by 1920, criticisms of inflation and high government spending were more powerful political forces. Spending was cut and prices were forced down by severe monetary restriction, which also produced a severe depression in 1921 and 1922. Even after recovery from this depression, the problems of staple industries remained, while the government and the Bank of England continued to worry about the repetition of inflation, a worry exacerbated by the German hyperinflation of 1922.

'The government' was not, of course, some monolithic entity. Rather, it consisted of various more or less powerful government departments and a set of politicians who would change from time to time, with all these being influenced by semi-autonomous institutions like the Bank of England. All of these components, which together produced the 'government' attitude, represented particular interests and also had specific functions, or considered that they ought to have these functions. Thus the Bank of England tended to represent the views of bankers in the City of London, but it also had its own ideas about its role, and its attitude was further shaped by the strong personality of its governor, Montague Norman. The Bank was concerned with the restoration and maintenance of the Gold Standard. It also believed that, while sectors of British industry needed reorganising, it was important to carry out this reorganisation through private enterprise rather than government agencies. An even more powerful institution was the Treasury. The vast increase in government expenditure needed to service the government debt and also meet the increased spending on social services had put it into a particularly strong position. The Treasury had always conceived of its function as the control of government expenditure and, since high taxes were politically unpopular, it could add political arguments to its traditional administrative ones in favour of restraints on spending. Another cogent Treasury argument for lower spending was that this facilitated its other main task, the management of government debt. If the government could run a budget surplus, it reduced the need to raise new loans when the old ones became due for repayment, a process known as refinancing.

Apart from these two major institutions, there were numerous other ministries and groups which helped shape economic policy, such as the Ministry of Labour, which dealt with trade unions and administered unemployment benefit. Also important, though more so at certain times than others, were the pressures imposed by events totally external to economics, notably the need to rearm in the 1930s. But for most of the period, the Bank of England and the Treasury were the two most dominant influences.

The post-war Coalition government soon disentangled itself from industries such as the railways and coalmining which had come under temporary government control during the war. The problems of the staples, however, remained. Occasionally, out of political expediency, governments opted for direct aid, most notably with the subsidy of 1925–6 for the coal industry, the withdrawal of which was one of the proximate causes of the General Strike. The favoured means of intervention, however, was to encourage the strengthening of private enterprise through amalgamation into larger units, a process which came to be known as rationalisation. (Rationalisation was a word frequently used at this time, presumably because it sounded modern and efficient. In practice, rationalisation schemes ranged from the genuine promotion of modernisation and greater efficiency, to the simple expedient of closing down plants in order to concentrate production.) Government interventions of this sort included the Railway Act of 1921, which provided for the amalgamation of the railways into four main companies, carried out in 1923; the Coal Mines Act of 1930 which, although passed by a Labour government, contained the same remedies of amalgamation and limitation of output to raise prices, neither with much success; and the various schemes to encourage the cooperative marketing of agricultural produce which were promoted in the early 1930s (see Ch. 31). The only really positive examples of intervention were the foundation of public corporations in electricity (the Central Electricity Board of 1926), broadcasting (the British Broadcasting Corporation of 1926) and London Transport (1933). These were financed by loan rather than equity capital, so limiting the profit they could distribute, and had statutory duties to provide efficient services. Government regulation of railways, as monopolies, was not of course new, and Docks and Harbours Boards and municipal trading enterprises had been forerunners of the public corporation idea. Nevertheless, the constitution of these corporations in major industries was an important development. This was not so much because of the potential for government intervention which they represented, since as in other cases the government, and the directors of the corporations, were both anxious to avoid direct government involvement. It was rather that the corporations, which were seen as agents of rationalisation and efficiency, represented one more step away from the uncontrolled competitive ideal of *laissez-faire* economics.

241

Rationalisation schemes were also promoted by the Bank of England, for a variety of motives. One, as with the Lancashire Cotton Corporation merger of spinning firms in 1929, was a desire to protect local banks, which were in a weak position, having overlent to the industry. Another, as previously noted, was the desire to minimise direct government involvement. The Bank's intervention contributed to the survival of some large firms by assisting in their financial reconstruction and did, therefore, have some benefit. Perhaps unfairly, the Bank is best known for its sponsorship of National Shipbuilders Security Ltd, set up in 1930 to rationalise the shipbuilding industry, which closed Palmers' Yard in the north-eastern town of Jarrow in 1934. The resulting heavy unemployment contributed to the famous Jarrow March of unemployed workers in 1936.

ECONOMIC THEORY AND ECONOMIC POLICY

It was governments' macro-economic policy or lack of it which was likely to have most effect on overall economic activity, however. As we have seen, there were important influences on government policy arising from practical considerations and from the particular functions which institutions had to carry out. Nevertheless, the overall view of what was possible and not possible in economic policy needs consideration.

The orthodox view of what economic policies the government should follow started with the assumption that, given the free working of markets, the demand for goods would equal the supply. As the supply was fixed, or only capable of increase through investment in productive capacity, attempts by government to influence the level of demand could only have adverse consequences. If, for instance, the government spent more than its revenue and financed the excess by borrowing short term from the Bank of England, thus increasing the money supply, inflation would occur as in 1914–19. It was accepted that this sort of inflationary boom could maintain full employment, since between 1918 and 1919 the policy was followed with the deliberate intention of providing employment for demobilised soldiers. Not unreasonably, it was not seen as a suitable policy in the long term. If the government financed the excess of expenditure by borrowing directly from savers, orthodox theory held that it would eat into the relatively inflexible total of savings, push up interest rates, and thus discourage private invest-ment. (Some economists did think that unemployment during the recession phase of business cycles could be alleviated by public works projects, but that the extent of this action should be limited because of its adverse effect on business confidence and because it would not solve the long-term problems of the industries concerned. The Treasury itself took this position, and was not as unreservedly orthodox in its economic ideas as historians used to think it was. It is not correct, therefore, to see the 'Treasury view', as it was often called, and contemporary economic orthodoxy, as identical.) Long-term unemployment was attributed in the orthodox view to the difficult conditions in export markets, compounded by the failure of wages to fall to levels at which they would clear the labour market. In other words, unemployment was partly caused by too high wages, a phenomenon often attributed to trade-union intransigence.

The policy prescription following from the orthodox view was that the government should avoid excessive expenditure, in order to minimise new borrowing and if possible allow repayment of government debt. This would help to reduce interest rates and would therefore encourage private investment. The Treasury supported these aims but, as was suggested above, not because it totally agreed with the economic analysis behind them. It was rather that the aims fitted in with the Treasury's concern to contain expenditure and therefore keep down taxation, as well as with its desire to ease the process of refinancing. Another strand of orthodox thinking, strongly supported by the Bank of England, was the desirability of Britain's return to the Gold Standard, if possible at sterling's pre-war parity against the dollar. There were apparently well-founded reasons for this widely-held belief. Before the war, Britain's position as the centre of world money markets had coincided with a period of success and stability for the world economy. Buoyant world trade was good for British industry, particularly for services like banking and shipping. Lending abroad had been closely associated with the prosperity of Britain's heavy industry, and a stable pound was thought to be attractive to borrowers. Less rationally, there was a general assumption that the economic relationships and price levels ruling before the war were somehow real and absolute in a way that their post-war equivalents were not. As Keynes said in the conclusion to the passage cited at the beginning of Chapter 24, discussing the ease with which the inhabitant of London could procure gold or invest and travel abroad: 'he regarded this state of affairs as normal, certain and permanent, and any deviation from it as aberrant, scandalous and avoidable'.

There was a cost, however, to keeping Britain on the Gold Standard. Foreigners had to be induced to buy sterling to maintain its value, when the currencies they preferred to hold were the franc and the dollar. The only way to do this was to maintain interest rates at a relatively high level – precisely the policy which, in the orthodox view, also hampered investment. Finally, we can note that the policy which should have flowed from the orthodox view had one more ingredient – measures to make wages more responsive to market forces. For reasons discussed in Chapter 29, the government was unwilling to take serious action on this.

The orthodox view therefore saw unemployment as a product of export difficulties and of too high wages which the government was unwilling or unable to reduce. Apart from the attempt to reconstruct the pre-war world economy by returning to the Gold Standard, governments had no real shots in their economic locker to deal with unemployment. Tariffs were disliked by Labour, and politically impossible for the Conservatives in the 1920s after they had been defeated on the issue in the 1923 election. When they were introduced, along with devaluation, in 1931, they were a response to overwhelming outside forces, not part of a coherent policy. The view came to be held, when world prices fell from 1929, that in the absence of wage-cutting policies, it was a good idea to raise prices, at least in home markets, in order to improve profits and hence the ability to invest. (This should be distinguished from advocacy of monetary inflation, since the idea was to raise prices back to what was conceived of as normal levels.) The various schemes for amalgamation and cartels, for instance in coalmining and agriculture, were in part a response to this. Given the downward pressures on prices from lack of world demand, however, there is little evidence that this fairly inchoate policy had any real effect. The result of this lack of any strong belief in economic cures for unemployment was that it began to seem inevitable, with the result that to governments it became primarily a matter for social policy, discussed in Chapter 34.

Alternatives to the orthodox view did exist. A school of thought, espoused by the Liberals and influenced by the economist John Maynard Keynes, advocated from the later 1920s a policy of large-scale public works construction to alleviate unemployment. Keynes developed these ideas into a theory which attributed to the government great potential power to control the level of economic activity, published in 1936 as *The General Theory of Employment,*

Interest and Money. Keynes saw no necessary mechanism by which, at a state of full employment, the desire to invest would exactly equal the desire to save. To orthodox economists, such a mechanism was provided by interest rates, which would change if there was any imbalance between potential savings and potential investment, falling if investment was less desirable than saving, or rising in the opposite case, until the imbalance was corrected. Keynes rejected this linking mechanism on theoretical grounds. He suggested instead that the level of employment was itself a linking mechanism, determining incomes, out of which savings were made. If the desire to save was greater than the desire to invest at the level of full employment, then employment would fall and only settle at a level where there was equilibrium between savings and investment. In this situation, which Keynes saw as the situation which obtained when he was writing, actual employment and output would stabilise at a level below that of maximum potential employment and output.

Keynes' remedy was to raise government expenditure, in particular by spending on public works. The increased spending would raise the level of employment, and those put into employment would themselves spend money which would lead to the employment of others. This is the so-called multiplier effect. Keynes' originality was to suggest that the raised level of employment would generate extra savings which could be tapped to pay for the higher levels of government expenditure; consequently this would not eat into the savings available for private investment.

In the long term, Keynes' ideas were to be influential, but in the 1930s they were not and so, given the theoretical standpoints of most economists and the political and institutional pressures on politicians, the economic policies of the inter-war period were very predictable. From 1920 there was a sharp cutback in government spending, called the 'Geddes axe' after the chairman of the committee which recommended economies, which was followed by return to and then maintenance of the Gold Standard. This, and a balanced budget, were the main planks of government policy until 1931, whether the government in question was Coalition, Conservative or Labour. The highly orthodox Philip Snowden, the Chancellor in both the Labour governments of 1923–4 and 1929–31, resisted the siren song of a few left-wingers for radically different policies. Labour's originality extended to a limited public works programme in 1929–31. The budget deficit in the latter year, which was an important reason for foreign loss of confidence in sterling, was not intentional but was an almost inevitable result of the fall in tax revenues and rise in unemployment payments consequent on depression.

The budget deficit and the current account deficit then combined to produce another significant influence on economic policy, the external pressure on sterling. In August and September 1931, the forces pushing sterling off gold were irresistible. But the events of this period should not be seen as the only influence on other subsequent policies, such as the tariff policy. There had since the early 1900s been elements in British industry and the Conservative Party favourable to tariffs, while in 1915 the so-called McKenna duties had been imposed on various luxury goods, notably cars. Given the collapse of existing economic relationships, therefore, it was politically quite easy to impose tariffs, first by temporary legislation in 1931, then more permanently in 1932. Their imposition, and the extension of imperial preferences, can be seen as partly a political move, although external pressures provided the opportunity.

In spite of the dramatic events of 1931–2 and the growth of government economic regulation, the ultimate aim both of the government and of Keynes, who was their strongest critic in economic affairs, was for a return to freer trade and a cohesive world economy. In terms of internal economic policy, the government after 1931 remained committed to a balanced budget, and although Treasury officials came to accept a case for a larger measure of public works should recession occur again, the government's basic standpoints on economic policy remained unchanged. Indeed, fiscal policy between September 1931 and 1933 was highly restrictive, the opposite to that prescribed by Keynes. The case for this was that it would allow interest rates to fall, an argument motivated both by orthodox economic theory and the Treasury's long-standing desire to convert War Loan to a lower rate of interest, thus saving interest payments. Interest rates did fall, and War Loan was converted from 5 per cent to 3.5 per cent in 1932. It may be, however, that this could have been achieved without such a stringent fiscal policy.

The 1930s did see, however, the first glimmerings of a regional policy, albeit a very limited one. The problems of the staple industries had, of course, raised unemployment in the regions in which they were located (see Table 31.7). The effect was not just on workers in the staple industries, for there was also less demand for new building, for transport, and for retail and miscellaneous services. Activity throughout the economies of these areas was adversely affected. In 1928 the Industrial Transference Board had been set up to assist workers in these areas to transfer elsewhere. Transference, whether voluntary or assisted, was however discouraged by the high levels of unemployment all over the country from 1929 on. The lack of labour mobility sparked in 1934 a tiny recognition of the problem of the worst hit areas, the Special Areas Act, which aimed to improve the infrastructure of these areas to attract industry. The completion of a few sewers was the main achievement in the early years of the scheme, but by the late 1930s there were some more practical initiatives. Refugee businessmen from Europe were directed to the depressed areas, while firms expanding to meet rearmament needs were asked to set up away from London and the South East.

An account of the inter-war decades therefore ends, as it begins, with an emphasis on how limited the government's economic policy initiatives were. Would a more active policy, by following Keynes' or some other prescription, have achieved more?

WAS THERE A SOLUTION?

There is little evidence that reducing real wages, as the orthodox theory prescribed, would have led to a substantial increase in employment in most staple industries. Since wages in most of these industries – the major exception being coal – formed only a small part of the cost of production, a very sharp reduction would have been necessary to lower costs significantly, and even then demand for most of the products of these industries was so low that increased sales would not necessarily have resulted. A fall in real wages should also encourage employers to shift from more capital intensive to more labour-intensive production, and so increase employment that way. This sounds all right in theory, but in practice is often not applicable because the existing capital equipment demands certain production techniques which are fixed whatever the wage level. So the fact that unions helped to keep wages up in most of the staple industries probably did not have much effect on unemployment. In mining, unions failed to keep wages up, but there was still substantial unemployment, which reinforces the argument that demand weakness or long-term structural change were the key factors.

In many other industries besides the staples, however, wages were not reduced substantially after 1921 even though prices continued to fall until 1932. Real wages therefore rose. In most cases, the reason for wage stickiness was probably the strong influence of custom on wage levels, although union influence may have been a factor, while in low-wage industries unemployment benefit formed a floor which prevented wages falling below a certain level. Supporters of falling real wages would argue that in these industries such falls would have enhanced profit levels, so encouraging investment and therefore increasing demand for labour. The biggest problem with this as a solution to inter-war unemployment is that although profit rates in the period were lower than before 1914, the fall was not massive, and much of it can be accounted for by the problems of the staples. In other words, low profit rates could not have been a particular disincentive to investment, and as a fall in real wages would have reduced consumer demand, its negative effects were likely to have outweighed any positive effects on investment.

It is true that in some service industries, a fall in real wages is likely to have added to employment even without new investment. In such industries, there was relatively little capital equipment and so less constraint on techniques; adding labour would increase the level of service, or make the employer's task a bit easier. As it was, however, labour productivity in major service sectors such as transport and retail actually fell in the inter-war period, as the rise in employment exceeded the rise in output. This suggests that the effect of further employment increase on output would have been minimal. The fall in wages would have encouraged shopkeepers to take on another man to sweep the floor or middle-class householders to employ another gardener. That is about all. The alternative to the state of affairs which existed, of a floor to wages accompanied by some unemployment, would have been lower wages accompanied by underemployment. The latter had been the fate of many people before the First World War, when unemployment benefit was virtually non-existent. Underemployment then manifested itself in a large volume of casual labour which, not surprisingly, was much less in evidence after 1918.

A more recent attempt to link unemployment benefit with the levels of recorded unemployment has been made through the application of search theory. This holds that the higher the levels of unemployment benefit, the longer those unemployed can afford to search for a suitable job and, hence, the larger the volume of unemployment. It seems *a priori* likely that this would occur, but technical difficulties with the data make it very hard to estimate whether its effect on unemployment will be large or small. The other problem with using this theory to explain away virtually all inter-war unemployment, as has been done, is that it assumes that unemployment levels could have fallen if people had been prepared to accept a high degree of social dislocation. Only by moving to other areas could those in the worst hit regions have obtained jobs, and such mobility was particularly difficult in the inter-war period for reasons discussed in Chapter 27. The search theory of unemployment, and that which sees high benefit levels as propping up real wages, both look on labour as a highly mobile factor of production with a flexible price. *In extremis* (as when people are starving) this is no doubt true; whether it is appropriate for a modern society is another matter.

Keynes' analysis, in contrast, held that unemployment existed because demand was insufficient to sustain full employment. The proposed solution – increased government spending – has had both supporters and critics. The practical difficulties of a Keynesian-type solution in this period can be seen by looking at one concrete proposal for public works, that made by the Liberals in 1929 which was entitled optimistically 'We Can Conquer Unemployment'. In the conditions of world-wide depression which was about to begin, demand reflation would have sucked in imports, thus worsening the current balance of payments with all the consequent problems of confidence in sterling which were to occur anyway in 1931. It may seem unfair to the proposals to test them in the light of what happened to the world economy, but it is in fact only realistic because Britain was so dependent on the world economy, at least until the floating of the pound and the institution of tariffs. Keynes realised this later, and became a supporter of tariffs. Another problem with his analysis was that, right or wrong, it was not accepted by most businessmen, and hence adoption of his policies might well have reduced business confidence, to which he attributed considerable importance. This was one of the Treasury's objections to public works programmes. Supporters could argue that the real benefits of increased government spending would soon outweigh the fears, and this may be true. It remains an imponderable. The final criticism of the Keynesian solution is the most cogent: much of the unemployment was either structural or arose from a deficiency in world-wide demand. Structural unemployment is that which results from the permanent loss of markets in certain industries, and the consequent creation of a pool of workers whose availability to do other work is limited by lack of appropriate skill and geographic immobility (discussed in Ch. 26). The unemployment which arose from a deficiency in world-wide demand was in practice similar to structural unemployment, since the deficiency persisted over such a lengthy period. Very broadly, coal and cotton experienced a permanent loss of markets, and also suffered from a deficiency of world demand; steel and shipbuilding suffered from a deficiency of world demand. The Keynesian solution of domestic reflation would not have solved the problems of these industries, while the expanding industries which would have been stimulated by domestic reflation tended not to set up in the areas where declining industries were located. For these areas, therefore, a much more powerful regional policy might have been appropriate. It is fair to say that both Keynes and the government recognised that world-wide demand deficiency was a major part of the problem, and in the 1920s the government had tried to remedy this, however ineptly, through the Gold Standard policy. Once that had failed, they were reluctant to consider alternatives involving domestic reflation.

Paradoxically, the government went some way to solving the unemployment problem by 1939 through rearmament. This, quite unintentionally, combined demand reflation with an attack on structural problems. Reflation occurred because the government had to borrow money to finance rearmament, which it managed to do without loss of confidence – presumably because when people had Hitler to worry about they were not worried by the lesser evil of government extravagance. Rearmament was also a structural unemployment policy because it benefited coal, steel and shipbuilding, and because firms were encouraged to expand away from the prosperous areas of London and the South East, which were vulnerable to air attack.

This discussion of inter-war problems may seem cynical, since it suggests that they were possibly insuperable. It is not meant to be. It should be realised that Britain was faced with fundamental constraints. Her previous world role boxed her in with an intellectual constraint – the idea that if this role could be recreated, things would improve – and with physical ones. For instance in the 1920s, when many industries still lived by international trade, attempts to lessen the current balance constraint by introducing tariffs were fraught with danger because other countries might retaliate. Yet internal reflation before 1931 without tariffs would have quickly posed current balance of payments problems. Paradoxically, the breakup of the world economy allowed a measure of domestic reflation through lower interest rates, while simultaneously worsening the problems of the staple industries. The domestic legacy of the First World War was also significant. Debt levels and the refinancing of debt were a serious problem, while inflation on the scale of 1914–20 or of Germany in the early 1920s was perceived as a threat, however unlikely in reality.

Given these constraints, the tendency of some historians to criticise anything the governments of the period did in economic affairs is not very illuminating. It is better to be more selective. In retrospect, the return to gold was a mistake because the world depression undid any benefit a stable pound might have brought to the world economy. Without foreknowledge of this, it could be argued that the Gold Standard policy was only one of a number of adverse influences on the staple industries and that its long-term effect might have been positive in other circumstances. For the depression period itself, the government is usually criticised for doing nothing or very little. There was not much it could have done, given world conditions, and what this criticism obscures is that Britain's experience during this period was much better than that of some other countries. The USA, for instance, saw unemployment rise from 3 to 24 per cent between 1929 and 1932, compared with a rise in Britain from 7 to 16 per cent. Historians' concentration on depression means that they rarely ask why the British economy did not suffer such a complete collapse as the American and German, but the possible reasons are worth investigating, although governments could only claim indirect credit for them.

One feature of the British experience was that there were no widespread bank collapses, as occurred in 1931 on the Continent and in the USA. British banks' large size and financial conservatism were both strengths in a depression, as it was precisely the opposite characteristics that proved so troublesome to Continental and American banks. The Bank of England also played a positive role in maintaining banking stability. Another feature was that investment in Britain remained at higher levels than in many industrial countries. Here, government policy was a positive factor, albeit inadvertently, through earlier government support for large amalgamated firms and financially strong public corporations. Thus investment in electrification by the Southern Railway continued throughout the period. Most significant, though, was the building of the National Grid in the late 1920s and early 1930s by the Central Electricity Board; this was estimated to have created 120,000 jobs directly and indirectly. The financial stability of local government was also important. Municipalities in the USA and Germany could and did go bankrupt, leading to further bank failures. Local government borrowing is secured on rate income in Britain, making bankruptcy almost impossible.

While governments should therefore be excused some of the

blame that has been attached to them, they cannot take much credit for the recovery from 1932 onwards. Tariffs must have had a positive impact on the industries which were protected, but this was to some extent negated by the fact that industries such as building actually suffered from the tariffs on certain of their manufactured inputs. The fall in the value of the pound which had occurred when it was first floated also discouraged imports, as well as helping exports. But here again the effect was small because world trade was so depressed at that period. Some measure of the overall effects of tariffs and devaluation on economic recovery can be obtained by comparing industrial production (which increased by 45 per cent between 1932 and 1937) with imports (which rose by only 20 per cent). Because imports were smaller in volume than industrial production, however, the effect of the former rising at the same rate as the latter, and at its expense, would only have reduced industrial growth to about 35 per cent, showing that tariffs and devaluation had limited, though not negligible, effects. Furthermore, there is little evidence that tariffs and devaluation had an immediate effect on industrial confidence, since manufacturing investment stagnated between 1931 and 1933 and only rose in 1934, by which time much of the benefit of devaluation had been lost because of changes in other countries' exchange rates. By this time, also, there were other important forces causing economic recovery.

One of the most important was the rise in consumer expenditure. Falling raw material and food prices had cut living costs, while the money incomes of those in work did not change much; consequently, their disposable income rose. The primary-product price fall, which had exacerbated the problems of the export industries, now acted to boost consumer incomes. Expenditure on durable goods, for example, increased by over 40 per cent between 1931 and 1936. Added to this force for recovery was the fall in interest rates. Here tariffs and the floating pound made an important contribution, as high rates were no longer needed to support the pound. 'Cheap money' now became a fundamental part of policy. The evidence suggests that investment in industry is not very sensitive to changes in interest rates, but depends more on factors like confidence. Investment in housing, however, is more interest-rate sensitive, since interest on borrowing is such a large component of housing expenditure. The early 1930s saw a housing boom, which has often been regarded as an important factor in recovery. The origins of this boom lay in more than interest-rate policy, however. Housebuilding had been depressed since before the First World War, and the consequence of this and the war itself, in which hardly any houses were built, was that by the 1920s there was an enormous pent-up demand for housing. Housebuilding had already reached a high level by the late 1920s, aided by government subsidies, but there was a further big increase between 1932 and 1934, from a rate of about 200,000 houses a year to one of about 350,000. Although slum clearance by local authorities was a factor in this, the main impetus came from the private sector. The initial stimulus had come from falling building costs, arising from efficiency gains and falling raw material prices which dated from the 1920s; associated with this was the rapid improvement of transport to the outskirts of large cities through the growth of bus transport and, in London, the electrification of railways. Since the bulk of the 1930s' housing customers were middle-class families with reasonably stable incomes, the fall in costs, and hence in house prices and rents, was a major impetus to move. Mortgage rates fell from late 1932, leading to a further fall in outgoings, which were reduced still more by financial innovations, notably the lengthening of the period of repayment of building-society mortgages from around sixteen years to the twenty-five years still standard today. The interest-rate fall therefore helped to stimulate the housing boom and keep it going, but was not its only cause.

The housing boom undoubtedly had a major effect on recovery, while the depression itself had been mitigated by the reasonably high level of construction between 1929 and 1932. Between 1932 and 1934, a conservative estimate is that 180,000 extra workers were drawn into building and closely allied industries such as bricks and cement. Taking account of the multiplier effects of the extra employment created, together with the enhanced demand for all sorts of complementary activities ranging from goods transport to estate agents' services, building must have made a big contribution to the fall in unemployment of 800,000 between 1932 and 1934.

A number of factors contributed to the economic recovery of the 1930s. It was important that some of the worst effects of the depression never reached Britain, since this meant that unemployment never exceeded 16 per cent while those in work often enjoyed rising real incomes as prices fell and wages and salaries remained stable. These were the people who contributed to rising expenditure on consumer goods and housing from 1932 on. Interest-rate falls, tariffs and devaluation all had some effect; while innovation in housing construction and finance, and in transport, all contributed to the building boom. Then from 1936 on, rearmament played a major part. Recovery, however, was extremely patchy in the early period, with the regions of the old staple industries much less affected. Even by 1939, industries like coal and cotton were still severely depressed.

CHAPTER TWENTY-SIX

Economic performance and government policy 1939–85

INTRODUCTION

The inter-war years had seen high unemployment and a few tentative government initiatives to reduce it. By contrast, for almost thirty years after the Second World War ended, Britain experienced very different economic conditions, while governments at one time or another interested themselves in almost every aspect of economic activity. This was a period of low unemployment, with economic growth proceeding at a rate faster than ever before (see Tables 26.1 and 26.2). This chapter will examine policy and the extent to which it really influenced economic performance. At the end of the chapter there is a discussion of the problems of recent years, when much higher unemployment and inflation have been accompanied by sharp doubts as to what government economic intervention can achieve.

THE WAR

It is a truism that the Second World War was as much a war of resources as of battles or strategy. Britain's ability to continue fighting depended on her achievements on the economic front, where she reached the very high proportion of 50 per cent of GNP devoted to the armed services and to the production of war material. The acceptance by both leaders and people that only the maximum mobilisation of resources and the consequent need for priorities and sacrifices could enable Britain to avoid defeat were the main factors in this achievement. Looking at the war economy from a global

Table 26.1 Unemployment averaged over five-year periods (UK)

	Halsey (%)	Maddison (%)
1946–50	2.1	
1951–55	1.6	2.4
1956–60	1.8	2.6
1961–65	1.9	2.6
1966–70		3.0
1971–75		3.6
1976–80		5.8
1981–85		12.4

Note: The use of different measures of the working population, and different criteria for counting unemployment, give slightly different results. The lower figures correspond to those usually cited for the 1950s and 1960s. Maddison's figures, however, are more comparable internationally

(*Sources:* Halsey; Maddison; *Annual Abstract* (1980 and 1981–5)

Table 26.2 Income and productivity growth 1937–1985

	National income (1)	Labour productivity (output per man-year) (2)	Total factor productivity (3)	Domestic investment ratio (%)
1937–51	1.8	1.0	1.4	n.a.
1951–73	2.8	2.4	2.3	18.7
1973–79	1.3	1.2	n.a.	n.a.
1979–85	1.3*	1.9*	n.a.	n.a.

Columns 1–3: Annual average percentage change
* To maintain consistency with the 1973–9 estimates, growth rates should be measured to the peak of a cyclical upswing; at the time of writing (early 1988), this had not been reached; the figures given therefore underestimate the trend growth rates over this cycle
(*Sources:* Matthews; *Economic Trends*)

perspective, Britain achieved gains from trade that eluded Germany. Britain could export products in which she had a comparative advantage or simply run up debts with sterling area countries in return for primary products. Germany had to devote correspondingly more of her resources to agriculture or the expensive production of synthetic materials. Britain's advantage should not be exaggerated, since it had a cost in terms of the need for shipping and for its protection, while Germany was able to compensate for her disadvantage by her control of raw material supplies in Central Europe and European Russia.

The high proportion of resources devoted to the war effort was achieved largely by physical controls over both materials and labour, although the allocation of the latter to necessary tasks was carried out very carefully with the successful intention of avoiding the industrial unrest of the First World War. Much diversion of resources was achieved by producing war materials in factories or maintenance shops built for other purposes. The use of physical controls, which took the form of central direction of industrial resources and rationing of consumer goods, was in contrast to the price mechanism which had been much more extensively used in the First World War. Controls were necessary because excess war profits were taxed at 100 per cent, thus removing any incentive which higher prices might have provided. Controls were also the most effective method when the need was to produce as rapidly as possible a fairly simple combination of products.

The changes in the government's macro-economic policy were almost as radical and were longer lasting. The problem during wartime was the opposite of the demand deficiency which Keynes had diagnosed in the 1930s. At full employment, the almost unlimited wartime spending requirement of the government was likely to far outrun the level of savings. Total spending in the economy – that is, consumers' expenditure, investment and government spending – would therefore exceed output, leading to rapid inflation, as in the First World War. The Keynesian remedy was for the government to maximise its revenue through taxation in order to reduce consumer spending. The 1941 Budget established this as a principle, using for the first time national income accounting. This estimated the main items of spending throughout the economy and thus arrived at a figure for the taxation needed to close the inflationary 'gap'. The propensity to save was also stimulated through devices like war credits, which were in effect taxes with the promise of eventual repayment. The upward pressure on prices was further reduced through the rationing of basic commodities and through food subsidies. The relatively low rate of wage and price inflation through the war testifies to the success of the policy, adopted partly because Keynes rapidly established an influential position in the Treasury.

DEMAND MANAGEMENT

The economic policy initiatives of the Second World War proved longer lasting than those of the First World War, although the post-war Labour government initially had other ideas about the best way of running the economy, discussed in the next section. By 1947, however, inflation and the convertibility debacle (see Ch. 24) convinced the Treasury that the pressure of demand in the economy was too high. Treasury officials accepted the Keynesian view that a budget surplus should be generated to reduce demand. This episode, and the subsequent sidetracking of other means of influencing the economy, set a pattern for British governments for the next twenty years or more. Macro-economic management, carried out by adjusting taxation and government spending, was to be the norm. Initially, many economists expected the post-war recovery boom to exhaust itself and be followed by a state of semi-permanent demand deficiency which would call for Keynesian counter measures. As the world economy expanded, the conviction grew that this would not happen. Economic management therefore became a matter of 'fine-tuning' the economy to prevent inflationary booms and serious recessions – in other words, to smooth the business cycle. The belief that governments could do this was an important by-product of Keynesianism, although the initial problem Keynes had devoted himself to was longer-run demand deficiency.

Since governments did not have to tackle the latter problem in the post-war period, some historians have asked whether it is helpful to refer to government policy as Keynesian at all. Certainly the idea that post-war prosperity was the result of governments pursuing Keynesian policies in the long-term sense is not acceptable. Most Western governments, including Britain, were fiscally orthodox over the longer term or, in other words, they did not consistently run deficits on their current spending, at least until the 1970s. A further point is that most governments, including Britain, used monetary as well as fiscal policy when attempting to smooth business cycles. Keynes believed monetary policy had a place, but attributed greater power to fiscal policy. In spite of these caveats, it does seem reasonable to say that British governments were strongly influenced by Keynesian thinking. Smoothing the business cycle was considered by both the public and governments themselves to be an extremely important task. Furthermore, in the 1960s it was hoped that short-run changes induced by Keynesian policies would open the way to longer-term benefits.

This discussion enables us to put into perspective the Keynesian-inspired commitment to maintaining employment levels made in the 1944 White Paper, when the government accepted 'as one of their primary aims and responsibilities . . . the maintenance of a high and stable level of employment after the war'. The making of this commitment does not of course prove that the actions of the British government were really the cause of post-war full employment. As was suggested in Chapter 24, the high level of world output growth provides an explanation and, whatever the causes of this, the actions of one country alone did not make much difference. Nevertheless, the full employment commitment did have meaning insofar as all governments up to the 1970s were extremely worried by even small rises in unemployment and saw the prevention of this as one of the tasks of fine-tuning.

THE FAILURE OF PLANNING: LABOUR 1945–51

The war also threw into prominence another tradition in economic management. The wartime dependence on physical controls fitted in well with an enthusiasm for planning which had developed among some members of the Labour Party in the 1930s. Their idea of planning partly stemmed from Soviet Russia, where the physical allocation of resources, rather than the price mechanism, was paramount. The post-war Labour government continued with physical controls, including the allocation of materials like steel, the licensing of new building, and the continued rationing of consumer goods. The development of planning culminated in the appointment in 1947 of Stafford Cripps, one of the ablest of the Labour ministers, as head of the newly-formed Ministry of Economic Affairs (MEA), which was set up to coordinate planning. At this point, events conspired to reverse the process. Dalton, the Chancellor, resigned and was replaced by Cripps, just as the forebodings of Keynesian economists about inflation were proving correct. This, and the fact that Cripps was more enthusiastic than Dalton about Keynesian analysis, conspired to divert attention from planning towards macro-economic management. The MEA was wound up, while the growing political unpopularity of controls led to the abolition of many of them in 1948, in Harold Wilson's 'bonfire of controls'. While planning, in the sense of physical controls, was at the mercy of chance events, it also suffered from the difficulties of predicting the demands of thousands of individual industries, let alone the demands of millions of consumers. In wartime, by contrast, the government had been the main buyer of industrial goods, while consumers were more willing to accept restrictions on their choice. Planning had practical limitations, but perhaps its failure was ultimately due to its lack of coherent intellectual underpinning, a lack in sharp contrast to Keynesianism. Whatever the reasons, the supply-side policies represented by planning and controls had effectively been vanquished by demand-side policies.

To the woollier minded of Labour's supporters, slogans about nationalisation were a substitute for the hard thought other economic policies required. Nationalisation had crept into the Labour Party Constitution in 1918 as the famous Clause IV. Socialists saw it as a step towards the millenium, trade unions liked it because abolition of private ownership also removed the constraint profits, or rather lack of them, imposed on wages. Less self-interested or less fanciful advocates could justify it as a means of rationalising industries which appeared to be badly run, like coal, and to that extent nationalisation was in a direct line of descent from the inter-war trend towards amalgamation in the name of efficiency. For that reason, there was widespread support for coal nationalisation, and not much hostility to that of railways. Nevertheless, the theoretical underpinnings of nationalisation were extremely weak when it was undertaken, and little or no attempt was made to fit it into the framework of national supply-side planning, which was itself becoming discredited by the later 1940s (see Table 26.3 for nationalisation dates).

Predictably, given nationalisation's intellectual antecedents, the organisational structure of the inter-war public corporations set a blueprint for that of nationalised industries. They were similarly run by professional managers and financed by fixed-interest loans, with the intention of breaking even, taking one year with another. Unlike the old public corporations, however, ministers had power to intervene in the new nationalised ones. The industries' organisational structure and lack of specific financial objectives encouraged their managers to indulge their penchant for costly and technically complicated schemes such as railway electrification in the 1950s or gas-cooled nuclear reactors in the 1960s. While control of such spending ultimately rested with ministers, they were not technically qualified to approve or disapprove. The criticism is often made that governments deleteriously cut back the investment plans of nationalised industries as a by-product of attempts at macro-economic control through the adjustment of government expenditure. This may have

Table 26.3 Dates of nationalisation or denationalisation (privatisation) of major industries (date given is that of actual transfer rather than that of Act)

Nationalisation		Denationalisation	
Bank of England	1946		
Coal	1947		
Electricity	1948		
Transport	1948		
Gas	1949		
Iron and steel	1951		
		Iron and steel	1953
		Road haulage	1953–56
Iron and steel	1967		
British Leyland (cars & trucks) (majority share holding)	1975		
Shipbuilding	1977		
Aircraft building	1977		
		British Petroleum (international oil company) (part sale)	1979, 1981, 1983, 1987
		British Aerospace (aircraft builder)	1981
		Cable and Wireless (international telecommunications)	1981, 1983
		Britoil (North Sea oil producer)	1982
		Jaguar (cars: part of old Leyland group)	1984
		British Telecom (telecommunications)	1984
		British Airways (airline)	1985
		British Gas (gas production and distribution)	1986

Note: There were a large number of other sales 1979–87; in most cases (as with some of those above), they involved miscellaneous activities which the government had become involved in over the years, and not the sale of the major nationalised industries listed above occurred in individual instances but it seems likely that, overall, there was too much rather than too little investment. Lack of financial objectives, and the fact that the government ultimately paid the interest on loans when the industry itself could not, also led to the acceptance in the later 1950s of mounting operating losses. These were particularly serious on the railways and in the coal industry, in both of which there were difficult political decisions to be taken on closures. It may well be that a proportion of such losses was justified on social grounds, but acceptance of a blanket loss further weakened financial discipline.

The year 1961 saw the publication of a White Paper, *The Financial and Economic Objectives of the Nationalised Industries*, which attempted to get to grips with the problems. Subsequently, specific targets on the rate of return on assets and guidelines on pricing policy have been formulated for each industry. 'Socially justifiable' services, such as railway suburban and provincial passenger services, or the use by the Central Electricity Generating Board of coal above a certain quantity, have been separately identified and subsidised. The changes constituted a definite advance. Nevertheless, the targets set have frequently not been met and the government has usually paid the difference; the targets can be set at different rates depending on a government's political complexion or priorities; and the concept of 'socially necessary' is extremely vague and can be modified to justify different levels of subsidy. The problem of financial control over nationalised industries, therefore, is not yet fully resolved.

If planning in the later 1940s came to nothing and nationalisation failed to substitute for it, Labour could claim more for its post-war regional policies. Building licences were used to discourage factory building in the most labour-short areas, and from 1948 Industrial Development Certificates were needed for all factories above a certain size. The Distribution of Industry Act of 1945 provided funds for the construction of factories, mainly in the former depressed areas which were now designated Development Areas. The wartime experience of how resources could be allocated to underemployed areas shaped these post-war policies as much as did the beginnings of a regional policy before the war. While the 1945 government deserves credit for the first serious regional policy, the actual effect of the policy at this time is not clear. Since the pressure of world demand was extremely high, the staple industries had revived. This and the intense shortage of labour in the London area and the Midlands, which discouraged industrialists from expanding there, must account for much of the disappearance of pre-war regional problems.

The definitive verdict on the economic policies of the post-war Labour government has still to be written. The increase in industrial production, 32 per cent between 1946 and 1951, was rapid by later standards, but it should be realised that it occurred in the context of a world-wide boom. Most European countries experienced similar or more growth. The freedom from the debilitating slump which had occurred in Britain only two years after the ending of the First World War was again largely a reflection of world conditions and of the USA's more positive role rather than of domestic policies. Nevertheless, the government may deserve some credit. Its physical allocation policies, especially of steel which was a crucial input to many manufactured goods, enabled it to favour exports and close the overseas earning gap by 1950. The maintenance of controls and rationing also damped down inflation, in spite of very low unemployment levels (see Tables 26.1 and 26.2). Inflation had been a serious problem after the First World War and had eventually led to restrictive monetary policies, which reduced prices but only by reducing economic activity. After 1945, inflation was moderate by international standards. Even when controls were reduced in 1948, it remained low. A contributory factor here may have been the wage-restraint policy from 1948 to 1950. Unlike most future wage policies, it had the voluntary support of the unions. Like most future policies, an acceleration in wage increases was experienced after the policy ended, which may indicate that it merely deferred inflation. In fairness, though, the early 1950s was a period of rapid price rises resulting from devaluation and the commodity price increases resulting from the Korean War, which exerted an independent upward pressure on wages.

The main criticism of the government at the time was that its generous housebuilding policy, and its attempt to continue the inter-war policy of low interest rates (cheap money), imposed upward pressures on demand which it then needed controls and rationing to diminish. Perhaps it could also be criticised for a failure to seize opportunities for the effective modernisation of British industry, opportunities which might have been conferred by different forms of nationalisation or other kinds of supply-side intervention in industry.

THE PROBLEM OF GROWTH

From the Conservative government of 1951 onwards, economic

policy came even more to mean demand management. Although fiscal policy was part of the armoury, monetary policy was also actively used to influence demand (see Ch. 30). Two examples will show how the policy was used. In 1952, the economy was still suffering from the inflationary aftermath of the Korean War. The Budget raised Bank Rate, which influenced the general level of interest rates in the economy, from 2 to 2.5 per cent, and tightened hire-purchase controls – a crude weapon for regulating the supply of credit in the economy. By 1953, inflationary pressures had eased and there were fears of unemployment. The Budget allowed fiscal expansion, cutting both income and indirect taxes. This sort of fine-tuning was the pattern of the 1950s and was continued with some modification into the 1960s.

Fine-tuning is a polite name for the policy. In common parlance, the label 'stop–go' has become attached to this period. It is misleading in that there were only two years before the 1970s with a nil growth rate, 1952 and 1958, but it highlights the fact that there were considerable fluctuations, with peak growth rates of 4 per cent or more being recorded in 1953, 1960 and 1964. Since the purpose of the fiscal and monetary policies was to avoid fluctuations, it seems that they failed, while some historians have suggested that they were actually destabilising or, in other words, accentuated fluctuations. Thus, paradoxically, while one widely expressed view of the 1950s and 1960s sees them as years of steady growth made possible by wise Keynesian policies of deficit financing, another sees inept Keynesian counter-cyclical policies causing more problems than they solved. As was shown earlier, the first view is mistaken; arguably, so is the second.

Econometric studies indicate that UK fiscal policies between 1955 and 1965 did have a modestly stabilising influence; in other words, fluctuations in economic activity would have been worse without them. This was achieved even though Britain's ability to carry out simple fine-tuning as between inflationary boom and recession was complicated by the balance of payments constraint. In general, sterling crises were caused by periods of rising inflation which would anyway have called for stabilising measures. However, there were important exceptions. In 1955, inflationary pressures had led to some tightening of policy, and by 1957 earnings and prices were rising quite slowly; however, there was further pressure against the pound in that year because of belief that the German mark would be revalued. The result was that for a lengthy period of declining inflation and a healthy current account surplus, monetary policy continued to be very restrictive in order to support the pound.

It was partly the low growth rate of the late 1950s which provoked an increase in intervention. Commentators were becoming increasingly aware of the rapid growth of other European countries, which could no longer be explained away as recovery from war. The 1960s saw a revival of supply-side policies which will be described below. On the demand side, incomes policies as a means of strengthening control of inflation again became popular. The Conservatives instituted a 'pay-pause' for public employees in 1961 and Labour a complete wages standstill in 1966–7, as well as setting up the National Board for Prices and Incomes, which monitored wage and price increases and issued guidelines and lasted from 1965–70. More traditional demand-management policies still had an important place. An expansionary policy had been launched in 1964 by the Chancellor, Reginald Maudling, in an attempt to 'go for growth'. The belief was strong that stop–go had imposed a burden on the economy by discouraging industrialists from developing long-term investment plans. Sustained growth, although it might initially cause balance of payments difficulties, would ultimately raise business confidence and investment and increase the productive potential of the economy. The logic was topsy-turvy. Fine-tuning was intended to smooth business cycles and had enjoyed a limited success, thus arguably aiding investment planning. Its success would have been greater but for balance of payments constraints. If modest expansionary policies in the 1950s had been limited by these constraints, what hope had an ambitious expansionary policy of avoiding them?

The Labour government of 1964 inherited the unfavourable current account legacy of Maudling's ill-conceived policy. It did not take substantial deflationary measures, and hence from 1966 experienced recurring balance of payments crises until it accepted devaluation in 1967. This opened the way for Keynesianism's penultimate flourish. With the pressure of demand still high, the Keynesian policy of reducing domestic demand by generating a negative Public Sector Borrowing Requirement (PSBR) or, in other words, repaying public debt was pursued and achieved in 1969. The policy was the opposite of Maudling's, and was more logical. Domestic deflation and devaluation should both promote an upward shift in exports which would finally remove the balance of payments constraint. The similarity with Maudling's policy is that Keynesian techniques were being used in an attempt to institute conditions for a higher long-term growth rate. The degree of success is difficult to judge. The current balance improved, but inflation tended to increase, exacerbated by devaluation which pushed up import prices.

The Conservatives, in keeping with the post-war consensus on important areas of policy, had retained Labour's interest in centralisation and coordination in major industries, and so a sort of unofficial supply-side policy continued throughout the 1950s. Thus when steel was denationalised in 1953, an Iron and Steel Board was set up with powers to regulate new investment; and apart from road haulage, no other industries were denationalised. The dissatisfaction with the 1950s growth rates, however, led to a more positive supply-side policy with the formation in 1962 of the National Economic Development Council (NEDC or 'Neddy'), a tripartite body composed of government, industry and trade unions. This imitated French 'indicative' planning – that is, the setting of targets rather than the use of physical controls. Neddy discussed national economic problems and, initially, set targets, while a host of 'little Neddies' discussed the problems of individual industries. In later years, Neddy did not produce anything too ambitious, its limited aims perhaps accounting for its survival to the present day. Then in 1964, Labour resuscitated the short-lived 1947 Ministry of Economic Affairs, this time as the Department of Economic Affairs. In 1965 it produced a National Plan. The ambitious targets made this something of a joke, but the subsequent rapid decline of planning stemmed from the same problems that had killed it in 1947. The persistence of sterling crises led to the Treasury and macro-economic management demanding and getting most time and attention from the government.

Supply-side policy was also concerned with increasing investment and strengthening the industrial base. The Industrial Reorganisation Corporation of 1966 fostered mergers, while the proportion of investment which could be immediately offset against company tax payments had been increased in 1954, effectively reducing the cost of such investment. This policy later dovetailed into a revived regional policy. While unemployment levels remained very low by inter-war standards, certain regions did have above-average levels, as shown in Table 31.7. The tax regime allowed for even greater offsets in these areas while, from 1966, cash grants were available for plant and machinery investment, again differentiated regionally. Total expenditure on regional incentives rose twentyfold in the 1960s. In addition, Industrial Development Certificates were used much more actively than in the 1950s to discourage development, while Office Development Permits were introduced in 1965 to fulfil the same purpose in the administrative sector. Regional incentives accounted for an estimated 330,000 jobs between 1960 and 1976; of course, the jobs might have been created elsewhere without subsidy. A common criticism is that the factories attracted through incentives tended to be the branch plants of larger organisations with headquarters elsewhere, and that in a recession branch plants are more likely to be closed. There is, in fact, no evidence for a differentially high closure rate of such plants. A more cogent criticism is that branch plants, and even branch offices, do not attract high value-added services such as those of lawyers and bankers. It is a matter of common observation that London continues to be the major centre for these activities, with large if unquantifiable income and employment benefits. A further point is that governmental emphasis on developing the major national airports in the South East, and the failure to encourage a major regional airport, represents a considerable bias towards the South East.

Regional policies, which since 1979 have been scaled down, have undoubtedly mitigated the effects of regional decline. But instead of attracting dynamic industries which would provide increasing employment opportunities over time, the policies tended to attract branch plants whose employment creation potential ended at the factory gate. An exaggerated example of this occurred in Northern Ireland, the recipient in 1979 of the highest regional aid per person in EEC countries outside Southern Ireland and Italy. Much of this money went on large plants such as the notorious De Lorean car plant, started in 1978 and closed in 1982, which even if successful would have had little external employment impact. The exception that proves the rule is Scotland where, since 1975, the Scottish Development Agency has set out to attract high-technology firms, both large and small. The result has been the growth of an area in Central Scotland, the so-called Silicon Glen, where such firms are concentrated. Concentration leads to external economies and the area is therefore likely to attract further firms, while employment in the existing ones is also likely to expand.

INFLATION AND UNEMPLOYMENT

The macro-economic policies of the 1970s and 1980s were again strongly influenced by the impact of world economic affairs, but in significantly different ways to those of the previous twenty years. The major characteristic of the world economy in this period – inflation and, after 1973, the slowdown in world growth and consequent unemployment – were also Britain's main concerns. The balance of payments constraint diminished after the mid-1970s, due to the floating of the pound in 1972 and North Sea oil revenues from the later 1970s which improved the current balance. The sterling crisis of 1976, marked by an unacceptably rapid fall in the value of the pound, was the last major one. For most of the 1970s, while unemployment and low growth were concerns, inflation was the biggest worry (Table 26.4).

Table 26.4 Inflation 1939–85 (percentage increase in consumer price index between first and last years of each five-year period)

1939–45	44
1945–50	25
1950–55	31
1955–60	14
1960–65	19
1965–70	25
1970–75	96
1975–80	94
1980–85	42

(*Sources:* Maddison (1939–80); *Annual Abstract* (1980–85)

The central problem of inflation in these years was that the apparently stable relationship between it and unemployment, in which inflation fell when unemployment rose to very modest levels, and vice versa, had broken down. Inflation in the 1970s rose at the same time as unemployment, and the levels of both, but particularly inflation, were higher than before. There are broadly speaking two explanations for this change. Cost-push theories see wages as increasingly liable to rise without necessarily experiencing pressure from rising demand. The possible reasons for this could include increasing pressure from trade unions; rising import prices, which themselves were inflationary but also exerted upward pressure on wages; and employee expectations of steadily increasing real wages which might lead to increased militancy if such expectations were not met. It is difficult to measure changes in union pressure, although the coalminers do seem to have become markedly more militant in the 1970s. There was certainly strong upward pressure on import prices in the early 1970s. In addition, wage inflation first began to accelerate in the late 1960s, at a time when real wages were rising slowly because of growth in public spending and consequent increases in the tax burden. This suggests that frustrated employee expectations may have been a factor. Cost-push theories would go on to point to factors which might make employers more susceptible to wage demands. Prime among these would be devaluation, or a floating currency which was considered to be unstable at its present rate. Firms which faced foreign competition, whether by exporting or in the domestic market, would be more willing to grant wage increases in these circumstances. These conditions too were present in the late 1960s and much of the 1970s, while the fall in inflation from 1980 came after a sharp rise in the value of sterling.

Cost-push theories assume that the supply of money will, broadly speaking, rise to meet the increased demand caused by wage and price increases. In this formulation, money supply is a passive factor in inflation. In contrast, monetarists believe that a rising supply of money, which will lower interest rates and increase money balances, therefore pushing up the demand for goods, is the prime cause of inflation. This can coexist with a high rate of unemployment because of imperfections in the labour market. For instance, unemployment benefit might reduce people's willingness to work at a wage which would clear the labour market, or it might increase their willingness to spend longer searching for jobs; and trade unions might force wages up beyond the market-clearing level. Monetarists are the lineal descendants of the orthodox economists of inter-war years: to both groups, unions are not the source of continuing inflation, but they might be the cause of unemployment through their insistence on excessive real wages.

Cost-push theories of inflation do not rule out the inflationary impact of money-supply expansion at periods when demand pressure is already high, although monetarists tend to be more dogmatic about accepting any role for cost-push influences. Most observers would accept that the very high money-supply increases of the early 1970s exacerbated inflation by leading to an extreme pressure of demand. Similarly, there is wide acceptance that there has been some increase in what monetarists call the natural level of unemployment – the level at which the labour market is in equilibrium as between demand and supply given existing wage rates. There may be a variety of reasons for this increase, and some were noted above. There is also evidence that long-term unemployment leads to a drop in the ability of people to take any sort of work, as their skills become increasingly outdated and their morale lower. Such people are effectively removed from the labour market, although still registered as unemployed, and therefore do not exert a moderating influence on demand-induced pressure on wage levels.

Government policies on inflation in the 1970s and 1980s have reflected the lack of theoretical agreement on its causes. In the early 1970s, the Conservative government, alarmed by a rise in unemployment in 1971, encouraged another expansionary boom. The basis for this was somewhat sounder than it had been for Maudling's attempt, since the floating pound of 1972 reduced the scope for sterling crises. Unfortunately, the lack of control over the money supply led to its rapid rise. Thus internal demand pressures added to cost-push pressures from oil and other commodity price increases. The government's reaction was to impose a policy limiting increases in prices and incomes, a policy which only makes sense if there is an acceptance that inflation is partly caused by domestic cost-push forces. Given the weight of domestic demand pressures and external cost-push forces, it is not surprising that the policy was challenged by the miners in 1973–4, a challenge which helped to bring down the Conservative government. The Labour government maintained support for incomes policies, however. In 1975 and 1976, it entered a voluntary agreement on wage limitation with the TUC, known as the Social Contract, which may have initially helped to reduce expectations for wage rises. Even on cost-push assumptions, however, wage policies, if effective, run into the problem that they frustrate expectations for real wage rises, thus leading to more forcefully pursued claims later. Earnings between 1976 and 1977 only rose by 9 per cent, compared with a 16 per cent rise in prices; but the following year, the relationship was reversed. Subsequently the government's continued attempts to limit public-sector pay increases resulted in growing unhappiness among public-sector employees and an explosion of demands in the 'winter of discontent' of 1978–79. The new Conservative government, in line with the monetarist thrust of its thinking, has eschewed overt incomes or prices policies.

As the earlier discussion of economic theory implies, the monetarist explanation of inflation also contains an explanation of unemployment. In this, unemployment is seen as an inevitable consequence of institutional factors, which increase the real wage payable to workers beyond the ability of some employers to pay. In monetarist theory, unemployment cannot be due to demand deficiency, since demand is not an independent variable as Keynes postulated. Monetarists therefore reject Keynesian policy prescriptions. As we have seen, there is justice in the monetarist view of unemployment insofar as the natural level of unemployment probably has increased in recent years. Monetarism does not provide a very coherent explanation for the sharp rise in unemployment which began in 1980, however (see Table 26.1). There is no reason for supposing that trade-union insistence on excessively high real wages has been any greater in the 1980s than in most of the post-war period; and unemployment benefit has been reduced slightly, relative to the wage level, since the late 1970s.

This suggests that unemployment in the 1980s has been largely due either to demand deficiency or to structural problems. In view of the continuation of some inflation, demand deficiency may seem an unsatisfactory explanation, but it should be remembered that, if cost-push explanations of inflation are accepted, then inflation could occur without there necessarily being any demand pressure. Certainly there have been changes in demand since the long boom of the post-war era. From the mid-1970s, world demand has grown at a much slower rate than previously; on the domestic side, the mid-1970s did see a very large government deficit which may have partially compensated for the shortfall in world demand but, since then, the deficit has fallen as a proportion of national income. Keynesian analysts, therefore, do see demand deficiency as a factor in recent unemployment. As in the inter-war period, however, structural unemployment is probably even more important. This seems particularly likely because, as in the 1930s, unemployment has remained high, particularly in certain regions, even though demand has risen since 1981. Viewing unemployment as partly structural also fits in with the pattern of its growth. In the mid and late 1970s, a very low growth in manufacturing productivity took place, but British industry remained internationally competitive due to the relative weakness of sterling. When sterling's international value increased sharply in 1979 and 1980, British costs rose relative to world costs, and large sections of industry rapidly lost competitiveness. Many plants in the steel, motor and engineering industries closed permanently, and between 1979 and 1982 the total number of jobs in manufacturing fell from 7.2 million to 5.8 million. The value of the pound fell somewhat after 1981, but remained relatively high compared with the late 1970s.

As with the treatment of inflation, monetarist ideas had increasing influence over government policy towards unemployment. In 1976, James Callaghan told the Labour Party Conference, 'We used to think that you could just spend your way out of a recession and increase employment by cutting taxes and boosting government spending. I tell you in all candour, that option no longer exists . . ..' The reasons for this change of tack are complex, and are not just to do with an intellectual rejection of Keynesianism – which many economists still support. As in the inter-war period, government policy was affected by real world problems and institutional pressures as much as, or more than, by changes in intellectual fashion.

One point is that although unemployment by the mid-1970s was worse than it had been in the recent past, inflation at that time seemed a greater menace. Hence an emphasis on the reduction of government spending was not altogether surprising, even in the light of Keynesian theory. Added to this was the influence of the IMF, whose loan to support sterling in 1976 entitled it to obtain assurances from the government about limiting the growth of the money supply, which the IMF saw as an important check on inflation; a reduction in government spending would help control of the money supply. Yet another factor was that government spending had actually reached unprecedented levels by the mid-1970s, and this had raised the PSBR to record levels. Callaghan's words could therefore be seen partly as a political manoeuvre designed to discourage Labour Party activists from expecting more government spending at a time when this was becoming increasingly difficult to deliver.

This focuses attention on the importance for economic policy of the secular rise in government spending, the reasons for which are discussed in Chapter 34. Throughout the 1950s, the decline of defence spending allowed some brake to be kept on overall spending, but it increased from around a third to 40 per cent of national income between 1960 and 1968, and by 1975 it had exceeded 45 per cent. The figure has fluctuated since then but had not markedly fallen by 1985. Any increase in spending threatens to raise the tax burden unless the government borrows. Increasing taxes is always unpopular, and raises the spectre of increasing inflation as workers try to maintain real wage levels. A growth in borrowing also poses problems, notably the perennial one of selling government debt. This became ever more difficult in the mid-1970s as the prospect of continued inflation made savers wary of fixed-interest investments, with the result that long-term interest rates rose to the unprecedented level of 17 per cent in 1974. Furthermore, each tranche of borrowing added a further lump of debt interest to the next year's budget. So a further rise in spending to counter unemployment would lead to an escalating borrowing requirement.

The Conservative government of 1979 has often been portrayed, and has portrayed itself, as introducing a radical change in attitudes to intervention by espousing monetarism and therefore rejecting the idea that governments could change the economy for the better by demand management. As we have seen, however, the formal rejection of Keynesianism had taken place earlier, while the reliance on monetary policy to curb inflation had also been accepted by Labour, albeit supported by incomes policies. The Conservatives did reduce the rate of growth of the money supply, although this was a task they found much harder than anticipated, with the supply consistently overshooting its targets. They also flouted Keynesianism by raising taxes in 1981 during the world recession. Inflation fell sharply, although on most analyses this was partly due to the rise in sterling which brought down import prices and to the subsequent fall in world commodity prices. A Keynesian approach would also suggest that raising taxes worsened still further the effect that the world recession and the rise in sterling had on British manufacturing industry and therefore on unemployment.

TRADE AND COMPETITION POLICY

In contrast to the inter-war years, British governments from 1945 took a more liberal attitude towards trade and competition both externally and internally, although there were important exceptions. The reaction of British industry to freer trade and increased competition was also generally favourable, reflecting the changed post-war conditions of the domestic and world economies in which selling was not difficult, at least until the 1970s.

In internal competition policy, the most important innovation was the Restrictive Practices Act of 1956. The network of agreements among British firms on prices and output, which had developed since the late nineteenth century, were made void unless they could satisfy certain conditions before a Restrictive Practices Court – most could not and were abandoned. Since 1976 the supply of services has been included and this has led to the removal of agreements on minimum charges and limits on advertising among important groups such as stockbrokers and solicitors. In 1964, Resale Price Maintenance, the enforcement by manufacturers of a schedule of prices on retailers, was also made illegal. No doubt the effect on competition was beneficial, but there were other forces acting the same way. Chain stores and supermarkets, for instance, could sell their own brands of goods at any price they liked. In other respects, government policies on competition were only consistent in their inconsistency. The Monopolies and Restrictive Practices Commission (now the Monopolies and Mergers Commission) had been established in 1948 to investigate individual cases of restricted competition, but only if they were referred by the government. There has never been a consistent policy of referral and at times there has been encouragement for mergers, as in the later 1960s. In contrast, the Conservative government of 1970–4 and that from 1979 did put considerable stress on increased competition as a way of improving British firms' efficiency. There is no strong evidence, however, that the rate of productivity growth has increased because of pro-competition policy or under the stimulus of the gradual increase in external competition. The effect of greater external competition may be to increase efficiency in the affected firms, or to bankrupt them. In Britain, as in the case of the shipbuilding and car industries, it often seems to have been the latter.

One of the main areas of restricted competition remaining until the 1980s was the nationalised industries. The Central Electricity Generating Board, for instance, controlled the sale of electricity to regional boards which monopolised distribution (while in Scotland two regional boards monopolised both generation and supply); the Post Office had a virtual monopoly of postal and telecommunications services. Such practices and agreements had grown up on the basis that such services were 'natural monopolies', that competition was likely to be disorderly and lead to wasteful duplication, and that regulation of charges and profit levels would be a sufficient safeguard against the abuse of monopoly powers. Since there is considerable force in these arguments, which up to the 1970s had been largely accepted by all parties, the shift towards a belief in greater competition can be partly explained by the apparently poor performance of many nationalised industries, and also by the public perception that this performance was unsatisfactory, and the consequent popularity of change. Changes in the industries mentioned and in others were introduced after 1979, although there were significant limits. Thus a licence was granted to one firm only to compete with British Telecom, which inherited the telecommunications section of the Post Office. The Central Electricity Generating Board was instructed to purchase externally generated electricity which was offered to it, but still maintained control over the ultimate sale to the consumer. The other main plank of the government policy towards nationalised industries was privatisation, that is their sale to the private sector. This could not be seen primarily as a competition policy, since it did not break up monopoly suppliers such as gas and telecommunications. Nevertheless, it was a radical policy in a number of ways. Apart from providing one marker for the end of the political consensus over certain areas of the economy which had existed since the 1950s, it removed the freedom of the government to manipulate the pricing policies and profit levels of the industries concerned – a freedom which had remained in practice, even after the disciplines imposed on nationalised industry pricing from the 1960s.

In spite of the intermittent trend towards increasing competition, there has always been a large area of economic activity where it has been much more restricted. This encompasses the whole area of government purchasing of materials, as well as the purchasing policy of nationalised industries, where government pressure, subtle or otherwise, has often been applied. While the government has always been a large purchaser of armaments, nationalisation enormously increased the quantity of government or quasi-government purchases as compared with any previous period. The restriction on competition has not just emanated from the government. Interested firms have lobbied to secure contracts which, for large capital items, can be enormously valuable. An illustration of this three-way pressure, from private firms to government to nationalised industries, is the purchase in the late 1950s by the British Transport Commission, at that time the supreme railway authority, of diesel locomotives from the North British Locomotive Company, which had little experience of diesel locomotive building. The locomotives subsequently proved unreliable. Another purchase influenced by government pressure occurred in the 1960s when British European Airways, one of the nationalised airlines, bought British rather than American aircraft. Here there were a complex of considerations, including the balance of payments implications of such a large foreign purchase. It is clear that lobbying skills have been an important part of the armoury of firms which are likely to be engaged on government contracts. The arguments of lobbyists have included the threat of unemployment if orders are not awarded, the need to retain or develop indigenous British technology and, as a last refuge, the appeal to patriotism.

A classic example of an industry which has been boosted by direct or indirect government patronage, at massive cost to the taxpayer, is aerospace. It has also absorbed a high proportion of Britain's research and development spending. In 1983–4, a quarter of all engineering research and development went on aerospace, both civil and military, and this excludes spending on electronics, much of which is associated with aircraft movement. These figures are usually taken to mean that Britain's supplies of scarce science and engineering personnel have been unduly absorbed by aerospace. The whole subject needs further research, however, since it is quite possible that aerospace's demand for scientists and engineers has helped to create its own supply from universities and polytechnics; in other words, without that demand it is not certain that the same numbers would have been trained and available to other industries. On the positive side, aerospace is an industry with many multiplier effects in its demands for special metals, components, and so on. Furthermore, the civil side, including a large part of the business of the important engine firm of Rolls-Royce, has in recent years had reduced levels of subsidy and less protection from government-sponsored purchasing, and yet has remained reasonably successful.

Whatever the limits to competition in sectors of domestic industry, there has been support by Britain for the gradual liberalisation of world trade, with occasional backslidings during balance of payments crises. This support was not surprising, since even in the 1930s policy makers had retained the ultimate aim of reconstructing the world economy, although their short-term policies were governed by more immediate constraints. There was no intellectual opposition to liberalisation until the formulation of the Alternative Economic Strategy by a group of Cambridge economists in the 1970s. This pointed to the rapid rise in manufactured imports and suggested that the reconstruction of British manufacturing industry which seemed to be needed would have to be carried out behind protective tariff barriers. Since the low international value of sterling when the plan was first mooted constituted a form of protection in itself, behind which British industry failed to modernise, the remedy seems a doubtful one, while the danger of retaliatory tariffs is obvious. Nevertheless, the inefficiency of British manufacturing industry which the strategy pointed to was real enough, while the intensity of Japanese competition in certain industries could be an argument for selective import controls.

CONCLUSION

The Alternative Economic Strategy was a child of the 1970s. Over the previous twenty years, many commentators had identified the main constraint on growth as the balance of payments. Historians have increasingly come to doubt this once strongly-held belief and to turn instead towards the diagnosis put forward in the 1960s by the economist Frank Paish. According to this, the central constraint was the rate of growth of the productive potential of the British economy, which was low. When economic activity was 'fine-tuned' towards the upper limits of productive potential, inflation occurred. This gradually pushed up the relative price of British exports and resulted in a less favourable current account position. The large destabilising flows of sterling which caused sterling crises were a result of the weak underlying position and not themselves an underlying cause of weakness. It is difficult to quarrel with much of this analysis. Britain's position in world trade after the Second World War was favourable, with a high proportion of exports in rapidly expanding sectors such as vehicles and machinery. There was a bias away from Europe and towards the slower-growing markets of Commonwealth countries, but to see this as a serious drawback implies that it would have been very difficult for Britain to establish new markets elsewhere; in a world of growing trade liberalisation, this is obvious nonsense. Yet from 1951 onwards, Britain's share of world exports of manufactures steadily declined, implying declining competitiveness.

Paish's analysis pointed to the 'go' or reflationary phases in fine-tuning as the problem rather than, as most commentators did, to the 'stop' or deflationary phases. This too seems justified. The usual complaint about the deflationary phases was that they discouraged long-term investment plans, especially in the consumer-durable industries which are always more vulnerable to cyclical fluctuations. Since fine-tuning actually had a modest stabilising effect, this criticism is unjustified. The downturns might have been even sharper without government action. The real problem here was not business cycles or government counter-cyclical policies, both of which existed throughout the Western world, but the low underlying growth rate. This meant, for instance, that whereas a deflationary phase for German industry meant only that the growth rate slowed, in Britain it really did stop.

We should continue to attach some importance to the balance of payments for two reasons. First, the occurrence of problems when they were not justified by the underlying state of the current account was caused primarily by London's position as a financial centre, exacerbated by the government and the Bank of England's failure to keep a high level of reserves. These problems may have led at times to restrictive policies over and above those necessary to counter inflation. These policies adversely affected investment plans and led to some long-term loss of growth. Second, and more important, the balance of payments diverted attention from the more fundamental problems of the British economy.

The origins of this diversion go back to the central role given to macro-economic management from 1947 onwards. While there may have been a justification for this in 1947, the ultimate verdict on the twenty years of fine-tuning which followed, given its limited stabilising effect, must be that it made very little difference. That is not what policy makers thought, however, and so the interference which balance of payments problems caused to the smooth operation of demand management was particularly galling. For a number of years before devaluation in 1967, the maintenance of the existing parity of £1 : $2.80 and the consequent sterling crises were seen by many economists, and by many in the Labour Party, as the only barriers to a Keynesian El Dorado of perpetual growth. The 'Gnomes of Zurich', as Labour politicians like to call the foreign bankers who bought and sold sterling with allegedly deleterious effects on the British economy, were a favourite target of left-wing criticism; although what moral obligation foreigners should have to finance British old-age pensions or infant schools is not entirely clear. No matter. Attention from both left and right was focused on stop–go and sterling crises, oblivious of the fact that the problems of the British economy were too deep-seated to be solved by demand management.

CHAPTER TWENTY-SEVEN

Population, migration and labour supply

POPULATION AND MIGRATION

The dominant population experience for the first half of this century was a continuation of the sharp fall in the rate of population increase which had begun in the 1870s. The two world wars, even the First World War which saw over 600,000 British soldiers and sailors killed in its four years, had only a small part to play in this secular decline. The rate of population growth continued to fall in the 1920s and 1930s, but actually rose in the 1940s. In spite of this rise, the growth rate remained at a much lower level than it had in the early years of the century, and by the 1970s it was falling again. The fall was steep enough to mean that the situation which had been feared in the 1930s, a decline in population, almost became a reality. By the mid-1980s the population was again growing slightly faster, as the large number of women born in the early 1960s reached their period of maximum fertility (see Table 27.1).

As in the late nineteenth century, the rate of population growth declined because fertility fell faster than mortality. The most important single component of the decrease in mortality was, as it had been in the Edwardian period, the decline of infant mortality. This fell from around 110 per thousand just before the First World War, to around seventy per thousand in the early 1930s, to around nine per thousand in 1985. The continued improvement in sanitary conditions and general cleanliness, together with better post-natal care, were the main reasons. Other age-specific death rates fell, but not so markedly. Higher incomes and the consequent improvement in the domestic environment continued to play a part, although the increase in smoking until the early 1970s could rank as an environmental deterioration. Since the 1950s there has also been a sharp drop in air pollution because of clean-air legislation. Unlike any earlier period in history, however, improved medical care and medical practice, notably the development and use from the 1930s of effective anti-bacterial drugs, deserves a large part of the credit for the decrease in mortality.

Table 27.1 Population 1901–81

	Population (millions)
1901	38.2
1911	42.1
1921	44.0
1931	46.0
1951	50.3
1961	52.8
1971	55.9
1981	56.4

Figures are for UK, i.e. including Northern Ireland
(*Source: Social Trends*)

The general decline in mortality, particularly infant mortality, has gone a long way towards equalising the expectation of life in different social classes. Nevertheless, there are still differences. Manual workers, for instance, are much more likely to die before retirement age than members of professional and managerial classes. These differences are reflected in different regional mortality experiences, with Wales, Scotland and the North East having a less favourable experience than other parts of the country. All are areas with a high proportion of lower-income groups in the population.

While the decline in mortality is fairly easy to explain, given the increase in medical knowledge during this century, the changes in fertility which have occurred are much less so. The possible factors leading to decline before the First World War were discussed in Chapter 11, and to some extent the continued inter-war fall can be explained as a result of more couples coming under the influence of these factors. Among them was the continued growth in education, which was likely to lead to greater equality between spouses and more discussion of the possibilities of family limitation. Actual knowledge of the possible techniques of limitation continued to spread and mechanical means of contraception became much better known and more widely available. Thus the percentage of the middle class using such means, particularly the sheath, rose from 9 to 40 per cent between 1910 and 1930, and of the working class from 1 to 28 per cent. There is plenty of testimony, however, to continued ignorance about contraception among many women. Better education was also a factor which could have led to greater aspirations, whether for material goods or for long-term career advancement. The shift towards white-collar and professional employment, which is much more likely to have a defined career pattern, is likely to have encouraged the second aspiration. It is not so clear that there was such a remarkable increase in the material goods available, to working-class families in particular, between the wars. Working-class consumption of some of the new consumer goods, such as cars and fridges, was negligible, while there were numerous goods which had already been affordable well before the First World War, such as gas cookers or improved sanitation, which were 'purchased' through higher rent. As Chapter 11 suggested, it was perhaps in the late nineteenth and early twentieth centuries, rather than between the wars, that growing material aspirations began to have a significant effect on fertility.

Short-term economic conditions are another possible variable, with inter-war unemployment suggesting itself as a factor in lowering the birth rate. On the other hand, many people were better off during this period than before. It is true that the birth rate increased in the 1950s, when conditions for practically everyone had improved, but it then began to fall from the early 1960s, hardly a time of economic pressure. Short-term conditions therefore seem only a marginal factor.

The post-war fertility experience points up the continued difficulty of finding explanations. The war saw a rapid increase in births, culminating in a post-war 'baby boom' in 1946. One factor here may have been the institution of family allowances in 1945. Yet after 1946 the birth rate fell again, although not quite to the level of the 1930s, before in 1956 beginning a sustained rise until the early 1960s. There was an increase in age-specific fertility across the age spectrum, most marked in younger women. The birth rate of women aged between twenty and twenty-four, for instance, increased by about 40 per cent between 1951 and 1961. One reason for this was a rise in the incidence of marriage, and a decline in the marriage age. But why this happened is not entirely clear, and so the post-war rise in fertility remains something of a mystery. It is much easier to explain the renewal of the decline from the mid-1960s, as the old factors were still at work, while new ones had become significant. In particular, opportunities for married women's employment had been increasing rapidly from the 1940s, and with this went a more gradual increase in the availability of progressive careers for women. The only substantial change in the 1960s itself which might have influenced family limitation was the availability of oral contraceptives from 1963.

The economic effect of the growth of population in this century has been less significant than in earlier periods, both because it has been slower and because the underlying rate of economic growth has been faster, particularly from the 1940s. Slower population growth has meant less pressure on housing provision, although this has been partly offset by the shortfall in housebuilding during the two world wars. There have also been short-term effects. In the 1950s, the gap between the demand for labour generated by economic growth and its supply, which was particularly low at that time as a result of the low birth rate of the 1930s, increased pressure for immigration. More recently, the children born in the high-fertility years of the early 1960s have entered the labour market at a time when employment opportunities are low. The final and perhaps most striking effect of modern population change has resulted from the decline in mortality, which has caused the expansion of the elderly population. The number of those over sixty-five has risen from 2.5 million in 1901 to 8.5 million in 1981. While this is partly a result of medical improvements, it has also resulted in a further increase in the demand for medical services, as well as fostering a vast industry which is devoted to catering for retirement.

The decline in population increase has been more or less coterminous with a decline in migration, which also started in the late nineteenth century. As in the nineteenth, twentieth-century migration has failed to equalise life chances, and severe regional inequalities have remained. In this century, however, it has tended to be unemployment which is the main variable between regions, rather than income levels. One can make sense of the fact that migration does not equalise life chances by seeing it as determined by a balance between promoting factors, notably wage and unemployment differentials, and retarding factors, which include the physical cost of moving, the risk of moving to an unknown location, and other factors discussed below.

From the late nineteenth century, the retarding factors began to have the upper hand, although before the First World War rather different factors were at work than after it. Among the initial factors which decreased the attractiveness of rural migration were the beginnings of decentralisation in industry, and the growth of personal mobility in rural areas because of that neglected but important invention, the bicycle. Industrial decentralisation and the growth of personal mobility have continued to increase throughout this century, so much so that by the 1960s much of the once rural South had become industrialised, while rural living, so long as it was not too remote, was no deterrent to the car owner. Hence much of the South has now become an area of inward migration. The more remote rural areas, however, such as mid-Wales, have suffered because although migration rates have declined, the continued absolute fall in population has meant a loss of services such as shopping facilities and schools. Tourism provides some antidote, but the employment it provides tends to be seasonal.

The problem of rural depopulation has been seen as a serious one for much of this century. In retrospect, some of this concern can be seen as a reflection of the nostalgic dream for a countryside full of sturdy independent yeomen, a state of affairs that has probably never existed and certainly did not exist by 1900. Effectively, the depopulation which occurred in some areas in this century was a coda to the dramatic change in agriculture's position in the national economy during the nineteenth century.

The decline in migration from rural Britain is fairly easy to explain. The relatively low levels of migration from the disadvantaged industrial regions of the inter-war period, and from those of today, needs a different set of explanations. The payment of unemployment benefit reduced the pressure to move in order to get a job at all costs, while the lack of work in other areas increased the risk involved in moving. At the height of the inter-war depression in 1931, unemployment even in the South East, the most prosperous region, was around 10 per cent. If you moved, what guarantee was there that you would get a job? Rent control, introduced in the First World War, was another disincentive. Up to 1933, houses remained controlled while there were sitting tenants there. People moving to another residence could expect to pay market rents, which were around a third higher than controlled rents.

In spite of disincentives, many did migrate. The Welsh could be found in large numbers on the route to London – in the Morris car factory in Oxford, in the light industry towns of High Wycombe and Slough, in London itself. Scottish steel workers moved en masse to Corby, in Northamptonshire, where steel making was expanding in the inter-war period.

Similar factors inhibit migration today, although housing is probably now a far worse problem. In 1933, the decontrol of the rents of cheaper housing when there were no sitting tenants was ended, while rent controls were strengthened further in the Second World War, although they have been eased since. The long-term effect of controls has been to weaken any incentive private landlords might have to own property for renting. Council housing has expanded enormously in lieu, but not enough to substitute in areas of high demand; hence it has not necessarily been available to those moving into an area, since there have usually been waiting lists for which local people have priority. Finally, and perhaps of equal importance in restricting housing supply and thus forcing up its cost, planning regulations have limited the amount of land available. The result has been to force up house prices fastest in the areas of greatest demand for housing, that is London and the South. A combination of good intentions and naked vote-winning (since there are always more tenants than landlords) has produced two major barriers to mobility: the dearth of freely available rented property, and regional house price imbalances. Migration has therefore been slow but, over a long period, cumulative. The regions of the nineteenth-century staple industries have seen a relative decline in population, while the South has experienced a relative gain. In the inter-war years, London and the South East were the chief gainers, together with the West Midlands as a centre of light industry. With the continued increase in personal mobility and further decentralisation of manufacturing and services, the South West and East Anglia have taken over as the regions of most rapid population growth (see Table 27.2).

It is an apparent paradox that net emigration ceased in the 1930s, after remaining at quite high levels in the 1920s, and was replaced by a net inflow. The paradox is apparent, not real. Economic conditions in much of the primary-producing Empire, which was the main recipient for emigration by this time, were even worse than in Britain. Since international migration has always been a two-way traffic, with a large number of returners even in the heyday of emigration, it only required a drying-up of outward movement for net emigration to become net immigration from Empire countries. Since the Second World War, there have been contrasting patterns. Over most of the period there has been a revival of net emigration, but immigrants from the New Commonwealth contributed towards a net inflow in the late 1950s. However, immigration restrictions sharply reduced the inflow from 1961. The total number of people who classified themselves as non-white amounted to about 2.5 million by the 1980s, of whom 60 per cent were immigrants.

Table 27.2 Population distribution by region (per cent)

	1901	*1951*	*1981*
South East	28.4	30.8	30.9
East Anglia	2.9	2.7	3.5
South West	7.0	6.8	8.0
West Midlands	8.1	9.1	9.5
East Midlands	6.5	7.1	7.0
North West	14.1	13.0	11.8
Yorkshire/Humberside	8.7	8.4	9.0
North	6.8	6.4	5.7
Wales	5.4	5.3	5.1
Scotland	12.1	10.4	9.5

(*Source:* Lee, C M 1986 *The British Economy since 1700*)

URBANISATION

As the discussion of migration implies, urbanisation, the most striking legacy of the rise of the industrial economy, had in relative terms largely taken place by 1900. Of course, the absolute population of urban areas continued to increase as the national population increased, but the proportion of the English and Welsh population which was urban rose only slightly, from 77 per cent in 1901 to a peak of 81 per cent in 1951, before falling to 76 per cent in 1981. The aggregate figures do conceal important changes within urban areas, however. One can generalise these by saying that, around the turn of the century, the process of concentration that had been so marked during the nineteenth century was reversed, and a process of decentralisation set in. The population living in city centres had already started to fall in the late nineteenth century. This was linked to transport improvements and the growing expense of land which forced out manufacturing in favour of high value-added service industries, whose employees could afford to commute. Throughout this century, these have continued to be the main influences on decentralisation, together with the decline of coal as a prime mover and the growth of road transport, both of which have positively encouraged manufacturing dispersion.

How can decentralisation be said to have taken place when there was an increase, up to 1951, in the proportion of the population which was urban? For a long time, the main effect of these decentralising tendencies was to move people from inner cities to suburbs, which became progressively further away from the centre as transport improvements and increased real incomes allowed longer journeys. The suburban living experience may have been very different from that in the inner cities, but the suburbanites were still classed as urban. Manufacturing decentralisation, too, reduced industrial concentration in large cities and conurbations, but it did not mean that manufacturing became rural. Between 1901 and 1961, the proportion of the population living in towns of between 50,000 and 200,000 people increased from 17 to 30 per cent in England and Wales. The losers were the very large cities and small towns. By the 1960s the growth of private motoring, and the freedom it gave from the constraints of fixed public-transport networks, initiated the overall decline in the urban share of the population noted earlier. The 'journey to work area', as planners call it, has been greatly enlarged and made much more flexible.

The decay and revival of the retirement industry is another factor which has had an influence on urbanisation, although the detail awaits study. The stagnation or even decline in the real value of income from investments over the First World War period must have had a deleterious effect on the wealthy leisured classes who had populated seaside resorts and the pleasanter inland towns. Cheltenham, for example, a town largely devoted to retirement, suffered a severe economic recession from the 1900s onward, as its elderly denizens sank into genteel poverty. The post-war period, however, saw the growth of a new group of retired people, the salariat with modest pensions. They flocked (and still do) to seaside resorts, whose capacity to absorb them increased as the seaside holiday declined from the 1960s. More recently still, the wealthy retired have again become a factor, as pensions have improved and become inflation-proofed. Observation would suggest that such people often make for smaller towns or villages.

The revival of rural areas highlights the problem of the economic decline of the inner cities. Until recently, the decline in job opportunities had gone hand in hand with the long-standing population decline, and had actually eased problems such as overcrowding. By the 1970s, job opportunities were declining faster than population. There were a variety of reasons for this. After the Second World War, planning restrictions added to the long-standing economic disadvantages of inner-city manufacturing and probably speeded up the latter's shift to other areas. Then in the

1960s and 1970s, dockwork and railway jobs declined. In the 1970s also, the opportunities for outward migration were reduced as the total stock of low-skilled jobs in the economy fell. The inner cities increasingly offered only relatively high-skilled service jobs, whose holders usually preferred to live in the outer suburbs or the country.

LABOUR SUPPLY

Before the twentieth century, the growth of the quantity of available labour moved more or less in step with the population. In this century, labour supply has lagged behind population increase. It is likely, however, that in a modern economy the quality of the labour supplied is more important than the quantity, and so discussion of quantity changes will be fairly brief, with the exception of the rise in the female participation rate, which has been of great importance to women.

The overall participation rate has remained remarkably stable over the long term. It was around 44 per cent in the mid and later nineteenth century and around 47 per cent in 1973 (it is expressed as the proportion of the total population available for work and so does not take account of unemployment). Apart from female participation, the other main influence has been changes in age-specific participation. The proportion of young people has fallen as the birth rate fell, although with an upwards jump after the Second World War, while the proportion of the elderly has risen. Within each of these age groups, there has been a declining participation rate throughout the period, as full-time education has increased for those at one end of the age spectrum and formal retirement has become the norm for those at the other. In recent years, the participation rate of men between sixty and the state retirement age of sixty-five has also decreased sharply, from 84 per cent in 1971 to 54 per cent in 1985, as early retirement, linked to occupational pension schemes, has become commonplace.

The first point to make about the rising female participation rate (see Table 27.3) is that it was not in any direct sense the result of either of the two world wars. Many women entered employment in each war, but left it afterwards, and the pre- and post-war participation rates in each case are not markedly different. The growth in women's participation has deeper roots.

One is the fact that types of employment which women were

already entering before the First World War, notably clerical work and its adjunct, typing, have been growing rapidly ever since. For a long time, however, this was counteracted by a decline in other types of women's paid work, notably employment in cotton textiles and domestic service. Up to the 1950s, therefore, total female participation did not change much.

Table 27.3 Female participation ratio (per cent)

	1901	1911	1921	1931	1951	1961	1971	1981
Total	35	36	34	34	35	37	44	48
Married women						30	42	49

1901 and 1951–61 over 15 years
1911–31 over 14 years
1971–81 over 16 years
(*Sources:* Lewis, J 1984 *Women in England 1870–1950; Social Trends*)

Changing types of work can only be a partial explanation for its subsequent rise, however. For as discussions in previous chapters have made clear, the work which people do, perhaps most particularly women, is the product not just of technical change, but also of social forces. Rising female participation rates can be seen as the consequence of the intersection of the demand for, and supply of, female labour, and both of these are subject to social as well as economic pressures. Apart from changes in the type of work available which increased the potential amount of women's employment, the long post-war boom also increased the demand for women workers. However, the continued rise in female participation after economic conditions worsened in the mid-1970s implies that demand was not the only factor. So does the failure of female wage rates to rise relative to male rates for most of the 1950s and 1960s, since if demand for female labour had been outrunning supply, relative wages should have risen. It therefore seems likely that supply-side forces equalled demand-side influences in their effect on participation. The falling birth rate was one supply-side factor which facilitated female employment, but this fall was most marked in the inter-war period, preceding any great increase in married women's employment. Similarly, female employment and the birth rate both rose in the 1950s. Birth-rate changes therefore give only a very general explanation. There is another link between the declining birth-rate and the rising supply of female labour, in that aspirations for higher family income may have influenced both the earlier birth-rate decline and the later desire to go out to work. This desire is not just income-orientated, however. Most people gain considerable non-monetary satisfaction from work, ranging from the opportunity for chat to the satisfaction of developing a career.

The ability to go out to work has clearly been facilitated by changes in household technology. These range from the more obvious appliances such as washing machines and electric irons, to fitted carpets, central heating and polyester/cotton sheets. Until these became common in the 1960s, housework was an even more time-consuming job than it is today. Yet even these developments do not provide more than a partial explanation for the growth in female participation, since better-off middle-class women were always relieved of most household chores by servants. So there must have been underlying changes in attitude, both among women themselves and among men in their various roles as husbands and as employers.

While the overall participation rate has held roughly constant in this century, the number of hours worked per person has fallen sharply. One reason for this has been a fall in the length of the working week, combined with longer holidays. The fall in manual workers' hours is shown in Table 35.3. By far the greatest fall came in 1919, with a sudden drop from around fifty-six hours, taking overtime into account, to forty-seven or slightly more. Subsequently, the fall in actual hours worked has been much slower as overtime has tended to increase. The usual explanation for this slow fall is that employers have preferred to incur extra costs through enhanced wage payments, rather than through paying workers the same for a shorter week. The shorter the working week, the less opportunity is there to recover overheads. Unions have adapted to this employer preference by using reductions in standard hours to enhance overtime payments; ostensible hours reductions, in other words, have frequently been disguised pay rises. This does not explain the 1919 reduction, of course; here one can only point to the complex of pressures for dramatic social change at that time. In spite of the slow fall in manual workers' hours after 1919, the rising proportion of workers in clerical and professional occupations, who tend to have shorter hours, and an increasing proportion of part-time workers, particularly among the female workforce, have both reduced the average of time spent at work. The proportion of part-timers rose from a negligible figure before 1939, to 42 per cent of the female workforce and 21 per cent of the total workforce in 1981.

Between 1918 and the 1960s, the varying movements of population, participation rates and hours worked more or less cancelled each other out, so that in spite of the rise in population, the total amount of labour supplied did not change much. The 1919 hours reduction had led to a sharp temporary fall, but this was subsequently counteracted by a rise in the population of working age. More recently, the downward effects have been stronger than the upward, with a particular impact from the raising of the school-leaving age to sixteen in 1972–3. Between 1964 and 1973, labour supply fell by around 10 per cent.

While enhanced education leads to falls in labour quantity, it is likely to improve its quality. Measuring all aspects of labour quality is extremely difficult, but it is theoretically possible to estimate its improvement through education by finding the extra income which accrues to those with an extra unit of education, say a year's schooling. In practice, this is virtually impossible to do for England except in the recent past, but there are also comparative studies for other countries available. These suggest that enhanced education does substantially improve income levels. However, there are methodological problems with this data. For instance, one theory, known as credentialism, holds that better-paid jobs may demand qualifications not for their educational worth, but as barriers to entry. Empirical studies suggest that, at least in this country, the remuneration of most work does more or less equate with its marginal productivity. In other words, extra remuneration is a reward for extra value and not just for artificial scarcity, and so credentialism is not a significant factor.

Assuming that this is the case and that enhanced education is of genuine economic value, Matthews has found that it accounts for an average increase in output of about 0.5 per cent per year cumulatively since before the First World War until 1973. There was a fairly steady increase in basic schooling throughout the period. Up to 1939, this was largely because an increasing number of children stayed on to fourteen. After the war, the extension of secondary education became more important. While poor basic education in Britain may have adversely affected economic performance before the First World War, international comparisons suggest that basic education levels are now more satisfactory. In 1976, everyone between fifteen and sixty-four had, on average, over ten years of formal educational experience, which is relatively high compared with most industrial countries. (The quality of education, which is not measured here, might alter the picture.) Technical education as measured by apprenticeship numbers did not change much between the wars, but then jumped as employers and unions cooperated to make apprenticeship more effective. In the 1950s and 1960s, the number of boys entering apprenticeships averaged around 100,000 per year, suggesting that about 25 per cent of those entering work underwent apprentice training. Another, smaller, proportion experienced other types of technical training. By the 1980s, around a third of the male manual workforce had experienced apprentice-level training or the equivalent, up from perhaps 20 per cent in the 1900s. International comparisons are much less favourable, however. In Germany, two-thirds of the workforce have equivalent qualifications. Since 1979, furthermore, the apprentice intake has collapsed, to 40,000 per year in 1983. On the other hand, increasing numbers of school leavers – by the mid-1980s all those who had not got some other form of job or training – secured places on one-year schemes which combined training and work experience. Whether these schemes provided effective training is a different matter.

International comparisons suggest that higher-level education may also have been too limited, or misdirected, in this country. The average quantity of higher education, if spread among the entire population, is relatively low, at 0.29 years per person in 1976, compared with 0.44 in Japan or 0.56 in France. Most notable has been the persistent lack of formal engineering training, a problem already identified before the First World War. Engineering training has implications for many other industries besides engineering itself, since from the late nineteenth century most forms of manufacturing have used sophisticated machinery which requires engineering knowledge. In the 1930s, Britain graduated under half the number of engineers that Germany did, while between 1925 and 1939 a total of under 1000 electrical engineers had graduated – for one of the most rapidly growing inter-war industries. By 1978, 10,000 engineers a year were graduating in Britain, 80,000 a year in Japan. Formal university-level education was supplemented before the Second World War by premium apprenticeship, which provided on-the-job training at higher levels; while many managers, in engineering and other disciplines, have obtained qualifications by part-time study. So a comparison of graduation levels does not tell the whole story. Nevertheless, there seems strong evidence that the provision of higher education in Britain has been insufficient.

CHAPTER TWENTY-EIGHT
Business organisation and management

Before the First World War, the larger part of business consisted of family-owned firms, whereas today the larger part consists of public companies. Parallel with this change, the average size of firms has increased. The two phenomena are related in that the greater capital needs of large companies make it increasingly unlikely that single or family owners will be able to provide all the finance themselves. This is not the only explanation for the decline of private ownership, however. The increase in estate duty as the century wore on made transferring assets to the next generation more difficult, although there were ways of mitigating this tax. Another problem was that, from the later 1950s, the distribution of profits above a certain level from family businesses became compulsory, thus enabling personal tax to be levied on the income. A long-term view, however, suggests that the decline of the family-owned business was inevitable when limited liability became available to all in the mid-nineteenth century, even though change was slow at first. For most sizeable firms, the time comes when the owners wish to diversify their assets. Issuing shares on the stock market is a way of doing this and retaining some interest in the firm if that is desired.

In spite of these long-term trends, about a fifth of national income in 1975 was produced by small companies not incorporated by limited liability, and by the self-employed. So these groups are still an important part of the economy, and certain forces make for their continued vitality. They exist primarily in the service sector, in which many businesses can be carried on with little more than a marketable skill and a telephone. Certainly many occupations which comprised a large proportion of this group in 1914, such as old-fashioned artisan trades, have declined sharply in numbers. Other groups such as the professional classes – doctors, lawyers and the like – and the providers of specialised household services, such as electricians and plumbers, have been much more buoyant.

In spite of the vitality of the small business, the share of the 100 largest manufacturing firms in net manufacturing output rose from 15 per cent in 1909 to 40 per cent in 1970. Retailing also experienced a steady growth in concentration, while in banking and railways concentration had occurred earlier and was much more marked than in other sectors by the 1920s. One explanation for this is that economies of scale make increasing size inevitable, although in only a few industries, such as iron and steel production, are there almost unlimited economies of scale for technical reasons. In most cases, the greatest economies come in purchasing, marketing, research and development, and the ability to pool knowledge of the best practice in production techniques. In Britain, however, many firms failed to exploit the potential gains from thorough integration of their operations. This had been the case with most pre-First World War mergers, and Alfred Chandler suggests that it continued to be the case up to the 1930s and in many cases beyond. There were important mergers before and after the First World War in the brewing, food-processing, soap, tobacco and machinery industries. Most of these resulted in decentralised amalgamated firms, in which there was cooperation in purchasing and overseas marketing, while competition among the constituent firms on the domestic market was limited. But otherwise, the constituent firms ran virtually autonomously, often under the direction of the original family owners. One of the last firms to be run on the old lines was Distillers, the spirits manufacturers, taken over by Guinness in 1986. There were exceptions, notably Imperial Chemical Industries (ICI), formed in 1926 from a number of chemical firms. These included the explosives firm Nobel Industries, which had already re-organised its management structure. Influenced by the developments at Nobel, ICI moved to the modern concept of a multi-divisional structure, in which operating divisions were separate entities and certain functions were centralised. The concept was very different from the old-style decentralised amalgamations. Operating divisions were constituted on a product basis, not because they happened to be separate organisations in the past; and, most important, financial control was one of the centralised activities.

It was only in the 1960s that the majority of large British firms adopted a multi-division structure, often under the guidance of the American management consultants McKinsey. Some very large and apparently successful firms such as the General Electric Company (GEC), Hanson Trust and BTR confine their head office operation to the monitoring of subsidiaries' budgets and approval of capital expenditure. GEC, which operates in the related areas of electrical and electronic goods manufacture, does however also have important central research and development facilities.

The inability of many large British firms, up to at least the 1950s, to reap the full benefits of their size must have had a deleterious effect on economic performance. The failure of these firms to maximise efficiency also suggests that the causes of the increase in concentration do not lie primarily in the force of competition driving out less efficient smaller firms. There have been other factors at work. Concentration in Britain has been largely achieved by mergers between firms or takeovers of one firm by another, rather than by organic growth within firms. Many of the early mergers, which produced the loosely-structured amalgamated firms described earlier, were primarily attempts to restrict competition, and can be seen as an extension of the price-fixing agreements of the late nineteenth century. Restriction of competition was stimulated by the difficult economic climate of the inter-war years. Another motive was the pursuit of speculative financial gain. The speculative boom of 1919–20 saw a wave of mergers, which were then used as an excuse to float the merged companies on the stock market at inflated prices. The 'asset-stripping' firms of the late 1960s and early 1970s, such as Slater Walker, were primarily financial operators who specialised in acquiring undervalued property assets. More often in recent years, mergers and hostile takeover bids, the latter dating from the 1950s, have had a mixed rationale. Professional managers, some with a financial stake in their company, have seen takeovers as a means of both acquiring assets cheaply and improving the profitability of the companies acquired. Thus conglomerates with a number of diverse activities have grown up, such as Sears Holdings, Charles Clore's 1950s creation, and more recently Hanson Trust and BTR. The usual rationale for mergers or takeovers in recent years, however, has been that firms have similar activities, so that the merger should give rise to economies of scale or enable rationalisation to take place. This was apparent as early as 1923 in the government-sponsored railway amalgamations; in the mergers, again with government blessing, which produced GEC and the car and lorry producer British Leyland in the 1960s; and in numerous private initiatives. The decline of the old type of loose amalgamation may have enhanced the economic benefits of mergers in recent years, insofar as they allowed economies of scale to be realised and enabled efficient managers to increase the scope of their activities. On the other hand, certain mergers clearly had a disastrous effect, most notably British Leyland where the effect seems to have been to widen the scope of bad management, so that it eventually destroyed almost the entire indigenous vehicle industry. Furthermore, the tendency of the stock market to value companies on their short-term earnings, rather than long-term aims, may have unduly enhanced the share price of certain companies and enabled them to take over other companies which were efficiently run and where there were no real economies of scale available.

The growth of large firms run by professional managers has led commentators to question the extent to which profit is in fact the goal of such firms or managers. There are a number of reasons for these doubts. A large number of managers have existed in an environment in which profit was not the only or even the main aim of the business. Notable among these have been the managers of the nationalised industries, but even before the Second World War observers such as Keynes noted that the managers of large firms, such as railway companies and banks, were highly visible to the public and government but not very accessible to shareholders. These managers, therefore, had as much or more incentive to satisfy the former as the latter. As average firm size has grown, and more firms have issued shares quoted on the stock exchange, this tendency has increased. Individual shareholders usually control only a small part of a company, and this shareholding is usually a small part of their assets. Unless the company's performance is very unsatisfactory, shareholders are unlikely to interfere. In recent years, the growth of shareholdings by large institutions such as pension funds has been some antidote to shareholder apathy, but even these institutions rarely interfere directly in management.

There may therefore be pressures on management other than to produce the maximum profit. Apart from the public and government, these might come from workers, colleagues, managers' own interests, and so on. The varying pressures on management are difficult to pinpoint easily, and the effects of the resulting diversity of aims are even harder to assess. It could be argued that since public opinion and the government are a fact of life, managers who fail to take account of these factors may not be acting in the best long-term interests of the firm. It seems likely that nationalised industries did suffer, particularly in their earlier years, from a lack of clear goals for management. However, the idea that the divorce of ownership and control has reduced managers' concern for profit can be taken too far. Apart from the problem of deciding whether short-term or long-term profit goals are the ones being aimed at, the growth since the 1970s in profit-linked salaries, and the increased use of budgets to set clear targets for cash generation and profits, are both ways of sharpening the emphasis on profits. The possibility of takeover has had the same effect. And since the 1960s, nationalised industries have had financial targets, although these have often been overriden.

The growth of a distinct group of professional managers is one thing; the growth of a management profession another. This apparently paradoxical statement highlights the fact that managers in Britain have had less formal training than those in most industrialised countries. The under-provision of higher education in general, and in engineering in particular, is discussed in Chapter 27. Education for management itself, or for allied disciplines such as personnel management or accountancy, has had some strengths but also considerable weaknesses. Formal training for financial accountants and bankers, carried out mainly by part-time study and examinations set by the relevant professional associations, has been thorough, although until recently there has been little provision for full-time higher education in these subjects. Cost accountancy, which is much more relevant than financial accountancy to the control of production costs, was neglected in Britain in the first half of this century, in contrast to Germany. General management education, through the provision of undergraduate courses in business studies, was limited before the 1960's, as was the growth of graduate business schools. This lack of management education, especially in some areas, reveals itself in surveys of the qualifications of existing managers. In 1977, nearly a half of production managers surveyed had left school before they were sixteen; and although a third had degrees, this compared with a half in Germany. As with engineering training and that in accountancy and banking, raw comparisons of this kind leave out the fact that part-time education for those already in work, leading to professional qualifications, has for a long time been much better developed in Britain than in most countries. This type of education has advantages in that it allows theory and practice to be related. The problem is that it can lead to an excessive respect for existing practice and can give an inadequate theoretical foundation for the development of new ideas.

While there may be deep-rooted social reasons for this neglect of formal management education, a proximate reason, mentioned earlier, quickly suggests itself. This is the continued domination of many British firms by members of the original family, at least up to the 1950s. This had two repercussions: almost automatic recruitment of family members reduced the demand for high-level managers, which must have reduced the incentive for institutions like universities to set up courses in management; and the lack of integration within amalgamated firms, and the consequent lack of any need to determine which were the most efficient plants and techniques, reduced the demand for standardised costing procedures. Both these lacunae were in sharp contrast to Germany and the USA, where amalgamated firms from the late nineteenth century demanded professional management which was applied throughout the organisation. Significantly, among the few sponsors of higher management education in Britain in the inter-war period were the railways, which had long had a bureaucratic management structure.

While a study of management training throws an indirect light on management practice, only a detailed study of what managers actually did can really help us here, and such studies hardly exist for the middle-management level of production, sales and other functions. Since formal training was so limited in the early years of this century, such general ideas as existed were disseminated by other means. From the 1890s or earlier, there were books dealing with the organisation of work on the shop floor, while the journals of the professional engineering associations which had been founded in the nineteenth century also dealt with this subject. One result was the rapid spread in the 1900s of the premium bonus system, a type of incentive payment used in engineering. These developments were independent of the 'Scientific Management' movement begun by the American F W Taylor at the same time. (Scientific Management, or Taylorism, had little direct impact anywhere in Europe, although it gave rise to techniques such as time and motion study which have become standard. The importance of Taylorism has been exaggerated by some historians. Much of it was no more than the elaboration of ideas already current in management textbooks.)

The First World War and afterwards saw considerable development in personnel management and in associated fields such as industrial psychology and industrial health. There was also an extension of welfare provision, ranging from company playing fields to works canteens. One influence on all this was a set of quite sophisticated ideas, developed by enlightened employers such as Seebohm Rowntree and Edward Cadbury, which echoed the inter-war American 'Human Relations' school of management theorists in laying an emphasis on the importance of inter-group relations and personal satisfaction at work. For most employers, however, welfare provision was probably little more than the expression of a sort of vague paternalism on the cheap, allied to government pressure for better working conditions which was exercised during the two world wars. Works canteens, for instance, spread in the Second World War due to the pressure of Ernest Bevin, the Minister of Labour.

The First World War also saw the beginnings of professional institutes concerned with personnel management, advertising and other functions, but until the Second World War their influence was very limited. Since then, they have grown rapidly. Perhaps it is now possible to speak of a management profession, symbolised by the senior management body, the British Institute of Management founded in 1947; but it is still a profession with apparently serious gaps in its education and training.

The lowest but one of the most important levels of management, the foreman on the shop floor, has also been neglected by historians. Certain facts stand out. Since the late nineteenth century, foremen have lost much of their autonomy to the professionalised groups discussed above. Their power to hire and fire has gone to personnel managers; much of their control over work organisation to production managers or work study specialists. On the other hand, a relic of their old status remains in that foremen in Britain have usually controlled quite large groups of workers; this has impinged on employee expectations, since up to the recent past it seems that even workers in routine jobs have expected a reasonable degree of freedom from constant supervision. A comparison with Japanese factories, where foremen control smaller groups but work much more closely with them, is instructive. British foremen also share with the workforce as a whole a lack of technical skill as measured by formal qualifications, at least as compared with Germany. It may be that problems of quality control and poor scheduling of work in British factories owe something to the ambivalent position and low qualifications of foremen as a group.

CHAPTER TWENTY-NINE
Trade unions in the twentieth century

During the twentieth century, unions have been far more influential, and far more in the public eye, than they ever were previously. For most of the time, they have enjoyed rising membership, although there were periods of decline such as the 1920s and the 1980s (Table 29.1). Their position in society has also changed. In 1900, only a minority of employers recognised and bargained with them, but an increasing number have come to do so, change occurring particularly rapidly over the period of the two world wars. In 1900, unions did not have regular contacts with government, while the government had very little concern with industrial disputes. This too has changed. Unions have become involved in quasi-governmental institutions, while the government has concerned itself with industrial disputes,

Table 29.1 Union membership (millions)

	Males	Density (%)	Females	Density (%)	Total	Density (%)
1918	5.3	42	1.2	22	6.5	36
1920	7.0	54	1.3	24	8.4	45
1925	4.7	37	0.8	15	5.5	30
1935	4.1	31	0.8	12	4.9	25
1946	7.2	52	1.6	24	8.8	43
1955	7.9	55	1.9	24	9.7	44
1965	8.0	52	2.2	25	10.2	43
1975	8.7	54	3.5	36	12.2	47
1984	n.a.	n.a.	n.a.	n.a.	11.1	41

Density = proportion of unionised workers as proportion of total work-
        force
Totals may differ due to rounding
(*Sources:* Halsey; *Annual Abstract*)

for a variety of reasons. In 1900, most union members were skilled workers, or at the least semi-skilled workers who commanded high wages, such as coalminers and cotton spinners. Since then the spectrum of membership has greatly widened, to include both unskilled workers on the one hand, and white-collar workers on the other. Finally, unions and their members have been involved in far wider-ranging and more spectacular strikes than was ever the case in the nineteenth century. There were strike waves in 1909–14 and in 1919–21; there was the 1926 General Strike, which involved one and a half million workers; and, more recently, there has been a heavy incidence of strike activity in the 1970s, followed by the year-long miners' strike of 1984–5 (see Fig. 29.1).

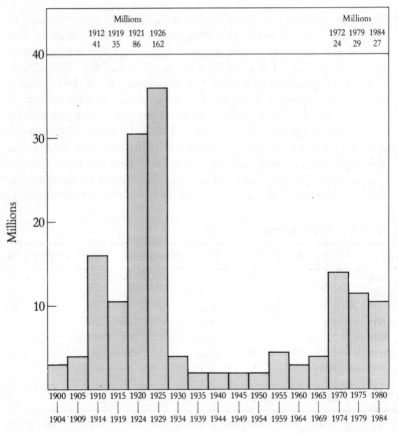

Figure 29.1 Days lost by strikes in the UK 1900–84 (annual averages) (based on Halsey; *Annual Abstracts*)

In spite of these changes, there have been important continuities in unions' fundamental objectives and in their methods of operation. For most unions, obtaining the highest possible wages has always been their foremost objective, but other considerations such as job security have usually been present. Furthermore, wages are part of a bargain which involves the worker expending effort; so unions have been concerned to limit or at least define the effort their members put into their work, so as to ensure that there is some link between effort and pay.

In the nineteenth century, most unions attempted to maintain control over wage levels by the limitation of access to certain jobs. In this way, they could limit competition for these jobs and have more chance of enforcing their wage scales. The greatest success went to unions in skilled occupations such as engineering and printing, in which access was limited anyway because of the technical qualifications needed for the work. The widening of union membership to include many semi- and unskilled workers has obviously led to change, although craft unions, which are in many cases the direct descendants of the skilled unions of the nineteenth century, have not changed at all in essence, at least until recently. The core of the policy of these unions has continued to be the attempt to enforce the manning of certain machines, or the performance of certain tasks, by time-served workers, that is those who have served an apprenticeship. Unions following this policy for a large proportion of their membership have included the Amalgamated Engineering Union (AEU – the successor to the ASE), the Electrical Trade Union (now the Electrical, Electronic, Telecommunications and Plumbing Trade Union or EETPU) and the National Graphical Association (NGA), which was formed in 1964 from various smaller printing unions. This policy has not just encompassed attempts to limit certain jobs to members of a particular union; even within unions, members of different trades considered that they had rights to certain tasks, and so separate groups such as millwrights, fitters and turners continued within engineering, and riveters, platers and welders within shipbuilding. As in the nineteenth century, most of these groups did not merely claim preference to certain kinds of jobs, but were the workers most technically capable of doing them. Consequently, their claims to higher pay have usually been accepted by employers. In some cases, however, the actual skill levels needed have declined since the nineteenth century. Newspaper printers, organised by the NGA, have had much of their work mechanised by the Linotype machine and yet have maintained high pay levels; in the 1930s, welding was successfully claimed by the Boilermakers Union as an apprenticed and, therefore, higher-paid job, even though the technical skill required was not great. In such cases, there have usually been special factors at work. Some groups of workers, for instance, have had a strategic position in the production process which gave them a high potential to create havoc by suddenly stopping work; newspaper printers, before the recent introduction of direct input typesetting, are a good example. In other cases, employers have been willing to give concessions to workers at the behest of a powerful union such as the Boilermakers; if the concessions were demanded only for a limited group, the employers might not bother to make too much fuss.

The majority of manual workers have not been able to follow the strategies outlined above. If everyone successfully claimed skill, then it would command no wage premium at all. However, workers without much skill or without a strategic position have sometimes tried to fulfil the same aim of limiting access. One way of doing this has been the pre-entry closed shop, once used among skilled artisan trades and kept up by the printers as part of their armoury of controls over labour supply. In this, workers have to be members of a union before they work and, in practice, the union is usually responsible for filling vacancies. A less skilled group with this privilege are the Smithfield meat porters, who gained it in the 1930s. The practice can clearly become an open sesame to nepotism and in printing certainly seems to have been associated with a high level of family recruitment. Fortunately, it has been quite rare in British trade unionism.

For most semi-skilled and unskilled workers, however, controls over labour suppply can only be very limited. In these circumstances, the ultimate weapon of the union is the strike; and it helps to have a high level of union membership in the workforce concerned, in order to persuade employers not to provoke strikes. One union aim, therefore, has been the post-entry closed shop, which simply means that everyone in a particular place of work, or firm, must join the union. Closed-shop agreements have expanded rapidly since the Second World War, and by 1978 almost 40 per cent of workers in manufacturing were covered by them. To back up strikes if they have occurred, unions in the past have looked to workers outside the dispute to support it by not dealing with the employers concerned. In 1913, a strike by agricultural workers in Lancashire was supported by railwaymen who refused to handle produce. The 1926 General Strike was essentially a large-scale sympathetic strike by railway and other workers in support of the coalminers, who were in dispute with their employers over proposed wage reductions. The strike failed partly because it lacked a clearly focused target. Sympathetic action by other workers has also been prone to founder on sectionalism. One reason why unions supported the General Strike was guilt at 'Black Friday' (15 April 1921), when the National Union of Railwaymen and other transport workers failed to support miners against another proposed wage reduction. So sympathetic action by those not on strike cannot be guaranteed. Consequently, the ability to discourage dealing with employers in dispute, by picketing the strikers' place of work, has been seen as a fundamental trade-union right since the later nineteenth century. In the National Union of Mineworkers' strikes of 1972 and 1974 and in other strikes in the 1970s, picketing was extended from the workers' own firm or place of work to other organisations whose operations might be detrimental to the success of the strike, such as, in the case of the NUM strikes, electricity power stations.

For the most part, however, unions have preferred not to strike but to bargain with employers. In order to make their bargaining effective without the use of strikes, unions have sometimes deployed other weapons, such as controls over effort. These have had a rationale in themselves, for instance as a means of preserving jobs; but essentially they can be seen as a recognition of the inseparable link between pay and effort, and of the consequent fact that employers have been willing to pay more to increase effort. Agreements over minimum manning levels were reached in some steel mills as early as the 1900s; informal agreements over assembly-line speeds appear to have existed in some car plants in the 1960s and 1970s, while lorry drivers have enforced mileage limitations. An alternative to limits on effort is to link pay directly with effort through piecework wage systems. Both unions and employers have had changing views on piecework; these changes have reflected genuine changes in technology, but also whichever system of pay determination has been most fashionable among personnel managers. Mining, textiles and shipbuilding were long-standing adherents of piecework payment, while in this century engineering has joined them, especially for mass-production sections of the industry such as car production. But mining, for instance, moved to day-work payment in the National Power Loading Agreement of 1966, as it was believed that mechanisation had broken the link between effort and output. Incentive payments based on output were then reintroduced in 1978.

Finally, unions have tried to better their wages or conditions by indirect means. One method has been support for legislation which might benefit their members and hostility to that which is seen as threatening the position of unions. Membership of quasi-governmental organisations, such as the National Economic Development Council, on which unions can try to influence government policy has been another. In addition, unions' support for nationalisation can be interpreted, perhaps cynically, as an attempt to remove the constraints which lack of profits might have on wages. The TUC's arguments for nationalisation of coalmining, put forward in 1936, stated that miners must have a 'proper level of wages', which would be fixed regardless of the price consumers were prepared to pay for the coal.

Unions have not operated in a vacuum in the twentieth century, however, any more than they did in the nineteenth. The attitudes of employers have throughout shaped the environment in which unions work, most crucially because it is only when employers formally recognise them that coherent and regular bargaining can take place. Employers' attitudes themselves have been shaped by external influences, notably the influence of government. In both the wars, the government put pressure on employers to recognise unions, in return for union cooperation in the war effort. Since the Second World War, central and local government organisations have themselves had an increasingly important role as employers; the central government of civil servants and, indirectly, of workers in the nationalised industries, and local government of employees ranging from teachers to dustmen. In this role, government bodies have tended to encourage unions by accepting their role in bargaining and by providing supportive facilities for them to service their membership. But many private employers have accepted unions since the nineteenth century without government pressure. There have been a variety of reasons for this. Employers may have felt certain moral obligations or have had a concept of themselves as 'good employers'. This has partly accounted for the acceptance of unions by government, or by government-owned organisations, but large firms such as ICI have increasingly put an emphasis on maintaining good labour relations by dealing with the appropriate unions. In the heavy industries, the home of pro-union employers in the nineteenth century, unions were perhaps accepted more as a convenience. They provided a means of negotiating coherent pay structures which prevented leapfrogging pay demands in times of good trade while, if agreements were comprehensive, they prevented fly-by-night employers undercutting on price by paying low wages. This acceptance of the role of unions became solidified by time, and only the most extreme outside pressure could disrupt it. In the coal industry, where inter-war depression saw severe pressure on prices and hence wages, even the conciliatory employers of the Durham coalfield joined in wage-cutting, putting severe strains on the previously friendly relationship between employers and unions. However, in other industries, union leaders and industrialists, whatever their public rhetoric, could see each other as fulfilling a necessary role. Harry Hopkins, President Roosevelt's special envoy during the Second World War, was impressed by the friendly relations between Ernest Bevin and Herbert Morrison, both Labour politicians and the former also an important trade union leader, and the industrialist Sir Andrew Duncan. Hopkins contrasted this with the situation in the USA.

Although the number of employers accepting unions has increased, at least until recently, there have always been those who were hostile or who gave unions so little active encouragement as to render them ineffectual. Such firms have often provided some alternative attraction for their workers, such as a degree of paternalism or higher than normal wages. An inter-war example was Morris Motors of Oxford. Today IBM, the multi-national computer firm, does not negotiate with unions but is said to provide attractive wages and other benefits. Many white-collar employers, both large and small, have resisted unions. The banks, for instance, did so between the wars, creating staff associations which reduced the scope for the one independent union, the Bank Officers Guild. In this and other cases, however, it is difficult to disentangle the adverse influences on union growth: there have been the employers' attitudes; the attitudes of white-collar employees, who were and are frequently hostile to unions; and the difficulty of organising a workforce which has mostly worked in fairly small offices rather than large factories.

The wartime pressure on employers by government was largely a result of the strong position that unions had at the time, and did not herald a long-run change in the essential neutrality of the state as between employers and unions. Contrary to a frequently repeated legend, the post-First World War governments did not act as agents of the employers. Government preparations against a General Strike were relatively small scale, although the idea of such a strike was frequently mooted during this period. Even after the strike, the Conservative government, by the 1927 Trade Disputes Act, made only limited changes to the labour laws. Sympathetic strikes were outlawed, and the system of union members 'contracting out' of paying a political levy (which usually went to the Labour Party) was altered to a system of 'contracting in'. In other words, a positive decision had to be made to pay the levy. The second measure did reduce the income of the Labour Party, but had little direct effect on unions. Given the economic views of the time, which saw high wages as one cause of unemployment, the forbearance of governments is worth emphasising, since stronger action might have forced down wage levels. The lack of action can be put down to the continued belief that state intervention in relations between capital and labour was wrong. In accordance with this attitude, the Second World War and the subsequent election of a Labour government did not lead to the unions receiving undue preference. The 1927 Act was repealed, but wage increases remained relatively low, with the unions themselves exercising restraint.

It was, paradoxically, the 1950s and a Conservative government which saw the flowering of union influence. The Conservatives were desperately anxious to prove their credentials as a party of the people and the Minister of Labour, Sir Walter Monckton, cultivated good relations with union leaders. Employers were encouraged to settle disputes which posed a serious threat to production, even if the terms were more generous than they wished. This tendency strengthened under the Labour government of the 1960s. Yet the public perception of unions was by now deteriorating, leading to the beginnings of a change in government attitudes. In 1969, the Labour government attempted unsuccessfully to introduce reforms of the labour laws, and by the 1980s, Conservative reforms were widely supported, even by union members. The 1980 Employment Act restricted lawful picketing to the pickets' own place of work. The 1982 Act went further: sympathetic strikes were, once again, made unlawful. Most important was the removal of the unions' legal immunity from civil actions, thus making them liable for damages if they carried out unlawful actions – such as picketing away from the place of work of those in dispute. The 1984 Act further required that, to be lawful, industrial action must be supported by a pre-strike ballot, rather than decided upon in whatever way an individual union's rules dictated. The reforms have introduced a radical change in the legislative framework of British industrial relations. The *laissez-faire* approach enshrined in the 1870s, and reaffirmed by the Liberal government of 1906, was swept away. No longer did government hold that unions' internal affairs were not the concern of the state. No longer was it accepted that almost any degree of interference with an employer's business was legitimate in pursuit of an industrial dispute.

Whatever the attitudes of government and employers, unions have ultimately depended on the support they get from individual workers. Certain circumstances have made unions attractive to workers. One influence has been size of workplace, since those with a large number of employees are much easier and cheaper for unions to service. For most of the period, the average size of workplace has been increasing, so union growth has been facilitated. On the other hand, scattered workers such as agricultural labourers have proved notoriously hard to organise. Another major influence on union growth has been inflation. This has led to anxiety among workers that their pay will fall behind rising prices, and has also made it relatively easy for unions to deliver pay increases, so giving them favourable publicity. The inflationary period just after the First World War, and the 1970s both saw a rapid growth in union membership. On the other hand, many workers, particularly in retailing and office employment, have proved resistant to unionisation. This has sometimes been because they work in small groups or their employers have been hostile to unions, but often because they themselves have had unfavourable attitudes towards unions. The growth in these lightly unionised sectors of the economy has tended to counteract the increase in union membership brought about by the growth of the closed shop and the increase in public service employment.

While many workers have resisted joining unions because they disliked them, most who have joined voluntarily have done so not out of commitment but for economic reasons. Surveys such as an extensive one of the Vauxhall car plant in Luton in the 1960s, carried out by J H Goldthorpe and others, showed that workers viewed unions in instrumental terms, as a means of delivering better wages and conditions. Interest in the union's political stance was minimal. This concentration on the here and now may often have led union members to support politically radical leaders in the belief that such leaders might fight industrial battles more energetically. The Nottinghamshire miners, whose moderation has twice led them to disassociate themselves from the national miners' union (in the inter-war years and after the 1984–5 coal strike), have nevertheless sometimes voted in a Communist as one of their senior officials.

The difficulties of maintaining contact between bureaucratic union structures and a membership which has usually been apathetic, but can be suddenly stirred by wage issues or by some shop-floor grievance, has led to a growth throughout the century in the number of shop stewards, elected and frequently unpaid representatives of the workforce. Many commentators have associated shop stewards with militancy. In the First World War, the 'Shop Stewards' Movement' was associated with large-scale unofficial (i.e. unrecognised by the union) strikes in engineering, and in the 1950s, 1960s and 1970s there were frequent disputes in the car industry in which shop stewards were prominent. However, the strikes in the First World War were based on a very strong groundswell of feeling among the workforce on certain issues, while in the car industry strikes have had many causes, including chaotic pay structures and weak management. For the most part, shop stewards have been conciliators, dealing with bread-and-butter issues such as the support of individual workers' grievances through the procedural channels. In a 1973 survey, 80 per cent of senior managers thought that stewards helped solve industrial relations problems.

To some extent the growth in the number of shop stewards was a natural counter to the pre-1914 extension of the geographic area and scope of collective agreements. One of the overarching aims of unions, to standardise wages and conditions in order to prevent undercutting and exploitation, was well served by this strategy; but it isolated workers in individual plants from the bargaining process and from the union structure. So the move to large-scale and even national agreements, which was given an enormous boost by the extension of collective bargaining in the First World War, has subsequently slowed and probably receded. Nationalisation extended such agreements in some industries, but the more recent trend towards decentralised management has militated against it; other influences have been union policy, which may favour centralised bargaining, as the miners have for many years, or may accept diversity and decentralised bargaining, as in the case of the Transport and General Workers Union.

To judge from unions' public rhetoric, it is largely they who have been responsible for the improvement in living standards this century; to judge from the rhetoric of some anti-union commentators, unions have been the major cause of the relative decline in Britain's economic standing. Both views are nonsense, but the question is, how much nonsense?

The first contention was discussed, in the context of the nineteenth century, in Chapter 22. There it was suggested that, when prices were stable, the upward pressure unions exerted on wages may have had beneficial effects on labour productivity and hence, ultimately, on incomes by forcing employers to modernise in order to stay competitive. It would be harder to support this contention for the post-1945 period, since it has been easier for employers to pass on cost increases. What has happened is that labour's share of national income has increased substantially, from around 55 per cent before the First World War to over 70 per cent in the 1970s. However, as discussed in Chapter 33, there are various explanations for this, of which trade-union pressure is only one. Certainly the influence of unions on income distribution should not be entirely discounted, since there is evidence that wages in unionised industries are higher than wages in equivalent non-unionised ones. Changes in income distribution, however, should be put in the context of the near-tripling of average per capita disposable income between 1913 and 1985. In other words, total national income, divided among everybody in the country, has grown enough to permit an almost threefold increase in average living standards – and this without taking into account tax revenues used to finance government expenditure, which provides indirect benefits for most people. This increase has come about because of economic growth, not because of redistribution which, for those who have benefited, has been a gilding on the lily. It has perhaps been more important in certain periods than in the longer term. In the inter-war period, in particular, unions may have contributed to the maintenance of wage levels and, therefore, the maintenance at a high level of labour's share of national income. The willingness of most employers to accept this position was, however, also a factor.

To the individual worker, the greatest value of unions has probably been the protection given against unfair treatment or dismissal. In theory, capitalist firms should operate in a rational profit-maximising way, treating individual workers as no more than units of production – concepts of fairness and unfairness should not apply. In practice, employers have run the full gamut from those who have consciously striven to be fair and afford good conditions of employment to those who have not, or who have allowed tyrannical foremen or managers full sway. Unions have offered an antidote to the latter.

If unions have not benefited workers' living standards much, have they had the opposite effect by deleteriously affecting national economic performance? There are a variety of possible ways in which this might have come about. It has been argued, for instance, that unions' insistence from the 1950s onwards on excessive wage rises forced up export costs, so exacerbating balance of payments problems and forcing governments to deflate demand. Hence the constant attempts in the 1960s and 1970s to find viable incomes policies. While some unions did become more aggressive in pursuing wage claims from the 1950s, there were other important factors at work. Governments themselves frequently encouraged employers to take a soft line. Perhaps even more important, union leaders' militancy usually reflected grass-roots pressure. The miners' strikes of 1972 and 1974, for instance, were foreshadowed by large unofficial disputes in Yorkshire in 1969 and 1970. And what lay at the heart of these and many other disputes was frustration at the slow rise in real wages. Poor national economic performance, allied to an increasing tax burden, has more probably been a cause rather than an effect of union pressure.

At the level of the individual firm, the insistence by unions on restrictive practices such as minimum manning levels or strict demarcation between different tasks, coupled with the debilitating effect of frequent stoppages, is often said to have hampered productivity. There is little doubt that the effects of all these must have been adverse. The problem is to decide how adverse, since it is extremely difficult to obtain quantitative measurements. Some wider perspectives may help in forming a judgement. Industries with bad strike records since 1945, such as vehicles and shipbuilding, have experienced increasing problems in remaining internationally competitive; but the same has been true of many industries with relatively good industrial relations records, such as textiles, consumer electrical goods or paper and board manufacturing. In addition, within individual industries, there have been firms with good industrial relations records but indifferent performance, such as the Vauxhall car firm in the 1950s and 1960s; and firms with the opposite experience, such as Ford. Demarcation between different trades, which has limited the flexible deployment of labour, may have hampered efficiency in maintenance work, but has been a systemic problem only in shipbuilding and in national newspaper printing. The latter is a special, limited, case. In shipbuilding, demarcation is not necessarily a serious problem if large numbers of a standardised product are being produced; it may simply reflect a high degree of specialisation. The problem seems to have been a reluctance by most British firms to concentrate on one type of product; an exception was the Sunderland firm of Austin and Pickersgill which, in the 1960s, achieved considerable success with a standard cargo ship, without experiencing major changes in labour relations.

The insistence by unions on demarcation and minimum manning levels has been both a defensive strategy to increase the number of jobs, and an attempt to weigh the effort bargain in favour of workers. The reasons behind this strategy are rooted in employment structures which go back a long way. In the nineteenth century many employers, particularly those in heavy industry, experienced sharp fluctuations in demand for their products; at the same time, they could count on an almost indefinite supply of labour which was adequately skilled for most of the tasks demanded. In the circumstances, it was rational for employers to lay off and re-employ workers as demand dictated. Of course there were exceptions, notably in industries such as the railways where there was relatively stable demand and where employers needed skills which were specific to the industry. In these, there was much greater stability of employment. In the twentieth century, other industries with a more stable pattern of demand, such as chemicals, food manufacturing and service occupations, have become more prominent and, hence, a more stable employment pattern has emerged. Nevertheless, many British employers have continued to find advantages in retaining a pattern of frequent hiring and firing.

In these circumstances, it has been natural for unions in many industries to defend jobs if possible; and, if not, to relate effort directly to pay by insistence on minimum manning levels and similar restrictions. Hence demarcation and issues of manning, while undoubtedly problems in British industrial relations, can be seen as a consequence of the intersection of employer and employee interests. They are not simply the product of bloody-minded unions and workers.

CHAPTER THIRTY
Banking and finance

In the years before the First World War, Britain had evolved
mechanisms of great sophistication for mobilising the savings of
middle-class investors and placing them in fixed-interest securities.
Much of the population hardly saved at all, however; and the
mechanisms for the supply of capital to domestic manufacturing
industry were relatively primitive. The twentieth century was to see
this situation change: savings media spread, while the whole direction
of stock market investment changed.

The extension of savings media was for a long time a slow affair.
Personal savings as a proportion of national income (the personal
savings ratio) fell sharply in the inter-war period, not surprisingly
given the attrition of rentier income due to inflation and then the
depression. Presumably the property-owning middle classes gave up
saving before they sacrificed their standard of living. The most
striking extension of savings media in the inter-war period, the
growth of building societies, was to a large extent the substitution of
one form of intermediary for another. Most houses during the
nineteenth century were owned by investors who rented them out
and who often financed ownership by mortgages from private
individuals arranged through solicitors. The inter-war period saw a
growth of home ownership. The provision of mortgages therefore
became a large-scale retail activity rather than a matter of small
individual transactions, and building societies, which were already
established on a small scale, were well placed to provide this service.
They had to attract savings to provide the mortgages, which they did
through branch extension and the provision of relatively attractive
interest rates. After 1945, as mortgage costs remained relatively low
compared with the capital gain from inflation in house prices, home

ownership became increasingly popular. In order to finance their increased lending, building societies by 1983 had attracted around 16 per cent of total personal savings and no less than 46 per cent of liquid savings.

The growth of the building societies was paralleled after the Second World War by the growth of a whole range of other savings media. Most obvious was National Savings, established as the Post Office Savings Bank in the nineteenth century. Essentially, this acts as another medium for government borrowing, supplementing the sale of bonds, and so is not remarkable. Less obvious, but more important, was the growth of contractual savings through life assurance, and pension schemes outside the national schemes. By 1985, pension fund assets amounted to £157 billion, 25 per cent more than the assets of building societies. The growth of contractual savings can be seen as a consequence of two forces. First, there were tax concessions on contributions. These go back a long way and initially cost relatively little in terms of forgone revenue, since the rate of income tax, on which the concessions were made, was low. Their survival into an age of high tax rates can be attributed to the political difficulty of abolishing concessions which benefited powerful vested interests, and a lot of individuals as well, although tax relief on life-assurance premiums was abolished in 1984. The second force behind the growth of contractual savings schemes was the revival after the Second World War, and continued growth, in the propensity to save.

The growth in this can be inferred from the fact that the personal savings ratio has steadily increased to exceed its pre-First World War level, even though real rates of interest for much of the post-war period have been low or negative, due to inflation. The idea that our ancestors were much more thrifty than we are is a myth. It seems likely that the reason behind this growing thrift is the increase in real incomes. To understand the mechanism behind this, consider savings not as deferred consumption, but as a form of immediate consumption which enhances feelings of security or stimulates a feeling of satisfaction because some future purchase is assured. On the general principle, which economic history seems to bear out, that as incomes rise consumption priorities will shift from food to manufactures, and then to services, we would expect increased incomes to eventually lead to a high priority being given to the intangible but real satisfaction provided by savings. Until the Second World War, working-class income was too low to reach this level. The extent of savings for most families remained a small weekly payment to friendly societies or industrial assurance companies to provide death benefit. The post-1945 rise in incomes was to shatter the constraint of low incomes on savings. There is nothing incompatible between the savings increase which has resulted and the concomitant rise in personal borrowing. Borrowings satisfy immediate consumption priorities; savings exist for the long term, or to provide for a reserve for emergencies. Their very existence may aid the propensity to borrow, since people will feel more confident about their ability to repay.

The history of personal borrowing – that is, borrowing for consumption rather than investment – can be traced back to pawnbrokers and shop credit, which formed the centre of a network of debt among many poorer working-class people in the nineteenth century. The inter-war period saw the spread of hire purchase as a means of financing spending on consumer durables. In hire purchase, the goods themselves constitute security, since they remain the property of the lender until all the instalments are paid. More recently the growth of home ownership has facilitated the growth of personal loans, since these often rely on houses as security. In both cases, the existence of security allows the loan to be cheaper. In effect, these types of lending are innovations which have made borrowing easier and cheaper. Borrowing for house purchase is technically different in that houses are classed as investment rather than consumption goods, although to the borrower the basic principle may appear the same.

There were, of course, other reasons for increased post-war savings besides higher personal incomes. Corporate saving increased, partly because as investment in fixed assets increased, there was a higher level of depreciation, that is the money set aside by companies as assets wear out. Another partial explanation for increased saving lies on the supply side. The tax concessions on life-assurance and pension contributions became more attractive as more people were drawn into the tax net. The number of building-society offices greatly increased, while contractual savings schemes became more ingenious and were much more heavily marketed. Although innovation and marketing in financial services are important, it seems likely that the crucial change was the increased volume of savings which higher incomes made available. One important side-effect of this was greatly increased employment in financial services.

The growth of these financial institutions occurred outside the clearing bank system, which remained the main market for short-term company saving and borrowing, for much personal saving and borrowing, and for money transmission. Change here was for a long time slow. The period from the First World War to the 1960s saw a slow attrition in the number of major clearing banks: there are now four in England and Wales, three in Scotland. This process strengthened the oligopoly which the joint-stock banks were already establishing before the First World War, so reducing competition but facilitating the high degree of stability which Britain's banking system has experienced relative to others in this century. It also made it easier for the Bank of England to control monetary conditions than a looser system would have done, as the Bank could act by means of informal requests, whose effectiveness was based on the frequency of contact among this small group of bankers. Such informal direction was important because controlling the supply of money had become more difficult without gold backing for the currency, which had been finally abandoned in 1931. (The Bank's own position had also changed since, although it retained some independence, its actions were much more strongly influenced by the government, especially from the Second World War onwards when the government assumed greater influence over monetary policy. The Bank was the agent, however, and the subsequent discussion will continue to refer to it.)

The Bank used open-market operations in the old way to influence monetary conditions. However, too active open-market operations would lead to violent fluctuations in interest rates, which the Bank disliked because they conflicted with other objectives. These included the maintenance of the desired rate for sterling and of an orderly market for the government debt which it was essential to sell, either to refinance existing debt or to meet necessary borrowing requirements. Requesting the clearing banks to restrict lending would avert the need to sell government securities in order to reduce the money supply, an action which would be likely to push up interest rates. What these controls over lending did, in effect, was to artificially restrict the velocity of circulation of the money already in supply. An acceleration in velocity has the same potential effect as a growth in money supply, that is it increases purchasing power. So the Bank's restrictions were a way of suppressing extra demands for goods and labour which, in post-1945 conditions when demand was already high, were likely to be inflationary.

The growth of other saving and lending institutions such as building societies posed problems. Attracted by higher rates of interest, savers might withdraw money from banks and deposit it in building societies. Since societies lay outside the sphere of gentle-manly agreement over restrictions on lending, they would lend this

315

money on to house buyers. It would eventually find its way back to the bank account of the house seller but, on the way, it would have financed a transaction and thus enhanced demand. To put it another way, building societies and other intermediaries such as hire purchase companies matched savers to borrowers in a way that banks were not allowed to do and, therefore, acted to increase the velocity of circulation. Concomitant with these developments, which increasingly threatened the old system of monetary control, was the revival in the 1960s of an intellectual doctrine, the theory of monetarism, discussed in Chapter 26. Taken together, these changes encouraged a move in 1971 towards a more market-based system of control, which relied much more on the Bank controlling the supply of money through open-market operations. This has proved fraught with difficulty, however, and targets for money-supply growth have consistently proved hard to meet. Expansion of the money supply in the early 1970s was almost certainly one reason for the subsequent inflation. One result of this has been that the Bank has continued, in practice, to utilise its more traditional forms of control. Money, it seems, is too awkward a commodity to be left to the market.

Although the Bank of England's relations with the clearing banks have always been close, it has largely confined itself to attempting to influence monetary conditions. Its inter-war attempt to develop a rather more interventionist industrial strategy never really got off the ground. The resistance of clearing banks themselves was one reason for this for, by the twentieth century, they were deeply imbued with the philosophy that they should not expose themselves to risk by making long-term investments. Although banks have been frequently criticised for this attitude, its practical effects have probably not been very great, for a variety of reasons.

The first and most important point is that industry has provided the great bulk of its long-term capital requirements itself, either from the cash generated by depreciation on its existing assets or from retained profits. In the inter-war period, investment was low and self-financing was relatively easy. In the post-war period, profits were higher, but investment rose even more steeply. To maintain this high level of investment from their own savings, companies paid out a lower proportion of their profits in dividends. One can conjecture that the main reason for this was the growth of large companies and the gradual decline of family influence. As professional managers came to the fore, companies more and more took a longer-term view and increased investment at the expense of immediate dividends. Another reason for high investment has been the tax structure.

Profits which are distributed in the form of dividends are taxed over and above the tax on corporate profits. With the high tax rates ruling after the Second World War, there was an incentive to reinvest profits rather than distribute them. In the long run, shareholders would gain through the increase in the company's earning power and hence, other things being equal, in its share price.

Although these changes increased the supply of funds for investment and help to account for its post-1945 rise, it should be realised that the increase in investment was world-wide. Britain's investment ratio rose to around 20 per cent by the late 1960s but as there was an increase in most industrial countries, Britain's ratio was still below the norm (Table 32.1). There are two probable reasons for this global increase which should be taken account of in assessing the reasons for the increase in any one country. The post-war period has generally seen favourable demand conditions, referred to in Chapter 24. On the supply side, there has been a growing realisation that research and development yield a high rate of return, and this realisation has stimulated an increase in research and development. The resulting innovations have opened the way for profit opportunities and have in consequence encouraged investment. The upward shift in Britain's investment ratio is therefore likely to have had both supply and demand causes, only some of which are peculiar to this country. The increase in investment has, of course, also had a major effect on the growth of national income. Investment has been the proximate cause of about a third of the overall growth of this between 1951 and 1973.

While reinvested profits have provided the main supply of investment funds for industry, the equity market developed to provide an additional source of finance. After the First World War it became much larger, and respectable merchant banks took a greater part in issuing shares, once the province of disreputable hucksters. The move was encouraged by the decline of the foreign loan market, as the current payments surplus declined, and the authorities exerted informal and later formal controls over foreign lending in order to protect sterling. In spite of its present large size and prominence, however, the equity market has never played more than a small part in raising capital for investment. Its capitalisation has developed as privately owned firms have been floated on the stock market or as existing quoted firms have issued new shares to acquire private companies. The equity market has therefore played a necessary role in the transition from an economy dominated by family firms to the corporate economy of today, dominated by large firms owned by

317

numerous shareholders. Whether its operation is wholly beneficial is another question, however. Although professional managers may wish to take a long-term view, many shareholders take a short-term one. This arises from the casino mentality of some private shareholders and the pressures on institutional shareholders, such as unit trusts, to produce good short-term performance. Since the inception of hostile 'takeovers' in the 1950s, therefore, there may at times have been pressure on managements to produce good short-term results which satisfy shareholders and so keep up share prices, consequently deterring possible bidders. Such over-concentration on the short term may be detrimental to long-term planning. Certainly there is no international evidence that active stock markets lead to high long-term economic growth. Germany and France, two countries with enviable post-war growth records, have both had relatively small and inactive stock markets for much of the period. Japan has a large and active market, but appears to have strong informal government controls over the direction of mergers and takeovers. In all these countries, banks have been much more involved in the provision of long-term industrial finance.

While existing firms have been able to generate most of their capital needs internally, the provision of capital for new firms, or small firms which wished to expand, was identified as a problem by the Macmillan Committee of 1931. Bank finance, as already noted, was difficult, while the overhead costs of a small equity issue made it relatively expensive. In response to this, the Bank of England encouraged in 1945 the formation of the Industrial and Commercial Finance Corporation, owned by the clearing banks, which, with various smaller equivalents, has helped to provide finance for such companies. More recently the Unlisted Securities Market, introduced in 1980, has cut the costs of equity finance by simplifying procedures. In recent years also, banks have become more flexible, developing 'term' loans which provide guaranteed finance for a lengthy period, say five years. To see banks' earlier unwillingness to lend long term as a serious restriction on industry would be incorrect, however. There is no evidence that large amounts of industrial investment were choked off by a lack of finance. Quite simply, industry has not asked for the money. If it had, banking attitudes might have been a problem but, on the other hand, they might have changed to accommodate the demand. The lower participation of banks in industry, as compared with other countries, had arisen essentially from a lower demand for finance because of Britain's lower rate of investment.

Another important source of investment in private industry has been direct investment by foreign companies in Britain. The origins of this date back to the nineteenth century, when a few mainly American manufacturing companies set up subsidiaries, notably Singer the sewing machine manufacturers. Until the First World War, inward investment was far overshadowed by British investment abroad; after the war, inward investment increased, and this increase has been even greater since the Second World War. It was given some impetus from 1931 by tariffs, but they are by no means the only reason why a foreign company should make an investment in Britain, or vice versa. The nearness to local markets, essential in the case of high-volume, low-value products such as breakfast cereals (Kellogg started in Britain between the wars); the ability to gauge local tastes and the possible need to manufacture products which are completely different from those sold domestically; the availability of cheaper labour than at home; all these might enter into a decision to manufacture overseas. Indeed, the growth of multi-national firms, (i.e. those operating in more than one country) is practically inevitable given that, with increasing specialisation, firms in different countries will develop expertise in different products. Consequently, since the Second World War, investment has also flowed outwards from Britain again, largely in the form of direct investment by British firms in overseas production.

Multi-national firms are often seen as undesirable because in many cases they are domiciled or controlled abroad, but there seems little rational basis for criticising them on this score. The opening up of international financial markets has meant that the ownership of many firms, whether nominally British or not, is split between shareholders in several countries. Even more fundamental to the understanding of multi-nationals is the fact that capitalist firms, wherever they operate, are ultimately concerned with profit, although this concern is tempered by a set of constraints which include government pressure, feelings of social responsibility, the desire to protect the corporate image, and so on. This being the case, the idea that multi-nationals necessarily act any differently from domestically-based companies, for instance in making decisions on opening or closing plants, has no firm basis. The most cogent criticism of foreign controlled multi-nationals is that they may keep the highest value-added activities, such as research, development and managerial services, in their country of origin, while eroding the market share of domestic companies and thus reducing their ability to carry out these activities. It is not clear how strong this tendency is. Large companies such as Ford and IBM, for example, do have research activities in this country. It is also arguable that a country like Britain, with relatively limited spending on research and management training by comparison with some other industrialised countries, can only benefit from the import of foreign knowledge and managerial technique.

So far this chapter has dealt with the provision of savings facilities and financial services to domestic customers, and the raising of money for investment. Apart from the provision of short-term trade finance, which continued to be largely the province of the clearing banks, the other main financial activity is the provision of international financial services, such as credit for international trade. Not surprisingly, this shrank in importance in the inter-war period. It was affected by American competition, but the fundamental reason for decline was the fall in world trade from 1929 on. Things recovered after the Second World War, although sterling was now the second trading currency after the dollar. More recently the situation has changed again. Since the 1960s, London has become the major centre for dealing in the Eurocurrency market, meaning the market in loans made outside the country of residence of the lender and borrower. The market for such lending and borrowing has greatly increased, partly because of the growth of multi-nationals which want to match their assets and liabilities in individual currencies. London has established its position by virtue of its existing financial expertise, an appropriate legislative framework and reasonable telecommunications. It was estimated that in 1985, turnover on the Eurocurrency market was around three times the level of stock exchange turnover, which gives some idea of its importance. Like the international financial services of the nineteenth century, it generates a multiplier effect through the demands for the services of lawyers, accountants and so on.

London is therefore still a world banking centre, although the type of business has changed and has only a tenuous connection with the developments of the nineteenth century. It is now a site on which multi-national banks operate, rather than the location of a largely domestic industry. More continuity can be traced in the provision of insurance. Insurance companies and the Lloyds unlimited liability market insure around 50 per cent of the world's shipping and its cargoes, and are important providers of aircraft and other types of insurance. There is also the domestic industry, whose size has increased vastly over the century as the demand for insurance has grown with the growth of personal and corporate assets. Quite why Britain has retained a strong position in the world insurance market is not clear, but the possible answer is that economies of scale act with a particular force in this industry. The larger the capacity of the market, the greater the specialisation and therefore the levels of expertise. In turn, this will lead to lower rates in the long term, and better levels of service. London's capacity being greater than that of any other market, it has an inbuilt advantage. In spite of these successes, Britain's share of the world market in exports of financial services appears to have declined between the 1960s and 1983 at the same rate as the market share of manufactures. This suggests that the overall picture may not be as bright as the prosperity of the City of London implies. There are problems in measuring the international earnings of insurance and banking services, however. Investment income is netted out in making the calculation but, in practice, investment income (as opposed to commission on banking operations, underwriting profit on insurance and so on) usually makes a large contribution to total profit. Without more refined calculations, it is too early to make a final assessment of recent international performance in financial services.

Britain's recent relative performance notwithstanding, the above average growth rate of financial services in all developed countries, taken together with Britain's historically strong position in such services, has ensured that they make a significant economic contribution. In 1985, finance institutions and insurance together accounted for 7 per cent of national income in Britain. Of other developed countries, only Switzerland reaches a comparable level. Financial services only accounted for 3.5 per cent of total employment, however. This reflects the relatively high productivity and income levels reached in these occupations.

CHAPTER THIRTY-ONE

Production and distribution

NEW INDUSTRIES 1918–39

After the First World War, British manufacturing industry enjoyed a brief boom as a result of reconstruction, restocking and high demand created by monetary inflation, before experiencing a depression which in some branches of industry lasted until the Second World War. Other branches, however, enjoyed considerable growth over the rest of the inter-war period, and long-term depression in output was concentrated in the staple industries, discussed in Chapter 24. The misfortunes of the staples have led some historians to suggest that Britain's problems in the inter-war period can be attributed partly to 'over-commitment' to these industries before the First World War. In one sense, this is simply another way of saying that Britain's problems were partly those of structural adjustment, a familiar proposition which few would disagree with. In another sense, the argument implies a misallocation of resources in the Edwardian period or earlier and is not, therefore, about the inter-war period at all. Again, many would agree that some sectors of British industry were not developed to their full potential before the First World War and, to that extent, the staples had greater relative importance than they deserved. Whether they absorbed too much investment in an absolute sense before the war is a different matter, since pre-1914 investors in cotton mills or coal mines could hardly be expected to take the First World War and all its effects into their calculations. Over-commitment makes some sense as an explanation of inter-war problems, if it is taken as a shorthand for the pre-1914 failure to invest heavily in advanced manufacturing sectors; it makes less sense as a criticism of the investment that did take place in staples.

Accepting that there were structural problems in the inter-war period is not contentious, however. A more positive but more debatable argument is that the inter-war period saw the rapid growth of 'new industries', such as vehicle production, chemicals and electrical engineering and that these together constituted a 'development block' which was such as to lift the economy on to a new growth path.

Undoubtedly there was significant growth in a number of industries, although 'new' is a handy phrase rather than an accurate description of an industry such as chemicals which had been around for 200 years. In chemicals itself there was reasonable qualitative success in producing more sophisticated varieties, although Britain's share of total world output declined. Motor vehicles and the production of electrical goods also did well compared with the pre-war period. In chemicals and vehicles especially, there was a shift towards a more concentrated production structure. Chemicals became dominated by ICI, produced by merger in 1926. In vehicles, Morris established a strong position in the 1920s, although there was some challenge to this, particularly from Ford, in the 1930s. The success of these and other industries was accompanied throughout the economy by a faster rate of growth in both labour productivity and total factor productivity than in the Edwardian period (see Table 31.1).

Table 31.1 Productivity growth before and after the First World War (annual average percentage change)

	Labour productivity (*output per man-year*)	*Total factor productivity*	*Labour productivity in manufacturing*	*Manu-facturing output*
1873–1913	0.9	0.5	1.2	2.0
1899–1913	0.5	0.1	n.a.	n.a.
1913-1937	0.7	n.a.	n.a.	n.a.
1924-1937	1.0	0.7	1.8	3.2

(*Source*: Matthews)

The development block idea, which constitutes one attempt to explain this growth, is very similar to Rostow's leading sector idea. On the one hand, a cluster of innovations occur, reducing the cost of certain products. On the other hand, demand for the same products is enhanced by favourable demand factors. In the inter-war period, the favourable demand factors were the fall in primary-product prices, which increased real incomes in spite of unemployment and therefore increased demand for consumer durables. Demand and supply together created opportunities for growth in the industries concerned. Like the leading sector idea, the idea of a development block is intellectually quite attractive. Unfortunately, it also resembles the leading sector idea in that it is not supported by the evidence during the period to which it is commonly applied. The actual share of 'new industries' in output was quite small, because only the middle classes had income levels which could sustain a substantial demand for durables; the rate of productivity growth in some of the old industries, such as steel, was as fast as the average for the new industries, suggesting that the new industries did not account for a major productivity breakthrough; and recovery in the 1930s seems to have been multifaceted. The latter depended on increased consumer demand for a wide range of goods, on the housing boom, on tariffs and interest-rate policies and, in the late 1930s, on rearmament.

In the long run, even the rise in labour productivity in manufacturing between 1924 and 1939 is much less impressive, because it came after stagnation between 1913 and 1924, the years of war and post-war instability (see Table 31.2). This occurred partly because of reductions in working hours, but also because capital investment had been so restricted during the war. This hampered the introduction of innovations, because these had to be embodied in capital assets. (In everyday language: it is not enough simply to invent something – you have to build the plant and machinery as well.) The First World War did not see a rapid introduction of new techniques, as is sometimes said. The growth of electricity supply, for instance, was actually slower during the war than before or after. Production processes in heavy industries experienced little change. Therefore there was by the 1920s a residue of product innovations and new production techniques, some of them American, which were ready for exploitation. The taking up of these opportunities goes a long way towards

Table 31.2 Income and productivity growth 1913–37

	National income (1)	Labour productivity (output per man-year) (2)	Total factor productivity (3)	Domestic investment ratio (%)
1913–24	−0.1	0.3	1.0	
1924–37	2.2	1.0	0.7	10

Columns 1–3: Annual average percentage change
(*Source:* Matthews)

explaining the improved productivity of the inter-war years. Even by the later 1930s, though, British labour productivity was far behind American – a fact which puts inter-war growth into perspective. Furthermore, labour productivity outside manufacturing appears to have fallen although, as in the Edwardian period, this can be partly accounted for by improving standards of service.

The most notable innovations, where Britain had seriously lagged before 1914, were the internal combustion engine and electricity. These constituted important production industries in themselves but, as has been noted, their share of output was too small for this alone to make a significant difference to growth rates. The beneficial influence of these innovations on efficiency in other sectors did facilitate overall productivity growth, however. The National Grid sharply reduced electricity prices by linking generating stations and enabling the most efficient to be used to the maximum. Here the main saving was of fuel, a saving enhanced by improved turbine design. Electric driving for machines was greatly extended: it eliminated the need for complex overhead belting and thus enhanced flexibility in factory layout. Better lighting and the use of electric furnaces were other improvements. Internal combustion engines were of less direct importance to manufacturing efficiency but, of course, did contribute to greater efficiency in distribution.

There were other innovations whose production was developed during this period. Rayon (artificial silk) had been discovered in the late nineteenth century, and bakelite, the first plastic, in 1908. Production of rayon, and to a lesser degree plastics, increased after the First World War. The aircraft industry shrank in size after the war, but it kept up with technical innovations such as the metal monoplane, while the aero-engine and aircraft component industry also saw innovation. The building industry, previously one of the most conservative both in materials and techniques, benefited from a number of innovations developed before or soon after the war. Cement manufacture had become much more efficient in the late nineteenth and early twentieth centuries, leading to the more widespread adoption of concrete for foundations and for civil engineering. The concrete roofing tile was another important cost-reducing innovation which was widely adopted in the inter-war period. Innovations in technique included the cement-mixer, but probably the most important was the replacement of the horse and cart by the lorry. In engineering, significant innovations included welding, and the availability of new steel alloys such as stainless steel, developed in 1914. While some of the innovations noted above related specifically to new industries, many had a much more general application and again show the problems of attaching too much attention to these industries, in isolation from others.

MANUFACTURING AND MINING 1945–85

For thirty years after 1945, the post-war boom almost submerged the very different experiences of the inter-war industries in a general prosperity. National income, manufacturing output and labour productivity in manufacturing all rose at faster rates than ever before. There were some exceptions, concentrated among the old staples, to the general prosperity. After a brief post-war boom, cotton continued its decline from the early 1950s. Coal output fell rapidly from 1957, although efficiency rose. Shipbuilding output remained more or less stable, but its share of world output fell sharply. Practically all the erstwhile new industries continued to experience rapid growth, however, and because their share of total output was now much larger, their growth had much more overall impact on the economy. Steel output also grew, as did building and construction output.

From the mid-1970s, the experience of most manufacturing industries and construction has been very different. Absolute output in many industries has fallen, in several cases catastrophically. Two particularly badly hit have been vehicles and shipbuilding. Not surprisingly, steel has also suffered. The volume of new construction and building has fallen, while in major industries such as clothing and footwear, output has fluctuated with little overall change. A few sectors have done better, notably defence equipment, chemicals, pharmaceuticals and food processing. Coal production, after a brief respite in the late 1970s, continued to decline; but oil production from the North Sea became a major industry (see Tables 31.3 and 31.4). The overall fortunes of industry since 1945 have been linked to the rapid growth of world production and trade until the mid-1970s, and its slower growth thereafter; and to Britain's changing competitive position in the world market. These are dealt with in other chapters, and here our concern is with the reasons for and effects of change in particular sectors.

The pattern of demand was one influence on change. As incomes rose, demand for consumer durables, notably cars but also kitchen appliances and leisure products such as television, rose more rapidly, since for many people it was the first time that these were affordable.

Table 31.3 Productivity growth after the Second World War (annual average percentage change)

	Labour productivity (output per man-year)	Total factor productivity	Labour productivity in manufacturing	Manu- facturing output
1951–64 } 1964–73 }	2.4	2.3	3.0 4.6	3.2 3.0
1973–79	1.2	n.a.	0.7	−0.7
1979–85	1.9*	n.a.	4.1*	−0.9*

* See note to Table 26.2
(*Sources:* Matthews; *Economic Trends*)

Table 31.4 Selected industrial output indicators (annual averages)

	A	B	C	D	E	F
1924–38	613	230	8.5	469	290	negligible
1951–64	308	211	20.4	1390	1351	negligible
1964–73	178	158	25.7	1107	2169	negligible
1973–79	110	122	21.9	1110	1754	1.6 (1975)
1979–85	54	122*	15.4	427	1267	127.5 (1985)

A = Raw cotton consumption (million kilos)
B = Output of coal (million metric tonnes)
C = Output of steel (million metric tonnes)
D = Tonnage of shipping (thousand tons)
E = Motor vehicle production (thousand)
F = Oil production (single years; million metric tonnes)

* 1979–83 only; 1984 and 1985 affected by miners' strike
(*Sources:* Lee, C H 1986 *The British Economy Since 1700*; *Annual Abstract*)

In economic terms, demand for them was income elastic. The share of these industries in output grew rapidly in the 1950s and 1960s. Since then, however, an increasing proportion of consumption has been met by imports, with adverse effects on British production.

On the other hand, the rise in incomes was accompanied by slower growth in the consumption of food and drink products and tobacco. Again, the relationship between incomes and demand is an important variable, but acting in the opposite direction, since demand for these products is income inelastic once higher levels of income have been reached. As with consumer products, however, a bald explanation is not sufficient. Since the 1970s, tobacco consumption has fallen, one probable reason being the link between smoking and lung cancer, first established in the 1960s. The relative price of tobacco products has also risen because of increased taxation, and this may constitute another factor in the consumption decline. On the other hand, the pre-consumption preparation of food products has become more sophisticated, with favourable implications for the food manufacturing industry, while alcohol consumption, having fallen up to the early 1950s, subsequently rose. Finally, import competition in all these areas has been less marked than in the durable-goods industries. So changes in taste and innovations in marketing and production techniques mean that recent changes in these industries have been complex and not all in the same direction, with food and drink manufacture faring better than tobacco products.

On the supply side, change has occurred in the fuel industries because of shifts in natural resource availability and pricing, both in Britain and world-wide. These shifts have manifested themselves in a continued pressure on coalmining and, more recently, in the exploitation of hydrocarbons in the North Sea, with gas in the 1960s preceding oil in the 1970s. In the coal industry, the problems of seam exhaustion which had begun before the First World War continued in the inter-war period, while competition from more modern European mines, notably in Poland, was also significant. The problems might be mitigated by mechanisation, but they would not go away. After the war, other cheap coal producers such as South Africa and Australia became significant. Even more important, however, was competition from oil. Advances in oil-production technology and reductions in transport costs meant that in the mid- to late 1950s there was a cross-over in relative prices, oil suddenly becoming more attractive for a host of purposes ranging from railway transport, to gas production, to domestic heating. The fall in coal production began during this period.

The switch in gas production from the use of coal to the use of oil as a feedstock, which proceeded rapidly in the late 1950s and early 1960s, enhanced the attractiveness of gas as an industrial fuel, but perhaps had most impact on domestic central heating. For the first time in history, people in Britain could actually be warm in winter in their own homes without crouching over a coal fire or spending a fortune in fuel bills. Subsequently, gas from the North Sea consolidated the revived position which the fuel enjoyed in the market. North Sea oil had much less effect on fuel use, since it arrived at a time of relative fuel scarcity, expressed in high prices. It therefore substituted for imported oil, rather than leading to a cheapening of prices and extension of fuel use. (At least in the short term; the effect that North Sea oil, together with Britain's relatively unrestricted depletion policy, had on the 1985–6 fall in oil prices is a fascinating topic for speculation, but at the time of writing no sound assessment has been made.) North Sea oil did have important direct and indirect employment effects, supporting around 100,000 jobs in Scotland by the 1980s; oil-platform building has intermittently given a substantial amount of work to shipyards, and led to some new construction of platform building yards.

Important though the shifts in fuel supply and use have been, a change of greater importance to manufacturing industry has been the trend towards greater capital intensity in production. Britain's low investment ratio in the later nineteenth and early twentieth centuries continued into the inter-war period, but after 1945 there was a marked upward shift (Ch. 30 and Table 32.1). Higher investment has been accompanied by an increased rate of technical innovation. While the direction of causality between the two is subject to much debate, we can note here that whichever is causal, in practice they go together. Innovations usually have to be embodied in investment and, therefore, a high rate of investment is likely to be accompanied by a high rate of innovation.

The first point to note about post-war innovations is that the most obvious ones have probably been the least important economically. A notable example is nuclear energy as used in power stations. At present about 20 per cent of Britain's electricity is generated by nuclear power stations, at a price somewhat, but not much, below that of coal-fired stations. Electricity generation accounts for about 15 per cent of total energy consumption. Adoption of a slightly more expensive method of providing a proportion of this would hardly have led to national bankruptcy. Rather similar remarks can be made about jet aircraft. The substitution of propeller-driven aircraft would have only a limited effect on costs, although it might have a greater one on travel habits.

Less visible innovations, however, have led to great changes in the techniques of production over the last forty years. Automatic transfer machines, which carry out a series of predetermined machining operations, have revolutionised the efficiency with which engineering components can be mass produced. In mining, where coal-cutting machines had been introduced widely in the inter-war period, the 1950s and 1960s saw the widespread adoption of power-loading, in which coal is both cut and loaded on to a conveyor mechanically. Both power-loading and automatic transfer machines illustrate the trend to mechanise the movement of components or raw materials within production, a trend whose best known example is the moving assembly line. Such mechanisation facilitates the breakdown of processes to discrete operations, which can themselves be mechanised. These developments are best suited to mass production, since they involve relatively expensive and inflexible machinery. More recent innovations have aimed to mechanise while retaining flexibility. Since the 1960s, growing numbers of numerical control (NC) machine tools, which use computer programs to control machining operations, have been introduced. These can machine more accurately than manually controlled tools and can be reset relatively easily. More recent still has been the use of robots for certain assembly operations. They can be reprogrammed to perform different tasks, although their introduction has been limited because they are still far less flexible than human beings.

Innovation in building has been much less successful in this period. The 1960s saw the widespread introduction of so-called system building in order to overcome shortages of traditional building labour. System building aimed to prefabricate large components, such as concrete floors and walls, so that site work would be largely semi-skilled assembly. It was more appropriate for flats than for houses and was heavily used for publicly owned dwellings. The subsequent discovery of faults revealed that there was often inadequate quality control on sites. Since the margin for tolerance of faults was much smaller than with traditional methods, serious problems have arisen with much construction of this kind, suggesting that its inclusion in output figures effectively inflates them, because of its poor quality. The more durable technical innovations in construction and in domestic building, therefore, have been incremental improvements in design which has led, for instance, to a reduction in the amount of material needed in load-bearing supports.

The most dramatic innovation in the post-war period has been the computer. During the 1960s, their main function was the automation of routine clerical functions such as payroll compilation and debtors' and creditors' ledgers. Subsequently their use in administrative and clerical work has widened and deepened through the development of mini- and micro-computers which can distribute information to every desk in an office. Drawing offices have made increasing use of computer-aided design since the mid-1970s, but the use of computers in manufacturing has proceeded slowly. Their main use has been in

NC machine tools, mentioned earlier, but although these originated in the 1950s, by 1976 they still comprised less than 1.5 per cent of all machine tools. A very broad way of judging the economic effect of computers is to look at the rate of growth of productivity in major industrialised countries. This has actually slowed down since the early 1970s, showing that even a pervasive innovation such as the computer is only one among many influences on productivity growth. Finally, the manufacture of computers and related equipment, and the provision of software, is an important industry in itself. In spite of carrying out much of the early development in the 1940s, Britain was rapidly outstripped by the USA, and there is now a substantial deficit in the 'information technology' balance of payments.

AGRICULTURE

During the First World War, the need to minimise imports led in 1917 to a system of guaranteed prices and government intervention to increase crop acreage, under the Corn Production Act. For a short time, agriculture was restored to prosperity, not just because of intervention but also because of a sharp increase in world prices. This brief boom had long-term effects because it gave farmers the wherewithal to buy their land and so aided the breakup of the estate system, which was already under way. In 1921, however, world prices collapsed and the cost of paying farmers a guaranteed price led to the abandonment of the support scheme. It was a cynical, if realistic, move. As in the nineteenth century, the smallness of the agricultural interest in terms of votes made them a relatively easy sacrifice. The reintroduction of protection in 1932 was not a special favour to agriculture, but merely the tail end of the protectionist bandwaggon. The Wheat Act of that year again provided a guaranteed minimum price, although not a very high one, which was paid to farmers whatever the world price. There were tariffs or quota restrictions on most other products. As with other intervention in the inter-war period, however, one intention of policy was to minimise government interference by encouraging voluntary schemes of restriction. The largest was the Milk Marketing Board, formed in 1933, which guaranteed a stable price for a fixed quantity of milk from each farmer. In spite of intervention, the low level of demand meant that prices generally remained low. The situation of agriculture had not changed much in reality from the 1920s or from pre-war. Mechanisation was slow, and there were still 400,000 horses on British farms in 1939. The only striking increases in output were in vegetables and sugar-beet. Market-gardens had been increasing their output before the First World War, since the diversification of diet resulting from higher incomes led to an increased consumption of vegetables. Sugar-beet was and remains a totally artificial industry, reliant on government support since its setting-up in 1925.

The Second World War saw a much more generous price-support policy, which was extended to most products and was accompanied by subsidies for ploughing up land and for land reclamation. Farmers' real incomes multiplied by almost three times over the war years, while labourers also gained from higher wages, with a guaranteed minimum. Once more, grain output rose, but now it continued to rise after the war. The grain farmers' seventy years of depression had ended, and their new prosperity was underpinned by the Agriculture Act of 1947, which maintained the price-support system. There were various pressures behind this. In contrast with 1921, the Labour government of 1945–50 was by nature interventionist; and small though the agricultural vote was, Labour was interested in it. There was support for the party among small farmers in areas such as rural Wales and the Scottish Highlands, as well as in areas which still had a large rural proletariat such as Norfolk. Since the price-support system guaranteed farm incomes without raising food prices, it was a cost-free policy in terms of urban votes, although not in terms of money. The dollar shortage provided a sort of rationale, since it was argued that increasing food production would save imports. Surviving free traders counter-argued that it was not very sensible to spend large sums of money on supporting an industry in which Britain was at a comparative disadvantage.

Since the war there has been a steady rise in the output of most agricultural products. This has been accompanied by a rise in labour productivity, encouraged by mechanisation. By 1945, the number of tractors had quadrupled to 200,000. Since then, innovations such as the milking machine and the combine harvester have reduced labour requirements further. The introduction of machinery to modern farming, together with the destruction of hedgerows, a grant-supported policy which was a legacy of the drive to increase production at almost any cost, are the changes in farming which strike the outsider most forcibly. In reality, the most important innovation has been the increase in yields, of grain, milk and meat. Grain yields have risen by three times over the century from 1885, most of the increase occurring after the Second World War. This has been achieved by a continued increase in fertiliser application, supported by pesticides and herbicides, by the increasingly rapid introduction and dissemination of improved seed varieties, and by the steady improvement in techniques (see Table 31.5).

Table 31.5 Agricultural statistics

	1960/2	1982/4	1913	1975/6	1981/2	1974/5	1978/9
Index of real output	100	180					
Index of labour productivity	100	363					
Wheat self-sufficiency			20	54	100		
Ratio of EEC agricultural prices to world prices						139	229
Net loss to Britain of CAP							$1500 million

(*Sources:* Artis; Boltho)

The fall in agricultural costs has not been as great as the increasing productivity of land and labour might imply. This is because the productivity increase has involved a big increase in capital inputs, in the form of machinery and fertilisers. High prices meant that high-input agriculture again became worthwhile. Nevertheless, the increase in total factor productivity, at 3.5 per cent per year between 1951 and 1973, has been substantial, and significantly better than in manufacturing.

For a long time, agricultural policy remained out of the limelight. More recently, the effects of increased output and the price-support mechanism have combined to make it once again the centre of attention. The old British price-support system was replaced gradually from 1973 by the EEC system, the Common Agricultural Policy (CAP). This aimed to bolster EEC prices, and hence farm incomes, by taxing imports and, if necessary, by further price support through 'intervention' buying of indigenous products and subsidies for exporting them. Compared with the old British system, CAP raised food prices to the consumer, unless world prices were higher than EEC prices; but it should cost less to governments, since tariff receipts would help to pay for any intervention buying which was necessary. Intervention buying would also build up a buffer stock against shortages. Like the previous British system, CAP aimed to bolster indigenous production, as well as support farm incomes. The idea was not as stupid as it seems today, because as late as the early 1970s there were serious fears of world food shortages. From the British point of view, the net cost if the CAP method of price support had been adopted in Britain alone would not necessarily have differed from that of the old system, although the burden would have fallen on the consumer rather than the taxpayer. In the real CAP, British taxpayers and consumers transferred a large amount of money to the European farming sector, while British farmers received a smaller quantity of money from European consumers and taxpayers. The difference occurs because the British farming sector is small relative to most EEC countries. This is one reason for the quarrels between Britain and other EEC members over CAP. The other reason, which also lies behind the more general problems of agriculture in the EEC, is the world-wide increase in yields, which has lowered world food prices and increased the amount of European produce that has to be bought by intervention or sold abroad at heavily subsidised prices. It is this that has caused the astronomic increase in the costs of CAP and led, with the milk quotas of 1984, to the beginnings of an output restriction policy. So, absurd though CAP always was from the British point of view, its wider problems today are connected with unforeseen changes in world agriculture.

The problems caused by agricultural support do not just end with the expense of CAP to the taxpayers and consumers, however. Resources put into agriculture have a much lower rate of return than resources put elsewhere, so overall growth is deleteriously affected; while the declining need for food imports raises the exchange rate, as discussed in Chapter 24, thus hampering exports of manufactures and services. A recent study suggests that the long-term effect of CAP may have been a fall of 2.5–3 per cent in the UK output of manufactures and services, and a rise of 0.5 million in unemployment.

SERVICES

Just as the nineteenth century saw a transport revolution, so did the twentieth. But in this century it is road traffic which has vanquished rail, rather than vice versa. The economics of road transport were transformed by the development of a lightweight prime mover, the internal combustion engine. Like most inventions, however, it took a long time for its full impact to be felt. This is partly because the growth of motoring has depended on demand as well as supply factors, and was limited until incomes across a wide range of society were able to sustain its expense. Even middle-class private motoring was restricted in the inter-war period, and it is only from the 1950s that the car has accounted for over a half of passenger mileage, rising to around 80 per cent today. The increase has come about not so much because other forms of transport have declined absolutely, but because the total amount of passenger travel has grown.

In the inter-war years, it was the bus which had more impact on both urban and rural transport than the car. While cheap mass transport was pioneered by the electric tram, the bus gave added flexibility and helped to make possible the spread of low-density suburban housing. In 1950, over 40 per cent of passenger mileage was by bus or coach, although by 1985 this had declined to 8 per cent. Nevertheless, almost 40 per cent of households did not possess a car in 1985, and for short-distance journeys such households are still heavily reliant on buses. Rail transport remains significant for commuting in the London area, a function it had continued to develop in the inter-war period.

The car has changed both leisure habits and the scope for living away from the workplace to an enormous extent. It has also affected the working habits of that unsung hero of economic and social history, the sales representative, once better known as the commercial traveller. (When did the name change?) Cars must have greatly increased travellers' productivity, since they could make far more visits with a car than when tied to the railway timetable.

The economic effects of road transport are even more striking in freight carriage. In the inter-war period, lorries mainly substituted for the horse and cart, since their running costs were too high to compete with rail or coastal ship over longer distances, at least until high speed diesel engines were developed in the 1930s. From the late 1940s, however, road haulage grew rapidly. By 1983, road transport accounted for almost 60 per cent of tonne-kilometres of freight, compared with 10 per cent for rail, 25 per cent for coastal shipping and about 6 per cent for pipelines. It is not so much the direct cost of the different transport modes that has been the crucial variable, but the ability of lorries to deliver door-to-door. This has cut transit times and hence the costs of carrying stock – the same reason as that which made railways preferable to canals in the nineteenth century.

The revival of road transport led, belatedly, to a revival of road building, and this and road maintenance are significant items of public expenditure. In the inter-war period, so-called arterial roads were built to bypass town centres, although the new roads quickly became built up too. From 1959, when the first stretch of the M1 was opened, the motorway network was developed. In theory, receipts from taxation on road vehicles have exceeded expenditure on road building and maintenance. In practice, the costs that road transport have inflicted through noise, injury and death, structural damage to buildings, and environmental pollution, have been substantial. It is not impossible, although extremely difficult, to estimate this cost. For instance, the cost of noise can be assessed by comparing the market value of houses beside main roads with those in side streets. Apart from the practical problems of assessing these costs, there is the counter-argument that motor vehicles have enhanced welfare by increasing accessibility. Rudyard Kipling bought his house, Batemans, at a knock-down price in 1902 because it was sited at the bottom of a remote Sussex valley. He correctly foresaw that the car would render it accessible and enhance its value, as has subsequently happened in villages all over the country.

Britain's shipping industry before 1914 was almost as important as the inland transport industry. The post-First World War merchant shipping industry has been criticised for technical conservatism, as it was slow to adopt motor ships and the oil tanker and lost market share. Much of this loss came about during the First World War, however, and the post-war decline in coal exports accounts for some of the subsequent loss. The renewed growth in post-Second World War world trade saw a growth in absolute fleet size, which had stagnated between the wars, and it reached a maximum size of fifty million deadweight tons in 1975. By this time, tankers were a high proportion of the fleet, which may be accounted for by the strong position of Britain in the international oil industry. In recent years the fleet has fallen sharply, to nineteen million deadweight tons in 1985. The fall would seem to be due to the decline in oil transport, to a less favourable tax regime than in other countries, and to the opportunities for owners to employ low-wage crew by registering under so-called 'flags of convenience'. The recent decline masks the fact that the value-added in Britain of British registered ships has been falling for a long time. The ships themselves have been decreasingly likely to be British built, while the crew size per ton has fallen drastically as ships have increased in size and engine rooms have been automated.

In many ways more important than the fortunes of the shipping fleet has been the revolution in ship operation from the 1960s, associated with containerisation and roll-on, roll-off ferry vessels. The fall in the number of workers in docks and inland water transport, from 146,000 in 1961 to 58,000 in 1981, demonstrates the impact of this change. The location of major port operations moved downriver and, apart from private wharves, the upriver London and Liverpool docks are now closed to freight traffic; but formerly small or specialised docks, notably Felixstowe and Dover, have become major ports. They were helped by their access to the road network and freedom from restrictive labour practices, but probably the single main reason for their success has been the growth of trade with Europe.

The other revolution in international transport operations has been air transport. Here Britain maintains a strong position as an international carrier, rather surprisingly as until recently the main airlines, the government-owned British European Airways and British Overseas Airways Corporation, and their successor from 1973, British Airways, were not particularly efficient and in the 1960s suffered from government pressure to buy unsuitable British aircraft. Britain's international position has probably depended on her subsidised development of Empire routes in the inter-war period and her strong position in air transport immediately after the war. These factors guaranteed a good share of international routes, which are negotiated between governments. The growth of air transport has led to the growth of another major industry, the provision of airport services.

Still in the realm of transport, but of information rather than goods or people, is the telecommunications industry. In 1985 there were twenty million telephone lines connected with the exchange in Great Britain, compared with three-quarters of a million in 1914. Unlike the postal service, which has remained labour-intensive, telephones have benefited from technical innovation which has reduced both labour requirements, through the introduction of direct dialling, and more recently capital requirements, through the application of electronics to exchange construction. On the demand side, telephones like cars have become more affordable as incomes have risen. Telecommunications growth has been accompanied by growth in other forms of data transmission, such as telex and facsimile.

Like transport, retail trading has also undergone remarkable

337

change over the last seventy years, although there are threads of continuity. In the inter-war years these were quite strong, the main developments having been foreshadowed before 1914. On the one hand, the market became more segmented, with multiples and cooperatives continuing to grow at the cheaper end of the price range and department stores at the upper end. By 1939, multiples had about 18 per cent of the retail market, coops 10 per cent and department stores 5 per cent. On the other hand, independent retail shops continued to hold the bulk of the market, and the levels of service provided became if anything greater. The errand boy on his cycle, collecting and delivering orders, was a familiar sight in the streets of inter-war Britain. Multiples followed the trend to enhancing service, in particular by improving the standard of shop interiors and providing modernistic facades. The style of an inter-war non-food multiple retailer would be recognisable today, whereas the cluttered interior and exterior of pre-1914 shops would not. A rather different development in the inter-war period was the provision of specialised sales and service facilities for motor vehicles. This seems to have been a haven for the small business, with no large suppliers outside the petrol trade, suggesting that growth was entirely demand-driven.

The war saw a sudden switch to a much less lavish provision of retail services. Labour became scarce, and since then there have been rapid shifts in retailing. The independent retailer has continued to decline and in 1984 held about 30 per cent of the market. Much of this is held by traders in small local shopping centres who do not compete with high-street shops, but cater for small purchases where price is not a major consideration. The growth has come in multiples, both food and non-food. Furthermore, ownership has become extremely concentrated. In food retailing, by 1987, five major groups held 52 per cent of the market. The coops, which have themselves become more concentrated, held another 12 per cent. Even the hitherto fragmented motor-vehicle sales and repair industry has become more concentrated and price competitive. Although concentration of ownership has been the most notable development in retailing, there have been more technical innovations than before the war. These have again tended towards reducing levels of service, but also costs. Most notable is self-service, which made rapid progress from the 1950s. The location of shops has changed relatively little until recently, however. Britain's high urban population and low levels of car ownership compared with, say, the USA, together with planning constraints, limited the growth of 'out-of-town' (or out-of-town-centre) shopping facilities before the 1980s.

The long-term trends in the wholesaling industry have been dominated by the growth of branding by manufacturers, together with the growth of multiples. These developments have encouraged direct dealing between manufacturer and retailer. The increasing concentration of ownership in retailing has therefore made the wholesaler almost redundant in many trades, although this has been a gradual process. They are still important in trades where specialised handling of produce may be necessary, such as meat and vegetables – both areas where the independent retailer also retains a niche because of the continued need for a degree of expertise in selection of goods.

These post-war trends in retailing are not yet subject to much analysis by historians. Clearly, one major force has been a shift upwards in the cost of labour as against the cost of goods, which has made the provision of high levels of service, in which the independent retailer was if anything at an advantage, so expensive that even wealthier purchasers moved to shops providing lower levels. Another encouragement to concentration of ownership may have been the fact that the operation of self-service shops needed considerable expertise, which was much more quickly accumulated by large firms. In the non-food sector, the independent retailer was hit by the abolition of resale price maintenance (RPM) in 1964. RPM had pre-1914 origins, but became enshrined in many trades in the inter-war period. Manufacturers refused to supply retailers who sold products below a recommended price. RPM was associated with the continued growth of branding, and with heavy advertising by manufacturers to promote branded products. Given these policies, manufacturers seem to have believed that breadth of distribution was more important than price. RPM ensured this, since it prevented the multiple driving the small retailer out of business by undercutting on price.

Branding itself has subsequently declined, perhaps as a consequence of the growth of the large firm in retailing. Such firms increasingly prefer to sell under their own label, thus reducing the cost of the product by avoiding the manufacturers' advertising costs. The success of own label, however, has only been possible because of the strong public perception of large chains. In effect, Sainsbury, Habitat or Laura Ashley are themselves brands. (A rather similar development in a completely different industry is the growth of large firms in housebuilding. Success in this today relies as much on skilful marketing as it does on the quality of the structure itself.)

The most fundamental systemic influence on retailing, therefore, has been size. This has given economies in purchasing and the provision of finance, and has enhanced expertise in store design and management and the location and development of new sites. Perhaps most important, it has been the quickest and most effective way of putting across an image. However, this has had dangers, for an outdated image can depress performance, as Woolworths and the coops have found to their cost.

Like retailing, the provision of leisure facilities was one of the more dynamic sectors of the economy before 1914, and the First World War did nothing to change this. There seems to have been no problem between the wars in raising money for investment in new leisure facilities, notably cinemas, although our knowledge at present on the financing of this and other leisure industries is limited. Apart from the cinema, demand for leisure in the inter-war years fell into well-established channels. The period marked the apotheosis of the seaside resort, as working-class holidaymaking began on a large scale, and one of the few areas of new investment by railways in the period was the provision of increased facilities for holiday traffic. Spectator sport maintained its popularity in the inter-war period, and this was to be followed in the 1940s by the highest attendance figures ever, as the scarcity of goods led to heavy spending on this and other forms of entertainment.

During the 1950s, the proportion of spending on leisure services stagnated as consumers switched their attention to goods that substituted for these services, notably television and the car. The 1960s, however, marked the beginning of a period of rapid change in leisure provision. One such change was the growth of cheap foreign holidays, one of the by-products of cheap air travel. The British tourist industry made an uncertain response to this competition. Many holiday resorts were shielded from its full impact by the growth of retirement provision; others decayed. (The author remembers a late summer visit a few years ago to Herne Bay, a small resort on the north Kent coast. There was no-one on the beach, and the middle of the pier had collapsed into the sea.) Recently there has been a growing investment by seaside resorts in all-weather leisure facilities and also in provision for conferences. The demand for leisure in inland areas has been much more buoyant. The flow of foreign tourists to Britain has been one reason, while indigenous leisure habits have become much more varied in the past twenty-five years. Attendance at stately homes, participation in sport rather than just watching it, meals out, and a taste for more exotic night-life than used to be provided by the pub, the cinema and the dance hall are all hallmarks of this change. It is difficult to say how far change has been simply demand-driven. The flexibility given by widespread car ownership is one important demand-side factor. On the other hand, areas of leisure as varied as the stately home industry and the keep-fit movement have seen significant innovation, which may have stimulated demand.

While leisure absorbs an increasing proportion of consumer spending, a great deal of spending on hotels, conferences, exhibitions and so forth is related to work. There has clearly been a considerable growth in this over time, and it now forms a major sector of employment. It has been estimated, for instance, that by the mid-1980s around 70,000 jobs in the West Midlands depended on tourism, broadly defined to include work-related spending. This compares with 20,000 or less before the opening of the National Exhibition Centre, near Birmingham, in 1976. While some of the increase will have come from the growth in local leisure spending, a large proportion of the extra demand must have come from outside.

The long-term growth of the conference industry (as it was already called by the 1930s) has not been the subject of much study. One can infer that there have been two primary factors behind it: the decentralisation of organisations, and the growing ease of travel. In the nineteenth century, most firms in any particular industry clustered around large regional centres such as Manchester and Glasgow, for reasons discussed earlier in the book. Exchange of information between businessmen therefore occurred in these centres. Nowadays, industry is much more decentralised, but since personal contact is essential to build up trust, the telephone cannot fully replace the contact that used to go on as part of everyday life. The substitute is the annual marketing convention, the exhibition for purchasing managers, and similar functions; and ease of travel makes attendance at these decreasingly costly in time. The individuals involved need hotel accommodation, as well as conference and exhibition accommodation. Of course, there are many other factors at work, such as the growing realisation that investment in acquiring knowledge has a high rate of return. Whatever the forces behind the growth of these activities, they are of increasing importance, and more and more have an international dimension.

Of equal economic importance to leisure spending has been the growth of professional and clerical services, as well as financial services, which were discussed in Chapter 30. Many of the first two are government provided and not traded on the market, and it is therefore difficult to analyse them in terms of demand and supply. Obviously there is a demand for better health services, more education and a quicker reply from the Inland Revenue to letters requesting a tax repayment. However, given that the greater part of these services are not priced, it is impossible to estimate how strong demand for them is in relation to the demand for other goods and services. Equally, the supply is not usually provided in terms of the normal economic criteria of return on investment, since there is no revenue directly attributable to each project. The provision of these government or government-subsidised services is therefore dealt with separately in Chapter 34.

STRUCTURAL AND REGIONAL CHANGE

While services, considered collectively, have formed the largest single element of the economy since the nineteenth century, their overall contribution has changed surprisingly little for most of the twentieth (Table 31.6). As the usual interpretation of economic development suggests that a rise in the share of manufacturing in national income will be followed by a rise in services' share, the latter's slow increase in Britain until recent years needs explaining. It seems likely that changes in income distribution are the main factor (Ch. 33). Before 1914, and to a lesser extent throughout the inter-war period, a large segment of discretionary purchasing power was still in the hands of the wealthier middle and upper classes. A high proportion of this expenditure went on domestic service and on retail services, which were provided on a lavish scale. The shift in income distribution over the Second World War period permanently cut this type of expenditure. Since then, as practically everyone's incomes have risen, the demand for services has reasserted itself, although now it is financial, professional and government-provided services which have been the fastest growing.

In the long term, the growth of these type of services has contributed to the shift which has seen the centre of economic dynamism pass from the North to the South. Change in the location of manufacturing has also been an important factor. Although in the inter-war period the new industries' share in output was quite small, they were responsible for much of the growth which did occur; and so

Table 31.6 Share of sectors in national income (%)

	Agriculture	Manufacturing, mining, construction	Other
1913	6	38	56
1937	3	41	56
1951	5	47	48
1973	3	43	54

(*Source:* Matthews)

growth was concentrated in the areas where they tended to be located. The most important new industry, vehicles, had already become established in the West Midlands and, consequently, this old industrial region enjoyed relative prosperity throughout the period and on until the 1970s. Vehicle manufacture also had important outposts in another old industrial area, Lancashire (commercial vehicles), as well as in the southern towns of Oxford (Morris) and Dagenham in East London (Ford). Another prosperous industry which was located in the established industrial areas was chemicals, where the main plants were in the North West and North East. Most new firms, however, were located near the biggest consumer markets – which meant not too far from London – or in areas where there was either cheap land, cheap labour, a pleasant environment, or all three. The older industrial areas had none of these. Land was expensive because so much had been built over, and the existing buildings were often unsuitable for new purposes; labour, although in surplus, was no cheaper than elsewhere because of the rigidity of wage rates; and the environment was certainly not pleasant, because air pollution co-existed with the detritus of heavy industry.

Much of the expansion took place around the fringes of London and the West Midlands conurbation, or slightly further out in towns such as Slough and Watford, where land was relatively cheap. The visibility of this development, whose depressing legacy can still be seen by anyone driving down the Great West Road or similar arterial roads of the inter-war period, is perhaps one reason why there has been an overemphasis on the importance of new industries. Towards the end of the inter-war period, the geographical range of industrial development widened, to the West and to the North, partly because of government pressure on firms producing strategic products to move away from the South and East, and partly because of growing

congestion in the London conurbation. The area around Cheltenham, for example, became a major location for aircraft component manufacture.

Increasingly since the Second World War, the demand for, and
supply of, services has had an important regional impact. Foreign
tourism into Britain has largely benefited London and a few other
centres. Governmental services were widely dispersed in the 1960s,
but the policy-making centres of major departments remain in
London. This means that the most highly-paid groups of civil servants
also remain predominantly in London. A less obvious regional factor
is the concentration of governmental research in the South, particularly Ministry of Defence research establishments which are all in
southern England. There are advantages for defence industries in
locating near such establishments to facilitate consultation and
liaison, so this may have exacerbated regional imbalance. It seems
likely, however, that the biggest contribution to uneven regional
growth has come from financial services. Here again, London has
been the chief beneficiary. The rest of the South has gained because
routine administration has often been moved out – but not too far.
Thus Swindon has become the administrative headquarters of the
insurance firm, Allied Dunbar; much of the administration for the
Lloyds insurance market is carried out at Chatham. Certain regional
centres, notably Liverpool and Edinburgh, developed a strong
financial sector in the nineteenth century which has continued to be
important; but they are exceptions.

The structure of service industry growth has reinforced the
problems of the old industrial regions. For thirty years after 1945, the
continued relative decline of their old industries had been masked by
the world boom. This revived demand for products such as steel and
heavy engineering goods, while the overall pressure of demand,
assisted by regional policies, pushed many manufacturing industries
towards the North and West. Nevertheless, these regions were always
running hard to stand still. There was still a loss of jobs in the old
industries, notably in cotton and shipbuilding in the 1950s and coal in
the 1960s. Regional unemployment, as shown in Table 31.7, was
always above the level of most of the South.

The relative prosperity of the South as a whole, not just of
London, now seems an immutable part of life. But it is, in fact, even
more recent than is the decline of the old industrial regions.
Employment in much of southern England in the inter-war period
still relied on the low-wage activities of agriculture and servicing the

Table 31.7 Regional unemployment in Britain 1931–85(%)

	1	2	3	4	5	6
1931*	19.2	12.2	9.6	9.4	7.8	8.1
1961	3.8	2.6	2.0	2.5	2.2	2.4
1985	18.8	14.9	12.4	10.3	9.7	11.7

	7	8	9	10	11	Total GB	Total UK
1931*	12.0	16.2	16.5	16.1	n.a.	12.0	n.a.
1961	2.1	3.5	4.2	4.5	9.4	2.8	3.0
1985	15.3	16.0	16.7	15.3	20.8	13.1	13.3

1 = North
2 = Yorkshire and Humberside
3 = East Midlands
4 = East Anglia
5 = South East
6 = South West
7 = West Midlands
8 = North West
9 = Wales
10 = Scotland
11 = Northern Ireland
* Based on census, and probably understates unemployment by about 20 per cent.
(*Sources:* Law, C M 1980 *British Regional Development Since World War I*; Feinstein; *Regional Trends*)

Table 31.8 Employment in staple industries

	1951 (UK)	1985 (GB)*
Coal	780,000	215,000
Cotton†	322,000	39,000
Railways	528,000	148,000
Shipbuilding	224,000	90,000

* Omission of N Ireland does not make a significant difference
† 1985: cotton and silk
(*Source: Annual Abstract*)

wealthy leisured classes – themselves less wealthy than before 1914. The 1930s saw the beginnings of an influx of industrial capital which has been sustained to the present day. Together with service industry decentralisation, it has caused an economic transformation of the cathedral cities and country towns of southern England.

CHAPTER THIRTY-TWO
Change and decay: economic performance in the long run

The theme of this chapter is Britain's relative decline from her mid-nineteenth-century position of world economic hegemony. At that time, Britain supplied around 40 per cent of the world's exports of manufactured goods; by 1985, this had fallen to 9 per cent, a fall commensurate with Britain's decline in other ways. By the 1980s, Britain's income per person was, on most measurements, below that of all Northern and Western European countries, of Japan, and of the North American and Australasian countries. Before the First World War, only Canada, the USA, the Australasian countries and possibly Argentina were superior to Britain in income per person. The situation had not changed markedly before the Second World War, although the USA had gone further ahead and most European countries had moved a little closer to British levels of prosperity. It was in the thirty years after 1945 that the main change came.

Explanations of the post-1945 relative decline tended to come at first from economists, politicians and journalists, until economic historians took an interest in linking recent problems with their explanations of relative decline in the late nineteenth century. It is, after all, something of a coincidence that decline should have gone on so long. Furthermore, so many of the explanations which have been put forward for Britain's recent problems seem, in the light of history, to be such palpable nonsense.

In Chapter 26, the demand-side explanation, which saw so-called 'stop–go' policies and overvaluation of sterling as the problems, was considered. This explanation or set of explanations is a serious one, but it is not one that can be accepted, for reasons already discussed. The most cogent of these is that other European countries followed very similar domestic demand policies, without the same deleterious effects; while the alleged overvaluation of sterling can be challenged on the grounds that devaluation in 1967, and subsequent falls in its relative value after floating in 1972, failed to achieve any significant improvement in industrial performance. British firms, it seemed, preferred to take higher profits on devaluation rather than use lower prices to aggressively pursue market share; and, anyway, wages quickly rose, so eroding the cost benefits of devaluation. The more fanciful explanations of Britain's post-war decline have tended to focus on the high level of government spending. This, it has been said, has discouraged private investment by raising interest rates. Since the domestic investment ratio in the post-war period has been roughly double that of any previous period, this explanation seems *a priori* unlikely. Of course, investment might have been higher still if government spending had been less, but those who put forward this argument would have to explain why investment was so low during that Golden Age of non-intervention, the late nineteenth century. The other major criticism of high government spending is that it results in very high rates of tax on upper incomes, which have discouraged enterprise. There may be something in this – it is difficult if not impossible to test – although it should be realised that high marginal rates of income tax (now significantly reduced) were a function of the British tax structure rather than of government spending *per se*. Other countries had high spending but lower tax rates on high incomes. It seems unlikely, however, that the effect of high tax rates on enterprise has been very great. The USA, a country with much lower rates, has experienced low economic growth, comparable with Britain, since the Second World War. Furthermore, there has been plenty of room for British firms to mitigate the effects of high tax rates on their senior managers. Tax-free pension contributions, company cars, flats and board-room lunches have all provided ways round. Finally, the late nineteenth century, with its low rates of tax and its low rates of growth, again provides a point of comparison which suggests that low taxes and enterprise do not necessarily go together.

Those who seek longer-term explanations of decline will find almost as many as there are economic historians (and the author intends to add another one). In addition, there are mavericks such as Donald McCloskey who deny that there was relative decline in the late nineteenth century, on the grounds that, by his calculation, total factor productivity rose as fast in Britain as elsewhere. This conveniently ignores the fact that the investment ratio in Britain and, consequently, the overall growth rate was much lower than in its main competitors (see Ch. 17). Apart from these Panglossian idiosyncracies, however, the numerous other explanations can perhaps be grouped into two main schools of thought.

The first, encapsulated recently in a book of essays edited by W Lazonick and B Elbaum, starts from the premise that a competitive market system is not a satisfactory guarantor of growth. A competitive market, in which information is easily accessible, will in theory maximise the efficient use of factors of production at any given time. Competitive operators in markets do not, however, possess mechanisms to overcome constraints which might hamper long-term growth – constraints such as union power, poor technical education and tariffs in foreign countries. Such constraints can only be overcome by larger organisations, most notably the state, which possess some coercive force. This school of thought, therefore, sees British industry as having been confronted over the years by a number of institutional constraints such as those outlined above, which could only have been overcome or mitigated by coordinated intervention. Intervention was limited, however, by the structure of the economy, and by reluctance or inability on the part of the state.

The second school of thought, while agreeing with the first in many of its specific diagnoses, sees the root cause of the problem as, if anything, even more intractable. Summed up in the title of Martin Wiener's book, *English Culture and the Decline of the Industrial Spirit 1850–1980*, it ascribes Britain's poor economic peformance to a disenchantment with industry which began in the mid-nineteenth century. The steady but gradual rise of industry in Britain up to that time meant that the aristocracy had survived, with much of its status still intact. This aristocracy provided an ideal for the English middle classes, who increasingly became seduced from the stern task of manufacturing and selling into aping the aristocracy by doing almost anything but manufacturing and selling. Instead, they sent their sons to public school, to prepare for careers in the army or the Indian Civil Service; and if in industry, remained in it only long enough to make enough money to retire to the country. Wiener, and others, see this ethos as leading to a downgrading of industry. The neglect of technical education and reluctance of the state to give primacy to manufacturing industry are perceived as stemming from this attitude, which is seen as still pervasive today. Commentators on Britain's decline also point to the maleficent influence of the City of London on manufacturing. Bankers, on this interpretation, knew little of industry and had little interest in financing it. On the other hand, the City had a higher social status than industry, and politicians were more likely to listen to its views – which might be antagonistic to manufacturing.

The two preceding paragraphs have provided a thumbnail sketch of two types of explanation for Britain's long-term economic decline. Many, although not all, of the details in these explanations are very cogent, being based on much research and evidence. The main criticism that can be levelled against them is that they attempt to be universal. In searching, quite properly, for phenomena which will link the economic decline of the late nineteenth century with that of the twentieth, they tend to treat all these phenomena as if they acted with the same force over the entire period of 100 years. This is hardly credible. What is needed is a long-term explanation which takes account of changes in the British economy over this period and, equally important, of changes in Britain's competitor economies. For it is essential to remember that the decline in question is a relative one. In absolute terms, the growth rate of the British economy has actually improved.

A helpful start would be to identify relationships which have changed between the periods. German economic performance will be taken as a point of comparison. Germany, having started as a country much poorer than Britain, has ended as one much wealthier, having lost two world wars on the way. The two main periods of relative change were the late nineteenth and early twentieth centuries, and the post-1945 period. The interim period does not constitute a good point of comparison, since it includes the disruption of two world wars and the inter-war depression. As Table 32.1 shows, there are important points of difference between the two periods. Comparing rows 1 and 2 with rows 3 and 4 reveals that the domestic investment ratio in Britain lagged much further behind in the earlier period than in the later. The lag in total factor productivity growth, on the other hand, was much less in the earlier period. Of course, measurement of the latter is problematical, but discrepancies of the order shown cannot be ignored. And, of course, Germany between 1950 and 1962 was undergoing a particularly rapid period of growth; but rows 5 and 6 show that, although the German growth rate subsequently slowed, there was only a slight reduction in the discrepancy between the British growth rate and that of all other European countries.

A less quantitative assessment also highlights differences between the two periods. Before the First World War, Britain was still the undisputed world leader in many economic sectors: she dominated the whole field of internationally traded services, notably banking, insurance and shipping, with apparently little challenge; much the same could be said about certain manufacturing industries, such as cotton textiles and shipbuilding. Only a few industries, notably steel and chemicals, had already suffered severe relative decline. In the post-Second World War period, by contrast, there were few sectors which were not increasingly challenged, if not by Germany then by other countries. Banking had already lost its international hegemony in the inter-war period; shipping came under challenge at that time, and by the 1980s Britain had become merely one among many shipping nations. Since 1945, most manufacturing industries have declined to the role of bit-part players on the world scene. On the other hand, in certain more limited areas, Britain has achieved some success. Her international oil-producing and trading companies, BP and Shell (strictly speaking, an Anglo-Dutch company), and the pharmaceutical sector are two such instances.

What is needed is an explanation of worsening relative performance, at least until the early 1980s, which also helps to explain the varying sectoral fortunes and the rise in the growth rate over the long term.

Table 32.1 International investment and productivity comparisons

Approximate dates	UK	Germany	All Europe
1. 1873–1913	0.5	0.9	
2. 1850–1914	9	20	
3. 1950–1962	1.2	4.5	
4. 1950–1964	15	23	
5. 1953–1961	2.9	7.2	4.9
6. 1961–1973	3.1	4.5	4.7

Rows 1 and 3: Total factor productivity growth, per cent per annum
Rows 2 and 4: Investment ratio (%)
Rows 5 and 6: National income growth, per cent per annum
Row 4 is the arithmetical average of three quinquennial figures; it is therefore approximate
Note: Row 1 includes added educational input, row 3 does not. British figures shown in row 3 are below Matthews' estimates of about 1.8 per cent per annum
(*Sources:* Rows 1 and 2: Matthews; Floud and McCloskey, Vol 2; row 3: Denison, E 1967 *Why Growth Rates Differ*; rows 4, 5, and 6: Boltho, A 1982 *The European Economy*

The explanation could start by focusing not on Britain's relative weaknesses in the pre-First World War period, but on her continuing enormous economic strengths. Behind these strengths lay Britain's accumulated practical expertise in manufacturing and selling. This was invaluable because scientific and organisational theory was weak, not just in Britain, but world-wide. Britain's practical training of managers and workmen, via the apprenticeship system which was increasingly topped up by night school, was unsurpassed. Similarly in commerce, trainee managers inherited a world of experience from their elders; so long as economic relationships changed only slowly, this was the best possible training. In certain areas, Britain's lack of theoretical training was already a drawback: these were in the technically advanced industries such as chemicals, and also in certain managerial techniques such as cost accountancy. It is important to realise, however, that weaknesses here came as much from a lack of demand for the products of such training, as from the initial failure to train. This lack of demand must have been the responsibility of the senior management or owners of existing firms. Even in the increasing number of large amalgamated firms, there were only tardy and limited attempts to institute centralised research departments, or allocate production to different plants on the basis of maximum cost-effectiveness. The largest firms of all, the railway companies, were notorious for their lack of cost control. Consequently there was limited demand for the appropriate staff.

It was at the level of top management and ownership, also, that decisions were taken to invest or not to invest. Britain's low domestic investment ratio can be put down partly to the decisions taken at this level to pay out dividends, rather than to plough back the money into the enterprise. This reluctance to invest was perhaps partly due to the relatively small size of firms, which inhibited their moving into new market areas. In that sense, the institutional constraints of a competitive market structure, as identified by Lazonick and Elbaum, were important. However, as pointed out in Chapter 17, many small firms could easily have amalgamated if the will had been there. Furthermore, when large amalgamated firms were formed, they did not necessarily follow more aggressive policies.

The problems of the inter-war period are harder to fit into a pattern, since so many of them were caused by demand weakness. Some commentators have attributed demand weakness entirely to particular government policies but, as Chapter 24 makes clear, it had essentially international causes, largely beyond the control of governments. It is fair to say that in many manufacturing industries, schemes for rationalisation were hampered by demand weakness. In steel, for instance, this was a disincentive to the building of large new plants. Nevertheless, some industries seem to have declined faster than would be warranted merely by changed world conditions. Among these were, in the service sector, international banking, where American competition now became formidable, and possibly shipping, where the Norwegians moved earlier than Britain into the oil-tanker market. In coalmining, also, it seems that spots of relative inefficiency before 1914 subsequently became raging sores. Furthermore, demand weakness does not explain why large sections of manufacturing industry continued under family control, even if floated on the stock market, with the big increase in the proportion of large amalgamated firms making little difference to patterns of management. So although international economic comparisons are difficult because of the world-wide depression, the inter-war period can be identified as a time when in many fields Britain stood still or only advanced slowly, while other countries were building the foundations for economic superiority. It was impossible, however, that the best practice of foreign countries would have no influence, and so there was a switch to large-scale organisation and more bureaucratic forms of management in some important firms. ICI in the private domain and the Central Electricity Board and London Transport in the semi-public domain were examples.

Paradoxically, one of the effects of the depression was to reduce rather than heighten the domestic impact of international competition, thus minimising the short-term effect of relative technical and managerial decline. Britain erected tariffs in the 1930s and mitigated internal competition by an extension of collusive price agreements. The lowering of tariffs from the 1950s and the revival of European competition exposed British firms in a new and much more devastating fashion. European countries had developed technical and organisational skills or imported them from the USA, for over fifty years; Britain had done so as well, but to much less effect. In the 1950s and 1960s, family control over large sections of British industry was finally eroded, and the big amalgamated firms at last adopted modern forms of organisation. However, the fifty years of relative stagnation had taken their toll. By now there was a new problem, the under-provision and under-training of middle management – the engineer, the sales manager, the production manager – compared with international competitors. Whereas in the 1900s this could only have been said of a few sectors, most branches of industry had now become more complex and demanded much more expertise. Britain had not kept pace.

In industry after industry, the weakness of middle management was exposed when the family owners finally retired or when international competition increased. In the hosiery industry, Courtaulds by 1968 controlled a fifth of capacity, achieved by buying up a series of family firms. By 1983, employment in the Courtauld-controlled plants had declined by 75 per cent, and its share of industry output was almost negligible. There had been no middle-management cadres to replace the family owners, and even amalgamation into a larger firm could not make up for the managerial deficiencies. In vehicle manufacturing, a much more important industry, the picture was even darker. In 1977, Michael Edwardes became chairman of British Leyland, the largest indigenous vehicle manufacturer with a peak annual output in the early 1970s of almost one million vehicles. It had evolved through a series of mergers over the previous twenty-five years. Edwardes found that 'the organisa-tion, including that at factory level, was a shambles'. At the factory level, his comments had been echoed by a *cri de coeur* from a Coventry worker in 1969: 'it is a myth that management manages on the shopfloor, when it comes down to detail they don't, they give instructions, and hope somehow they will be implemented . . . .' A report by the National Institute of Economic and Social Research in 1985, comparing British and German factories making relatively simple engineering products, itemised some of the British defects in production techniques. These were not the result of under-investment or restrictive labour practices, but of inattention to detail and inadequate training. Maintenance was poorer in Britain, so machine breakdowns were more frequent; the lack of skilled staff meant that repairs then took longer to complete; the German firms paid more attention to the design of products, so that they were easier to make.

The progressive weakening, as production techniques have be-come more sophisticated, of management's ability to organise production has been replicated in other areas, notably marketing. Before the First World War British firms often seem to have been relatively good at selling. However, as the century wore on, it was not enough just to sell: it became necessary to develop marketing, a more comprehensive function which is concerned with deciding market objectives and integrating a number of other functions such as research, design and advertising, so that these objectives are met. A survey in 1987, which compared British and Japanese firms in a number of fields, found that with certain exceptions British firms lacked clear marketing strategies. Almost half the British companies, for instance, were unclear about the main types of customer in their market area, and what the needs of those customers were. Only 13 per cent of Japanese firms were similarly uncertain.

The thrust of this account of British industry's progress in this century has been to emphasise the common origins of problems which have themselves differed in different periods. Before the First World War, British technology and organisational skills were usually equal to those of the competition. Investment was much lower, however, and this can be attributed primarily to decisions taken (or not taken) by owners and top managers. As the century wore on, the failure to institute coherent managerial structures in large firms became more marked as the number of these firms increased. In the post-war period, reorganisation on a large scale at last began to take place, and control became increasingly divorced from ownership. Company boards were less susceptible to pressures for high dividend payouts and could devote a higher proportion of profits to investment. However, by that time technology and organisational skills had developed world-wide, while British management at the operations level had not. Again, the earlier failure of top management to reorganise and to demand better trained personnel can be seen as the root cause.

There were, of course, individual exceptions to this pattern, some of which have been mentioned. In one sector, moreover – retailing – Britain has not been a laggard at all. Indeed, the British distribution system is often contrasted favourably with the Japanese. Again the historical development of the sector may offer a clue. There was no legacy of existing expertise when large-scale retailing first developed in the late nineteenth century. From the beginning, therefore, firms had to devise appropriate techniques for controlling operations, since there were no rule-of-thumb methods on which to rely. Thus a managerial infrastructure existed from the earliest days. Although there was a degree of stagnation between the wars when devices like resale price maintenance limited competition, firms were still better placed to cope with the combination of faster growth and enhanced competition in the post-1945 period.

The account above, and other evidence, contradicts some elements of other explanations for Britain's decline. The alleged bifurcation of finance and industry is something of a myth. While financial institutions with international business have influenced policy on exchange and interest rates, there is little evidence that these have had a significant impact on British industry in the long term. The clearing banks, which have been the main suppliers of funds to industry within the banking system, have retained close links with industry. Until the 1930s, they had little contact with other financial institutions, and even subsequently their priorities were different. If British industry failed to invest enough in the late nineteenth century, this can be put down more to its own decisions than to the banks'. If industrialists preferred to pay dividends, why should the banks provide the missing investment capital? It is true that neither merchant banks nor clearing banks performed much of a role in encouraging or coordinating amalgamations, as banking institutions did in the USA and Germany. Industrialists in Britain, however, were quite capable of amalgamating their firms themselves, and often did. Their problem lay in organising the resulting combines.

Blanket criticisms of Britain's provision of technical and scientific education are almost as misplaced. Provision has not been as limited as has often been said, either in lower-level education or in higher scientific education. In the league table of scientific publications per head of population, Britain in recent years has come almost as high as does the USA, with Germany, Japan and France all behind; and in some fields, such as organic chemistry and several medical fields, Britain is today extremely strong. This suggests that a combination of demand from the large research-orientated concerns such as ICI and Glaxo which emerged in the inter-war period, and supply from the university sector, could transform Britain's standing in specific industries. In organic chemicals and pharmaceuticals, areas where before the First World War Britain had been notoriously weak, the country's relative position has improved. Where there has been increasingly relative weakness has been engineering and management education. The premium apprenticeship system, once a satisfactory form of training, became decreasingly so as technology became more complex, and was not adequately replaced by theoretical training. Formal management education has also been late to develop in this country (see Ch. 28). Training in electrical engineering and electronics was stepped up after the Second World War, but here the increased human resources were to a large extent absorbed by defence research. This has consistently taken between a quarter and a third of Britain's total spending on research and development since the Second World War, compared with small fractions of that figure in Germany and Japan. Although British firms have become world leaders in some areas of electrical application – a striking contrast to the pre-First World War situation – these areas are specialised and often in the related areas of defence and aerospace. It is well-established that spin-offs from these specialised sectors to the rest of industry are limited. So Britain's strong position in some sectors has only had minor effects on the rest of the economy.

This is not to suggest that state intervention in areas of industry has always been deleterious, as is often assumed. As Chapter 26 suggested, the alternative to research and development on defence and aerospace may have been none at all. A bigger problem has been that state purchasing decisions, in defence or otherwise, have frequently been conceived of as grandiose national projects, and have swamped the technical and managerial resources available. The results, as with the advanced gas-cooled nuclear reactors, have been costly delays and technical problems. Lack of managerial resources also seems to lie behind the mixed results from the nationalised industries and from the state-encouraged mergers of the 1960s. The inter-war public corporations, the London Passenger Transport Board and Central Electricity Board, were relatively successful; the National Coal Board (now British Coal) was not a great success story but contrasted favourably with the disastrous record of private enterprise between the wars; the nationalised railways, on the other hand, suffered from managerial uncertainty and government interference and, until the 1960s, their record was fairly appalling. Of the 1960s mergers, GEC was reasonably successful, British Leyland a terrible failure.

The importance of managerial structure, and of the calibre of the managers themselves, highlights both the strength and weakness of the argument that greater state intervention would have remedied Britain's past economic failures. The strength lies in the perception that private enterprise itself has all too frequently not supplied efficient management. The weakness lies in the assumption that the state could necessarily fill the gap. It is not the state which ultimately organises production and marketing, but the individual organisation; and if management in that organisation is inadequate, any state remedy will, at best, have only a very long-term effect. The fact that, throughout the period of Britain's relative decline, some organisations have been successful is perhaps the most telling rebuttal of those who see Britain's problems as irredeemable except through enhanced state intervention. If some firms have been successful in the past, could not others have emulated them?

Criticism of the state's alleged inactivity has another side to it. The gravamen of the critics' charge is that, in spite of its sporadic intervention in industry from the First World War onwards, the British state has had a bias towards consumers rather than producers. Compared with other countries, this is probably true. The reluctance to impose tariffs has been a classic example. Yet this bias helped to produce a buoyant consumer sector in the late nineteenth century, as food prices fell, and this in turn helped to produce a strong retailing sector. In the long run, of course, a higher growth rate in manufacturing industry would have benefited everybody. However, much of the gains from an efficient manufacturing sector can be swallowed up by an inefficient distribution sector, something which accounts for the failure of the Japanese standard of living to rise commensurate with that country's manufacturing efficiency. Those who advocate state support of manufacturing at the expense of all else are the modern equivalent of seventeenth century mercantilists: they believe that a country's wealth is measured by its sales abroad; more realistically, wealth is measured by a country's ability to consume.

Finally, those whipping boys of historians and politicians, the trade unions, deserve some mention. It was suggested in Chapter 29 that management attitudes have had much to do with the restrictive practices that have undoubtedly existed. The fact that these practices have flourished in modern industries such as vehicle manufacture, as well as in old-established ones such as cotton, bears this out. In the inter-war period, trade unionism among the semi-skilled workforce of most car firms was weak or non-existent. Instead of developing effective methods of control of this workforce, however, the car firms preferred to follow the semi-autonomous working practices of older industries, exercising loose management control and relying on piecework payment to encourage effort. Consequently, after the war, as technology became more complex and unionisation developed, most firms had no effective managerial structure. Such middle management as existed had to spend its time coping with day-to-day problems of production or industrial relations, with the disastrous results outlined by Michael Edwardes.

This account has tried to suggest that the blame for much of industry's long-term decline lies with owners and senior managers. In other words, in the last analysis the reason for British industry's long relative decline lies with industry itself and not with the variety of scapegoats which have been put forward over the years. However, there is still one unanswered question – why did this group of people fail? If the initial problems began with the failures to invest and to reorganise in the late nineteenth century, then the generation most to blame are the owners and managers of that period – those whose careers were beginning in the middle of the century; and this fits in with the chronology suggested by Martin Wiener. In focusing on the low esteem accorded to business, however, Wiener misses one point. The occupation accorded even lower esteem in Britain, if relative pay rankings are anything to go by, is education. The low esteem in which those in the academic world think business is held is more than matched by the low practical worth which society accords to academics and teachers. It is this disassociation between business and education which has been the essential theme of this chapter. Businessmen as a group have not wished to employ highly trained technicians or qualified managers. There may have been defects in the supply of such people by educational institutions but, as Britain's standing in the scientific world proves, educationalists have responded to the once-valid criticism that Britain neglected science education. Presumably they would have responded to other demands if these had been made.

This disassociation between business and education did not exist in the eighteenth century. Then, businessmen thought it natural to be members of societies which discussed philosophy and science. To explain the change, perhaps we need to go back even further than 1850. J H Plumb has suggested that in the late eighteenth century the American and French Revolutions had a cathartic effect on English society. Fear of revolution meant that political radicalism, once widespread in the middle classes, became marginalised. Reason became treason, and the questioning attitude which had led both to political radicalism and an interest in science was quenched. Throughout the first half of the nineteenth century, the industrial middle classes became increasingly assimilated to an essentially conservative view of society and to the pseudo-aristocratic values which Wiener describes. Among those engaged in manufacturing industry, original thought and questioning were devalued and have never since been reinstated to their former position.

PART FIVE

Economy and Society 1914–85

CHAPTER THIRTY-THREE
Prosperity and poverty

INCOMES

By the turn of the twentieth century, most people in Britain had become more prosperous than they had ever been before. Nevertheless, large segments of the population, including most unskilled urban workers and the agricultural workforce, had standards of housing and diet which would today seem unimaginably bleak to most people; while, except among the upper and middle class, the consumption of durable goods was extremely low. This chapter charts the course of transition to the relative prosperity of today.

The increase in disposable incomes and spending is shown in Table 33.1. The growing incidence of taxation means that national income per person does not accurately measure the amount available for spending. This is better captured by measuring consumer spending direct, or by measuring personal disposable incomes, that is incomes after tax but before saving. Between 1914 and the mid-1920s, there was little change in either of these measures. This apparent stability, however, cloaks a shift in income in favour of wage- and salary-earners, and away from those who owned property of any kind, and who therefore received profits, rents and income from foreign investments. As Table 33.2 shows, between 1913 and 1924, the share of property owners in national income fell steeply, the advantage going to wage- and salary-earners. Consequently, real incomes for those in work rose, with increases of around 15 per cent for wage-earners and possibly more for low-paid salary-earners. Over the subsequent decade or so, there was another rise of about 15 per cent, this time more evenly distributed. A contributory factor to this increase was the decline in primary-product prices, which shifted the terms of trade in favour of industrialised countries. Low food prices helped to buoy up real incomes, an effect that was most marked at the height of the depression.

Table 33.1 Income and spending 1913–85

| | Consumer expenditure and personal disposable income, per person, 1913–1985, constant prices | |
	1	2
1913	100	
1924	100	
1937	120	
1951	122	
1961	153	153
1971		185
1985		259

1 = Consumer expenditure per person*
2 = Personal disposable income per person†
* Note that the savings ratio reached about 10 per cent by 1961, and has only increased slightly since then. Consumers' expenditure will therefore have moved at a similar rate to personal disposable incomes
† Personal disposable income is estimated after tax on incomes and national insurance payments, with cash benefits (state pensions, unemployment benefit etc.) added back. It does not, therefore, reflect the full burden of income tax on taxpayers
(*Sources:* Feinstein; *Social Trends*)

Within the overall increase in earned incomes of around 30 per cent between 1914 and the late 1930s, there were important variations. Top salary-earners did not do quite so well and, more important, they now paid much more income tax than before the war – as did those in receipt of property income. Income tax fell much more heavily on higher incomes, rather than affecting practically all earners, as it does today; and the standard rate had risen to 25 per cent, as against 6 per cent before the war. A large slice of the revenue from this went to the poorer sections of society, in the form of unemployment benefit and pensions. Within the working class, some groups did better, some worse. Skilled workers in general did less well than average. Even more striking, coalminers' real wages probably fell between the war and the mid-1920s: from being among the best paid of British industrial workers, they were now among the lower-paid groups. Agricultural workers, always low paid, continued to do badly; but their relative position did improve quite sharply in the early 1930s, when agricultural protection was instituted. Women industrial workers, on the other hand, also low paid, did reasonably well, with average real wage increases of 20 per cent or more over the wartime period. Furthermore, the existing trend for women to move into better-paid occupations such as clerical work had accelerated during the war, and continued after it. Finally, most semi- and unskilled male workers improved their position by at least the average or better.

The inter-war period therefore saw a considerable evening out in income distribution, in spite of unemployment. Among manual workers, the relative position of the low-paid groups improved. The old pattern, in which workers in the South, outside London, were considerably poorer than those in the major industrial areas was decisively broken. The latter now suffered disproportionately from unemployment, with coalminers again badly hit. However, the sort of widespread poverty which had still existed in the South and other low-wage areas before the First World War was now much less in evidence, even in the industrial areas. Unemployment benefit provided some floor to incomes in families which had unemployed members; the low paid had experienced a significant jump in their real incomes; and the reduction in family size also helped to reduce poverty. Seebohm Rowntree, who thought that 10 per cent of the population of York were without sufficient means of subsistence in 1899, found, using the same criteria, that only 4 per cent were in 1935–6. As before, poverty disproportionately hit children, since low-earners tended to have larger families.

Income trends during and after the Second World War bore many resemblances to the equivalent period between 1914 and the 1930s. There was redistribution over the wartime period, through changes in property income's share of total income, through changes in relative earnings, and through taxation. Property income's share again fell, although less drastically than over the First World War period. There was also a big squeeze on the incomes of the professional groups such as civil servants and teachers. By contrast, the relative share of manual workers of all skill levels improved, so that they achieved a real wage rise, by 1950, of a third compared with 1938. Finally, tax levels once again increased, income tax reaching 50 per cent during the war and continuing at a high rate afterwards. Even manual workers were now paying tax on a large scale, so reducing their real gain. The combination of increased tax levels to pay for government spending and increased saving to finance increased investment meant that consumer spending rose much slower than national income per person.

Table 33.2 Income shares 1913–85

| | *Factor shares of national income + relative salaries and wages* | | | |
	1	*2*	*3*	*4*
1913	56	44	77	44
1924	67	33	64	45
1937	65	35	68	45
1951	71	29	77	54
1973	73	27	76	61
1985	74	26	n.a.	n.a.

1 = Total labour income (wages, salaries, employers' contributions to national insurance, income from self-employment) as percentage of GNP

2 = Total property income (profits, rent, from abroad) as percentage of GNP

3 = Skilled manual workers' wages as a percentage of the simple average of all male pay

4 = Unskilled manual workers' wages as a percentage of the simple average of all male pay

Note: Dates for columns 3 and 4 are slightly different to those shown

(*Sources:* Matthews; Rubinstein; *Annual Abstract*)

After 1950, there was a sustained rise in living standards, more so than in the inter-war period, and until the late 1970s it was not marred by the large-scale unemployment which blighted the lives of so many in the 1920s and 1930s. The relative earnings position of manual workers continued to improve slightly. However, they also experienced increasing levels of taxation, as income tax was levied on a larger and larger share of personal incomes, while taxation of higher incomes diminished somewhat. So the post-tax distribution of incomes as between upper- and lower-income levels has not changed much since the 1940s (Table 33.3). Income tax was therefore at its most progressive during the 1940s, but has subsequently become less so.

The changing relationship between the earnings of the lower paid and average earnings is also reflected in women's earnings. Women's relative earnings increased over the Second World War period and then stagnated until the Equal Pay Act, which came into effect in 1970 and saw a further reduction in the differential with men (Table 33.4). There is no doubt, however, that although women had become

Table 33.3 Income shares 1949–85

| | Share of national income accruing to different groups of earners, after tax (%) | | |
	1949	1976–7	1984–5
Top 1%	6.4	3.5	4.9
Top 10%	27.1	22.4	26.5
11–50%	46.4	50.0	48.6
51–100%	26.5	27.6	24.9
Bottom 10%	n.a.	3.1	2.7

(*Sources:* Rubinstein; Central Statistical Office)

legally entitled to the same pay as men when doing the same job, discrimination still took place. Women have tended to dominate certain jobs in individual firms or workplaces, often low-paid ones such as catering or cleaning work, with the result that there are no substantial bodies of men holding the same job against whose pay the women's can be compared. In effect, women may have been doing work of equal value to men's but, because there is not a direct comparison, they may still receive less pay for it. The Equal Pay Act was amended in 1984 to take account of this, by making it possible to compare occupations largely staffed by women with ones dominated by men.

The growth of women's employment, particularly married women's, has had an impact on family incomes as the number of households with husband and wife earning has risen. However, the decline in juvenile employment, as children stayed at school longer, and in recent years the rise in unemployment, have had the opposite effect; so the average number of earners per household has fallen

Table 33.4 Women's wages 1938–78

	Women manual workers' hourly earnings as a % of male workers' hourly earnings
1938	52
1948	61
1969	59
1978	72

(*Sources:* Wright; Taylor, R 1980 *The Fifth Estate*)

from 1.4 in 1969 to 1.2 in 1984. Furthermore, in low-income households the adult woman is often the only earner, either because the husband is unemployed or because there is no male. Households with unemployed members and single-parent families, together with old people, constitute the main areas of relative poverty today. Poverty of the type still to be found before the war – almost total destitution – now does not exist except by choice. Child benefits, and the national assistance (later called supplementary benefit) introduced in 1948 as a 'safety net' for those below a certain level of income, ensure that this is the case. Poverty today usually takes the form of a lack of command over resources so that choice, even of basics such as food and housing, is sharply limited. The relatively low levels of pension and child benefit introduced at the inception of the welfare state meant that this sort of poverty has remained common, and a large number of people were forced to claim national assistance from the time it started. Although the level of real income provided by national assistance has increased over the years, in relative terms there has been little or no improvement in the position of the poorest groups. Furthermore, although there is objectively no reason for anyone to be in dire poverty, many people dislike drawing supplementary benefit. It is means-tested and still, to some, carries the connotation of charity. This idea lingers from the inception of the welfare state, when great stress was laid on the insurance principle as legitimating the notion of the right of the genuinely unemployed, the sick and the old to receive support. It is ironic that the low level of benefits undermined this idea from the beginning (see Ch. 34).

In spite of the continued existence of relative poverty over the whole range of incomes, there has been a substantial reduction in inequality since 1914. This has been matched by a reduction in inequalities in wealth. The two are not synonymous, since most people have continued to gain the bulk of their income from earnings, and changes in wealth-holding have made only small differences to changes in relative incomes. Nevertheless, inequalities in wealth have been reduced, and the change is the more striking in that wealth had been far more unequally distributed than income. The figures shown in Table 33.5 probably minimise the fall in inequality, because to a large extent the figures for any one year relate to an historic state of affairs, being based on probate records. They miss, for instance, much of the recent extension of home ownership because the people concerned are still living.

As in the nineteenth century, the fundamental mechanism behind the great twentieth-century rise in real incomes has been rising labour productivity. The causes of this are dealt with in other chapters, and only one point needs to be made here. However poor Britain's relative economic performance has been, in absolute terms the period from 1945 onwards has seen a faster growth in output per person, and hence a faster growth in real incomes, than ever before. The consequence is the paradox that, while Britain is no longer of great significance in the economic league of nations, the average family is far better off than their equivalent of one hundred, fifty or even twenty-five years ago.

What has also occurred in this century, and did not in the nineteenth, is a substantial shift in relative incomes. There are three reasons for this. First are the tax changes which have sharply reduced income differentials as compared with the pre-1914 position; the factors leading to these tax changes are discussed in Chapter 34. The other aspects of change in relative incomes are connected with the declining share of property income within total income, and the increase in the wages of lower-paid workers relative to all earners. The relative decline in property incomes is difficult to explain. A contributory factor may be changes in market power between capital and labour. By the mid-twentieth century, the stream of surplus labour from agriculture, which for centuries had exerted a downward pressure on labour's share of national income, dried up. The volume was already reducing by the inter-war period and became a trickle after the Second World War.

The growing strength of trade unions may have also exerted a downward pressure on property's share of national income. Such a hypothesis appears to fit in with the fact that it has been the relative wages of unskilled and semi-skilled workers, the most weakly unionised groups in the past, which have risen most over the whole period. On the other hand, it is precisely these workers who have gained most from the reduction in the supply of surplus labour from agriculture, since agricultural labourers did not usually compete with skilled craftsmen. So trade-union pressure, although probably helping to raise labour's share of national income and also compress-ing differentials, should not have its effects overestimated. Perhaps equally important in determining both income shares and pay relativities have been non-economic forces such as custom, institu-tional pressures and external factors, notably war. A striking example is provided by the experience of banks over the period of the First World War. Although their profits did not rise markedly, they were willing to adjust the salary levels of bank employees upwards. The increase could not be put down to unionisation, which was not very effective in banking. It seems rather that the banks, whose previous profit levels had been high, were willing to readjust their priorities in favour of their employees. Another example, this time involving legislation, is the increase in women's relative pay as a result of the Equal Pay Act. If women's pay before the Act had been determined solely by demand and supply, the Act should have led to a decline in the demand for paid female labour as such labour became more expensive. But, in fact, the number of women workers continued to increase subsequent to the Act, suggesting that female wages before it were artificially low due to the force of custom, which stigmatised women as inferior workers.

Changes in wealth distribution can be fairly easily explained. On the one hand, graduated taxes on the estates of the deceased (once called estate duty, subsequently capital transfer tax, and now inheritance tax) have had an erosive effect on larger blocks of family wealth. Although there are ways round these taxes, for instance by giving up assets before death, plenty of people have not, for one reason or another, taken advantage of them. On the other hand, the rise in incomes led after the Second World War to a rise in the personal savings ratio. Savings are no longer a prerogative of the wealthy, but of the many. Combined with the increase in home ownership, the result has been a reduction in wealth inequality which is likely to continue. Taking into account pension entitlements, because they form an 'asset' producing a stream of income, inequality has fallen still more steeply, as shown in Table 33.5.

Table 33.5 Wealth distribution 1924–81

| | Share of wealth held by different groups (%) | | |
	1924–30	1981	1981a*
Top 1%	58	23	12
Top 10%	88	60	35
Top 50%	n.a.	94	78–82
Bottom 50%	n.a.	6	18–22
Bottom 80%	6	n.a.	n.a.

* Includes value of occupational and state pension rights
(*Sources:* Harrison, A J in Aubrey Jones (ed) 1976 *Economics and Equality* (cited in Rubinstein); Inland Revenue statistics cited in Rubinstein)

Table 33.6 Housing by tenure 1914–84

	Owner-occupied	Local authority (%)	Rented from private landlord (%)‡
1914	10*	†	90
1938	25	10	65
1951	29	18	53
1960	42	26	32
1970	50	30	20
1984	59	29	12

* Some authorities believe the owner-occupied figure to have been higher, e.g. *c.*15 per cent
† Very small; included in private rented sector
‡ Includes housing provided as part of employment
(*Sources:* Rubinstein; *Social Trends*)

CONSUMPTION

In his book *The Stages of Economic Growth*, W W Rostow described the final stage as 'the age of high mass consumption'. Whatever the analytic value of this concept, it has some use as an evocative description. Its meaning is clear – that most people are consuming a lot of things besides the basics of food and shelter. Few would disagree that this age is now with us. But when did it arrive?

Total consumer expenditure stagnated between 1914 and the early 1920s, before rising slowly in the inter-war period (Table 33.1). The Second World War again saw stagnation, before a rise which has continued to the present day. Table 33.7 throws further light on these figures. The first thing to notice is the extraordinary persistence of relationships. Food has only just been overtaken by housing as the largest component of consumer expenditure. The proportion of spending on major items such as clothing, and fuel and power has not changed all that much over the years. Spending on motor vehicles has soared, but the proportion of incomes going on other consumer durables has not changed as quickly.

In reality, some of this apparent stability cloaks major changes in relative prices. The relative price of food, having fallen in the inter-war period, has subsequently increased, in spite of the improvements in agricultural productivity. The increase is related to the post-war improvement in agricultural prices and, subsequently, to the Common Agricultural Policy. The relative price of drink and tobacco has also increased. This was caused, particularly in the early post-war period, by heavier taxation on these products. On the other hand, the relative price of cars and other consumer durables has fallen. So a given proportion of income today will buy a far larger quantity of consumer durables than in the past; but this would not be the case to the same extent for food, drink or tobacco. Since incomes themselves have risen steeply, the actual consumption of consumer durables has gone up manyfold.

So when did the age of high mass consumption arrive? Like so much else in history, it is really a question of definition. By the beginning of the twentieth century, 70 per cent of consumer expenditure in Britain was going on non-food items; around a fifth of the population, the middle class, had constituted a mass market for consumer goods since the eighteenth century; around two-fifths, the better-paid segment of the working class, were increasingly constituting such a market. Their main items of spending were still food, drink, fuel, clothing and housing, but much of this spending was to increase quality or variety – in other words, these things were not being purchased simply as necessities. On one, perfectly acceptable, definition, the age of high mass consumption had already arrived. On the other hand, if the age of high mass consumption is to be defined as involving the purchase of large quantities of consumer durables, then it only began in the 1950s. The inter-war period only saw a modest rise in spending on these items and, at that time, the relative price effects were not enough to have made a great difference to quantitative consumption. Items like refrigerators were still luxuries. The main exception was car purchase but, although growing rapidly, this was still a middle-class market. It is likely that the First World War, far from promoting consumption by reducing income differentials, actually held back the growth of a mass market for consumer durables. The best-paid pre-war manual workers – skilled workers and coalminers – suffered a sharp decline in relative incomes. It was the poorer groups who gained, and their increase in spending power was largely directed towards increasing the consumption of basic necessities, such as food and clothing. By the late 1950s, although the proportion of spending on cars and other durables had not increased massively, the fall in these products' relative prices meant that the quantity sold was rising rapidly. The affluent society, as it was often called, had arrived.

Today the ownership of electrical gadgets such as washing

machines, vacuum cleaners and televisions is almost ubiquitous – so much so that many commentators have suggested that the demand for manufactures will decline, as wants are satisfied, in favour of services. Services are certainly a major component of spending, and always have been. Excluding a few items such as expenditure on reading matter (not very large), most consumer spending not listed in Table 33.7 has gone on services such as recreation, meals out and financial services; and, of course, expenditure on goods includes a large service element, since it incorporates the proportion which goes to the retailer. Furthermore, the consumption of largely unpriced services, notably health care and education, has increased sharply. A glance at Table 33.7, however, shows that over a period of seventy years the proportion of income spent on major items of consumer goods, excluding food, housing and power, has increased by 5 per cent. History suggests, therefore, that whatever happens to British industry's ability to supply manufactures, the demand for them is unlikely to suddenly dry up.

Table 33.7 Consumer spending 1913–85

| | Spending on various consumption items as a percentage of total consumer spending | | | |
	1913	1937	1965	1985
Food	28	26	22	14
Alcoholic drink	8	6	6	8
Tobacco	2	4	6	3
Housing	11	10	11	15
Fuel, light & power	4	4	5	5
Clothing	10	10	9	7
Cars & motor cycle purchase	0.6	1	3	5
Furniture, floor coverings, electricals ⎫	4	4	5	5
other household textiles, hardware etc ⎭		2	2	2
	68	67	69	64

Note: All figures rounded to nearest whole number except spending on motor vehicles in 1913
(*Sources:* Feinstein; *Annual Abstract*)

CHAPTER THIRTY-FOUR

Social policy 1914-1985

The growth of central government activity and spending since 1914 has been remarkable. Before the First World War, only a small number of people were covered by state-subsidised unemployment insurance; a rather larger, but still limited, number by state-subsidised health insurance. Both these schemes, together with a means-tested pension scheme, had only been introduced a few years previously. Government regulation of hours of work and safety at work had taken place from a much earlier date, while the central government had increasingly intervened to ensure adequate provision of local government services such as sewerage; but most of these interventions only cost a limited amount or were paid for largely out of local rates. Only in education was there a free, national system, but even here local provision was a very important element, while the education provided was basic. Many children left before they were fourteen, and only a few stayed after that age.

The first and most important thing to realise about the subsequent growth of government activity is that it has been practically universal throughout the developed countries of the world and that it has occurred at roughly the same rate in different countries – it is not unique to Britain. This growth has been explained in a number of different ways.

One explanation points to the rise of universal adult suffrage. In most countries there have been more people with relatively low incomes than with relatively high ones. This has meant that the majority of voters have benefited (or think they have) from high government spending on social services, since the taxes needed to pay for it have apparently come only from the better-off. There has, therefore, been pressure on politicians to increase such spending.

Table 34.1 Government expenditure 1913–81

	1	2	3	4	5	6	7
1913	12	2.4	8	n.a.	2	0	10
1925	24	6.2	13	n.a.	3	2	8
1935	25	8.5	18	n.a.	4	4	8
1951	37	14.4	13	2	9	8	7
1961	35	15.7	17	2	10	6	10
1971	41	19.3	17	2	10	5	13
1981	46	24.8	25	2	11	4	12

1 = All public expenditure (capital and current) as percentage of national income

2 = Columns 3–7 as percentage of national income

3 = Social security expenditure (poor law, pensions, unemployment benefit, family allowance) as percentage of all public expenditure

4 = Personal social service spending as percentage of all public expenditure

5 = Public health spending as percentage of all public expenditure

6 = Housing expenditure as percentage of all public expenditure

7 = Education spending as percentage of all public expenditure

In most cases, columns 3–7 include capital and current spending, although there are omissions between 1913 and 1935

(*Sources:* Feinstein; Halsey; Mitchell and Deane; *Annual Abstract*)

Another explanation would point to changing ideas. In the nineteenth century, the idea of *laissez-faire* became modified by the idea that collective action might be both beneficial in the treatment of some of society's ills and also morally right. Subsequently, the growing influence of socialism has reinforced this emphasis on collectivism. A more cynical view would see increased government action as a conscious or unconscious attempt by capitalist societies to nullify working-class discontent by a modest redistribution of income. This view, which exists in more and less subtle versions, is associated with much Marxist writing on the growth of welfare, although one would not have to be Marxist to hold it. Both this and the second explanation see an increasingly active social policy as a reflection of systemic forces which have also led to greater government intervention in the economy.

Some would argue, however, that neither the power of ideas nor the self-interest of groups is a sufficient explanation for the growth of government activity. The secret lies in the inner logic of collectivism, which creates an almost inexorable tendency for it to increase. Government departments, pressure groups and other interested parties will constantly spot defects and loopholes in legislation designed to curb some evil or help some disadvantaged group, and will seek to strengthen such legislation; while professionals such as educationalists and doctors constantly press for the use of more sophisticated techniques, which almost always cost money. This process will be familiar to readers of Chapter 23 as that outlined by Professor MacDonagh when explaining the more limited growth of government in the nineteenth century. In this century, a new dimension has been added because of the growth in numbers of a major group already enrolled as recipients of welfare – the elderly – who not only receive pensions but also require enhanced medical care.

An alternative to this view, which stresses long-term forces, is that which stresses the disruptive impact of wars. The twentieth century has seen two major wars, affecting most countries in the world to some degree or other. Long-standing expectations about government spending and levels of taxation have been altered. Could it be this which has provided the motive power for the growth in government intervention?

To explain a world-wide phenomenon is beyond the scope of this book, and so there will be no attempt to reach some final conclusion about the correctness or otherwise of the various explanations which have, in a very simplified form, been listed above. Most of them are not mutually exclusive and might coexist together as partial explanations. However, in the subsequent course of the chapter we will see how well or badly some of them seem to fit the British evidence; the coverage will be confined to the main items of welfare expenditure. Government spending on, and legislative control over, all sorts of other areas has also increased: educational provision has burgeoned, with an economic impact discussed elsewhere; social work has become a professionalised occupation rather than a largely voluntary activity; legislation on health and safety requirements has multiplied; planning controls over the use of land have become a major instrument of policy. Leaving these out is not to suggest that they are less important; but it is possible to outline the major stages in the increase in government activity, and some of the reasons behind it, without referring to every activity in which the government has been engaged. A comprehensive treatment would need a book rather than a chapter, and there are good and easily accessible books available.

Inseparable from the subject of increased government spending is the subject of taxation, and this is a logical place to start, since in Britain and in other countries tax revenues have risen at about the same rate as government spending. The alternative to increasing tax revenues is borrowing, a high level of which cannot be sustained for long without leading either to excessive inflation or to an unacceptable increase in interest payments. In the nineteenth century, growth in revenue had been achieved painlessly by the increase in national income, which enhanced the yield from a given level of taxation. This enabled governments to increase spending modestly without increasing rates of taxation. In this century, however, the growth in spending has far outstripped the growth in national income, and so tax levels have had to increase sharply. What has persuaded taxpayers to foot the bill, given that at any time before 1914 the political opposition to increased taxation was immense?

The most obvious answer is the two world wars. Tax rates increased sharply during each war and very little during periods of peace, at least until the 1960s. Acceptance of increased tax rates in wartime can be easily explained as a consequence of patriotism and necessity. The increased rates having been accepted, their continuation in times of peace was less painful to taxpayers, although spending was diverted from arms to welfare. While there must be a great deal of truth in this as an explanation of the acceptance of higher taxation, it cannot be the entire explanation. The Napoleonic Wars had involved relatively high tax rates over a long period, but the propertied classes had not continued with these a moment longer than necessary. Another comparison is with countries which have not been involved in wars in this century. One such is Sweden which, nonetheless, has high tax rates and levels of government expenditure. It seems likely, therefore, that in the long run, tax increases have been endorsed by the electorate because more people appeared to gain than to lose from the consequent increases in welfare. Added to this has been the growing belief that social justice demanded some degree of income redistribution.

While wars may not have been the only reason for acceptance of higher taxation, they undoubtedly accelerated the process and, thereby, speeded the delivery of higher levels of social welfare spending. Wars also seem to have facilitated the acceptance of a particularly high rate of increase in taxation on incomes. The more traditional sources of revenue, mainly consisting of taxes on goods and services such as customs and excise revenue and stamp duty, increased by less.

While the increase in welfare spending has been an international phenomenon, there are significant national differences in how it is allocated. Compared with the average of other European countries,

Britain has allocated relatively large amounts to housing and, until recently, made relatively generous provision for health care; child allowances and pensions have fared worse. Historians often 'explain' the growth of welfare in purely national terms, a procedure which, as this chapter has already made clear, is unacceptable. What such explanations do help with, however, is understanding why particular components of welfare have become more important in some countries than in others.

The First World War generated strong working class demands for some amelioration of conditions as a recompense for the sacrifices of war. However, these demands had distinct limits, not surprisingly, as before the war there seems to have been little popular support for spending on welfare. The wartime demands centred on housing improvement: in many areas, particularly the North East and Scotland, there had always been considerable overcrowding, and the war made this worse as workers flocked to these areas to make munitions and build ships. Promises to build more houses had considerable political resonance in the 1918 election. The Coalition Prime Minister, Lloyd George, played this up with the slogan 'homes fit for heroes'. It would be quite wrong to conclude from this that British housing was significantly worse than Continental. On the contrary, most British workers were much better housed than Continental workers, who often lived in tenement flats. The focus in Britain on housing improvement perhaps occurred because of the relatively high standards of the average dwelling, which cast a spotlight on lower-quality housing and overcrowding. Once housing had been highlighted as a 'problem', it continued to be seen as one. Furthermore, rent control, which was introduced in 1915 in response to protests about rapid rent increases in Scotland, made things worse in the long term by discouraging landlords from building houses to rent and by reducing the incentive for existing landlords to keep their houses in good repair. The result of all this was an upsurge in public housing provision, which had previously been negligible. At the end of the war, the government made generous subsidies, in the form of annual payments continuing over a number of years, available for housebuilding. These schemes were withdrawn in 1921 when inflation and high government expenditure once more made 'economy' a politically powerful word. Historians have tended to highlight this withdrawal as a turning back on the earlier promises for social reconstruction. But the long-term involvement of government in the provision of housing was now established, and continued with less generous schemes. Because the earlier subsidies were still being paid, central and local government current spending on housing rose steadily to over £40 million per year by the 1930s, compared to less than £1 million a year before 1914. The heavy level of subsidy reveals a dichotomy in the policy which emerged from the First World War. The striving for high standards encapsulated in the phrase 'homes fit for heroes' made public housing relatively expensive to build, but the inability or unwillingness of people to pay high rents led to rent subsidies, and rent controls in the private sector. The politicians and the people wanted both cheap and better housing. The cost of achieving both together has always been so great that it has prevented either objective being achieved for all the population.

Nevertheless, by the 1930s the upsurge of private building, and a concentration of public provision on slum clearance, gave some hope that the genuine housing problems of many areas might eventually be solved. The Second World War, however, saw another six years' hiatus in housebuilding, the destruction or deterioration of much existing housing, and the re-imposition of strict rent controls. Once more after the war, housing became a political football, suggesting that the advent of mass democracy has had a significant impact on this area of social policy. Whether or not voters actually cared about housing, the politicians certainly thought that they did. The Conservative government of 1951 promised 300,000 houses per year, and Harold Macmillan's reputation as a political wizard partly depended on his achievement of that target in 1954, while he was the minister responsible. In the 1960s, Labour briefly hoped to build 500,000 houses per year. From the 1940s to the 1960s, housebuilding diverted resources which might, under the ruling conditions of excess demand, have gone to exports or to investment in manufacturing. The obsession with numbers led to much poor-quality housing being produced and a neglect of the possibilities of renovation of the existing stock. From the early 1970s, rather more sensible policies have prevailed, although the poor quality of much post-war housing is now producing its own problems.

Housing policies have therefore developed from *ad-hoc* responses to particular problems. The British still enjoy, on average, good housing conditions compared with most developed countries, although a significant proportion of public housing is in poor condition. These housing conditions have been achieved at the cost of very heavy subsidies, both for public rented housing and for private owners through tax relief on mortgages. The decline of the private rented sector has reduced choice for those too poor, or unwilling, to buy, since they are dependent on the availability of public housing.

Finally, the value of private landlords' assets has been squeezed since rent control was first imposed in 1915. Private landlords rarely excite sympathy; but since much working-class housing was owned by other members of the working class, and since rent control has always been most strictly maintained on such housing, the policy has not even had the merit of being redistributionist – it has just been unfair.

The First World War and the problems it created help to explain subsequent housing policies. It also had a lasting influence on unemployment policy, although the mass unemployment of the inter-war period made its own contribution. Before the First World War, there existed only an unemployment insurance scheme applicable to a few industries, such as shipbuilding, which were subject to cyclical unemployment. The scheme provided benefit for only a limited period. Apart from that, the Poor Law was a safety net for those who had no other means of support. After the war, the Coalition government provided 'out-of-work donations' (nicknamed the dole) for discharged servicemen, as it feared social discontent if those who fought in the war came home with no work and no money. In the event, the post-war boom quickly mopped up surplus labour. The government meanwhile extended the unemployment insurance scheme to other manual workers. The element of government subsidy in the scheme was expected to be small, since both workers and employers paid a contribution. So the government anticipated a temporary dole scheme, and a permanent, but small, contribution to an insurance scheme. In the event, the extension of the insurance scheme in 1920 was soon followed by the beginnings of the first post-war depression, and from then on unemployment remained high. There was never a chance to build up reserves in the insurance scheme, so the government either had to reduce benefit levels sharply or accept the need for a much larger subsidy. Furthermore, many people had never built up sufficient credit in the insurance scheme for their unemployment benefit to last for long. By 1921, the government was faced with the prospect of a mass of destitute unemployed, as it had feared immediately after the war, and a bankrupt insurance scheme. It chose the politically easier route out of its dilemmas. The unemployed were allowed to continue drawing benefit after their entitlement had technically expired, while the unemployment insurance fund was topped up to keep it solvent. This continued throughout the 1920s. In 1931, in an attempt to make the insurance scheme viable, those whose entitlement had expired were required to draw a means-tested benefit administered by local Public Assistance Committees, which in 1929 had taken over the functions of the old

Poor Law Guardians. Although this scheme was very unpopular (and the nickname 'the dole' persisted), it was in reality only a minor regression. The old Poor Law ideal that there should be no relief for the able-bodied outside the workhouse had long been forgotten.

The First World War and the aftermath of mass unemployment had set the tenor of public policy towards the unemployed. The out-of-work donation had established a precedent for paying benefit to those whose insurance had run out. This provided a convenient escape route in 1921 when the government was faced with a mass of unemployed such as no nineteenth-century government had ever experienced. Once the insurance principle had been breached, it was regarded as politically impossible to go back.

The Second World War, on the face of it, caused more radical changes in social policy. William Beveridge's famous report of 1942 proposed universal social insurance against unemployment, ill-health and old age. The reaffirmation of the insurance principle meant that benefits could be regarded as obtainable by right, so that the connotation of the dole, and the reality of the means test, were dispensed with. Beveridge's proposals excited great popular support, rather as the promises for better housing had in the First World War. The wartime Coalition government accepted many of the proposals, while the post-war Labour government, in establishing the 'welfare state', put them into practice, with some modifications. How far was it the will to change, generated by the war and made effective by the voters, which led to the foundation of the welfare state?

Pre-war health provision had been something of a jumble: manual workers had the existing government-subsidised insurance scheme, but it was administered by existing bodies such as trade unions and industrial assurance societies; hospitals were provided partly by local authorities, who had taken over the old Poor Law hospitals, and partly by voluntary agencies. Many manual workers, as well as the better-off, made their own insurance arrangements to cover dependents, since the state scheme only covered wage-earners. Many simply went without health care except *in extremis*. The post-war change was dramatic. The National Health Service, established in 1948, provided an entirely free service (although prescription charges for some items, such as dentures and spectacles, were introduced later and have subsequently been extended). Many other countries have continued to rely on a system under which individuals meet their own medical bills and are then reimbursed. In other words, the state and the provision of medical services are kept separate. In Britain the war, and the expectations aroused by Beveridge, do seem to have had a major influence on the pattern of health care.

The other major post-war innovation was child allowances, introduced with all-party support in 1945. Here the war was arguably only an accelerator of change – if that. Concern for the health and fitness of children went back to the 1900s, if not before, and the widespread belief at that time that 'national efficiency' was deteriorating because of urban living conditions. This belief was held strongly by those on the right as well as the left of the political spectrum, and it revived in the 1930s as medical reports showed widespread evidence of malnutrition among children. Concern was exacerbated by the decline in the birth rate. As a result of this, the idea of child allowances was being tentatively considered by the Conservatives before the war, and it is significant that all European countries, whether combatant or not, had introduced them by 1950. In some countries, such as France, they were far more generous than in Britain. This leads to an important conclusion. Although the war may have accelerated the payment of child allowances in Britain, it may also have restricted their generosity. Because the war also accelerated the introduction of welfare schemes such as the health service and possibly made them more generous than they would otherwise have been, it reduced the resources available to other schemes. Child allowances were fixed at 5s per week for the second and each subsequent child, as against the 8s per week which Beveridge had recommended.

Similarly, the effect of the war and its associated effects on old-age pensions and unemployment benefits should be put in perspective. The number of people covered by old-age pensions had been gradually widened since their introduction in 1909, when they were limited to those over seventy, and means-tested. Their value increased sharply in 1946, when the present age limits of sixty-five for men and sixty for women were also adopted. However, when adjustment was made for inflation, the level was still below Beveridge's recommendation. Unemployment benefit for single men was increased very little and, allowing for inflation, was less generous than before the war. Again, a consequence of the wide scope and hence expense of the post-war changes was that changes in individual programmes, or levels of benefit, were sometimes small.

The structure of the welfare state then remained little changed until the mid-1960s. The Conservatives' acceptance of Beveridge during the war had owed itself largely to popular pressure and to pressure from Labour, who shared government. However, as had happened so often with welfare provision in the past, once the welfare state was established it became politically almost impossible to erode. The perception, right or wrong, that welfare was extremely popular, meant that the Conservatives became enthusiastic supporters. From their election in 1951 they were concerned to prove that their party was as safe a custodian of the welfare state as Labour. The Conservatives' task was eased by the fact that Labour had set many benefits at low levels in the 1940s; consequently it was not too expensive to keep up this relatively meagre provision. In the longer run, this provoked an intellectual reaction in the form of the 'rediscovery' of poverty in the late 1950s and early 1960s. In absolute terms, poverty was decreasing throughout the period (see Ch. 33) The rediscovery of poverty involved its redefinition as relative rather than absolute. On this definition, poverty had not been reduced, as the proportion of national income received by the poorest fifth of the population was little changed. The rediscovery of poverty coincided with an attempt by Labour to differentiate themselves from the Conservatives, who had taken over the mantle of guardians of the welfare state. Competition between the parties to raise benefits therefore increased: Labour, for instance, raised old-age pensions sharply in 1965; in 1972, the Conservatives introduced a 'Christmas Bonus' of £10 for pensioners. Then in 1975, annual increases in pensions were linked to whichever was the higher of the increase in average incomes or average prices.

While spending on benefits was restricted until the 1960s, the cost of one element of welfare proved almost impossible to control: this was the health service. A spectrum of reasons combined to raise spending: the initial unsatisfied demand for services; the fact that most of the services were unpriced; the increasing number of elderly; and the pressure from professionals for greater spending in a field where technology was developing, and so costs rising. Combined with these was the fact that, as with other government services such as education, health care was labour-intensive and had only limited scope for improvements in productivity. In 1946 it was estimated that the cost to central government of the National Health Service, excluding the receipts from national insurance contributions, would be £110 million per year. In the financial year 1949–50, the actual cost was over £300 million. These large unplanned running costs inhibited new hospital building, so that by the late 1960s there was a backlog of construction. By the mid-1970s, real capital spending on hospitals was running at seven times the level of 1949, while real current spending had increased by 90 per cent.

The proportion of national income taken by welfare, broadly

interpreted to mean state benefits and health spending, has therefore risen substantially in two stages in the post-war period: first during the inception of the welfare state and then during the 1960s and 1970s. Since 1979 the Conservative government has attempted to limit expenditure, for instance by reducing spending on housing and by ending the link between increases in pensions and increases in average incomes. However, there are strong underlying forces which keep welfare spending up: the continued increase in the number of elderly; the continued perception by politicians that welfare, especially the health service, is a vote winner; and, of course, the recent increase in unemployment.

In 1932 a Treasury official, Sir Richard Hopkins, referred to the 'onward march' of the cost of social services. As the beginning of this chapter made clear, the onward march has not been confined to Britain, and its general causes lie beyond the scope of this book. However, some points about the British experience stand out. As with all countries, the scope of welfare has been limited by its cost. However much politicians would like to deliver welfare programmes to the voters, they have to consider that voters also pay taxes and at some stage may resent increases more than they cherish welfare benefits. Furthermore, as was shown in Chapter 25, the Treasury has had its own reasons for wishing to restrain spending, which have strengthened the political arguments. The influence of cost can be seen at the very beginning of the welfare state, when economic constraints led to substantial modification of the Beveridge blueprint. Later, in the 1960s and 1970s, Britain's per capita spending on health care, hitherto among the highest internationally, continued to rise in absolute terms. But other countries' spending rose even faster, as their higher economic growth rate enabled them to allocate a larger proportion of national income to health, and Britain's international position declined. Within the general constraints of cost, however, the structure, generosity and timing of particular programmes have been related to events and pressures within individual countries.

While the resources that the economy can make available have affected its scope, welfare itself has had an economic impact. Its impact on income distribution and the amelioration of poverty was discussed in Chapter 33. It has also absorbed resources that could have been used elsewhere – for private consumption, investment or exports – particularly during the post-war years of high demand. On the other hand, it is fair to say that Britain's post-Second World War economic peformance was so much better than in the inter-war period that resources could be taken for welfare and yet still leave enough for a much higher investment ratio and for a steady rise in the standard of living. Furthermore, one explanation of the developed world's high post-war growth lays the emphasis on the favourable demand conditions created by high government spending, of which Britain's was a part. So the economic effects of welfare may have been positive. From the 1960s, the renewed competition by politicians to raise welfare spending may have had more deleterious effects. The higher tax rates needed to pay for it frustrated wage-earners' expectations that their incomes would continue to rise rapidly. It could be that this was one reason for the high level of wage claims seen in the late 1960s and throughout the 1970s.

CHAPTER THIRTY-FIVE
Work and leisure

OCCUPATIONAL PATTERNS

At the beginning of the twentieth century the factory worker, the miner and the railwayman could stand as symbols of the working population. However, just as in the nineteenth century they had usurped the position of the agricultural labourer, so in the twentieth century their dominance has been challenged. Today the nurse, the sales representative and the receptionist are as or more typical.

Behind this change lie more complex shifts than occurred in the nineteenth century. Then the proportion of manual workers remained more or less constant, although the occupational structure changed with the shift from agriculture to industry. However, in this century there have been occupational shifts both between and within sectors. The long-term growth in service employment has continued, with the shake-out in low-productivity services such as domestic service and distribution during the Second World War being counteracted by long-term growth in professional occupations, notably medicine and teaching, in the civil service and in finance. All these are predominantly salaried occupations, often with middle-class status, though their pay levels are not necessarily very high. There has also been a shift towards white-collar jobs in manufacturing, which has further increased the proportion of middle-class jobs in the population. And the female working population has increased substantially, with its composition changing even more radically than has the male. The predominance of textile employment and domestic service has been replaced by a more variegated pattern, with clerical work, nursing, teaching and shopwork all being important. The results of all these changes are shown in Tables 35.1 and 35.2.

Table 35.1 Share of labour force in sectors 1913–74 (per cent)

	Agriculture	Manufacturing mining construction	Services
1913	8	46	46
1974	2	43	55

(*Sources:* Deane and Cole; Wright)

Table 35.2 Occupational class of the employed population in 1911 and 1971

	1911			1971		
	% M	% F	Total	% M	% F	Total
Higher professional	1.3	0.2	1.0	4.9	0.5	3.3
Lower professional	1.6	6.5	3.0	5.9	10.9	7.8
Employers	7.7	4.3	6.7	5.0	2.7	4.2
Managers & administration	3.9	2.3	3.4	10.9	3.5	8.2
Clerical workers	5.5	3.3	4.8	6.4	27.0	13.9
Foremen, inspectors, supervisors	1.7	0.2	1.3	5.0	1.8	3.9
All middle class	21.7	17.8	20.2	38.1	46.4	41.3
Skilled manual	33.0	24.8	30.6	29.1	8.5	21.6
Semi-skilled manual*	33.6	53.4	39.5	20.8	32.9	25.2
Unskilled manual*	11.5	5.0	9.6	11.9	12.0	11.9

Figures are rounded, so columns do not sum to 100 per cent

* In the textual reference to these figures in Chapter 20, agricultural labourers (approximately 5 per cent of the total working population) were transferred from the semi-skilled to the unskilled sector for 1911. This table shows the original figures

Note: In this classification, sales representatives are classified under 'managers and administration'; shop assistants are classed under 'semi-skilled manual'; domestic servants are also under 'semi-skilled manual', which helps to account for the large fall in the proportion of female semi-skilled workers

(*Source:* Routh)

THE ENTRY TO WORK

The entry to work has been given little consideration by historians, yet for many people the initial decision to enter one job or another is of vital importance. The British pattern of training has virtually excluded those above the age of sixteen from entering an apprenticeship, the usual route to skilled manual work. It has been possible to enter such work by other routes, but the difficulties of acquiring the relevant technical knowledge and skill, together with trade-union restrictions, have hampered such entry. Entry to non-manual work requiring qualifications has presented different barriers, such as lack of finance for the further education needed to acquire them. The British tradition of providing good night-school facilities accessible to adults has helped to lower these barriers, but vocational qualifications such as those in banking and accountancy, which can be acquired by part-time study, are most useful to people already in those occupations. So, again, the initial decision on what job to enter has been important.

The entry to work, then, is a serious matter. Yet most young people have undertaken it with little idea of its importance, not because they were feckless, but simply because they were ignorant of the alternatives. A survey in an East Midlands town in 1953, for instance, found that half the school leavers did not know if their parents had any views about the jobs they should enter. Other investigations have found similar levels of apparent uninterest by parents. Careers advice from schools has been patchy and often ignored, while school leavers themselves have hardly been in a position to make a reasoned judgement. Much entry to work has therefore been by personal or family contact with individual firms. In this way, firms have saved themselves the trouble and expense of advertising and of elaborate formal hiring procedures. Vacancies have been filled simply by asking around or by notifying existing employees, who then contact friends or relatives. For workers, there have been advantages and disadvantages. The advantages have included an almost guaranteed entrée, for those in the right place at the right time, to a job. Others have been less fortunate: black people, in particular, seem to have suffered from their lack of a network of informal contacts, which may help to account for their less favourable employment experience.

Although reliance on personal contacts has helped many to some sort of a job, it has clearly had deleterious effects. Manual-worker parents and their children have downgraded the value of further education because of their lack of knowledge of the possibilities it might open up. This has reduced the potential stock of human capital in the community, as well as adversely affecting the life chances of those who have left school early. People have found themselves virtually locked in to types of work to which they were not suited. This lack of knowledge of the spectrum of future opportunities has, of course, applied to girls as well as boys. One of the strongest forces behind both sexes' choice of occupation has been knowledge of an individual in that occupation. In a recent sample of school leavers, nearly half the girls wanted to go into one of three jobs – nursing, hairdressing and clerical work. All three are classic female occupations, and the youngsters usually knew a close relative in one of them. The 'labelling' of particular occupations as female, a process discussed in Chapter 2, has been the crucial influence on the emergence of the female job structure. The continuity of this job structure, however, has been powerfully reinforced through the processes by which people enter work, which have led most of them to accept certain structures as not merely inalienable, but also desirable. So the Sex Discrimination Act of 1975, while in theory removing discriminatory barriers to women's employment, has not in practice led to rapid change in the female employment structure.

So far, this section has been pessimistic, but pessimism should not be taken too far. As Table 35.2 shows, the occupational structure has changed over this century, and for men and women the change has been towards the provision of generally higher-grade jobs. The influence of custom and ignorance on the entry to work has been strong, but it has not been strong enough to prevent a steady outflow from manual to non-manual work. In 1972, for instance, almost a third of the male children of manual workers were in a non-manual occupation ten years after entering work. There was also intergenerational movement from non-manual to manual, but at a slightly lower rate, while within the middle class there was a shift from lower- to higher-status occupations. This kind of movement seems to have been going on all through the twentieth century and to have accelerated in the last forty years or so. This acceleration is not surprising, because about two-thirds of the shift in the male occupational structure, from manual to non-manual, has taken place since 1951.

THE EXPERIENCE OF WORK

No-one seems to have asked nineteenth- and early twentieth-century workers whether they enjoyed their work or not. Since 1945, surveys on attitudes to work have become quite commonplace and have emerged with some surprising, and some predictable, findings.

Most semi-skilled factory workers, and even many skilled ones, tolerate their jobs without finding great satisfaction in the work itself. The reasons for this are familiar ones – the relative monotony of much assembly-line work and of repetitive machining work, together with high stress levels in jobs where pay is linked to high output targets. Whether there has been any significant change compared with earlier periods is difficult to say. Much factory work was repetitive by the late nineteenth century, and certain jobs, particularly in textiles, also involved a high pace of work as well as effort-related pay. Most male workers find some compensation in relations with workmates, but in factory jobs these tend to be limited in terms of depth; most friends are found away from work. Again, most writing on late nineteenth-century work tends to stress the growing separation between home and work; it is not a new phenomenon. Workers' attitudes to jobs like these have been described as instrumental. The biggest attraction of the job is the pay packet, rather than the work itself. Many workers who have taken such jobs, however, have done so out of choice; in other words, they could have taken more satisfying jobs – they chose less satisfying ones because these paid better. This points up the fact that, as in the nineteenth century, there are many sorts of employment outside factories. Consequently, manual workers have had a degree of choice between high earnings and job satisfaction, subject to the broad constraints on job choice imposed by education and the early years of work. Drivers, for instance, often take up that line of work because they enjoy the degree of autonomy and independence that it gives. It is not highly skilled work and so entry is easy.

In contrast with many manual workers, most of those in non-manual jobs, according to surveys, experience relatively high levels of job satisfaction. They also experience a much higher degree of linkage between work and home: colleagues at work are often friends outside work. This tendency is particularly marked among professionals, who often do not make any meaningful distinction between leisure and work. Work becomes the central interest of the worker.

Many women appear to have a slightly different attitude to paid work than do men. Women have a fairly instrumental view of such work in the main, seeing it as a way of earning money. Their expectations of the intrinsic satisfaction of work seem to be lower, so their toleration of the unpleasant aspects is greater. Furthermore, women in routine jobs enjoy social relations with their workmates and appear to gain greater satisfaction from these than do men. None of these things are surprising, in view of the way women have been acclimatised to approach paid work – as something which will cease on the birth of children, perhaps to reappear in part-time form later on.

Although there is no firm evidence as to changes over time in the satisfaction given by work, there have been more tangible changes in working conditions. While the entry to work has only gradually become more regularised, there has been increasing formalisation of the process of ending work through disciplinary dismissal or redundancy. Up to the Second World War, there were in most firms no formal procedures for dismissal – the employer could, in theory, dismiss at will. (This does not mean that workers were necessarily in constant danger of dismissal. In practice, paternalism and informal codes of conduct must have often limited arbitrary dismissal.) From the Second World War onwards, a variety of pressures led to change. A major impetus came from the growth of personnel management as a profession: part of the rationale of this segment of management was the formalisation of procedures relating to employment within the firm. Trade-union pressure for less arbitrary dismissal procedures was another factor. The law also intervened in various ways in the 1960s and 1970s. Most notable was the setting up of industrial tribunals by the Industrial Relations Act of 1971, which gave employees a legal redress for unfair dismissal; and the Redundancy Payments Act of 1965, which instituted compulsory payments for employees made redundant. The latter measure, of relatively minor importance when it was set up at a time of full employment, was extensively used in the late 1970s and early 1980s when mass redundancies became commonplace.

In recent years, job security has probably decreased as unemployment has risen. Leaving aside the overall economic position, however, workers' security has otherwise been measurably increased in a variety of ways by the changes outlined above. Subject to a certain qualifying period, there are now rights to compensation in case of redundancy. Whereas in 1969 only 8 per cent of plants had a written disciplinary procedure, by the 1980s over 80 per cent had one. Whether these changes constitute a qualitative shift in the power of labour *vis-à-vis* capital is another matter. Management's control of information, and its economic power compared with that of the individual worker, still puts it in a position of advantage.

In other respects, there have been positive changes in the employment relationship, particularly for manual workers who enjoyed few benefits, apart from their wages, before the First World War. Hours of work have fallen and holiday entitlements have increased (see the next section). Up to the Second World War, sick pay and pension schemes for manual workers were only to be found in the railway companies and a few other paternalistic firms. They became commonplace after the war, with about half of all firms providing schemes by the 1960s. Since then there has been a further, but slow, growth. The result has been a steady increase in the proportion that payments for sick benefit, pensions and other subsidised services bear to the total wage. Before 1939, it was probably no more than 4–5 per cent. By 1964 the cost of benefits in manfacturing industry ran at 11 per cent of the total wage bill, in 1981 at 19 per cent. Since the increase in these benefits has resulted more from employers' initiatives than from trade-union or government pressure, they can be seen as an attempt to generate a higher degree of employee commitment to the firm. Perhaps the underlying rationale for this has been post-war full employment, which made it difficult if not impossible for firms to recruit labour at short notice as they needed it. Consequently, firms wished to hold on to labour, which they did partly by building employee loyalty through benefits.

The improvement of conditions has, however, been more marked in some industries and firms than in others. Enterprises with a relatively stable demand for their products or services, which have therefore been less reluctant to incur high fixed costs, have been in the forefront. These include firms in industries such as chemicals, oil refining and modern sectors of engineering. In non-manual work, which had always enjoyed relatively better conditions, firms such as banks and insurance companies, and certain retail chains, have provided the best benefits. Central and local government is another relatively high benefit provider, for both manual and non-manual employees. Not surprisingly, such firms and enterprises appear to have relatively low levels of staff turnover. Furthermore, in some cases, although more often with non-manual employment, they offer a definite career pattern. All this has led some commentators to suggest that such enterprises have been characterised by the growth of internal labour markets; in other words, labour markets which are internal to the firm and which segment the workforce from the outside world. A further extension of this idea is that those who are excluded from these favourable conditions of employment constitute another segment of the workforce altogether. This segment would encompass workers in, for instance, jobbing engineering, building, low-grade assembly work, much catering work, and contract cleaning. This dual labour market theory hypothesises that movement from the secondary, or inferior, sector of the labour market to the primary sector is low.

So far as there has been historical study of this subject, it suggests that there has not been increasing duality in the labour market. There have always been better jobs and worse jobs, and it has always been difficult to move from certain types of work to others. What has happened is that the type of labour market segmentation that existed in the past has changed because the stability of employment has emerged as an important determinant, to be added to the long-standing forces of custom, the sexual division of labour and, of course, the training or education required for individual jobs. As before, however, the labour market remains essentially a spectrum of individual markets merging into one another, rather than a rigidly segmented structure. Even the idea that internal labour markets exert a much stronger influence on the overall pattern of the labour market than in the past must be open to question. Few occupations are so firm-specific that they do not allow some job mobility, although clearly the risk of losing benefits is a disincentive to changing jobs.

An excessive focus on hypothetical changes in labour markets can distract attention from the very real variations in workers' life chances occurring as a result of macro-economic changes in the economy, which can alter the desirability of certain jobs. In these circumstances, opportunities for people in those jobs will also change if their ability to take up other work is limited. The inter-war depression, for instance, sharply reduced the desirability of employment in the staple industries. Exogenous non-economic factors also affect life chances. The Second World War, in particular, provided large numbers of people with a training in marketable skills, for instance driving, as well as offering a significant number a status enhancement through promotion which would not otherwise have been available. This must have favourably affected their future employment prospects.

The single largest sector of work is not entered via a market: this is unpaid domestic work. Although the amount of time the average family spends on domestic work has been estimated, with a view to establishing its cash value, such estimates seem fairly worthless. How much of such work is choice, how much necessity? What does seem well established, both by sociological surveys and by common observation, is that women do far more domestic work than men, even when it is interpreted to include jobs like car cleaning and house repairs. And if some credence is given to estimates of the time spent on domestic work, then women who also do paid work are known to spend more hours in total on paid and unpaid work than do men. How much this pattern, established by fairly recent surveys, has changed from the past is anyone's guess. Clearly the availability of labour-saving innovations has reduced the time needed to keep a home running, and it was suggested in Chapter 27 that this was one factor behind the growth in women's paid employment. On the other hand, women who do not go out to work may have partly absorbed the benefit of innovations in higher standards of household care and may, therefore, spend just as long on housework and childcare as did earlier generations.

LEISURE

Work is necessary to produce a reasonable income. To most people, this income is a means to a variety of ends, one of which is leisure. This century has seen an increase in the time most people have available for leisure, although the increase has been surprisingly slow given the rise in the economy's productive capacity. Table 35.3 shows the decline in the number of hours worked by manual workers; the reasons for the slowness of the decline, after the drop in 1919, were discussed in Chapter 27. More of an impact has come from the growth in non-manual employment, where the work week for men has in recent years been around seven hours shorter than that of manual workers. Finally, there has been a growth in paid holidays, virtually non-existent for manual workers before the First World War (although most workers did have around two weeks off, including public holidays). Paid holidays, usually of a week or so, became widespread after the Holidays with Pay Act of 1938. By the 1960s, all full-time employees had at least two weeks' paid holiday, while by 1985 the majority had four weeks or more.

How have people used this extra time? It has been a common observation of sociologists, made for instance in the classic study of the 'Affluent Worker' by Goldthorpe, Lockwood and others in the 1960s, that for manual workers at least, leisure has become 'privatised' – enclosed within the family. It may be that this is a change, for many of the working class, from a community-centred existence, as described by Young and Willmott in their study of Bethnal Green in the 1950s. This was an old established working-

Table 35.3 Hours of work 1913–85

	1	2	3	4	5
1913	54	56	56.4		
1924	47	46.8*	46.6		
1951	44.4	46.3	44.6		
1973	40.0	43.9	38.1	43.8	37.8
1985	39.1	44.5	n.a.	41.9	37.3

1 = Hours in standard working week (i.e. those not paid
    at overtime rates) of full-time manual workers
2 = Hours in actual working week (i.e. including over-
    time and short-time working) of above
3 = Hours in average working week (all workers)
4 = Hours of all full-time male workers
5 = Hours of full-time female workers
* Negative figure = short-time working
(*Sources:* Matthews; *Social Trends; Annual Abstract*)

class area, destined like many others to be broken up by slum
clearance and rehousing in the 1950s and 1960s. Clearly this process
must have had an important influence on the degree of interaction
within the local community. A more positive aspect of housing
change, and the growth of home ownership, is the enhanced
opportunity these have given for home-centred activities. These
include gardening, difficult in most nineteenth-century working-class
housing, since it only offered a yard; and DIY, whose scope had been
limited by the smallness of many houses and by the fact that they
were rented.

The change which observers like Young and Willmott noted is
undoubted, but the apparently dramatic break with past patterns of
behaviour which it represents must be put in perspective. The
cohesion of many working-class communities may well have developed only during the period of economic stagnation and low
migration between the wars. There is no real evidence of a linear
trend away from community and towards privatisation. The 'Affluent
Worker' study explicitly contrasted the family-centred life styles of
manual workers with the life styles of non-manual workers, whose
leisure pursuits involved more interaction with colleagues at work.
Yet in the nineteenth century, it was the middle classes, retreating to
their suburban castles, who were seen as isolated from each other. So
here, there may have been an increase in social interaction over time.
Furthermore, many of the working class also led isolated lives by the

early twentieth century, as described for instance by Mrs Pember Reeves in *Round About a Pound a Week*. Important though the pub still was as a centre for male communal activity, many men did not go to it, either through disinclination or poverty. So the idea that manual workers have experienced a uniform decline in social interaction over time should be viewed with caution.

The pattern of holiday making also suggests the lack of a clear trend in sociability. For instance, there was a massive extension of seaside holidaymaking, a fairly matey sort of activity, in the inter-war period. Communal, if not community, jollification reached its apotheosis in the holiday camps. The first Butlins started at Skegness in 1937, and the camps grew fastest in the 1940s and early 1950s. Furthermore, the leisure of young people has never shown any signs of being constrained by trends dreamed up by historians or sociologists. Youth leisure has increasingly moved off the streets where, at least for the purpose of meeting the opposite sex, it was centred before the First World War and into a diverse range of locations such as the cinema and the dance hall or, latterly, the disco. The main systemic influence on young people's leisure has probably been the increase in disposable incomes, which has widened the range of activities available. It seems likely that, if anything, this has made youth leisure less family-orientated, rather than more so.

It is true that, for anyone over twenty-five or so, the home has been the focus for most leisure activities in recent years. By the late 1970s, the government's General Household Survey, with over 20,000 respondents, found that 50 per cent of men had carried out some DIY in the previous month, and the same proportion had gardened. By a rather odd coincidence, the same proportion had spent some time reading books. Women were less keen on DIY, but a third gardened, 57 per cent had been reading books, and 50 per cent had done some needlework. Predictably, people spent a long time watching TV – around seventeen hours on average a week in winter and thirteen in summer for employed adults; unemployed men and housewives spent about four hours longer than this. The sort of pattern this represents, if not the actual activities, were becoming increasingly widespread in the inter-war period, although the detailed statistics available today are lacking. Gardening, as already noted, was increasingly a possibility; listening as a family to the radio is an enduring image in reminiscences of the time.

While the average home today offers far greater opportunities for leisure than was the case in the nineteenth century, there is not much in the statistics cited above to suggest that the Victorian middle-class ideal, of the workers actively improving themselves in their time off, has come to pass. But in fact, when people in the recent past have gone out of their home for leisure purposes they have, surprisingly often, pursued some educational purpose. The 1977 General Household Survey found that 8 per cent of adults had visited an historic building within the previous month, an amazingly high figure, but one which is confirmed by the growing membership of the National Trust, from 25,000 in 1950 to three-quarters of a million in the late 1970s. Furthermore, these activities were not confined only to people in non-manual occupations. As Table 35.4 shows, they were more likely to go, but many manual workers participated as well.

One cannot draw many conclusions from citing further statistics, such as the 4 per cent going to museums and art galleries, since many of the same people might have been involved in both. However, added to the host of voluntary clubs and societies catering for musicians, would-be actors, botanists and so on, the impression is of a keen interest by many people in pursuits which would have quite impressed Victorians dedicated to improving the minds of the people.

Ironically, one group today, those with more leisure time than

Table 35.4 Participation in social and cultural activities, 1977

	Visiting historic buildings	Theatre/ opera/ ballet	Museums/ art galleries	Amateur music/drama
Participation in 4-weekly period				
All adults (%)	8	5	4	3
Participants in various social groups as proportion of total				
Professional (%)	5	7	6	6
Intermediate and junior non-manual (%)	40	46	44	43
Skilled manual (%)	18	12	17	14
Semi-skilled and unskilled manual (%)	18	15	14	11

Note: Certain groups are omitted so figures in last four rows do not sum to 100
(*Source Social Trends*, 9 (1979))

most, have a low participation in active leisure pursuits – the unemployed. Unemployment, by reducing income, cuts opportunities for activities like DIY. This not only costs money but, on a large scale, virtually necessitates having access to a car, which many of the unemployed, and others with low incomes, do not have. Lack of a car also constrains other leisure activities. Furthermore, the loss of morale caused by long-term unemployment inhibits the unemployed's desire to participate actively in leisure.

It is impossible to summarise properly the long-term trends in leisure in this century. As has already been noted, groups in society such as the young and the unemployed have had their own opportunities and problems. The apparent growth of a 'privatised' life style in the post-Second World War period may have had more to do with the break-up of a type of community which itself was a recent creation than the herald of a complete and permanent change in customs and habits. For the student of the economic past, two points stand out. The first is the influence on leisure of income growth, which has widened choice by permitting home and car ownership, and by enhancing access to other kinds of leisure which involve expensive technology. The other, less obvious, is the influence of relative price changes, and also quality changes in the goods and services consumed in the pursuit of leisure. In the inter-war period, technical change improved the quality of services such as the cinema and public road transport, the latter enhancing access to holiday resorts and spectator sports. Incomes were not large enough for most people to purchase cars, so the radio and the gramophone were the only important leisure-orientated consumer goods. As a result, the consumption of services rather than goods was, from the economic point of view, the dominant feature of leisure.

In the 1950s and 1960s, the car and the television became widely affordable – the latter almost universally so. They encouraged a more domestic pattern of leisure, while there was a poor response from the established providers of leisure services, such as seaside resorts, cinemas and spectator sports, to the new competition from leisure goods. This feeble response can be evidenced by the pathetic inability of cinema managements to abolish queueing, although cinemas were half empty, and by the inability of football clubs to respond to the demand for reasonably comfortable family entertainment. Nevertheless, other leisure providers, such as the stately home industry, have gradually filled the gap, while tourist provision in general has been greatly enhanced and improved in recent years. Cars, which for many first-time owners may have initially inhibited participation in other leisure activities because of the expense of running them, have increasingly provided access to a wider range as incomes have grown.

One of Karl Marx's rare glimpses into the future of society under Communism occurs in the *German Ideology*. With the division of labour abolished, it would be possible for one '. . . to hunt in the morning, fish in the afternoon, rear cattle in the evening, [and] criticise after dinner . . . .' While these may not be everyone's preferred activities, the point is fairly clear. In making more income and free time available to most people, Western capitalist society seems to be achieving the Communist ideal without anyone noticing.

CHAPTER THIRTY-SIX

A middle-class society?

The social divisions in the early twentieth century between a wealthy few and the rest were clear and stark: 10 per cent of the population received around half the income. The distribution of wealth was more uneven still, for the bulk of the population depended on their labour for their income: 10 per cent of the population owned 90 per cent of the wealth. There was a fairly clear distinction, therefore, between a propertied middle class and a propertyless working class. In spite of this divide, there is little evidence of a strong dissatisfaction with the existing state of affairs. Although people were conscious of being working class or middle class, it was not a consciousness of a mutually antagonistic economic situation. In sociological terms, people's self-description of themselves as belonging to one class or another was essentially a status description. This apparent contradiction arises because class, in sociological terms, is an economic strata in society (Ch. 21). However, when people in the early twentieth century described themselves as being in one class or another, they were generally referring not just to their economic position but also to the way other people saw them, and the way they wished to be seen. This in itself was a complex calculation. To describe oneself as working class did not imply that one was inferior, but rather that one did not aspire to a status one did not possess. It encapsulated a belief in political and moral equality with others, together with an acceptance of economic inferiority.

On the face of it, the growth of support for the Labour Party, which was most marked between 1918 and the party's peak in terms of Parliamentary seats in 1945, suggests a radical change in the pre-1914 acquiescence in existing economic and social relations. And certainly there was less acquiescence, and a growing belief that the share of labour in the fruits of the economy should be greater. Nevertheless, some important caveats should be entered. In voting for the Labour Party, people might have been endorsing some redistribution from the rich to the poor; but they were not necessarily endorsing an abolition of private property or even a major change in the social structure. Furthermore, they might have had other motives altogether for voting Labour. They might have been supporting the party's policy towards a particular industry, such as the coal industry; in this case, their motives would have been sectional rather than class-based. They might have been endorsing Labour's mantle, which it inherited from radical liberalism, as the party of peace, an important attraction in the early 1930s; or they might have been endorsing Labour's equally frequent attempts to project itself as the party of patriotism, the party which was independent of international finance and other undesirable outside influences. In other words, there might have been, and probably were, all sorts of reasons why people turned to the Labour Party. There is no strong evidence that they turned to it because it was a class-conscious party which aimed to radically change social relations. On the contrary, the early Labour governments were anxious to give an impression of moderation by doing practically nothing. And while the 1945–50 Labour government achieved much more in the way of redistribution and collectivisation, it was very concerned to project itself as acting in the national interest, rather than in a narrow class-based interest.

The same points might be made with equal or greater force about the trade unions, which grew rapidly at the same time as the Labour Party. While trade unionists have from time to time engaged in bitter industrial conflict with capital, there is no evidence, as Chapters 22 and 29 make clear, that most have seen their unions as fundamentally antagonistic to capital. Members have seen unions as useful implements to defend or increase living standards. In recent years, surveys have demonstrated that the majority of union members do not think their unions should be involved in politics any more than is necessary to defend their immediate interests. The same sort of evidence is not available for earlier periods, but there are other pointers which suggest that joining unions was a matter of expediency rather than principle. For instance, most unions had a high turnover of members, which hardly suggests a strongly-held sense of allegiance.

The 1950s were to see a decline in Labour support, a decline that was renewed in the 1970s. And as shown in earlier chapters, the post-war period has also seen a marked shift in the occupational structure towards non-manual jobs, a general and fairly rapid rise in the standard of living, and a continuing fall in income and wealth differentials. Just as it would be wrong to see the rise of the Labour Party as the consequence of a Gadarene rush towards militant economic class consciousness, though, so it would be wrong to see its stuttering decline as marking the end of any sort of class divisions or class consciousness. The idea that class might cease to be an issue or even a useful category became embodied in the 'embourgeoisement' hypothesis of the 1950s. Put simply, this was the idea that everyone was becoming a bourgeois, or like the bourgeoisie (the word Marxists use for the middle class). Careful study of the affluent manual workers of the 1960s, in car factories and the like, showed, however, that even when their incomes reached or exceeded non-manual levels, their attitudes remained distinguishable. This was true of attitudes to work, discussed in the previous chapter, but also in voting behaviour and in the continuing tendency of manual workers to identify themselves as working class.

The embourgeoisement hypothesis, therefore, has plainly exaggerated the extent to which change has been perceived by manual workers. The fact remains, however, that over the last eighty years a large proportion of the working population has shifted from manual to non-manual work and that most of these people would identify themselves as middle class. Furthermore, the shift towards non-manual occupations (which will from now on be referred to as middle-class occupations) has been accompanied, obviously enough, by an increase in the opportunities that working-class children have to rise in the social scale and, as noted in Chapter 35, the rate of increase has accelerated since 1945. Sociologists, a pessimistic lot, tend to conclude in spite of this acceleration that there has been no change in relative mobility chances, because the increasing chances for working-class children to enter middle-class jobs have been matched by increasing chances for middle-class children to enter middle-class jobs (and a consequent decrease in downward mobility). Most people would call this progress. The overall effects of mobility, both up and down, have meant that in the recent past almost half – 45 per cent – of adult males were, ten years after entering work, in a different social class than that occupied by their parents. The point was made in Chapter 21 that mobility into or out of classes can be one index of the degree to which they actually constitute meaningful categories. If this is accepted, then Britain's class structure has a major weakness.

There are two main conclusions to be reached about the history of class in twentieth-century Britain. The first is that, if class is taken as an economic category which reflects individuals' market situations, there has been a marked equalisation over the years. Comparing the position in the 1900s with the position now, the following major changes are evident. There is less inequality in post-tax income, for a variety of reasons outlined in Chapter 33. There is much less inequality in wealth, a fact particularly associated with the rise in house ownership and the growth in pension entitlements. There is less inequality in health and education chances, as a result of government intervention. And there is a considerable degree of intergenerational occupational mobility, from manual to non-manual and vice versa. In all these things, people who start in the middle class still have a much better chance of ending up in a favourable position than do those who start in the working class. So Britain isn't a very equal society. On the other hand, it is a great deal more equal than it was.

Furthermore, the old distinction between a middle class distinguished by property ownership or the possession of educational capital, and a working class distinguished by not having very much of either, is now obsolescent. House ownership and pension entitlements have made many manual workers as much owners of property as are non-manual workers; there is no meaningful distinction between them in this dimension of class. This process of equalisation suggests that the labelling of certain occupations as middle class and others as working class has less and less meaning in economic terms, and is more and more an attribution of status, so far as it is anything at all. The individuals who work in these jobs actually occupy a variety of market situations. Middle-class job holders are more likely to be in a favourable position, but this is not necessarily the case. The process of equalisation, in other words, has proceeded beyond the usually accepted class boundaries. The converse of this is that people whose only property of any value is their rights to state welfare are now in a minority. In some senses, this makes them more deprived: when most people were poor, so most people were to that extent equal; now it is no longer so.

Marxist historians and sociologists would reject the entire basis of the preceding interpretation of social change, one which sees society as becoming increasingly middle-class in economic terms. This rejection would be based on the idea that the labour of most people, whether manual or non-manual workers, is controlled by something other than the workers themselves. That something other is capital. Although recent Marxist interpretations of social change differ in detail, they are basically all saying one thing, which is that most people are still quasi-proletarian because they still work for wages or salaries and are therefore subject to capital. It is hard to argue with this proposition, because in a sense it is true. The question is whether it actually means anything. As has been seen, the distribution of the ownership of capital has become increasingly widespread, as growing numbers of people participate in pension and life-assurance schemes and in direct share ownership. These people own capital which is then used for setting other people to work: capital and labour remain separate entities, but many workers do have a stake in capital. The abolition of capital so that the worker remains in entire control of his or her labour has not occurred, as Marx dreamed that it would; but equally, the division between capitalist and proletarian now seems problematical, since many proletarians are now also capitalists and most capitalists are now also proletarians.

In one sense, the distinction between capital and labour has been entirely abolished: this is when people own their homes. Within those homes, people can labour without any fear of the surplus being appropriated by capitalists. In ignoring the unpaid work which people carry out in their own homes, Marxists are ignoring an activity which shatters the divide between capital and labour. While it might be difficult for most people in a suburban semi to fulfil Marx's suggestion that they should hunt in the morning and rear cattle in the evening, they have some opportunity to reintegrate the divided self by reintegrating their labour and the objects of their labour. (Marx seems to have seen this division of the self, or alienation, as the ultimate evil, one which sprang from the division of labour; the author is not suggesting that this view is necessarily correct, but merely that, on Marx's own terms, home ownership allows the division to be surmounted.)

Pace the followers of Marx, most observers would conclude that the economic categories of class have become increasingly blurred in twentieth-century Britain. The second conclusion we can come to about class relates to people's perception of it, that is their degree of class consciousness. It was suggested earlier that the widespread use of the language of class in the early part of this century did not mean that people were in fact highly conscious of classes as antagonistic economic categories, but rather that they were conscious of broad social distinctions which were labelled as class distinctions. In sociological terms, class was used as a shorthand for status. Various social surveys suggest that this is the case as much today as it was in the early part of the century. The 1960s survey of affluent workers, for instance, showed that although they mainly viewed themselves as working class, this self-image owed itself as much or more to perceived behavioural differences with middle-class (that is non-manual) families as to any strong sense of belonging to a particular economic strata. Comparative evidence, notably with France, also suggests that British manual workers' sense of class solidarity with other manual workers is relatively weak. Whereas a large number of French manual workers have, at least until the recent past, voted Communist, only a tiny minority of British workers have ever done so. Attitude surveys also reveal that while many French manual workers perceive society as unequal and want to do something about it, British workers have a less strong perception of inequality and, even more important, see inequality between classes as more or less irrelevant to themselves.

W G Runciman has provided an explanation for this live-and-let-live attitude. Most people's horizons of comparison are sharply limited. People in Britain have no great awareness of or, if they are aware, no strong feelings about the wealth of other people outside their own social network. So far as there is comparison, it is with those whose general economic position is not unlike that of the comparor. Relative deprivation is not, therefore, generally perceived of as a function of economic class. There are a variety of reasons for the adoption of this limited frame of reference. It is adopted to some extent because people are unaware of the true state of affairs, and to some extent because of the widespread existence of certain concepts of fairness and justice, which attach more importance to the stability of existing relationships in society than to the promotion of radical egalitarianism. But probably most important is that habits of comparison with some entities, and not with others, are inculcated almost from birth. As Runciman says, 'The denial of equal opportunity begins in infancy, and with it the long process of habituation to inequality without which society would be forever in a state of civil war.'

Appendix: changing price levels 1750–1985

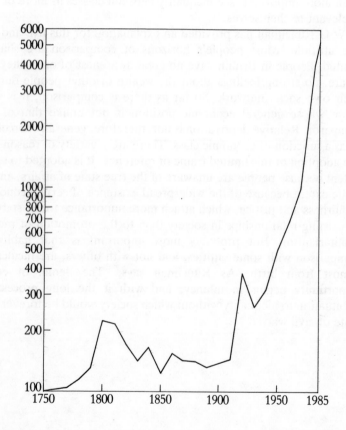

The graph shows changes in a composite index of prices, with a base in 1750 of 100. Up to 1820, the index constitutes a rough guide to consumer prices;

from 1820–1870 it consists of wholesale prices, which are liable to greater fluctuations than consumer prices; only from 1870 does it start to become a fairly precise guide to consumer price changes. Another point to note is that the composition of the goods whose prices make up the index has changed over time: for the eighteenth century tallow candles, felt hats, and blue yarn stockings were among the constituents; today cars and other consumer durables are among the goods included.

The graph is drawn on a semi-log scale, which ensures that the index reflects the rate of change of prices over each decade (the index was calculated at decadal intervals up to 1980, and does not show year by year fluctuations).

Sources: Schumpeter – Gilboy (1750–1820) and Rousseaux (1820–1870) indices cited in Mitchell and Dean; Feinstein (1870–1965); *Economic Trends* (1965–1985).

Bibliography

The purpose of this bibliography is to indicate to the reader the most helpful general textbooks and surveys of particular areas, the most widely-used statistical surveys, and a limited selection of recent specialist works. It is selective because most of the books listed themselves contain bibliographies of the more specialised literature.

STATISTICAL SURVEYS

Annual Abstract of Statistics, annually, HMSO
Economic Trends, annually, HMSO
Regional Trends, annually, HMSO
Social Trends, annually, HMSO
(Invaluable for up-to-date statistical information)

Feinstein, C H 1972 *National Income, Expenditure and Output of the United Kingdom 1855–1965* (the established source for all macro-economic statistics in the period covered)
Halsey, A H (ed) 1972 *Trends in British Society since 1900* (a wide range of social and economic statistics)
Maddison, A 1982 *Phases of Capitalist Development* (a wide range of international comparative statistics)
Mitchell, B R, Deane, P 1962 *Abstract of British Historical Statistics* (still the basic source for economic data broken down by industry or sector, although specialist studies often contain modifications)

Mitchell, B R, Jones, H R 1971 *Second Abstract of British Historical Statistics* (contains series beyond 1945)

Routh, G 1980 *Occupation and Pay in Great Britain 1906–1979*

HISTORICAL ATLAS

Langton, J, Morris, R J (eds) 1986 *The Atlas of Industrialising Britain 1780–1914*

PERIODICALS AND SERIES

The Economic History Society's 'Studies in Economic History' are an invaluable series of short paperbacks covering a wide range of topics. They are published by Macmillan.

The *Economic History Review* is the best-known journal, publishing articles on specialist topics and also more general surveys. Its List of Publications on Economic and Social History is published in the November issue for the preceding year.

The Economic History Society also publishes REFRESH, a publication for sixth-formers and teachers with up-to-date surveys of areas of debate.

TEXTBOOKS – GENERAL

Floud, R, McCloskey, D (eds) 1981 *The Economic History of Britain Since 1700, Vols I and II* (quite high level; it is an excellent foundation for most topics, although sometimes the reader will find that different chapters put forward quite different views about the same subject)

Lee, C M 1986 *The British Economy Since 1700* (not a comprehensive textbook, as it is focused on growth, but an important book with a particular emphasis on service industries and the regional dimension)

Mathias, P 1983 *The First Industrial Nation 1700–1914* 2nd edn (a comprehensive and detailed textbook)

May, T 1987 *An Economic and Social History of Britain 1760–1970* (a particular emphasis on social history)

Bibliography

SURVEYS

Class

Halsey, A H 1981 *Change in British Society*

Economic growth

Crafts, N F R 1985 *British Economic Growth During the Industrial Revolution* (an important reinterpretation, with much recent statistical material)

Deane, P, Cole, W A 1967 *British Economic Growth, 1688–1959* 2nd edn (while its statistical material has sometimes been superseded, this is still a valuable source)

Matthews, R C O, Feinstein, C H, Odling-Smee, J C 1982 *British Economic Growth, 1856–1973* (an indispensable source of statistics and ideas for anyone engaged on a serious study of the subject)

Economic policy

Peden, G C 1985 *British Economic and Social Policy: Lloyd George to Margaret Thatcher*

Incomes and living standards

Hunt, E H 1981 *British Labour History 1815–1914*
Rubinstein, W D 1986 *Wealth and Inequality in Britain*

Industrial relations

Currie, R 1979 *Industrial Politics*
Gospel, H 1988 *Markets, Firms and the Management of Labour*
Hunt, E H 1981 *British Labour History 1815–1914*

International economic relations

Foreman-Peck, J 1983 *A History of the World Economy*

Manufacturing

Musson, A E 1978 *The Growth of British Industry*

Period studies

Aldcroft, O 1983 *The British Economy Between the Wars*

Artis, J (ed) 1986 *Prest and Coppock's the UK Economy* (an invaluable survey of the contemporary scene and the recent past, updated every two years)

Ashworth, W 1960 *An Economic History of England 1870–1939* (still a book of great value)

Berg, M 1985 *The Age of Manufactures 1700–1820* (not a straightforward textbook, but a pathbreaking study in the relationship between technology and work organisation in the period)

Boltho, A (ed) 1982 *The European Economy, Growth and Crisis* (compendium of information on post-war Europe, including Britain)

Crouzet, F 1982 *The Victorian Economy*

Wright, J F 1979 *Britain in the Age of Economic Management: an Economic History Since 1939*

Scotland

Lythe, S G E, Butt, J 1975 *An Economic History of Scotland 1100–1939*

Social history

Bedarida, F 1979 *A Social History of England 1851–1975*

Social policy

MacDonagh, O 1977 *Early Victorian Government 1830–1870*

Peden, G C 1985 *British Economic and Social Policy: Lloyd George to Margaret Thatcher*

Women in the economy

Lewis, J 1984 *Women in England 1870–1950*

Roberts, E 1984 *A Woman's Place: an Oral History of Working-Class Women 1890–1940*

SPECIALISED WORKS

These comprise either books which may be too recent to be listed in other bibliographies, or monographs or articles which have been referred to in the text.

Industrial Revolution period

Crouzet, F 1985 *The First Industrialists: the Problem of Origins*

Davis, R 1979 *The Industrial Revolution and British Overseas Trade*

Dutton, H 1984 *The Patent System and Inventive Activity during the Industrial Revolution 1750–1852*

Harris, J R 1976 Skills, coal and British industry in the eighteenth century. *History* Vol 61 (No 202): 167–82

Lindert, P H, Williamson, J G 1983 English workers' living standards during the industrial revolution: a new look. *Economic History Review* 2nd series, Vol XXXVI, (No 1): 1–25

O'Brien, P K 1982 European economic development: the contribution of the periphery. *Economic History Review* 2nd series, Vol XXXV (No 1): 1–18

Plumb, J H 1972 *In the Light of History* (especially Chs 1 and 6)

Sanderson, M 1983 *Education, Economic Change and Society in England 1780–1870*

Wrigley, E A, Schofield, R S 1981 *The Population History of England 1541–1871: a Reconstruction*

Nineteenth century

Anderson, M 1974 *Family Structures in Nineteenth Century Lancashire*

Baines, D 1985 *Migration in a Mature Economy: Emigration and Internal Migration in England and Wales 1861–1900*

Church, R 1986 *The History of the British Coal Industry,* Vol 3

Cunningham, H 1980 *Leisure in the Industrial Revolution*

Davis, L, Huttenback, R 1986 *Mammon and the Pursuit of Empire: the Political Economy of British Imperialism 1860–1912*

Rubinstein, W 1981 *Men of Property: the Very Wealthy in Britain Since the Industrial Revolution*

Wiener, M 1982 *English Culture and the Decline of the Industrial Spirit 1850–1980*

Twentieth century

Chandler, A D 1980 The growth of the transnational industrial firm in the United States and the United Kingdom: a comparative analysis. *Economic History Review* 2nd series, Vol XXXIII, (No 3): 396–410

Goldthorpe, J H 1969 *The Affluent Worker in the Class Structure*

Hannah, L 1983 *The Rise of the Corporate Economy*

Holmes, A R, Green, E 1986 *Midland: 150 Years of Banking Business*

Lazonick, W, Elbaum, B 1986 *The Decline of the British Economy*

Middleton, R 1987 The rise and fall of the managed economy. *Refresh* No 5: 5–8 (this short guide is the best introduction to the increasingly complex debate over the application of Keynesianism)

Runciman, W 1966 *Relative Deprivation and Social Justice*

Sources for quotations

N.B. Details are listed by page and line number.

p.129, ll.1-2. Jefferies R 1966 edn *Hodge and his Masters* p. 127

p.173, ll.23-9. Shadwell A 1906 *Industrial Efficiency* Vol. 1 pp. 77–8

p.178, ll.17-20. Bourne G 1955 edn *Change in the Village* p. 30

pp. 201–2 ll.41-3. Slater Lewis J 1986 *The Commercial Organization of Factories* p. 468

p.217 ll.17-18 Kitson Clark G 1967 *An Expanding Society: Britain 1830–1900* p. 162

p. 221 ll.11-20 Keynes J M 1920 *The Economic Consequences of the Peace* p. 9

pp. 243–4 ll.41-1 ibid p. 9

p.259 ll.3-5 White Paper 1944 *Employment Policy* Command 6527

p.354 ll.18-19 Edwardes M 1983 *Back from the Brink* p. 82

p.354 ll.21-3 cited in Nichols T 1986 *The British Worker Question* p. 227

p.405 ll.30-3 Runciman W G 1966 *Relative Deprivation and Social Justice* p. 294

Glossary of terms

balance of payments The state of a country's (say Britain's) payments with the outside world. Divided into current and capital accounts. The items in the current account which contribute either positively or negatively to payments are exports and imports, both visible and invisible (*see* p. 136). The net result of these transactions will be a surplus of payments in over payments out (surplus on current account) or vice versa (deficit on current account). The capital account includes investments by residents of Britain in other countries, foreign investments in Britain, and international grants and loans. If the combined current and capital account movements do not balance out, the overall deficit or surplus is brought into balance through purchase or sales of gold (under the Gold Standard) or foreign currency by the central bank.

best practice The best in current use; used of techniques (e.g. in agriculture) or organisation (e.g. of a factory).

bonds (of companies) Fixed interest stock; if secured on the company's assets, they are known as debentures.

budget Prediction of income and expenditure (i. and e.). The Budget is the government's estimate of its i. and e. for the forthcoming financial year. A balanced Budget indicates an equality of i. and e., a Budget surplus an excess of i. over e. (and therefore an opportunity to repay government debt), a Budget deficit the opposite. *See also* fiscal policy.

by-employment Part-time employment.

capital (overhead) Investment in facilities which are necessary to the functioning of a modern economy, and which do not necessarily yield a return to private investors (e.g. canals, roads, schools).

capitalism Hard to define, as there are so many competing usages. A reasonable definition would probably include the following widely accepted characteristics: private ownership of property; systematic pursuit of profit; elements of a market economy, although this might be distorted by (e.g.) monopolies.

capitalist Owner of substantial amounts of capital, in the sense of financial assets.

casual work Work characterised by short and irregular periods of hiring; endemic in certain occupations in the nineteenth century (and probably before) e.g. building, dockwork.

consumer durables Consumer goods with a lengthy but finite life: e.g. pianos, television sets, cars. (Semi-durables – goods with an in-between life, e.g. clothes).

co-operation Nowadays associated (in Great Britain) only with the retail co-operative movement (Coops). In the early nineteenth century, both retail and manufacturing co-operatives existed on a small scale. Co-operation implies mutuality, between employees (in manufacturing) or purchasers (in retailing). In retailing, mutuality in early co-operatives took different forms. The Rochdale Society (*see* text) successfully pioneered the payment of dividends in proportion to purchases, which became the model for future large scale retail co-operation; their claim to primacy rests on this basis. From the 1960s, co-operatives dropped this distinctive feature.

currency Until 1971, the pound sterling was divided into shillings (twenty shillings equalled one pound); shillings were divided into pence (twelve pence equalled one shilling).

demand The desire and ability to pay a sum of money for a particular good. In general, individuals' demand for a good will fall as its price rises and vice-versa.

A rise in aggregate national income, e.g. because of rising population, will lead to rising demand at any one price; if supply is fixed, the result will be a rise in prices until the demand of individuals has fallen to an extent that demand and supply are again in equilibrium. In practice, supply is likely to rise in response to price and the eventual price will depend on the price elasticity of demand and supply.

Demand-side forces are the forces which, by acting on price in the way described above, stimulate increases in supply.

Dissent Nowadays usually called Nonconformity. In the eighteenth and nineteenth centuries, Old Dissent included groups like the Quakers and Unitarians, which originated in the seventeenth century. The most notable new group was the Methodists.

economies of scale The economies to be gained from enlarging the size of a process, a firm or an industry. These economies are achieved particularly through the enhanced opportunities for specialisation, but in other ways too: e.g. enlarging the size of a blast furnace or a ship will enhance their capacity without increasing their capital or operating costs in the same proportion.

elasticity The price elasticity of demand and of supply is a numerical measure of the extent to which the volume of goods demanded or supplied rises or falls in response to changes in price. (Income elasticity of demand – *see* page 88).

entrepreneur The supplier of capital, organiser of production, and bearer of risk. His or her reward is profit.

fertility The incidence of live births in a specified population – e.g. all women between 20 and 29 (age-specific fertility). Measures of fertility give a more precise indication of change than do crude birth-rates, which are simply the incidence of live births per 1000 population.

fiscal policy Policy which is concerned with the level and distribution of government expenditure and taxation. Before the 1940s, policy aimed broadly at a balanced budget or budget surplus; with the advent of Keynesianism (index), the actual level of surplus or deficit became a tool of economic management, and hence part of policy (*see* full discussion in text). From the 1970s, the pre-Keynesian view of the budget was revived.

free trade The absence of protective tariffs or other restraints on trade.

gains from trade   The gains accruing to a country from the exercise of its absolute and comparative advantages.

Gold Standard   The situation in which the currency of a country is exchangeable for gold. Also used colloquially to mean the state of affairs, only ruling between the late nineteenth century and 1914, when the majority of the world's larger trading nations accepted a Gold Standard for their currencies.

   If two or more countries are on the Gold Standard, their currencies are effectively fixed in price against each other.

GNP/GDP   *see* national income.

index numbers   An expression of the collective value of a related set of items over a time period, in proportion to their collective value in a base year (or month etc.), e.g., index numbers of industrial production with a base in 1980: the index will include items such as steel and motor vehicle production, weighted in accordance with their relative importance in total production (the more sophisticated the weighting procedure, the more accurate the index); in subsequent years, the index will fluctuate in accordance with the changes in output of all its component items, taking account of their weighting, e.g. index numbers of wages with a base of 1750: this index will include wage figures from as many occupations as possible; but weighting in such retrospective indices is often haphazard or not done, because of the difficulties of obtaining accurate figures, thus reducing their accuracy; again, the index will fluctuate in accordance with the wage levels of its component groups. Index numbers of changes in a single item (e.g. steel production) are, strictly speaking, called ratio series. By convention, index numbers and ratio series are expressed with a base of 100 (or, sometimes, the terminating year is shown with a value of 100).

innovation and invention   The latter means a totally new product or process. Innovation is a rather more flexible term; its application to a product or process implies a degree of novelty but not total originality. In addition, 'innovation' can be used of a new agricultural or managerial technique, or a new service industry product, for which 'invention' is not an appropriate term. In the text, the terms have been used without any attempt at exact precision.

macroeconomics The part of economics concerned with broad aggregates in the economy, e.g. saving and investment, consumers' expenditure, money supply, national income and the relationships between them. Macroeconomic policy is, therefore, policy directed to influencing these variables. In general governments did not see it as their business (or within their ability) to exert such influence until the 1940s.

means test Assessment of a person's or family's wealth or income, in order to determine whether they should receive social security benefits.

monetary policy Control (or the attempt to control) either or both of the supply of and demand for money, e.g. by open-market operations (index). The intention of monetary policy was and is to influence either the capital account of the balance of payments (high interest rates attract funds from abroad and vice versa; this was the main purpose of monetary policy in the nineteenth century), or inflation, or employment, or all three. The agent is the Bank of England, although since the First World War the Treasury has become increasingly involved with the formulation of policy.

money supply The supply of money in the economy. It is almost impossible to define. It always includes notes and coins, and holdings in clearing bank current accounts; deposit account holdings and other bank account holdings may be included. There is considerable controversy as to whether the money supply is controllable by the central bank, as monetarists believe (*see* open market operations).

monopoly The control of the supply of a particular good or service by a single seller. It will usually suit monopolists to restrict supply in order to obtain a higher price – hence the concern of public policy since the eighteenth century to restrict or control monopolies.

mortality The incidence of deaths in a specified population, e.g. all children under one (infant mortality). As with fertility, mortality rates give a more precise indication of change than do crude death-rates, which are the incidence of deaths per 1000 population.

national income The money value of the total amount of goods and services produced in the economy over a period of time (normally one year).

Strictly speaking, national income, also known as Gross National Product (GNP) includes income from investments abroad by British residents, while net income paid to foreign holders of British investments should be subtracted. Gross Domestic Product (GDP) excludes such income altogether. The textual and tabular references to national income may refer to either GNP or GDP, and rarely differentiate. In most cases it makes relatively little difference as to which measurement is used.

oligopoly The control of the supply of a particular good or service by a limited number of sellers. This has a number of likely outcomes, the most significant being a restriction of price competition and an emphasis instead on product quality or levels of service. The clearing banks were a classic example, at least until recent banking deregulation.

personal savings ratio The ratio of savings by individuals (rather than companies or government), less their personal borrowings, to national income; usually expressed as a percentage. The reference in table 33.1 to this as stable at around 10% has been overtaken by events; by 1988 the ratio had fallen to around 5%, suggesting that nine years of the inculcation of Victorian values by Conservative governments had resulted in less thrift, not more.

piece-rate wages Wages which are paid according to the production achieved (rather than being paid by the day, week or month). Modern variants are often referred to as incentive bonus schemes, in which only a proportion of the total wage varies with output.

productivity The efficiency with which the inputs to a productive process are utilised (hence efficiency has been used in the text as a synonym).

Reference to the productivity of one input, i.e. capital, labour or land, is usually taken as meaning simply output per unit of input.

See the Index for total factor productivity.

profit Usage in economics is somewhat different from everyday usage. 'Profit' in economics is the net income accruing to individuals or firms, taking account of the alternative use of the factors entering into productions, e.g. a building owned and used by a firm could be rented out as an alternative; the possible rent obtainable should be deducted from the income to show profit. This would be different from the normal accounting procedure. (*See also* Index for opportunity cost.)

In effect, the profit should be enough to keep an entrepreneur in the line of business. If profits are inadequate, entrepreneurs will transfer their capital and willingness to accept risks to some other activity. If profits are above normal, entrepreneurs from outside will enter the business, enlarge supply and so drive down prices and profits.

public company   Limited liability company with shares quoted on the stock market (hence also 'quoted company').

Public Sector Borrowing Requirement   The net borrowing of the government and publicly-owned industries during a financial year. Thus it comprises net borrowing for nationalised industry capital projects, plus the budget deficit (or minus the budget surplus).

rates   The basic system of local taxation until the time of writing; levied on property, in approximate relationship to its value.

rentier   A person who lives on interest or dividends from capital (French – *rente* – interest).

service sector   The sector of the economy encompassing the supply of services – notably retailing, wholesaling, transport, public and professional services, and financial services.

smallpox (inoculation and vaccination)   Inoculation – the administration of the smallpox virus to induce a mild form of the disease. Vaccination – the administration of a variation of the virus (in this case, the cowpox virus), a process which also gives immunity and is less risky.

stock (government)   In most cases, fixed interest stock, quoted and tradeable on the stock market. It comprises the greater part of government debt. Some stock whose yield rises in line with inflation (index-linked) has been issued.

supply   The amount of goods that producers and distributors are prepared to sell at a particular price. In general, supply will rise and fall with price (and *see* elasticity). However, a fall in the cost of production will lead in the long term to a willingness to supply the same quantity of goods (or more) at a lower price, as the large profits available attract more entrepreneurs to the industry. Hence supply-side forces are those forces which lower the cost of production (e.g. by reducing the cost of capital or by making available innovations) and so increase supply without there necessarily having been a change in aggregate demand.

sweated trades   Usually, occupations carried on in houses or small workshops and characterised by low wages and poor working conditions; frequently involving female and/or immigrant labour – i.e. workers who found (and often still find) entry into other occupations difficult. Clothing manufacture frequently was, and sometimes still is, a sweated trade.

underemployment   A state of affairs where workers are not continuously employed on productive work, but are not formally unemployed. Underemployment could manifest itself in casual work, or (as often in agriculture in the eighteenth and nineteenth centuries), by 'makework' in inactive periods – thus agricultural workers would spend endless hours in the winter cleaning out ditches or picking stones.

waggonways   Primitive railways on which ran horse-drawn waggons.

wollens and worsteds   Both refer to cloth made from wool; the difference lies in the technique of manufacture which produces, in worsteds, a lighter cloth.

Maps

Maps

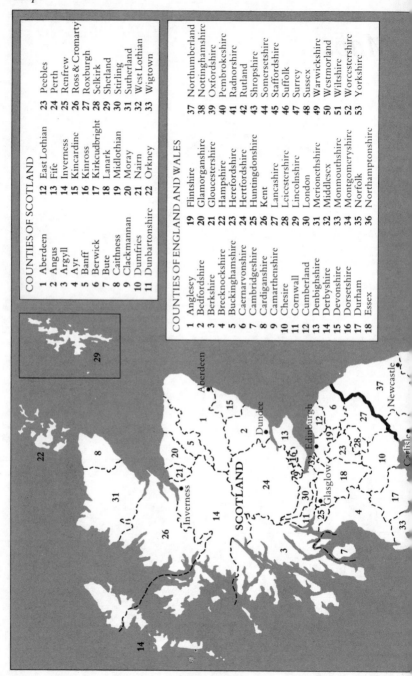

COUNTIES OF SCOTLAND

1	Aberdeen	12	East Lothian
2	Angus	13	Fife
3	Argyll	14	Inverness
4	Ayr	15	Kincardine
5	Banff	16	Kinross
6	Berwick	17	Kirkcudbright
7	Bute	18	Lanark
8	Caithness	19	Midlothian
9	Clackmannan	20	Moray
10	Dumfries	21	Nairn
11	Dunbartonshire	22	Orkney

23	Peebles
24	Perth
25	Renfrew
26	Ross & Cromarty
27	Roxburgh
28	Selkirk
29	Shetland
30	Stirling
31	Sutherland
32	West Lothian
33	Wigtown

COUNTIES OF ENGLAND AND WALES

1	Anglesey	19	Flintshire
2	Bedfordshire	20	Glamorganshire
3	Berkshire	21	Gloucestershire
4	Brecknockshire	22	Hampshire
5	Buckinghamshire	23	Herefordshire
6	Caernarvonshire	24	Hertfordshire
7	Cardiganshire	25	Huntingdonshire
8	Camarthenshire	26	Kent
9	Chesire	27	Lancashire
10	Cornwall	28	Leicestershire
11	Cumberland	29	Lincolnshire
12	Denbighshire	30	London
13	Derbyshire	31	Merioneothshire
14	Devonshire	32	Middlesex
15	Dorsetshire	33	Monmouthshire
16	Durham	34	Montgomeryshire
17	Essex	35	Norfolk
18		36	Northamptonshire

37	Northumberland
38	Nottinghamshire
39	Oxfordshire
40	Pembrokeshire
41	Radnorshire
42	Rutland
43	Shropshire
44	Somersetshire
45	Staffordshire
46	Suffolk
47	Surrey
48	Sussex
49	Warwickshire
50	Westmorland
51	Wiltshire
52	Worcestershire
53	Yorkshire

424

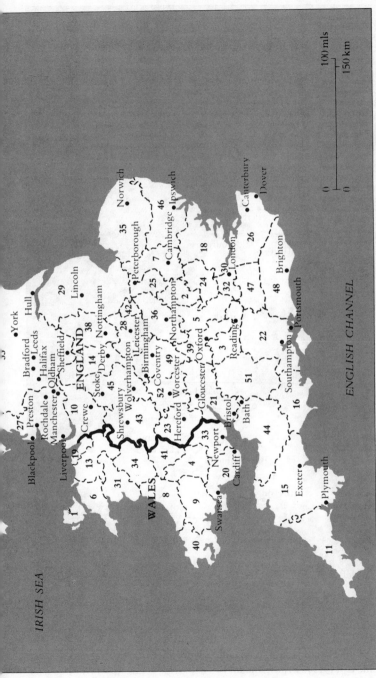

Map 1 Pre-1974 counties and major towns

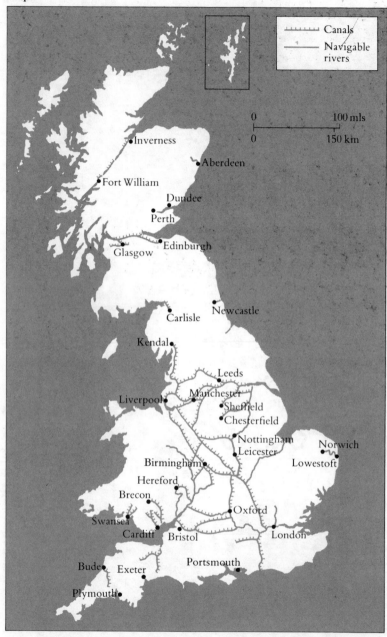

Map 2 Canals and major navigable rivers in Britain by *c.* 1830 (after Hadfield, C. (1959), *British Canals*)

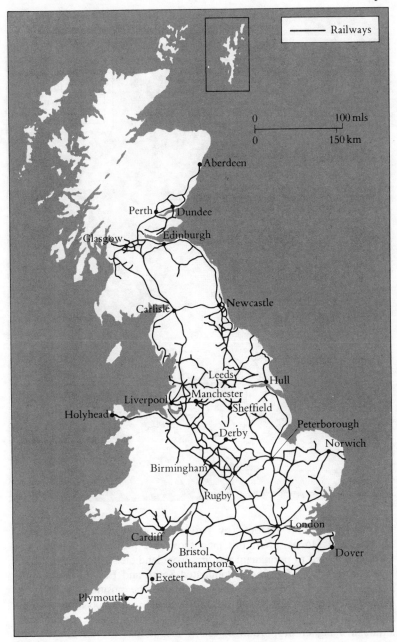

Map 3 The railway network in 1852 (after Langton and Morris; and Pollins, M. (1971), *Britain's Railways: an Industrial History*)

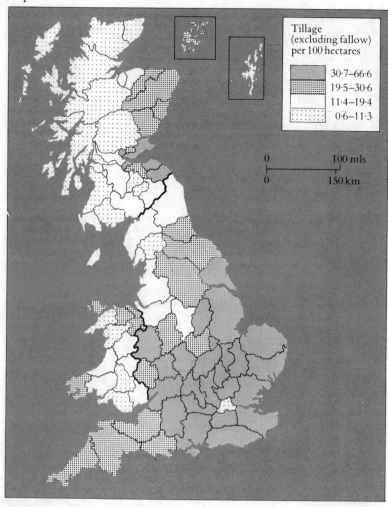

Map 4 Agricultural regions (by percentage of tillage) in 1871 (after Langton and Morris) (NB: this map shows the proportion of cultivated land, as opposed to permanent pasture, woodland etc. It brings out clearly the transition from the arable-dominated South and East to the pasture-dominated North and West. The map shows the position in 1871, the earliest period for which full data is available. The position was not significantly different in the late eighteenth and early nineteenth centuries, although a higher proportion of fallow meant that overall tillage ratios were lower)

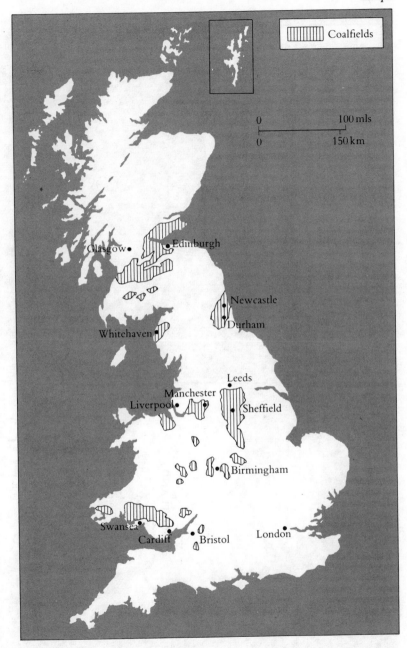

Map 5   Coalfields in Britain *c*. 1900 (after Checkland, S. G. (1964), *The Rise of Industrial Society in England 1815–1885*)

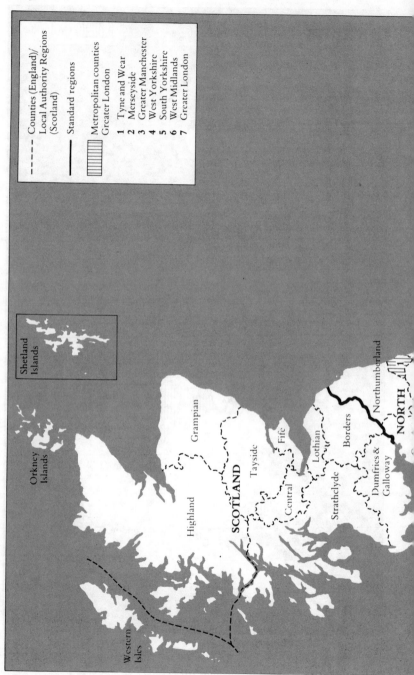

Counties (England)/
Local Authority Regions
(Scotland)

Standard regions

Metropolitan counties
Greater London

1 Tyne and Wear
2 Merseyside
3 Greater Manchester
4 West Yorkshire
5 South Yorkshire
6 West Midlands
7 Greater London

Shetland
Islands

Orkney
Islands

Western
Isles

Highland

SCOTLAND

Grampian

Tayside

Central

Fife

Lothian

Strathclyde

Borders

Dumfries &
Galloway

Northumberland

NORTH

Map 6 Counties and local authority regions in England, Wales and Scotland in 1985

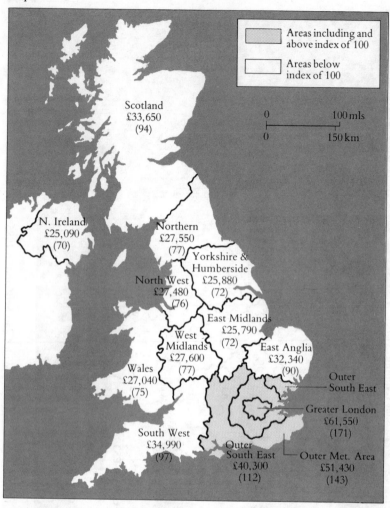

Map 7 House price differentials in Britain in 1985 (after data issued by the Nationwide/Anglia Building Society; and Fleming, D. and Nellis, J. (1987), *Spon's House Price Data Book*) (NB: the map shows prices for semi-detached houses in the fourth quarter of 1985, followed by relative value (UK average = 100 (£35,930). Prices are an approximate, but not an exact, indication of regional house price differentials, since the quality of this particular housing type may differ slightly in different areas; it is likely that this accounts for the relatively high price in Scotland)

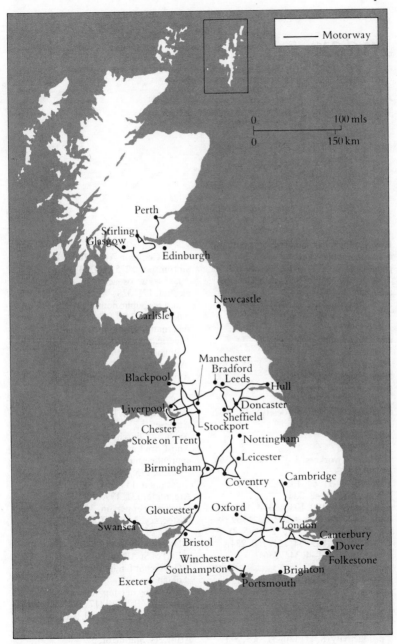

Map 8   Motorways in 1986

433

Index

Page numbers in italic indicate that there is an explanation of the term on that page. *G* indicates a glossary entry.

accepting houses, 146
accounting (and accountancy), 156, 296, 388
 cost, 296, 352
advantage (in trade)
 absolute, *34–5*, 36
 comparative, 34–5, 36, 51, 139
advertising, 118, 126–7, 339
aerospace (and aircraft) industry, 275–6, 325, 357
affluence (and affluent society), 372, 402, 404
Africa, 31, 140
 South, 328
agricultural workers, 3, 179–80, 203, 363, 364–5, 369
 farmers, 3–11, 64, 105, 129–34, 179–80, 198, 331–2, 334
 labourers, 3, 100, 103, 133–4, 164–5, 182, 188, 198–9, 202, 332, 369, 386
agriculture, 1–11, 22, 67, 72, 74–5, 81–3, 97–8, 111, 129–34, 151, 168, 234, 244, 283, 331–4, 344, 386
 Act (1947), 332
 depression of, 105, 131–3
 innovations and improvements, 6–8, 10–11, 130–31, 332–3
 investment, 6, 69–70, 131, 333
 price support, 333–4
 productivity, 8, 11, 130–31, 333, 371
 techniques, 5–7
 and see agricultural workers,
  commons, enclosure, harvests,
  ownership, rotation, yields,
  Common Agricultural Policy
air transport, 275, 329, 337, 340
 and see aerospace
alcohol, 171, 328
 and see public houses
Alkali Acts, 210, 217
Alternative Economic Strategy, 276
American colonies, 32–3
 Revolution, 359
'American system', 119
Americas (and New World), 31, 34–5, 92, 99, 129, 131, 157, 228
 and see Canada, North America, South America, USA, West Indies
Anglesey, 55
Anglican Church, 12, 78
Anti-Corn Law League, 208
apprenticeship, 19, 59–60, 109–10, 147, 155, 175, 186, 200, 301, 388
 premium, 155, 291, 356
Argentine, 131, 139, 148
 income per person, 347
aristocracy, 3, 78, 80, 132, 349
 Duke of Devonshire, 133
 Duke of Portland, 133
 Earl of St Albans, 133
 Grosvenor family, 133
 of labour, 195
 and see ownership of land
Arkwright, Richard (1732–1792), 49, 57
armaments industry, 120, 326, 356–7
 spin-off from, 357
Artificers, Statute of, 59
Ashley, Lord (1801–1885), 211, 213
attorneys, *see* solicitors
Australia (and Australasia, Antipodes),

31, 131, 139, 223
coal production, 328
emigration to, 105
food supply, 99, 103
income per head, 347
investment in, 148
land, 129, 137,
tariff concessions, 225
Austro-Hungarian Empire, 222

Bacup, 182
Bakewell, Robert (1768–1843), 7
balance of payments, *see* payments
Baltic, 30
Banbury, 98
banks (and banking), 23, 37, 38–44, 52,
    136–7, 139, 143–9, 154, 239, 242,
    251, 267, 318, 320, 349
  Bank Charter Act, 143, 145, 208
  Bank of England (The Bank), 40,
    42–4, 143–6, 240, 242–3, 251,
    315–16, 318
  Bank Rate, 145, 264
  central, 43, 145
  clearing, 144, 146, 314–16, 356
  concentration in, 293
  country, *38–41*
  international, 224–5, 350–51
  investment, 146
  joint-stock, 40, 43, 143–4, 147, 208
  merchant, 146, 317, 356
  management of, 295
  multi-national, 320
  pay in, 369–70
  Post Office Savings, 147, 313
  Scottish joint-stock, 40–43, 143–4
  Trustee Savings, 147
  and see bills
banking and investment, 316, 318, 356
Barrow-in-Furness, 177
Bath, 21, 23, 24, 95, 100, 165, 187
Bazalgette, Joseph (1819–1891), 101, 213
Bentham, Jeremy (1748–1832), 211
Bermondsey, 51
Bessemer, Henry (1813–1898), 114
Bethnal Green, 177, 395
Beveridge, William (1879–1963)
  Report, 381–2, 384
Bevin, Ernest (1881–1951), 104, 298, 305
bills, *38–9*, 40–43, 52, 145–6
  bill-brokers, 41–2, 143
Birmingham, 24, 46
  canals, 26
  metalware, 51, 116
  water supply, 209

birth control, 14
  and see contraception
birth-rate, *see* fertility
Black Country, the, 24, 26, 51, 56, 151
Black Death, 13
'Black Friday', 303
Blackpool, 95
Bolton, 173
bonds (of companies), G 154
  and see stock (of government)
borrowing (and loans), 39, 41–42, 144,
    149, 316, 377
  foreign, 317
  hire purchase, 314
  international, 223
  personal, 314–15
  Public Sector Borrowing Requirement
    (PSBR), G 265, 272
Boulton, Matthew (1782–1809), 54, 76
Bradford-on-Avon, 166
branding (of consumer products), *118*,
  339
Bretton Woods, 227–9
Bridgewater
  canal, 26, 27
  Duke of (1736–1803), 26
Brighton, 23, 95, 127
Bristol, 21, 23, 25, 90, 104
British Institute of Management, 298
British Broadcasting Corporation, 241
British Transport Commission, 275
Bubble Act, 40, 43, 57, 59
budget, G 257, 264
  deficit, 225, 246, 264
  surplus, 258
building (and building industry), 55, 63,
    69, 112, 326
  house, 252–3, 282, 378–9
  innovation in, 325, 330
  societies, 147, 253, 312–13, 315–16
  system building, 330
  work in, 184, 392
Burton-upon-Trent, 169
bus
  horse, 123
  motor, 124, 253, 335
by-employment, G 17, 64

Cadbury, Edward (1873–1948), 297
Callaghan, James, 271–2
Canada, 32, 105, 139, 148, 226, 228
canals, 7, 26–7, 28, 36, 41, 63, 81
capital, 36, 39–40, 74, 75, 80, 82, 91, 95,
    97, 99, 110, 146, 149, 152–5, 157–8,
    167, 192, 195, 312, 316, 345, 391,
    401, 403–4

capital-intensive, 247, 329
circulating, 39, 41-2, 69-70, 154
export of, 136, 139
fixed, *39*, 41, 66, 69-70
human, *18*-19, 110, 147, 152, 167, 192, 195, 388
for new firms, 318
overhead, *G* 8
public corporations', 241
capitalism (and capitalist), *G* 79, 93, 143, 148, 166, *192*-3, 195, 201, 309, 319, 375, 399, 404
cars, *see* motor vehicles, motor industry
Cardiff, 97
Catholics, 193
census, 12, 191
Chadwick, Edwina (1800–1890), 211, 212
Chamberlain, Joseph (1836–1914), 152, 209
charity, 198, 214
Organisation Society, 214–15
Chartism, 194–5
Chatham, 23, 344
Chelmsford, 98
Cheltenham, 21, 28, 95, 104, 187, 344
decay of, 286
chemical industry, 54–5, 76–7, 119–20, 155, 156, 323, 326, 343, 350, 392
concentration, 323
firms in, 293
organic, 356
Cheshire, 16, 48, 49
children, 13–14, 100–3, 106, 169, 174–6, 178, 210, 213, 215
child benefit, 368, 382
China, 117, 139
cholera, 101
Church of England, *see* Anglican Church
cities, *see* towns, urbanisation
class, 100–3, 105, 191–7, 400–5
class-consciousness, 193–7, 401–2, 404–5
middle, 123, 127, 147, 169, 171, 173–4, 177–8, 179–80, 186–90, 191, 194, 196–7, 202, 221, 248, 342, 359, 363, 372, 386, 395, 400, 402–3, 405
working, 124, 126, 147, 168–9, 170, 172–3, 175, 177–8, 187, 188–90, 191, 194–7, 281, 313, 340, 372, 380, 394–5, 400, 402–3, 405
upper, 177–8, 179, 187, 190, 191, 202, 221, 342, 363
Clore, Charles (1904–1979), 294
Clyde, The (and Clydeside), 116, 125
coaches, coach services, 27–8, 92, 94, 123

coal (and coal industry), 53–4, 73, 81, 87, 111, 112–13, 172, 222–3, 262, 344, 401
Coal Mines Act, 241
coke, 53, 62, 76, 79
depression in, 237, 249, 255
export of, 113, 135, 231
fall in output, 326, 328
and industrial location, 95, 97, 285
investment in, 322
nationalisation, 260
rearmament and, 250
subsidy for, 241
and see mines
Coalbrookdale, 39, 53, 79, 115
Cobden-Chevalier Treaty, 140
collective bargaining, 203
collectivism, 201, 214–15, 375
colonies, 32–3, 140–1
Combination Acts, 202
commercial travellers, 124, 128, 335
and see sales representatives
Common Agricultural Policy, 231, 333–4
common land, *5*–6, 165
Commonwealth, 231, 277
preference, 228, 231
New, 284
Communism, 399, 405
Communist party, 307
Companies Act (1879), 145
companies, limited, *40*, 120–2, 146–8, 292
computers, 330–1
conferences, 340–1
Conservative party, 140, 382
Conspiracy and Protection of Property Act, 202
consumer durables, *G* 117, 119, 173, 252, 314, 324, 326–7, 371–2
imports, 328
semi-durables, *G* 171
consumer goods, 25, 81, 253, 281, 372–3
industries, 45–6, 111, 117–18, 122, 139, 156
rationing, 259
and see consumer durables
consumption (and consumers), 25, 73–5, 165, 169–71, 173, 358
markets, 343
mass, 371–2
spending, 257, 340, 363, 366, 371–3
contraception, 102, 280–2
convertibility, 225–6, 227–9
cooperation, *G* 126, 338, 340
Corby, 283

Corn Laws, 59, 129–30, 139–40, 194–5
Corn Production Act (1917), 331
Cornwall (and Cornish), 54, 55, 56, 105, 112
corporate economy, 317
Cort, Henry (1740–1800), 54
Cotswolds, 4
Cotton Famine, the, 89
cotton textiles, 36–7, 55–6, 135–6, 207, 344, 351
  advantage in, 35
  clothing, 13
  depression in, 237, 249, 255
  exports, 31, 117, 135–6, 231
  fall in output, 326
  industry, 48–50, 55–6, 68, 72–3, 80, 83, 111–12, 117, 156, 223
  investment, 322
  productivity, 142, 157
  strikes, 204
  'counter-factual', *91*
Coventry, 354
Crewe, 95
Cripps, Sir Stafford (1889–1952), 259
Crompton, Samuel (1753–1827), 49
Cumberland, 115
  West, 237
Customs
  records of, 65
  revenues, 216
  and see tariffs
cycles (economic), 89, 94, 215, 238, 264

Dagenham, 343
Dalton, Hugh (1887–1962), 259
Darby (family, of Coalbrookdale), 39, 53, 79, 199
  Abraham (1677–1717), 53, 80
death-rate, *see* mortality
Department of Economic Affairs, 266
defence, *see* armaments
deference, 197, 198
De Lorean, 267
demand, *G* 81, 93, 117–18, 128, 139, 153, 229, 315, 337, 342, 347
  for consumer goods, 118, 323–4, 326-7
  deficiency of, 249–50, 257, 270–71, 352–3
  elasticity of, *88*, 327
  for foodstuffs, 8–9, 131, 133–4
  for goods, 62, 315
  and government, 242, 258, 264–5, 273, 278
  for houses, 253, 284
  and industry, 74–6

  for iron, 93
  for labour, 284, 288
  for leisure, 190, 340–1
  for medical services, 282, 342
  for motoring, 335, 338,
  and price 8–9, 19, 73
  and technical change, 11
  and transport, 29
  and see inflation
depreciation, 314
depression, 89
  agricultural, 131–3
  Great, 150, 224
  of 1921–2, 240, 380
  of 1930s, 224, 226, 237, 249, 253
  of 1980s, 233–4, 326
  of staple industries, 322, 393
Derbyshire, 48
deskilling, 185
devaluation, *see* pound sterling
development block, 323–4
Devon, 48
discounting (of bills), *41*, 145–6
Dissent, *G* 76, 79, 80
  Dissenting Academics, 76–7
dividends, 154, 225, 316–17, 352, 355–6
division of labour, 45–6, 47, 185–6, 192, 199
  sexual, 186
  and see specialisation
dole, *see* unemployment
dollar, the, 222, 227–8, 230, 244
  dollar gap, 228
domestic industry, 47, 52, 120, 166, 199
Duncan, Sir Andrew (1884–1952), 305
Durham (county of), 26, 169
  employers in, 305
Dutch, *see* Netherlands

earnings, *see* income
East Anglia, 48, 50, 97
East India Company (British), 32, 40
Eastbourne, 95, 133
Eastern England, 5, 7, 26
economies of scale, *G* 24, 46, 56, 76, 153, 293–5
  external, 56
Edinburgh, 21, 24, 54, 97
  financial sector, 344
education (and schools), 18–19, 80, 103, 109–10, 207, 214, 217, 280, 290–1, 359, 373, 374, 376, 403
  further, 388
  higher, 291, 296, 356
  management, 155–6, 296–7, 356

scientific, 356
technical, 110, 290–91
and see polytechnics, universities
Edwardes, Sir Michael, 354, 358
Edwardian period, 133, 157–9, 178, 181
Egypt, 226
Eldon, Lord (1751–1838), 60
electricity, 142, 155–6, 241, 324–5, 356
Central Electricity Board, 241, 251, 353
Central Electricity Generating Board, 262, 274
electrical industry, 119–20, 154, 323
electrification, 251, 253, 260
electronics, 275, 337
training in, 356
and see National Grid
emigration (and emigrants), 100, 104–6, 134, 158, 234
and see migration
Empire (and imperialism), 105, 140–1, 225–6, 231, 337
First British, 32–4
immigration from, 284
imperialism of free trade, 208
imperial preference, 225, 227–8, 231
Employment Acts (1980, 1982, 1984), 306
Employers and Workmen Act, 202
enclosure, 5–7, 75, 165
Engels, F. (1820–1895), 195
engineering, 87, 89, 93, 109, 111, 119, 147, 168, 200, 271
agricultural, 98
exports, 231
heavy, 115–16
innovations in, 325, 329
light, 98, 116–17
personnel, 276
training, 291
work in, 181, 184, 392
engines
internal combustion, 114, 325, 335
diesel, 335
and see power
entrepreneurs (and entrepreneurship), *G* 77–80, 156, 159
Equal Pay Acts, 366–7, 370
equities, *see* stock (of companies)
Eurocurrency, *320*
Europe (and the Continent), 58, 74, 82–3, 107, 138, 142, 158, 353
Central, 222, 225, 257
Eastern, 222
Northern, 347

Southern, 30
Western, 175, 347
agriculture, 3–5, 9, 129–30, 334
banking, 251
coalmining, 328
expansion, 81
financial crisis, 224
growth, 263, 265, 350
hotels, 128
housing, 378
income per person, 347
population 12
refugees from, 247
science, 77
technical education, 110
trade, 30–31, 36, 231, 234, 277
urbanisation, 21
wealth, 47
welfare, 377
European Economic Community (EEC), 231, 267, 333–4
European Free Trade Association (EFTA), 231
Evangelicalism, 198, 211
Exeter, 28
canal, 26
exports, 30, 31, 35–7, 135–142, 153, 157, 223–225, 228, 231, 234–5, 253, 263, 265, 277, 347
of coal, 113, 222
of cotton, 31, 117, 135–6, 222–3
invisible, *136*, 225, 233, 235
of oil, 233–5
price of, 222, 277

factories (and mills), 17, 18, 36, 49, 72, 114, 120, 167, 175, 194–5, 201, 267, 354
electricity in, 325
reform, 213, 217
work in, 180, 183–6, 199, 390
Factory Acts, 204
factors of production, *66*, 152, 349
family, the, 174–8
family-owned firms, 292–3, 297, 316–17, 353
farmers, *see* agricultural workers
Far East, 222
fertilisers, 131, 132, 333
fertility, *G* 12, 13–14, 100–3, 174, 177, 279–81, 382
fiscal policy, *G* 216, 230, 246, 258, 264–5
fine-tuning, 258–9, 264, 278
and see demand deficiency, Keynes
food, 368

canned, 118
consumption, 170–71, 371–3
imports of, 136, 234–5
manufacture, 328
output, 8, 157
price, 11, 75, 129, 157–8, 168, 358, 364, 371–2
processing, 156
foremen, 298
franc, 222, 244
France (and French), 25, 58, 64, 77, 82–3, 91, 140, 193, 223, 405
agriculture, 4
allowances, 382
exports, 222
literacy, 19
planning, 266
population, 11
railways, 91
Revolution, 83, 194, 202, 359
science, 77
stock market, 318
taxation, 61
trade, 30
war, 33
free trade, *G* 139–40, 207–8, 227
within EEC, 231
friendly societies, *147*, 214, 314

gas (and gas industry), 118, 172–3, 187, 275, 328
GATT, 229
'Geddes axe', 245
gentry, landed, 3, 132
and see ownership
George, D. Lloyd (1863–1945), 378
Georgian period, 171
Germany, 153–6, 225, 231–2, 251, 256–7, 350, 354
apprenticeship, 291
banking, 356
competition from, 151–2, 351
foremen, 297
industry, 119–20, 277
management, 296–7
mark, 264
migration to Britain, 107
railways, 90
steel, 115–16
stockmarket, 318
Glasgow, 23, 37, 56, 106, 169, 209, 341
Gloucester, 22, 28
Gloucestershire, 48, 104
gnomes (of Zurich), 278
gold (bullion), 38, 42, 43, 64, 143, 145, 150, 223–4, 227, 243, 246
Gold Standard, *G* 145, 222, 225, 227, 240, 243, 245, 250
government (and the state), 32, 58–63, 207–17, 240–7, 250–1, 295, 349, 352–3, 357–8, 374–85, 403
Coalition, 241, 245, 378, 380, 381
and competition, 273–6
Conservative, 244–5, 263, 265–6, 270, 274, 306, 379, 383, 384
debt, 62–3, 166, 194, 216, 239, 315
and economic activity, 237–8, 242–5, 249–51, 255
and inflation, 270
Labour, 225, 241, 244–5, 263, 265–6, 270, 306, 379, 381, 383, 401
Liberal, 204, 215
local, 209, 213, 251
and macro-economic policy, *G* 242, 257–8, 267, 273, 277–8
National, 225
overseas spending, 233
purchasing, 275, 357
spending, 62–4, 164, 216–17, 225, 234, 239–40, 249, 257, 272, 365, 376–8, 383–5
and unions, 201–2, 204, 299, 304–7
and see fiscal and monetary policies, stock (government), welfare state, regional policy, nationalisation and working conditions, 298
Greenwich Mean Time, 94
Guest (family), 57
guilds, 47, 52, 59, 199–200

Halifax, 24
Hampshire, 98
Hargreaves, James (?–1778), 48
harvest (and harvesting), 3, 89, 131
health, 101–2, 381–4, 403
insurance, 215, 374
public, 211–13, 215, 217
Herne Bay, 340
high farming, 131
High Wycombe, 283
hobbies, 189–90
holidays (and holidaymaking), 94, 188–9, 394, 396
camps, 396
St Monday, 182
seaside, 123, 127, 188–9, 286, 340, 396
and see leisure
Holland, *see* Netherlands
Holyhead, 28, 58

Hopkins, Sir Richard (1880–1955), 384
Hornby, John, 213
hospitals, 102, 212, 214, 381, 383
hotels, 127–8, 341
hours of work, 17, 107–8, 210, 213, 289,
    394
houses (and housing), 24, 63, 99, 171–3,
    210, 213, 252–4, 263, 363, 368,
    371–3, 395–6
  council (local authority), 213, 284
  demand for, 253, 284
  ownership of, 312–13, 370, 379–80,
    403–4
  price of, 284
  rent, 283, 378–9
  rent control, 283–4, 378–9
  and see building
Hull, 23

immigration (and immigrants), 106–7,
    282, 284
  and see migration
imperialism, *see* Empire
imports (and importing), 30–31, 35, 74,
    89, 99, 136, 153, 226, 234–5, 252
  of agricultural produce, 130–1
  of manufactures, 231–2, 235
  of oil, 234–5
  of steel, 115
income (and earnings), 133, 164, 168–9,
    170, 279, 363–70, 371–3
  and birth-rate, 289
  craftsmens', 61
  distribution, 164, 342, 363–6, 369–70,
    372, 374, 377, 400-03
  family, 163, 367–8
  farmers', 130, 133, 169
  handloom weavers', 166
  and leisure, 399
  policy, *see* wage policy
  real, 253, 364, 369
  and saving, 313, 370
  working class, 147
  and see wages, living standards
income per head, 66–7, 69, 71, 82–3,
    150, 164, 309, 363–4
India, 32, 36, 105, 138–9, 222, 226
  Civil Service, 349
  exports to, 117, 141–2, 152
  trade, 31, 208
  wheat production, 131
individualism, 200
Industrial Relations Act (1971), 391
Industrial Reorganisation Corporation,
    266

Industrial Revolution, the, 26, 35, 45, 52,
    72–3, 77, 83, 87, 165, 167
Industrial Transference Board, 247
inflation, 42, 225, 233–4, 238, 242, 250,
    255, 264, 266, 268, 322, 377
  control of, 257, 263, 265, 273
  cost-push, 268–71
  demand, 239–40, 269, 271–2
  and see prices
innovation (and invention), G 19, 54,
    76–7, 80, 84, 139, 253–4, 323–4,
    328–31, 394
  agricultural, 10, 130–31, 332–3
  in building, 325, 330
  computers, 330–1
  in cotton, 48–9
  electricity, 325, 329
  in finance, 253, 314
  internal combustion engine, 325
  and investment, 324, 329
  in iron, 53
  in leisure, 341
  in marketing, 328
  in mining, 113, 329–30
  and see technical change
insurance (and assurance), 23, 37, 136–7,
    313, 321, 350
  health, 215, 374, 381
  industrial, 147, 314, 381
  old-age, 381
  principle, 368, 381
  unemployment, 215, 374, 380–81
  valuation, 65
interest rates, 145, 154, 224, 230, 246,
    263–4
  eighteenth century, 41–2
  and investment, 243, 252–3
  long-term, 42, 272
  and see monetary policy
International Monetary Fund, 227–8,
    230, 234, 272
investment, 19, 36–7, 39–40, 43, 62, 66,
    73, 79, 89, 93, 99, 106, 139, 148–9,
    150, 153–6, 164, 169, 228, 248, 251,
    257, 265, 316–18, 320, 358, 365
  in agriculture, 6, 75
  banks and, 144, 316, 356
  desire to invest, 245
  direct, 148, 318–19
  and interest rates, 242–4, 252–3
  and innovation, 324, 329
  in leisure, 340
  nationalised industries, 260–1
  overseas, 99, 106, 141, 143, 147–8,
    152, 225–6, 227, 235

portfolio, 148
ratio, *69*–70, 141, 148, 153, 158, 317, 348, 350, 352, 385
and tax incentives, 266, 317
in transport, 72
war and, 63
invisible earnings, 136, 233, 235
Ireland (and Irish), 16, 26, 58, 106–7, 168, 172, 267
Northern (Ulster), 26, 48, 267
potato famine, 208
iron (and iron industry), 52, 54, 57, 68, 71, 72, 81, 87, 111, 116, 140, 151
in agriculture, 7, 130
exports, 135
Iron and Steel Board, 266
manufacture of, 52–3, 113–14, 121
in railways, 93
in shipbuilding, 116
and war, 62
work in, 183
and see steel
Italy, 52
Northern 21

Jamaica, 32
and see West Indies
Japan, 138, 222–3, 231, 355, 356, 358
competition, 236
foremen, 298
higher education, 291
income per person, 347
retailing, 355
stock market, 318
Jarrow, 242
Jews (and Jewish), 107
joint-stock, *40*, 42, 146–7
and see banking, companies

Kent, 133
Weald of, 5
King, Gregory (1648–1712), 193
Keynes, J. Maynard (1883–1946), 63, 93, 221, 244–7, 249–50, 257–8, 270
Keynesian theory, 63, 93, 245, 249–50, 257–60, 264–5, 270–73, 278

labour market, 196, 200, 205, 215, 243, 269, 392–3
dual, 393
internal, 392–3
Labour party, 204, 260, 271–2, 278, 382, 400–01
and agricultural vote, 332
and political levy, 306

and see government
labour process, 187
Labour Representation Committee, 204
laissez-faire, 200, 207–11, 213, 217, 241, 375
Lake District, 16
Lancashire, 16, 41, 87, 173, 175–6, 186, 194, 199, 203, 208, 210
canals, 26
Cotton Corporation, 242
cotton industry, 48–9, 56, 117, 223
holidays, 188
mining, 55
unemployment, 237
vehicle industry, 343
wages, 97, 165
Lancaster, 196
landlords (and landowners), *see* ownership of land
law (and lawyers, legal system), 43–34, 58–60, 82, 199, 207
and trade unions, 202, 204, 306
and see solicitors
leading sector, *73*, 323–4
Le Blanc, Nicholas (1742–1806), 54
Leeds, 24, 107, 209
Leicestershire, 7
leisure (and recreation), 22, 23, 95–7, 127–8, 187–90, 340–41, 394–9
and see holidays
lend-lease, 226
Lenin, V.I., 141, 143, 148, 195
Liberal party, 133, 140, 244, 249
and see government
limited liability, *40*, 57, 208, 292
and see companies, limited
Lincoln, 98
Lincolnshire, 4
literacy, 18–19, 77, 109
female, 188
Liverpool, 23, 28, 37, 97, 106, 172
financial sector, 344
living standards, 63, 69, 99, 134, 165–7, 169, 385
middle-class, 169, 312
and see income per head, wages
loans, *see* borrowing
Locomotion, the, 90
Lombard Street, 146, 149
London, 9, 23, 25, 27, 28, 61, 96–8, 117, 125, 167, 194, 203, 214, 224, 243, 247, 250, 253, 262
banking, 40–2, 320
City of, 221, 240, 321, 349
employment, 107–8

engineering, 116
financial services, 97, 146, 277, 320–21, 344
house prices, 284
manufacturing, 24, 56, 97–8
market, 47, 343
migration to, 104
mortality, 101
population, 21
railways, 125
services, 267
tourism, 344
Transport, 243, 353
wages, 165
Welsh in, 283
Luton, 307
Lyons, 82
Lytham St Annes, 127

MacAdam, John (1756–1836), 28
Macaulay, T. B. (1800–1859), 210–11
machinery (and mechanisation), 51, 52, 54–6, 72–3, 111–18, 182
in agriculture, 7, 131–2
export of, 145
investment in, 70
lathes, 54, 119
machine tools, *115*, 119, 330–31
in textiles, 48–50
Macmillan, Harold (1894–1986), 379
Maidstone, 22
Malthus, T. (1766–1834), 211–12
management (and managers), 57, 121, 155–6, 159, 293–8, 353–5, 357–9, 391
consultants, 293
education, 296–7, 320, 352, 356
and investment, 316, 318, 352
middle, 297, 353–4, 358
personnel, 121, 297–8, 391
profession, 296–8
scientific, 297
Manchester, 56, 107, 169, 341
canals, 26
housing, 172
Manchester School, 208
mortality, 100
water-supply, 209
wholesaling, 28
manual workers, 169, 180, 184, 186, 188, 191, 193, 195, 197, 380, 386, 388–9, 390–2, 402–3, 405
and apprenticeship, 291
holidays, 394
and mortality, 280
relative incomes, 365–6
and see work, working-class
marketing, *see* sales
markets, *9*, 74, 80–81, 203, 244, 349, 352
consumer, 343
mass–, 45–47, 51
and see labour market, money market, stock exchange
marriage, 14–15, 102, 281–2
Marshall Aid, 228
Marx, Karl (1818–1883) (and Marxism), 36, 107, 143, 185, 192–6, 345, 399, 403–4
Maudling, Reginald (1917–1979), 265, 270
Maudslay, Henry (1771–1831), 54
measles, 13
mechanisation, *see* machinery
medicine, 13, 101–2, 280
demand for, 282
and see hospitals
mercantilism, *31*, 64, 359
merger (and amalgamation), 120–1, 155, 241–2, 293–5, 318, 352–4, 356–7
of banks, 144
government policy and, 241, 255, 266, 274
metal (and metal industry), 168, 180, 221, 223
non-ferrous, 62
in machinery, 54
and see iron, steel, mining
Middlesbrough, 188
Midlands (of England), 5, 25–7, 49, 83, 131, 165, 172, 262
East, 48, 51, 112–13, 199
West, 55, 97–8, 113, 115, 117, 182, 184, 341, 343
migration (and migrants), 16, 94, 97, 100, 104–7, 134, 167, 176, 282–5
and see emigration, immigration
Milk Marketing Board, 331
mills, *see* factories
mines (and mining), 17, 45, 57, 147–8, 167–8, 180
coal, 54, 104–5, 112–13, 221–2, 247
iron and non–ferrous, 54
miners' challenge to government, 270
work in, 182–4, 186
Ministry of Defence, 344
Ministry of Economic Affairs, 259, 266
Ministry of Labour, 240
Monckton, Sir Walter (1891–1965), 306
monetarism, *269*–71, 273, 316
money (and currency, monetary system),

38–9, 41–2, 64, 143–4, 148, 239,
  315, 316
cheap money, 263
hot money, *223*–4
G monetary policy, 264, 316
G supply 224, 242, 269–70, 272
velocity, 315–16
and see banking, monetarism, gold
  bullion, money market, pound
  sterling
money market, *143*, 146
monopoly, monopolies, G 59, 121, 207,
  209, 217, 241, 274–5 Monopolies
  and Mergers Commission, 274
Morrison, Herbert (1888–1965), 305
mortality, G 12–15, 100–2, 279–80
  infant, 13–14, 102, 279–80
mortgages, 39, 43, 63, 312
  building-society, 253, 312
  tax-relief, 379
motor industry (and car industry, vehicle
  industry), 98, 116, 119, 156, 271,
  274, 295, 323, 327, 354, 358
  concentration, 323
  exports, 231
  industrial relations, 310, 358
  tariffs, 246
motor vehicles
  cars, 283, 286, 326, 335–6, 372, 398
  lorries, 325, 335
  sales and service facilities, 338
  spending on, 371, 373
multi-nationals, 319
  banks, 320
multiplier, 245, 253
municipal corporations, 209

national assistance, 368
National Board for Prices and Incomes,
  265
National Economic Development
  Council, 267, 304
National Exhibition Centre, 341
National Grid, 251, 325
national income, G 65–9, 71, 83, 164,
  216, 309, 317
  accounting, 257
  export's share, 62, 272
  GNP, 255
  labour's share, 309
  large firms' share, 293
  personal share, 164
  sectoral shares, 45, 68, 88, 342
  welfare's share, 385
National Institute of Economic and

  Social Research, 354
nationalisation, 260, 304
  denationalisation (privatisation), 266,
    274–5
  nationalised industries, 260–2, 274–5,
    295–6, 357
National Plan, 267
National Savings, 313
National Trust, 397
Navigation Acts, 32–3, 59, 139, 207
Netherlands (and Holland; Dutch), 4, 21,
  30, 82
Newcastle, 23
new industries, 323–4, 326, 342
  location of, 343
New Lanark, 57
New Zealand, 105
Norfolk, 332
Norman, Montague (1871–1950), 240
North America, 30–2, 137–8, 347
  and see Canada, USA, The Americas
Northampton, 169
North (of England), 28, 83, 167, 342, 344
  agriculture, 132
  canals, 26
  housing, 172
  industry, 56
  textiles, 51, 167
  wages, 16, 165–6, 169
  and see North-East, North-West
North-East (of England), 25, 48, 107,
  126, 210
  canals, 26
  chemicals, 343
  housing, 172, 378
  mining, 54–5, 113
  mortality, 280
  railways, 90
  shipbuilding, 116
  steel, 115
  unemployment, 237, 242
  wages, 97
North-West (of England), 48, 196
  canals, 26
  chemicals, 343
  manufacturing, 24
  population, 97
  wages, 16
Northumberland, 26
Norwich, 21
Nottinghamshire
  miners,
  nuclear energy, 260, 329, 357

Oastler, Richard (1789–1861), 213

oil, 233–5, 328, 336, 351
  North Sea, 234–5, 268, 326, 328–9
  transport, 336
  work in, 392
oligopoly, *G* 144, 315
OPEC, 233, 235
open-market operations, *145*, 315
opportunity cost, 93–4
'over-commitment', 322
Owen, Robert (1771–1858), 57
ownership
  of houses, 312–13, 368, 370, 379–80,
    395, 403–4
  of land, 3, 5, 10, 74, 78, 132–3, 169,
    174, 191, 193–4, 198, 208
  of property, 179, 191–2, 196–7, 312,
    363, 377, 403–4
  and see family
Oxford, 343

Paish, Frank, 277
Paris, 21, 82
Parliament, 58, 194, 217, 401
  members of, 58, 60
Parsons, Charles (1854–1931), 114
participation rate, *17*–18, 100, 287–90
  female, 17–18, 108, 287–9
  male, 17, 107–8, 287
patents (and patent system), 49, 54, 77
paternalism, 185, 194–5, 197, 198, 201
patronage, 193
Paul, Lewis (?–1759), 48
payments
  balance of, *G* 136, 137–9, 222, 226,
    230, 233–4, 264, 277
  multilateral, 137–8, 223
  and see pound sterling
Peel (family), 57
  Sir Robert (1788–1850), 208
peerage, *see* aristocracy
Pennines, 55
pensions, 95, 179, 214–15, 286, 364, 368,
    370, 377, 382–3, 384, 392, 403, 404
  pension funds, 295, 313
pharmaceutical industry, 326, 351, 356
pipelines, 335
Place, Francis (1771–1854), 194
planning, 259–60
  indicative, 266
  and land supply, 284, 286
plastics, 325
Plymouth, 23, 91, 172
Poland
  coalmining in, 328
polytechnics, 276

Poor Law, 16, 176, 211–12, 214, 381
population, 12–15, 34, 67, 72, 74, 99–
    103, 130, 166, 168, 279, 282, 287
  and demand, 8–9, 19, 75, 81, 99, 153
  and migration, 106
  and Poor law, 211
  regional, 284
  urban, 21–2
ports, 23, 37, 97, 337
Portsmouth, 23
post, Post Office, 109, 125, 209, 275, 337
  Savings Bank, 147, 313
  and see Royal Mail
Potteries, the, 24, 26, 56
pound sterling, 145–6, 208, 226, 278–30,
    234, 243–4, 246, 249, 251, 264, 273,
    278, 347
  area, *226*, 256
  devaluation of, 228, 230, 234, 265, 348
  floating, *225*, 230, 252, 269
poverty (and the poor), 168–9, 173,
    216–17, 364–5, 368, 383
  and see Poor Law
power, 81, 373
  steam (and steam engines), 49, 51, 54,
    73, 90, 111, 113–14, 115, 182
  water, 49, 51
  and see engines (internal combustion)
Preston, 175–6, 196
prices, 42, 50–51, 65, 80–81, 88, 157,
    205–6, 222, 244, 257, 259, 274, 372,
    398
  agricultural, 9–10, 130–2, 140, 331–4,
    372
  controls on, 265, 270
  electricity, 325
  fall in, 64, 150–51, 240, 247
  food, 11, 63–4, 74–5, 89, 358, 364, 371
  fuel, 328–9
  grain, 226
  index, 163–4
  primary products, 223–4, 323, 363
  retail, 239
  tobacco, 328, 372
  and see inflation
producer goods, *45*, 52–5, 111
productivity (and efficiency), *G* 11, 72,
    81, 88, 91–2, 157–8, 323–6, 331
  in agriculture, 74–5, 130–1, 157, 332–3
  in cotton, 73, 142, 157
  in Japan, 236
  labour, 8, 66, 69, 71, 79, 131, 150,
    152–3, 323–6, 368–9
  in mining, 113, 326
  in shipbuilding, 116

total factor, *152*–3, 155, 159, 323, 348, 350
unions and, 205–6
professions (and professionals), 179, 192, 194, 212–13, 215, 341, 376, 383, 386
incomes, 365
management profession, 295–8
mortality, 280
self-employed, 292–3
profit, *G* 36–7, 62, 64, 80, 150, 154–5, 205, 241, 296–7
family businesses, 292
inter-war, 248
proletariat (and proletarianisation), 174, 177, 192
property, 294
and see ownership
protection, *see* tariffs
Protestantism, 78
proto-industrialisation, 52
Public Assistance Committees, 380
public corporations, 241, 251, 260
public houses, 127, 396
public works, 243, 244–6, 249

Quakers, 39, 79
quarantine, 13

Railway Mania, the, 90
railways, 87, 89–95, 104, 111, 124–5, 139, 146, 148, 154, 155, 157, 180, 209, 335, 340
amalgamation, 241
concentration, 293
electrification, 251, 253, 260
Great Western, 90
Liverpool and Manchester, 90
London and Birmingham, 90
management, 295, 297, 352
Midland, 124
nationalisation, 260–2
oil use, 328
Southern, 251
Stockton and Darlington, 90
work on, 184
rank, 193
rationalisation, 241–2, 260
rationing, 257, 259, 263
rayon, 325
Reading, 169
rearmament, 226, 250, 254
Redundancy Payments Act, 391
regions (and regional), 97, 165–6, 172, 237, 266–7

Distribution of Industry Act, 262
policy, 250, 262, 266–7
population, 284–5
unemployment, 246
rent, 6, 63, 64, 132–3, 194
control, 283–4
Resale Price Maintenance, 273, 339, 355
research and development, 275, 294, 319–20, 352, 356
governmental, 344
Restrictive Practices Act, 273
retailing (and retail trade), *see* shops
retirement, 95, 286
and see pensions
Ricardo, David (1772–1823), 207, 212
riots, 193
Luddite, 198
Swing, 198
river navigations, 7, 26
roads (and road transport), 27–8, 285, 335–6, 398
building, 336
and see buses, coaches, motor vehicles
Roberts, Richard (1789–1864), 117
robots, 330
Rochdale, 196
Pioneers, 126
Rocket, the, 90
Rocky Mountains, 105
Roebuck, John (1718–1794), 76
rotation (of crops), 7, 130
Rowntree, S (1871–1954), 168–9, 171, 187, 297, 365
Royal Mail, 27
and see post

Saint Domingue, 31
sales (and selling, marketing), 121–2, 127, 339–40, 341, 352, 354–5
financial services, 318
representatives, 335
and see commercial travellers, shops, branding
Sankey navigation, 26
saving (and savings), 38, *39*, 41, 42, 43, 62, 147–8, 179, 242–3, 257, 312–16, 320, 365
building societies, 312–13
corporate, 314
desire (or propensity) to save, 245, 313
personal savings ratio, *G* 313–14
science, 76–7, 82, 183, 275
Scotland (and Scots), 26, 27, 47, 54–5, 57, 80, 83, 100, 107, 115, 144, 165, 267

banking, 40–43, 89, 144
  Central, 56, 97
  diet, 170
  Eastern, 48
  electricity, 274
  Highlands, 10, 16, 97, 106–7, 332
  housing, 171–2, 378
  Lowlands, 6, 10, 16, 19, 90, 107
  migration from, 283
  mining, 113
  mortality, 280
  North Sea oil, 329
  population, 97
  railways, 91
  Scottish Development Agency, 267
  steel, 115
  urbanisation, 22
  wages, 165
  West of, 24, 49, 55, 186, 237
securities (financial), 145, 146–9
  and see stock
Senior, Nassau (1790–1864), 207
servants (and service), 175
  domestic, 95, 104, 108, 175–6, 180–1,
    186–7, 288, 342, 386
  farm, 104, 175
service (sector of industry), *G* 83, 88,
    94–8, 158, 248, 273, 292, 342–4, 373,
    386, 398
  financial, 37, 96–7, 146, 149, 159, 314,
    320–1, 343, 373
  and unions, 203
Severn (river), 25
Sex Discrimination Act, 389
shares, *see* stock
Sheffield, 51
shipbuilding, 115–16, 120, 147, 274, 326,
    344, 351
  depression in, 237, 250
  industrial relations, 310
  rationalisation, 242
  rearmament and 250
  unemployment, 380
  work in, 182
ships and shipping, 30, 32, 111, 116,
    136–7, 157, 159, 225, 243, 336–7,
    350–1, 353
  coastal, 335
  containerisation, 337
  sailing, 26, 105, 137
  steam, 26, 105, 137
shop stewards, *307–8,*
  Shop Stewards Movement, 308
shops (and shopping, retailing), 22, 28,
    95, 125–7, 156, 188, 337–40, 355,
    358, 373

concentration, 293, 338
  shopkeepers, 179, 248
Shropshire, 16, 39, 53, 57
Slough, 283, 343
smallpox (and inoculation and
    vaccination against), *G* 13, 101
  Smeaton, John (1724–1792), 76
Smith, Adam (1723–1790), 34, 36, 58,
    207–8
Smith, Dr T. Southwood, (1788–1861),
    212
smuggling, 34.
Snow, Dr John (1813–1858), 212
Snowden, Philip (1864–1937), 245
Social Contract, 270
socialism, 143, 204, 260, 375
social mobility, 192, 196–7, 386–7, 402–3
social saving, *91–*92, 94
solicitors (and attorneys), 22, 39, 42, 82,
    149, 273, 312
  and see law
Somerset, 4, 48, 104
South America, 64
  and see The Americas
South East of England, 97, 247, 250, 284
  unemployment, 283
Southern England (and the South), 16,
    25, 83, 104, 167, 343–4, 346, 365
  agriculture, 131
  canals, 26
  domestic industry, 56, 64, 166
  housing, 172
  land tenure, 5
  migration from, 94
  migration to, 283
  research in, 344
  wages, 134, 165, 169, 365
South Sea Bubble, 40
South West (of England), 5, 55, 97
  and see West of England
Spain (and Spanish), 33
spas, 23, 95–6
Special Areas Act, 247
specialisation, 4, 8, 9, 35, 45–7, 56, 119,
    149
  international, 232
sport, 128, 188–90, 340
St Helens, 210
Staffordshire, 16, 50
Stanby, 169
staple industries, *135*, 237, 322
state, the, *see* government
status, 180, 192, 196–7, 400, 403, 404
steam, see power
steel (and steel industry), 111, 116, 121,
    136, 140, 151, 153, 271, 326, 351, 353

allocation, 259, 263
depression in, 237, 250
manufacture of, 114–15
productivity in, 324
rearmament and, 250
work in, 183
Stephenson, George (1781–1848), 90
sterling, *see* pound sterling
stock (of companies) (and equities,
    shares, shareholders), *40*, 91, 146–8,
    154–5, 292, 295, 317–18, 404
    and see stock exchange
stock (government) (and bonds,
    bondholders), *G* 40, 62–3, 154, 166,
    216
    and see government debt
Stock Exchange (and stockmarket), 96,
    133, 147, 292, 294–5, 312, 317–18,
    353
    London, 40, 147
    Unlisted Securities Market, 318
stocks (of goods), 28, 69–70, 75, 92, 154
strikes, 193, 199, 201, 203–5, 300, 302–3,
    305–8, 310
    General, 241, 300, 303, 305
    shop stewards and, 308
    sympathetic, 302–3, 306
    unofficial, *308*
sub-contracting, 122, 183, 184, 199
Suffolk, 3
Sunderland, 23
supply (of goods and services), *G* 10, 29,
    74, 76, 81––2, 150, 335 supply-side
    policies, 260, 262, 266
Surrey, 178
Sussex, 97, 336
sweated trades, *G* 120, 215
Sweden, 110
    tax rates, 377
Swindon, 95, 344
Switzerland, 321

Taff Vale, 204
'take-off', *73*, 83
tariffs (and customs duties, protection),
    33–4, 59–61, 64, 115, 117, 135, 140,
    142, 152, 207-8, 216, 225, 227, 229,
    231, 238, 246, 252, 276, 331, 334,
    349, 353, 358
    railway goods tariff, 209
    McKenna, 246
    and see Corn Laws, Wheat Act,
        Common Agricultural Policy
taxation, 60–63, 166, 216, 238–40, 243,
    257, 264, 272, 365-6, 369-70, 374,
    375-6, 384-5

Cider Tax, 60
concessions, 313–14, 379
and dividends, 316–17
and enterprise, 348
estate duty (and death duty), 133, 292,
    370
excise duties, 61–2, 377
income tax, 216, 264, 292, 364–6, 377
on road vehicles, 336
and see tariffs
technical (and technological) change, 36,
    71, 74, 82, 116–18, 151–2
and output growth, 229
in services, 398
in textiles, 50–1
and see innovation, machinery
technical education, 155–6, 159, 290–1,
    349, 356
technology
    British, 355
    high, 267
    household, 289
    mass production, 119, 156, 330
    medical, 383
    production, 329
    steel, 115
    and work, 186, 192
Teesside, 151
telecommunications, 274–5, 337
    telegraph, 94, 209
    telephone, 123, 125, 209, 337
Tennant, Charles (1763–1838), 55
textiles (and textile industry), 17, 47–51,
    71, 80, 87, 111, 117, 135, 166–7, 199,
    221
    industrial relations, 310
    work in, 182
    and see cotton, linen, wool textiles,
        domestic industry, factories, proto-
        industrialisation
Tewkesbury, 28
Thrale (family), 52
threshing machines, 7
Tolpuddle Martyrs, 202–3
total factor productivity, *see* productivity
tourism, 340, 398
    employment in, 283
    and see holidays
towns (and cities), 9, 21–5, 167, 171–2,
    286
    and mortality, 100–2
    and see municipal corporation,
        urbanisation
Townshend, Charles 2nd Viscount
    (1674–1738), 10
trade

composition, 135–6, 235
foreign, 23, 30–7, 82–3, 135–8, 142,
    231
internal, 25, 28–9
terms of, *157*–8, 233
world, 135, 137, 223, 225, 228–9, 231,
    233–4, 252
and see exports, free trade, imports,
    shops, wholesaling
Trade Boards Act, 215
trade unions (and trade unionists), 89,
    163, 183, 198–206, 214, 299–311,
    381, 388, 391, 401,
    bargaining, 203–4, 303, 308
    closed shop, 302, 307
    demarcation, 310
    and hours of work, 289
    and inflation, 268
    and national economic performance,
        157, 309–10, 349, 358
    New, 203–4
    picketing, 303, 306
    and unemployment, 247, 269
    and wages, 205–6, 243, 247–8, 271,
        309, 369
    and see government, law, strikes, shop
        stewards
Trades Union Congress (TUC), 202, 270.
    304
training, 19
trams (and tramways), 147, 148
    electric, 125
    horse, 124–5
transport, 4, 8, 22, 25–9, 75, 76, 81,
    123–4, 146, 158, 188, 253– 4, 334-7
    investment in, 69–70
    public, 95
    and see air, buses, canals, coaches,
        roads, railways, ships, turnpikes,
        trams
    transaction costs, *46*
Treasury 240, 243, 246, 249, 384
    and Keynes, 257–8
    Treasury view, 243
trusts, 120
tuberculosis, 101–2
turnpikes, 26, 41, 48
Tyne, the, 116

underdeveloped countries, 235
underemployment, *G* 63, 75, 107, 163,
    248
unemployment, 89, 163–4, 215, 365–6,
    368, 380–81, 384, 398
    benefit, 248–9, 283, 364, 380-81, 382

and CAP, 334
demand-deficient, 249–50, 271
dole, 380–1
in staple industries, 237, 246–7
inter-war, 237, 243–4, 248–50, 253,
    281
insurance, 215, 374, 380–1
natural level, 269–71
post-war, 259, 263, 268, 271–3
regional, 283
search theory, explanation of, 248–9
structures, *249*, 271
universities, 155, 276
urbanisation, 21–5, 81, 94–7, 167, 176–7,
    188, 210, 285–6
    suburbs, 286, 335
USA, 117, 119–22, 138, 141–2, 155–6,
    186, 222–3, 227–9, 231, 251, 324
    and class, 193–4
    computers, 331
    competition from, 150–1
    financial services, 159
    investment from, 319
    investment in, 148, 153
    labour productivity, 325
    lend-lease, 226
    management, 297
    migration to, 105
    railways, 125
    recession in, 224
    shipbuilding, 116
    shipping, 137
    steel, 115
    trams, 124
USSR, planning, 259
Usury Laws, 59, *63*
    repeal of, 208
Utilitarian, 211, 212

Vale of Evesham, 133
Victorian period, 123, 131, 144, 147,
    157–8, 171, 175, 177–8, 396–7

wages (and salaries), 16, 73, 97, 113, 116,
    134, 163–9, 200, 221– 2, 253, 288,
    363–5, 369–70
    differentials, 119, 186, 301–2
    low, 215, 365
    piece rate, *G* 157, 303
    policy, 263, 265, 270
    profit-linked, 296
    real, *163*–8, 205–6, 247–9
    and unemployment, 243–4
    unions and, 205–6
    women's, 288, 365–7, 370

and see incomes, living standards
waggonways, *G* 26, 90
Wales, 5, 22, 40, 47, 83, 97, 100
  Central and Mid, 91, 104, 106, 283, 332
  migration from, 283
  mortality, 280
  North, 16, 91, 106
  South, 16, 28, 55, 57, 87, 97, 104, 112,
    115, 237
  West, 55
Wall Street, 224
war, 62–4, 369, 377
  American Civil, 117
  American War of Independence, 33,
    62
  Boer, 216
  credits, 257
  First World, 221–2, 225, 226,237–8,
    250, 252, 257, 263, 280, 293, 297–
    8, 324, 331, 336, 369, 372, 378–81
  Korean, 228, 233, 263
  Napoleonic (and Revolutionary), 6,
    11, 31, 33, 37, 62–4, 131, 143, 166,
    182, 216, 377
  Second World, 227, 231, 233, 255, 258,
    277, 332, 371, 379, 381–2, 366, 393
  Seven Years, 33
  and social policy, 377, 380–2
Watford, 343
Watt, James (1736–1819), 54, 113
wealth, 169, 191–2, 368, 370, 400, 403
Wear, the, 116
Weber, Max (1864–1920), 78, 191–2

Wedgewood, Josiah (1730–1795), 51, 76
welfare state, 229, 368, 381–4
West (of England) (and West Country),
  48, 50, 104, 106, 132, 199, 343–4
  and see South-West of England
West Indies, 30–32, 64, 137–8
Wheat Act (1932), 331
Whitehaven, 23
wholesaling, 28, 127, 339
Williams, Thomas, 55
Wilson, Harold, 259
wool textiles, 47–50, 117
  export of, 30–31, 135
work, 107–9, 181–7, 188–90, 389–94
  casual, 107–8, 248
  children's, 109
  domestic, 393–4
  entry to, 387–9
  men's, 107–8, 181–2, 184, 390
  women's, 18, 108–9, 182, 186–7, 282,
    288, 390–1, 393–4
  and see hours of work, manual
    workers, participation rate, labour
    market

yield (of crops), 11, 130, 132, 332–4
  per hectare, 8
  ratio, *4*, 8
York, 169, 171, 365
Yorkshire, 28, 97, 112, 117, 199
  industrial disputes, 309
  West Riding, 24, 48, 79
Young, Arthur (1741–1820), 8